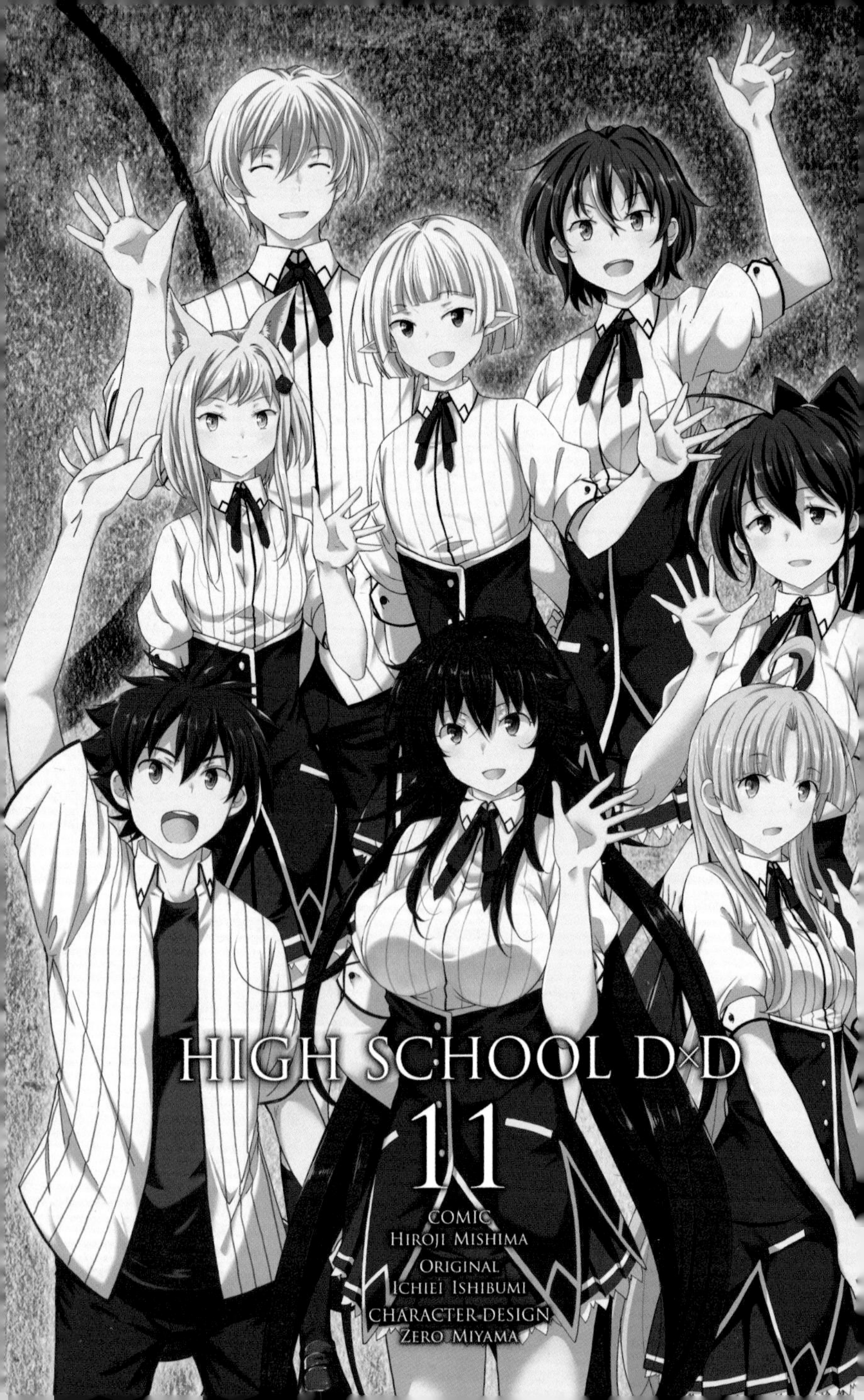
HIGH SCHOOL D×D
11
COMIC
Hiroji Mishima
ORIGINAL
Ichiei Ishibumi
CHARACTER DESIGN
Zero Miyama

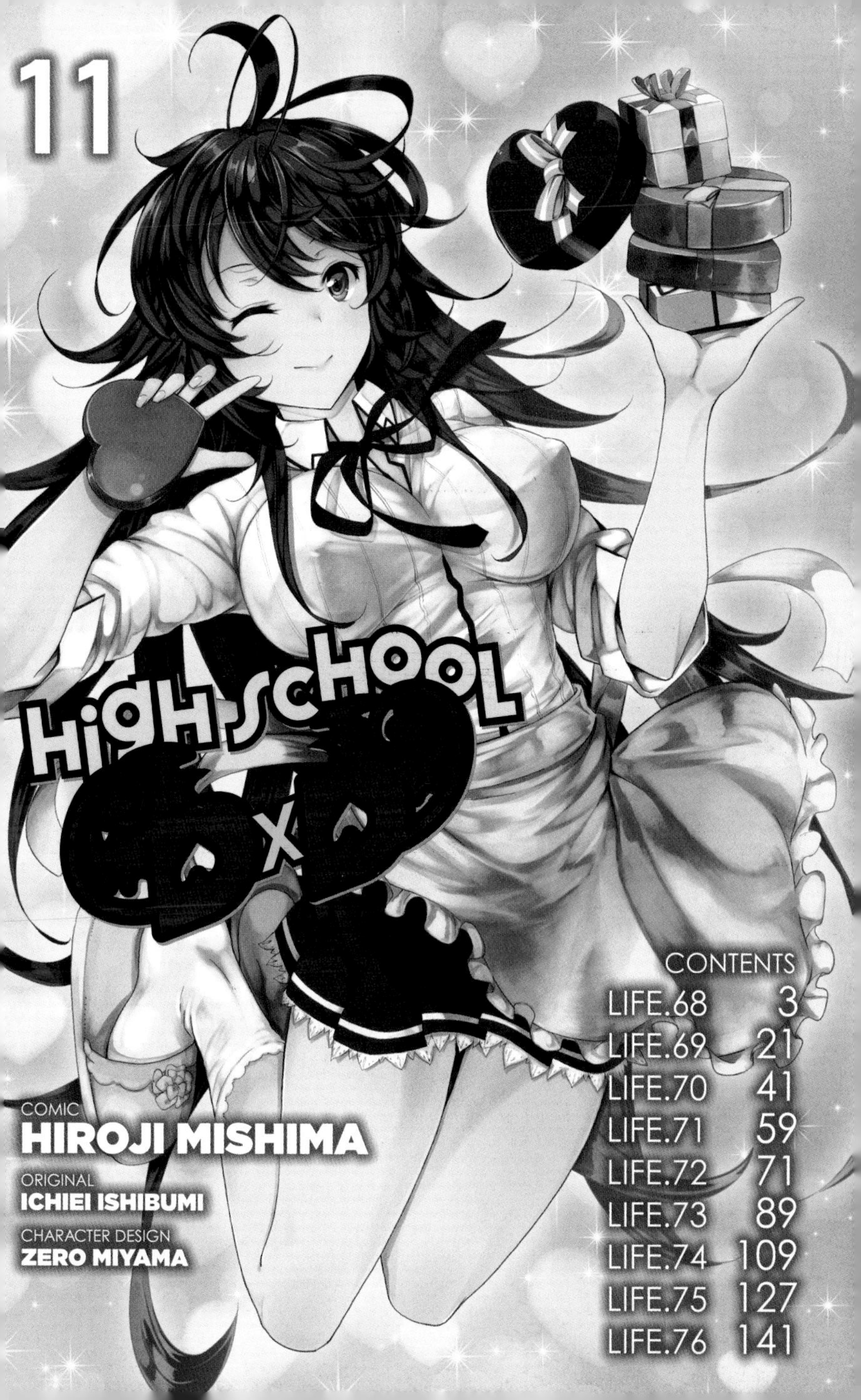

11

HIGH SCHOOL DxD

COMIC
HIROJI MISHIMA
ORIGINAL
ICHIEI ISHIBUMI
CHARACTER DESIGN
ZERO MIYAMA

CONTENTS

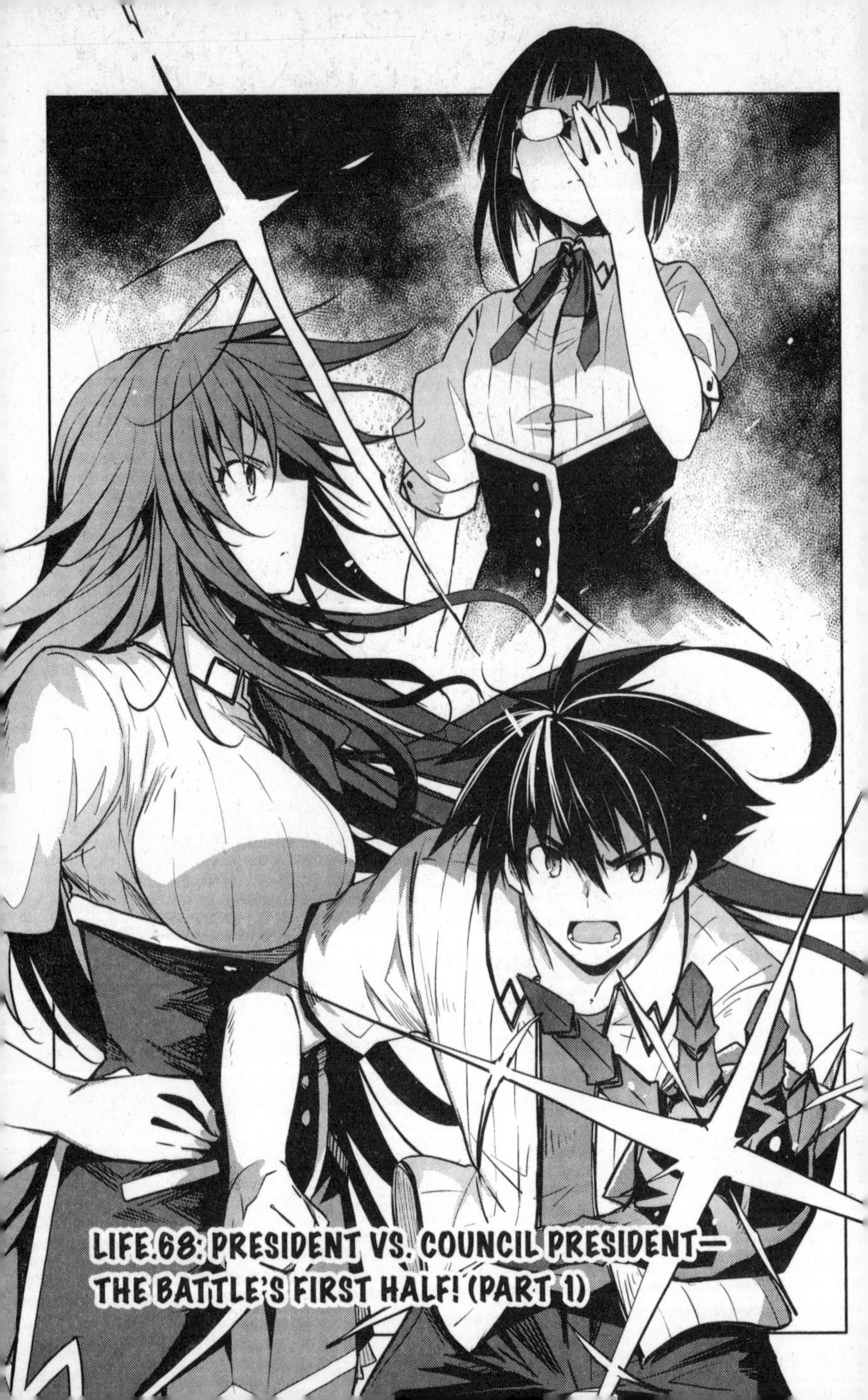
LIFE.68: PRESIDENT VS. COUNCIL PRESIDENT—
THE BATTLE'S FIRST HALF! (PART 1)

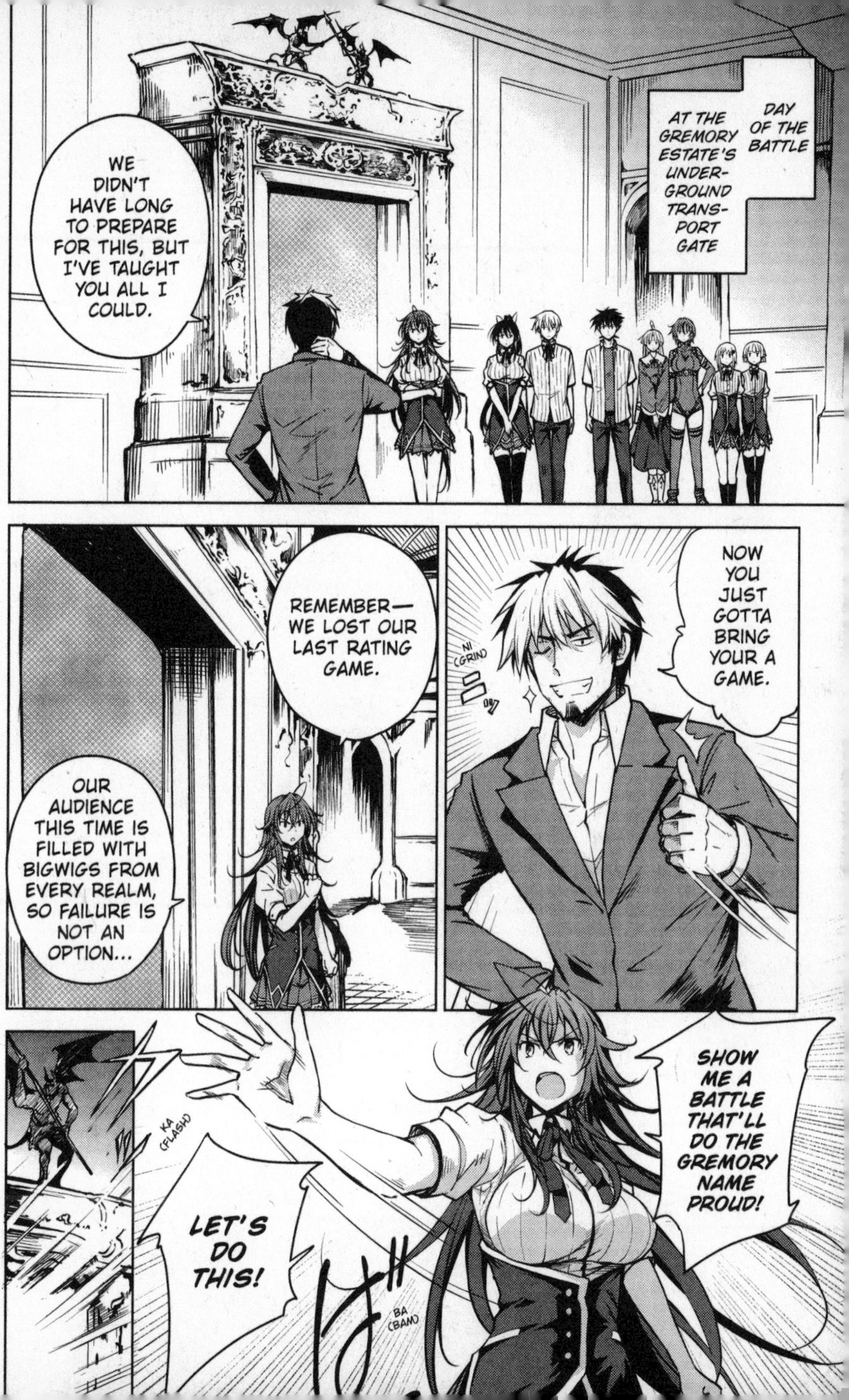
DAY OF THE BATTLE
AT THE GREMORY ESTATE'S UNDER-GROUND TRANS-PORT GATE
WE DIDN'T HAVE LONG TO PREPARE FOR THIS, BUT I'VE TAUGHT YOU ALL I COULD.
NOW YOU JUST GOTTA BRING YOUR A GAME.
NI (GRIND)
REMEMBER—WE LOST OUR LAST RATING GAME.
OUR AUDIENCE THIS TIME IS FILLED WITH BIGWIGS FROM EVERY REALM, SO FAILURE IS NOT AN OPTION...
SHOW ME A BATTLE THAT'LL DO THE GREMORY NAME PROUD!
LET'S DO THIS!
BA (BAM)
KA (FLASH)

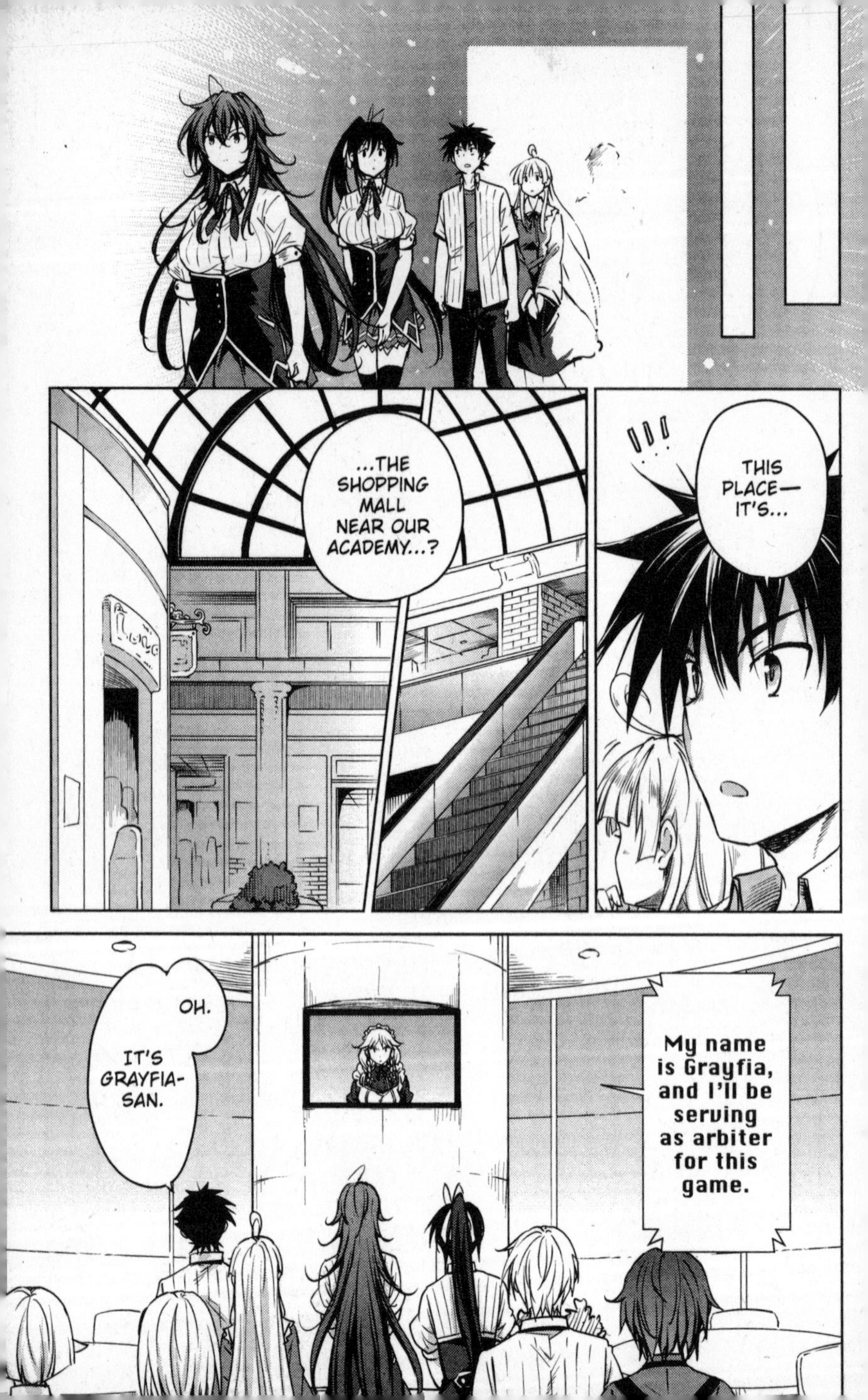
!!!
THIS PLACE—IT'S...
...THE SHOPPING MALL NEAR OUR ACADEMY...?
My name is Grayfia, and I'll be serving as arbiter for this game.
OH.
IT'S GRAYFIA-SAN.

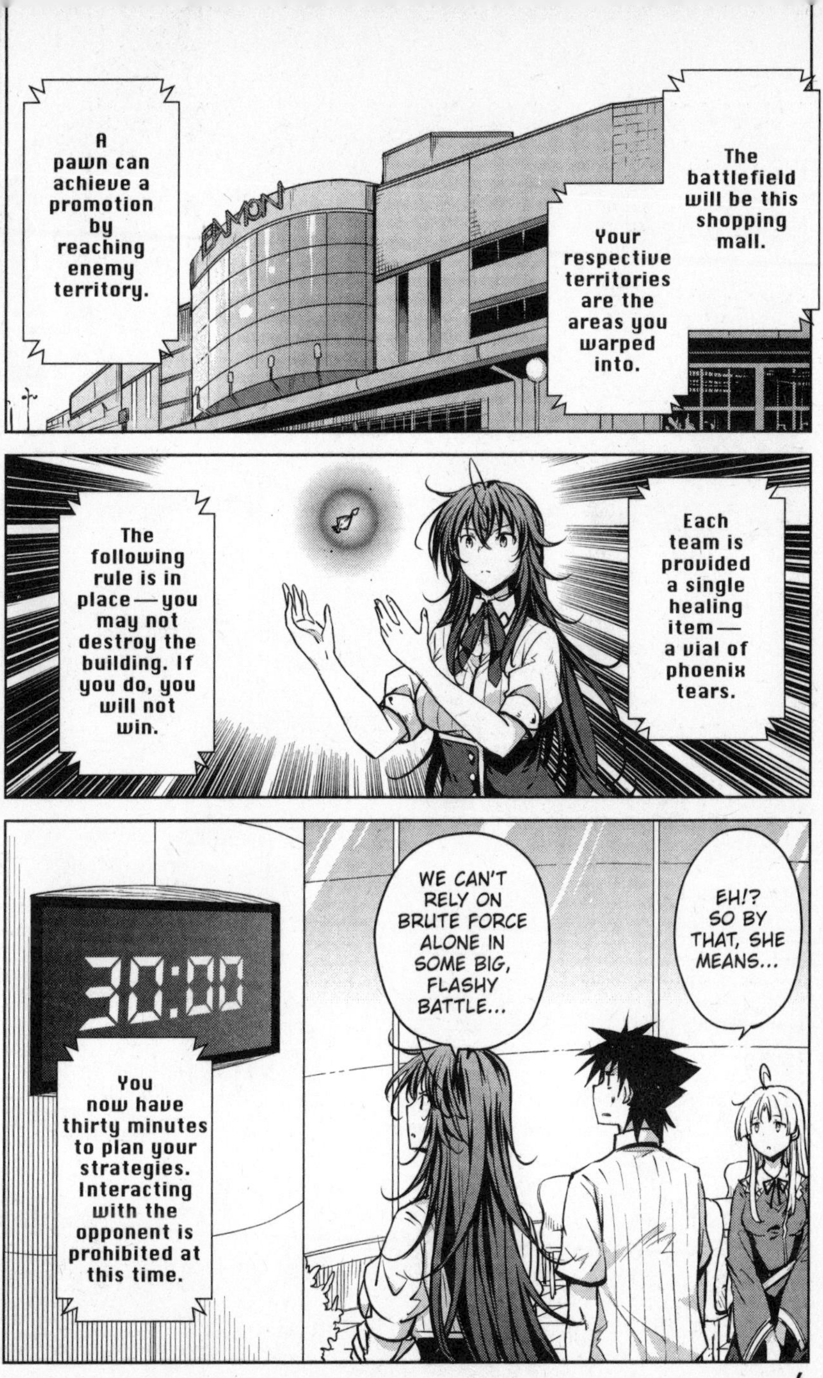
The battlefield will be this shopping mall.
Your respective territories are the areas you warped into.
A pawn can achieve a promotion by reaching enemy territory.
Each team is provided a single healing item—a vial of phoenix tears.
The following rule is in place—you may not destroy the building. If you do, you will not win.
EH!? SO BY THAT, SHE MEANS...
WE CAN'T RELY ON BRUTE FORCE ALONE IN SOME BIG, FLASHY BATTLE...
30:00
You now have thirty minutes to plan your strategies. Interacting with the opponent is prohibited at this time.

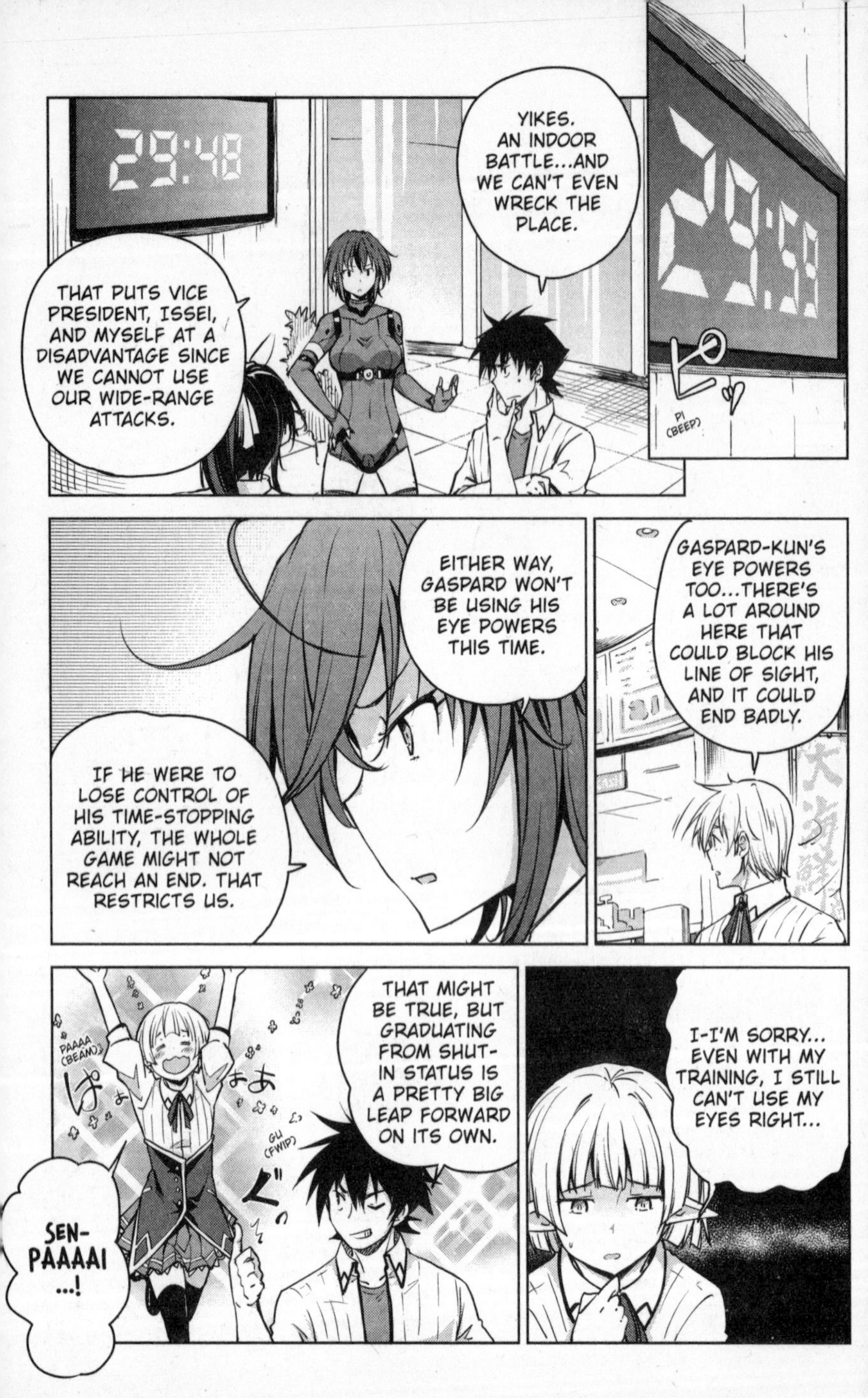
29:59
PI (BEEP)
29:48
YIKES. AN INDOOR BATTLE...AND WE CAN'T EVEN WRECK THE PLACE.
THAT PUTS VICE PRESIDENT, ISSEI, AND MYSELF AT A DISADVANTAGE SINCE WE CANNOT USE OUR WIDE-RANGE ATTACKS.
GASPARD-KUN'S EYE POWERS TOO...THERE'S A LOT AROUND HERE THAT COULD BLOCK HIS LINE OF SIGHT, AND IT COULD END BADLY.
EITHER WAY, GASPARD WON'T BE USING HIS EYE POWERS THIS TIME.
IF HE WERE TO LOSE CONTROL OF HIS TIME-STOPPING ABILITY, THE WHOLE GAME MIGHT NOT REACH AN END. THAT RESTRICTS US.
I-I'M SORRY... EVEN WITH MY TRAINING, I STILL CAN'T USE MY EYES RIGHT...
THAT MIGHT BE TRUE, BUT GRADUATING FROM SHUT-IN STATUS IS A PRETTY BIG LEAP FORWARD ON ITS OWN.
GU (FWIP)
PAAAA (BEAM)
SEN-PAAAAI ...!

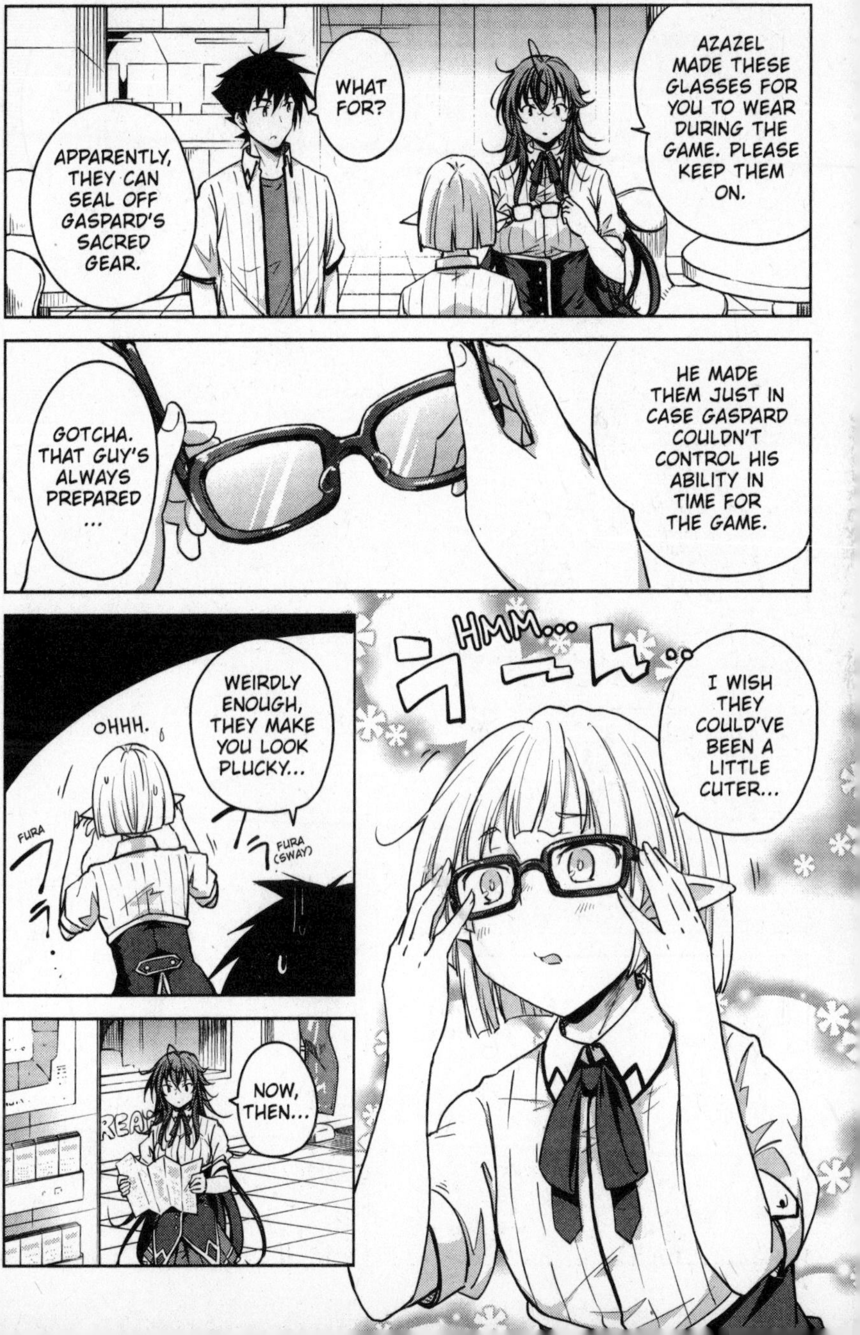
AZAZEL MADE THESE GLASSES FOR YOU TO WEAR DURING THE GAME. PLEASE KEEP THEM ON.
WHAT FOR?
APPARENTLY, THEY CAN SEAL OFF GASPARD'S SACRED GEAR.
HE MADE THEM JUST IN CASE GASPARD COULDN'T CONTROL HIS ABILITY IN TIME FOR THE GAME.
GOTCHA. THAT GUY'S ALWAYS PREPARED ...
うーん..
HMM...
I WISH THEY COULD'VE BEEN A LITTLE CUTER...
WEIRDLY ENOUGH, THEY MAKE YOU LOOK PLUCKY...
OHHH.
FURA (SWAY)
FURA
NOW, THEN...

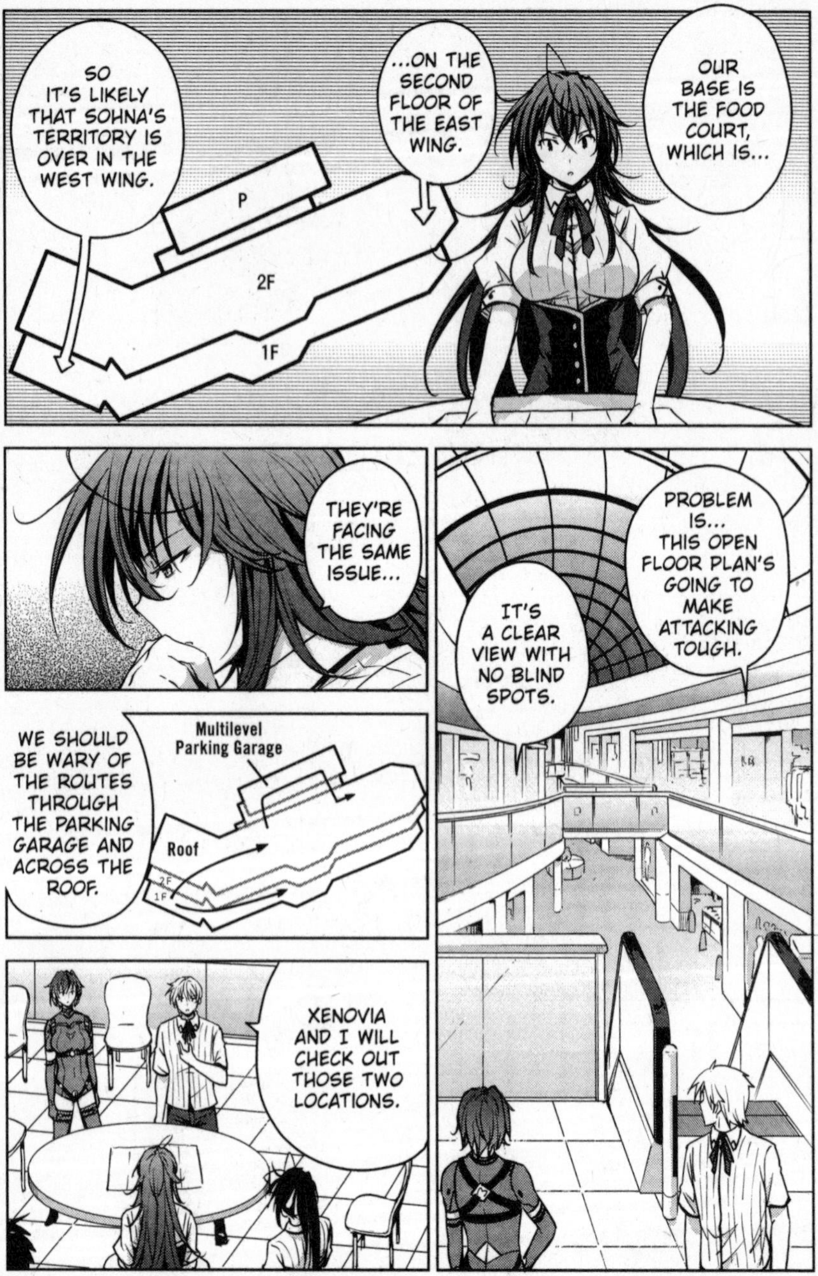
OUR BASE IS THE FOOD COURT, WHICH IS...
...ON THE SECOND FLOOR OF THE EAST WING.
SO IT'S LIKELY THAT SOHNA'S TERRITORY IS OVER IN THE WEST WING.
P
2F
1F
PROBLEM IS... THIS OPEN FLOOR PLAN'S GOING TO MAKE ATTACKING TOUGH.
IT'S A CLEAR VIEW WITH NO BLIND SPOTS.
THEY'RE FACING THE SAME ISSUE...
WE SHOULD BE WARY OF THE ROUTES THROUGH THE PARKING GARAGE AND ACROSS THE ROOF.
Multilevel Parking Garage
Roof
2F
1F
XENOVIA AND I WILL CHECK OUT THOSE TWO LOCATIONS.

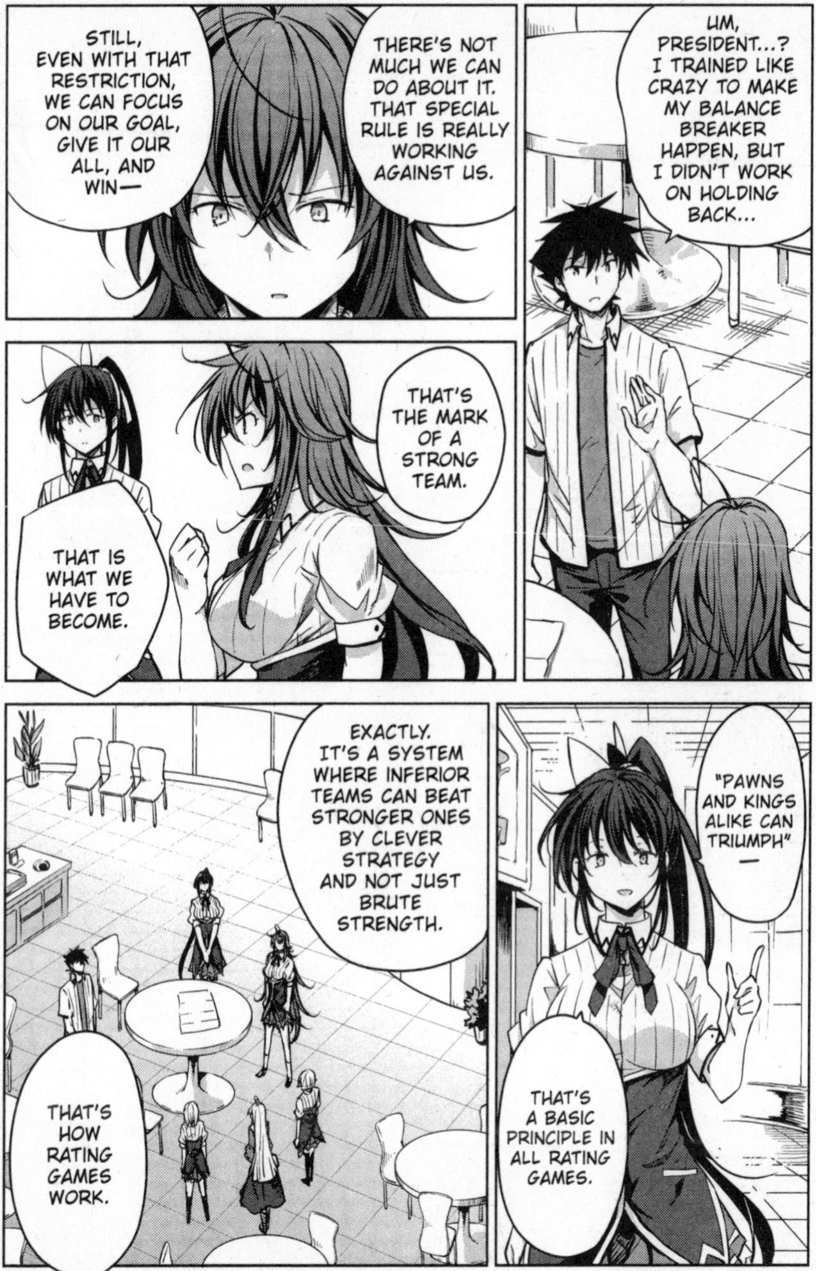
UM, PRESIDENT...? I TRAINED LIKE CRAZY TO MAKE MY BALANCE BREAKER HAPPEN, BUT I DIDN'T WORK ON HOLDING BACK...
THERE'S NOT MUCH WE CAN DO ABOUT IT. THAT SPECIAL RULE IS REALLY WORKING AGAINST US.
STILL, EVEN WITH THAT RESTRICTION, WE CAN FOCUS ON OUR GOAL, GIVE IT OUR ALL, AND WIN—
THAT'S THE MARK OF A STRONG TEAM.
THAT IS WHAT WE HAVE TO BECOME.
"PAWNS AND KINGS ALIKE CAN TRIUMPH"—
THAT'S A BASIC PRINCIPLE IN ALL RATING GAMES.
EXACTLY. IT'S A SYSTEM WHERE INFERIOR TEAMS CAN BEAT STRONGER ONES BY CLEVER STRATEGY AND NOT JUST BRUTE STRENGTH.
THAT'S HOW RATING GAMES WORK.

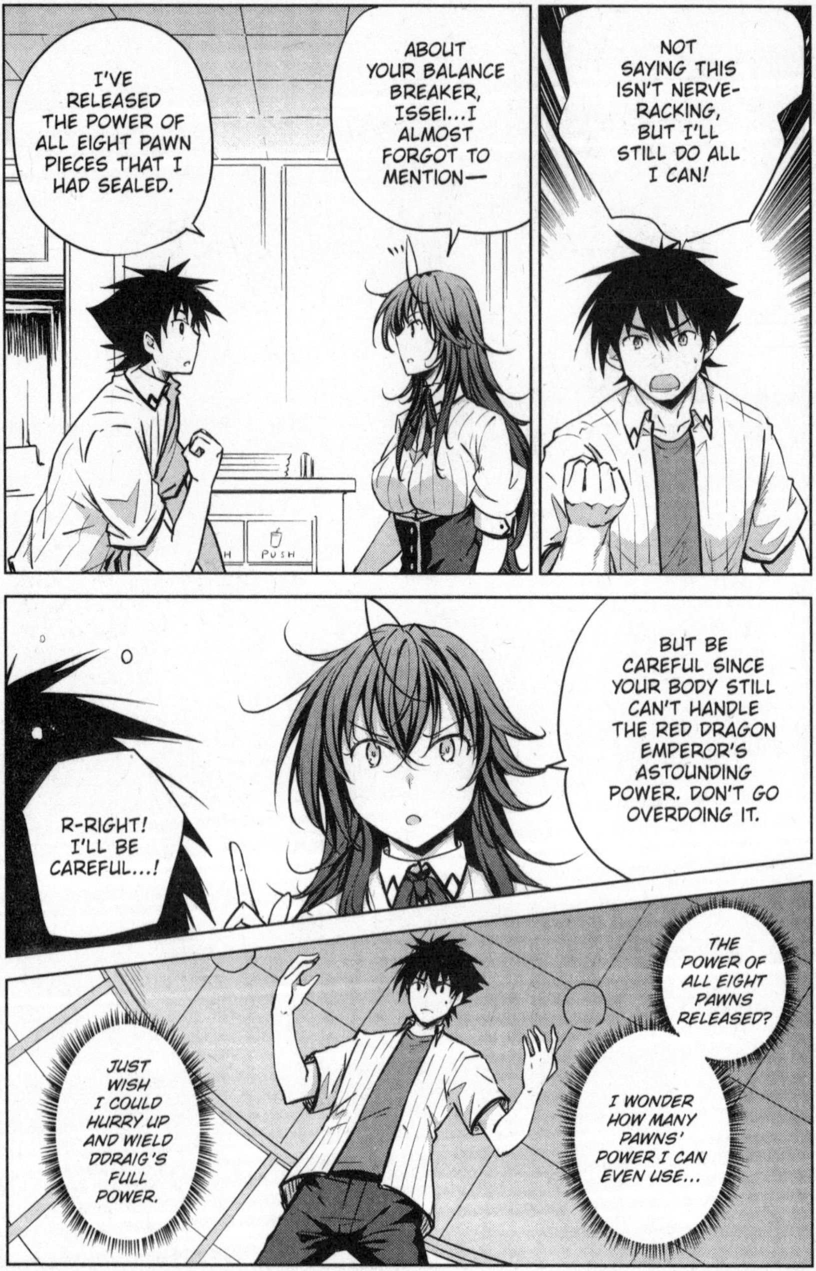
NOT SAYING THIS ISN'T NERVE-RACKING, BUT I'LL STILL DO ALL I CAN!
ABOUT YOUR BALANCE BREAKER, ISSEI...I ALMOST FORGOT TO MENTION—
I'VE RELEASED THE POWER OF ALL EIGHT PAWN PIECES THAT I HAD SEALED.
PUSH
BUT BE CAREFUL SINCE YOUR BODY STILL CAN'T HANDLE THE RED DRAGON EMPEROR'S ASTOUNDING POWER. DON'T GO OVERDOING IT.
R-RIGHT! I'LL BE CAREFUL...!
THE POWER OF ALL EIGHT PAWNS RELEASED?
I WONDER HOW MANY PAWNS' POWER I CAN EVEN USE...
JUST WISH I COULD HURRY UP AND WIELD DDRAIG'S FULL POWER.

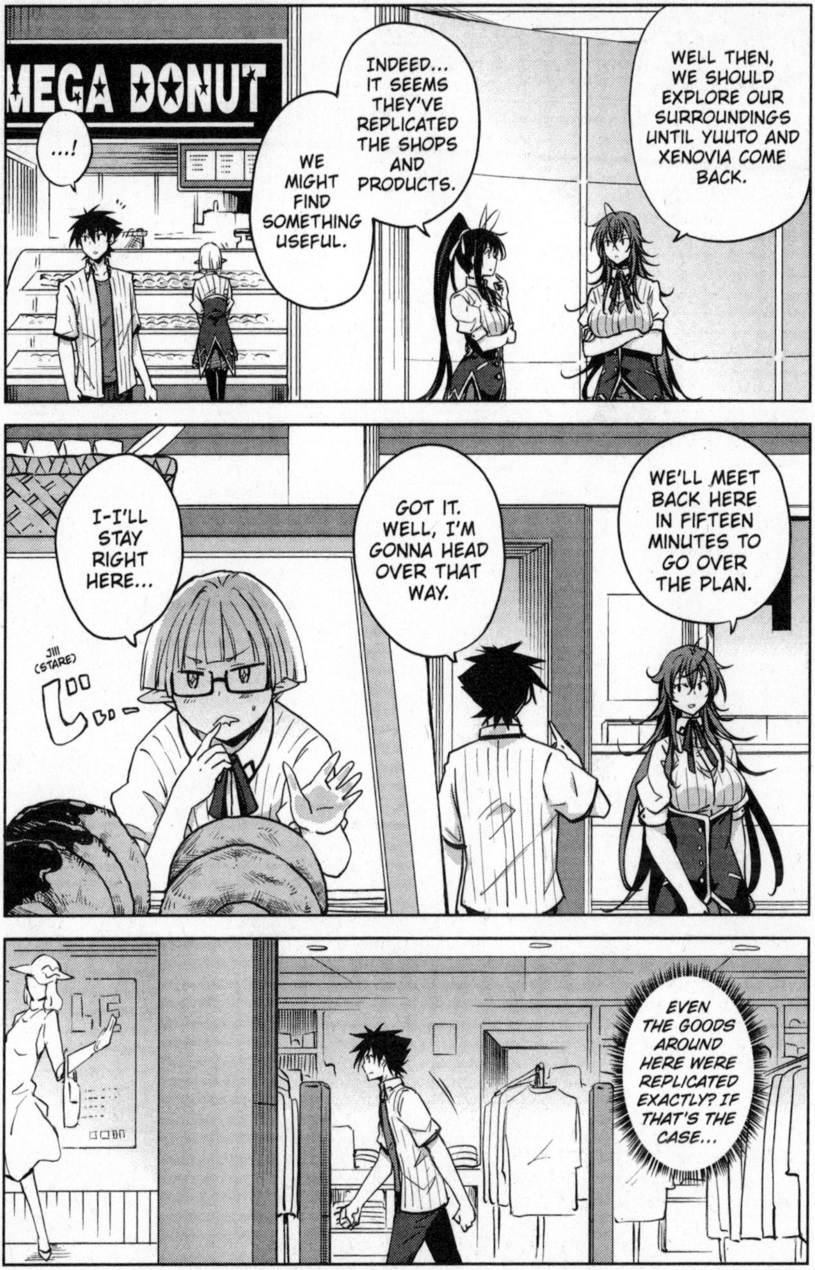

MEGA DONUT
WELL THEN, WE SHOULD EXPLORE OUR SURROUNDINGS UNTIL YUUTO AND XENOVIA COME BACK.
INDEED... IT SEEMS THEY'VE REPLICATED THE SHOPS AND PRODUCTS.
WE MIGHT FIND SOMETHING USEFUL.
...!
WE'LL MEET BACK HERE IN FIFTEEN MINUTES TO GO OVER THE PLAN.
GOT IT. WELL, I'M GONNA HEAD OVER THAT WAY.
I-I'LL STAY RIGHT HERE...
JIII (STARE)
EVEN THE GOODS AROUND HERE WERE REPLICATED EXACTLY? IF THAT'S THE CASE...

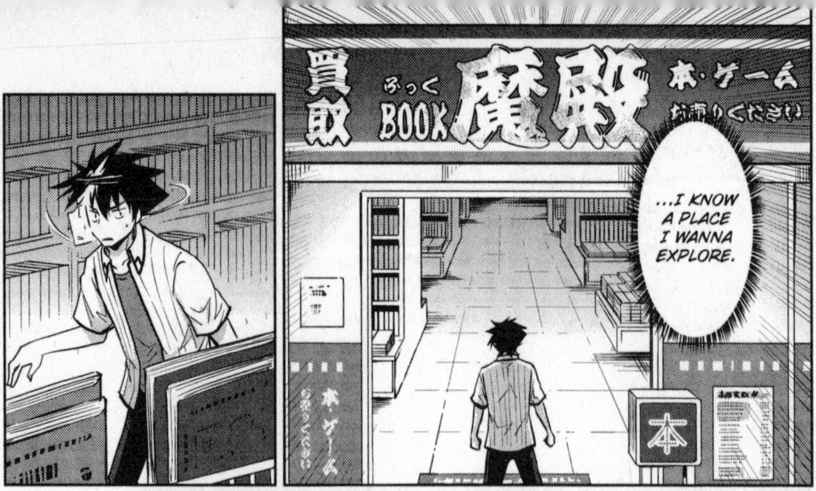
買取
BOOK 魔殿
本・ゲーム
...I KNOW A PLACE I WANNA EXPLORE.

SIGNS RIGHT TO LEFT: SELL US YOUR BOOKS AND VIDEO GAMES, DEVIL PALACE BOOKS, SECONDHAND STORE

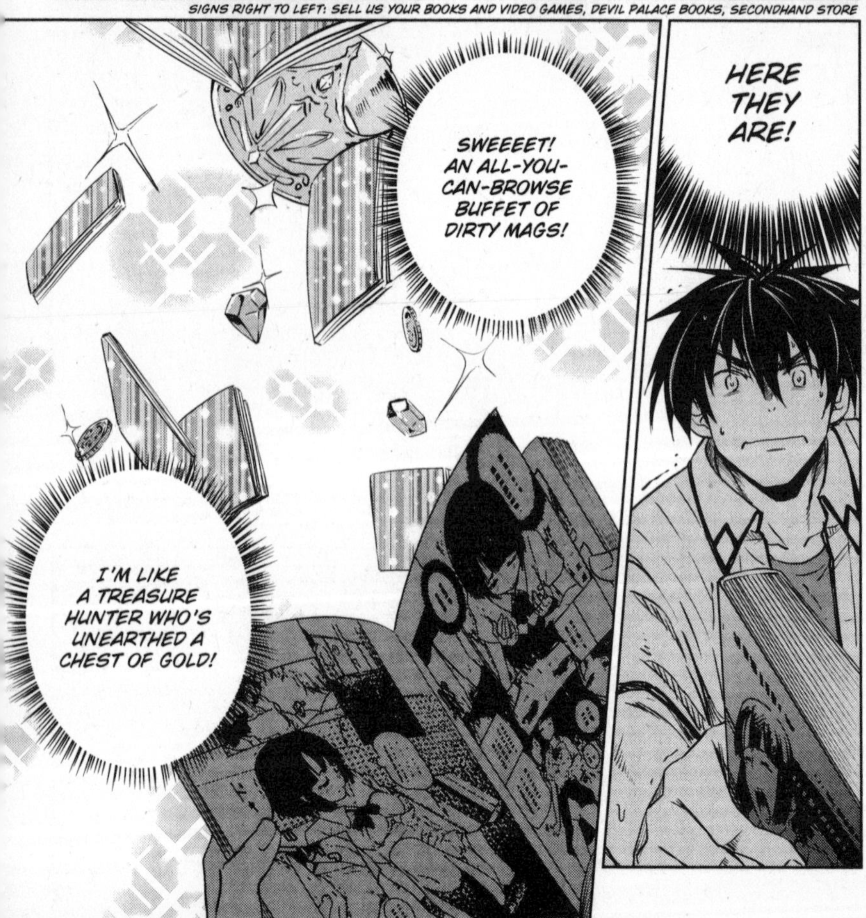
HERE THEY ARE!
SWEEEET! AN ALL-YOU-CAN-BROWSE BUFFET OF DIRTY MAGS!
I'M LIKE A TREASURE HUNTER WHO'S UNEARTHED A CHEST OF GOLD!

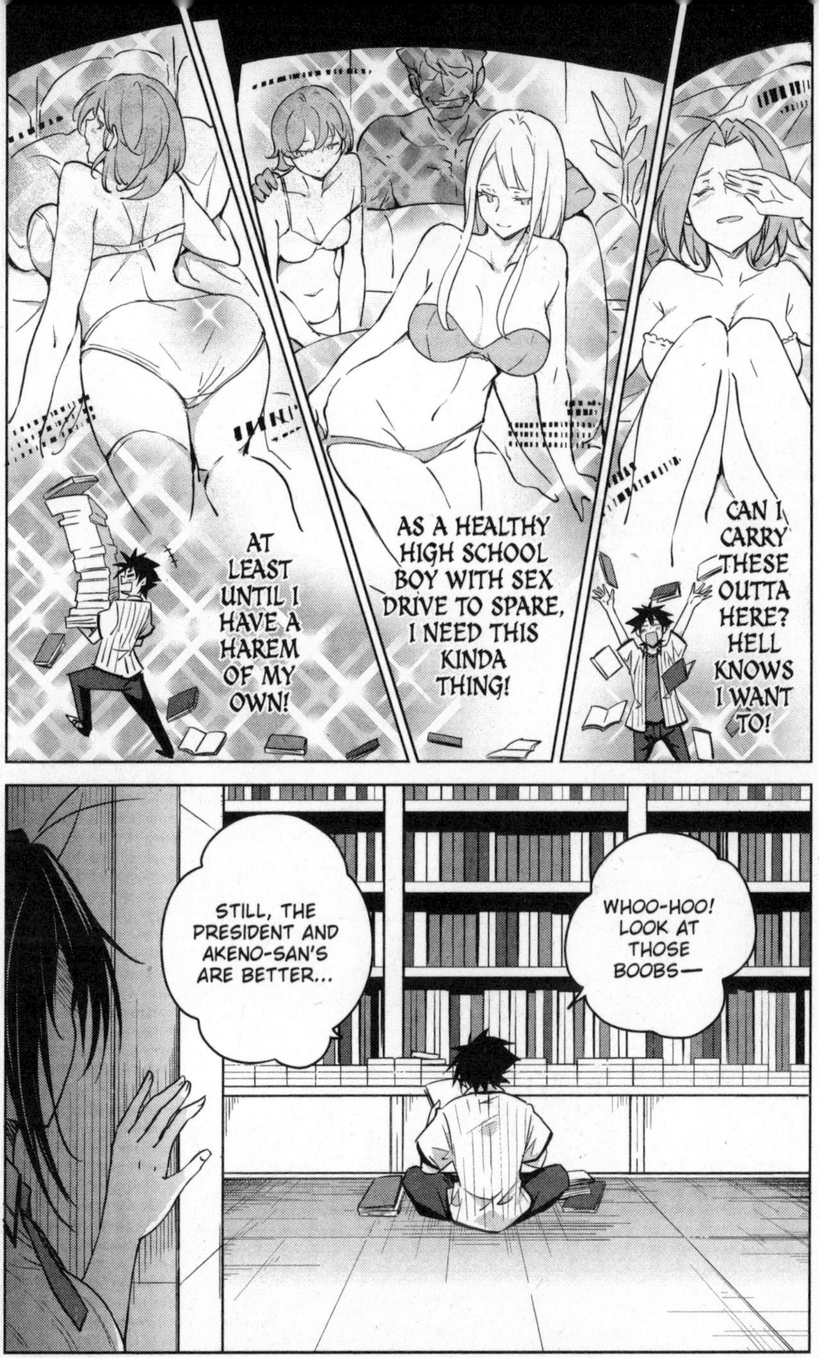
CAN I CARRY THESE OUTTA HERE? HELL KNOWS I WANT TO!
AS A HEALTHY HIGH SCHOOL BOY WITH SEX DRIVE TO SPARE, I NEED THIS KINDA THING!
AT LEAST UNTIL I HAVE A HAREM OF MY OWN!
WHOO-HOO! LOOK AT THOSE BOOBS—
STILL, THE PRESIDENT AND AKENO-SAN'S ARE BETTER...

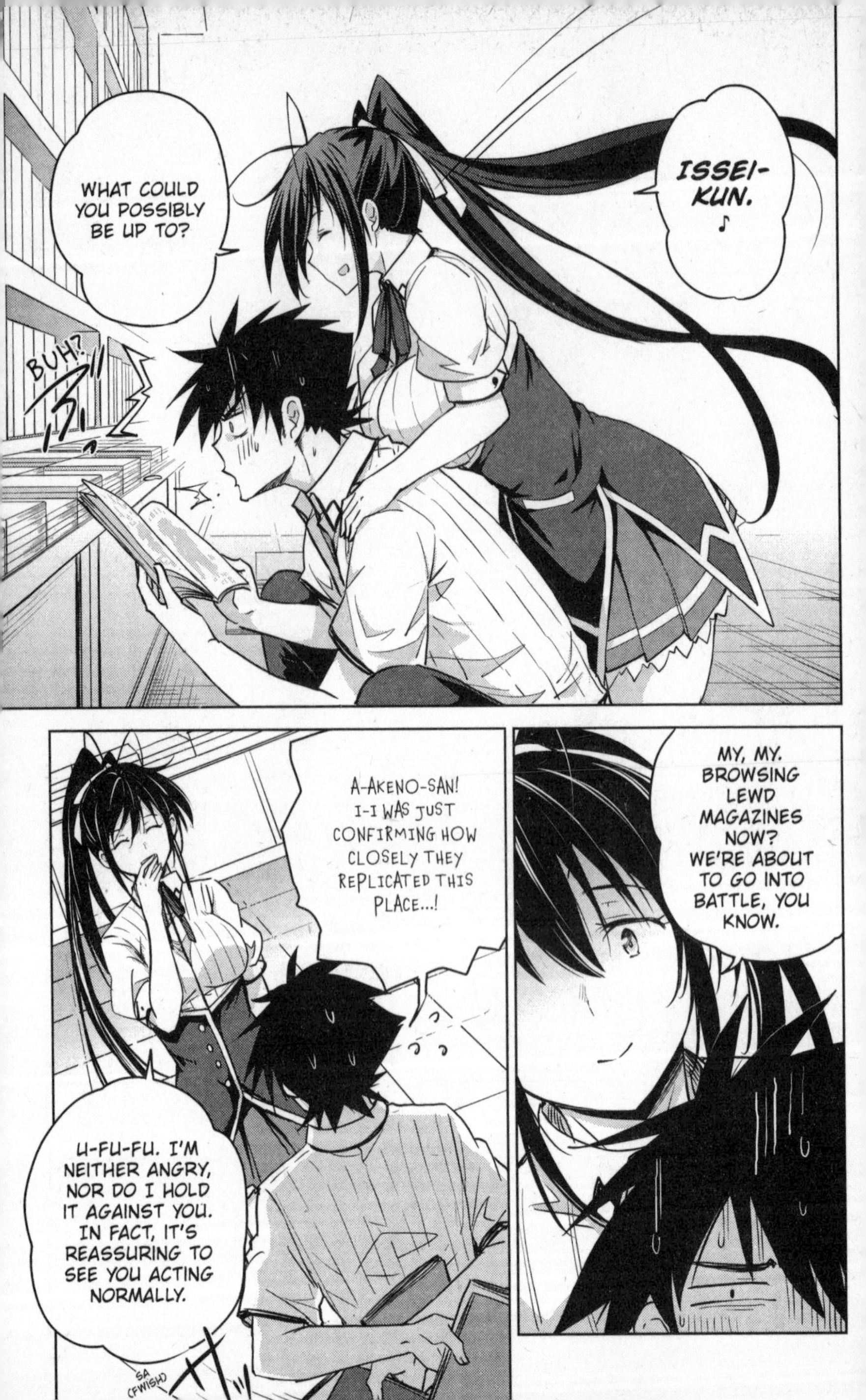
ISSEI-KUN. ♪
WHAT COULD YOU POSSIBLY BE UP TO?
BUH?!
MY, MY. BROWSING LEWD MAGAZINES NOW? WE'RE ABOUT TO GO INTO BATTLE, YOU KNOW.
A-AKENO-SAN! I-I WAS JUST CONFIRMING HOW CLOSELY THEY REPLICATED THIS PLACE...!
U-FU-FU. I'M NEITHER ANGRY, NOR DO I HOLD IT AGAINST YOU. IN FACT, IT'S REASSURING TO SEE YOU ACTING NORMALLY.
SA (FWISH)

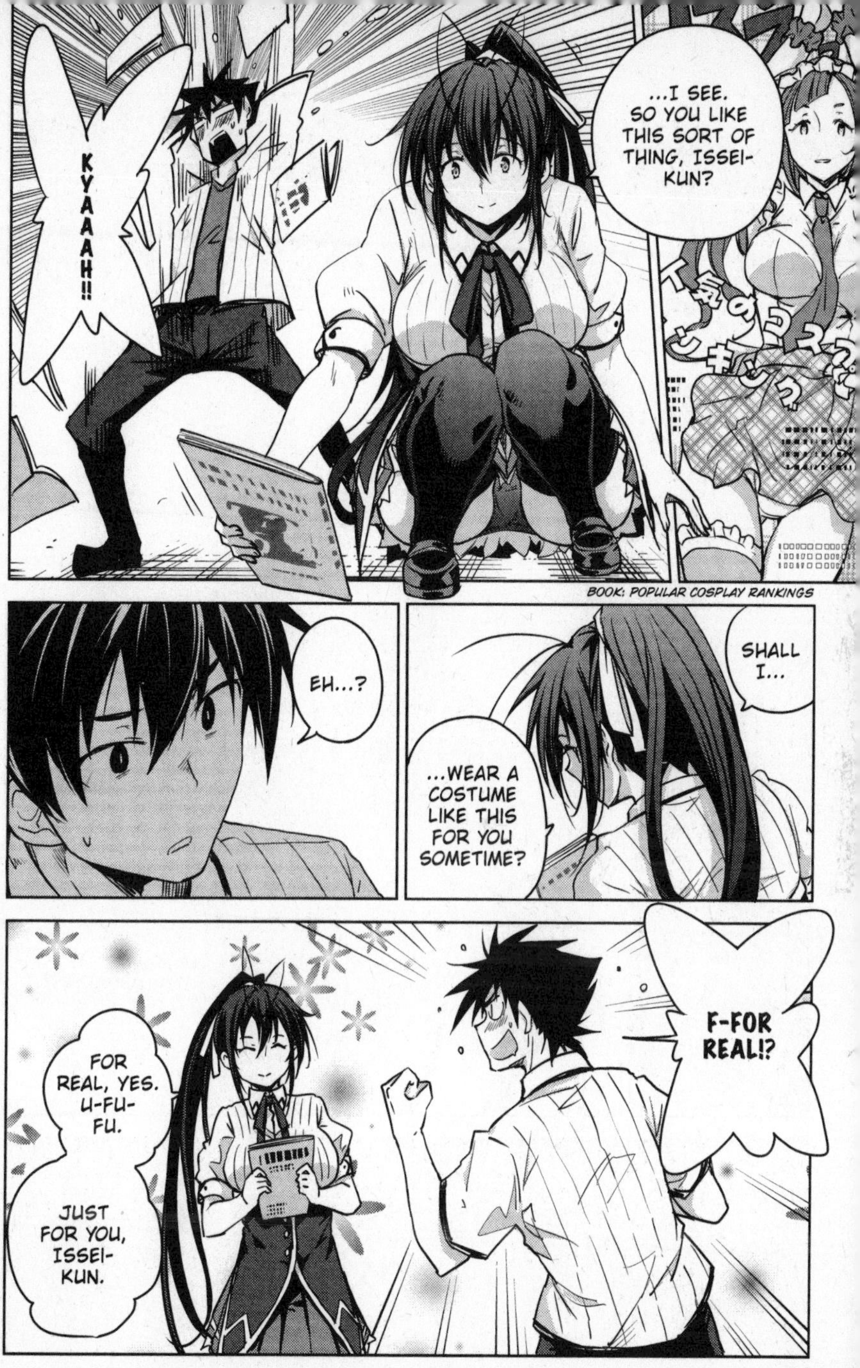
...I SEE. SO YOU LIKE THIS SORT OF THING, ISSEI-KUN?
KYAAAAH!!
BOOK: POPULAR COSPLAY RANKINGS
SHALL I...
...WEAR A COSTUME LIKE THIS FOR YOU SOMETIME?
EH...?
F-FOR REAL!?
FOR REAL, YES. U-FU-FU.
JUST FOR YOU, ISSEI-KUN.

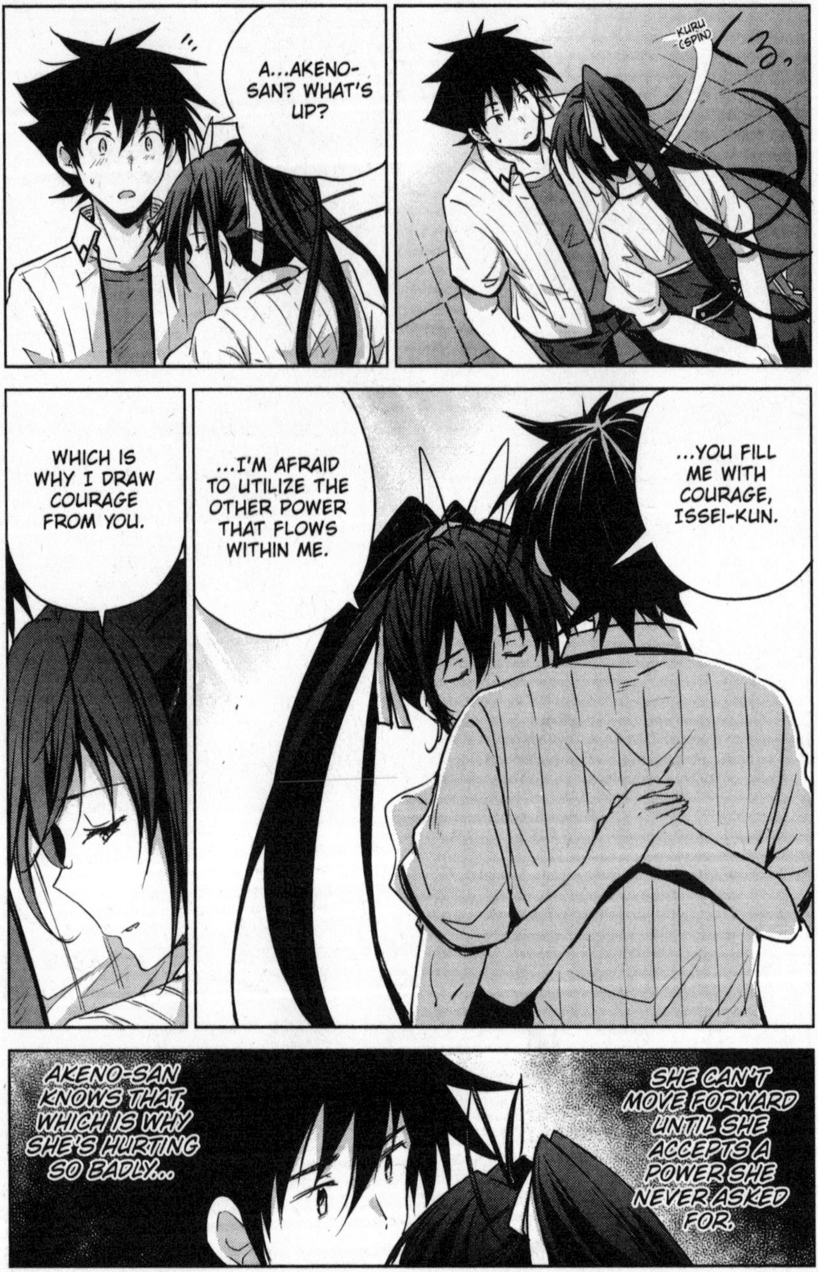
KURU (SPIN)
A...AKENO-SAN? WHAT'S UP?
...YOU FILL ME WITH COURAGE, ISSEI-KUN.
...I'M AFRAID TO UTILIZE THE OTHER POWER THAT FLOWS WITHIN ME.
WHICH IS WHY I DRAW COURAGE FROM YOU.
SHE CAN'T MOVE FORWARD UNTIL SHE ACCEPTS A POWER SHE NEVER ASKED FOR.
AKENO-SAN KNOWS THAT, WHICH IS WHY SHE'S HURTING SO BADLY...

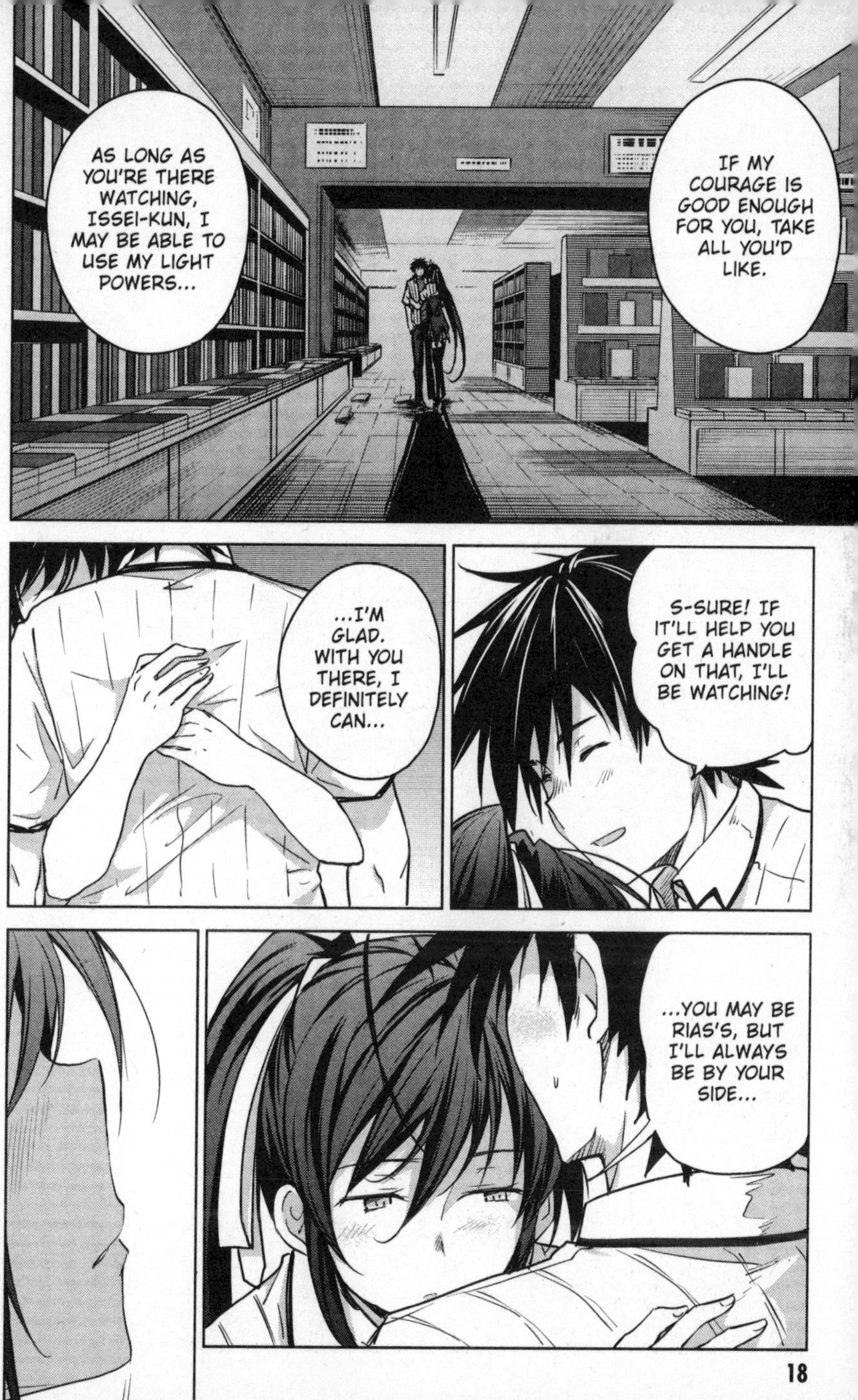
IF MY COURAGE IS GOOD ENOUGH FOR YOU, TAKE ALL YOU'D LIKE.
AS LONG AS YOU'RE THERE WATCHING, ISSEI-KUN, I MAY BE ABLE TO USE MY LIGHT POWERS...
S-SURE! IF IT'LL HELP YOU GET A HANDLE ON THAT, I'LL BE WATCHING!
...I'M GLAD. WITH YOU THERE, I DEFINITELY CAN...
...YOU MAY BE RIAS'S, BUT I'LL ALWAYS BE BY YOUR SIDE...

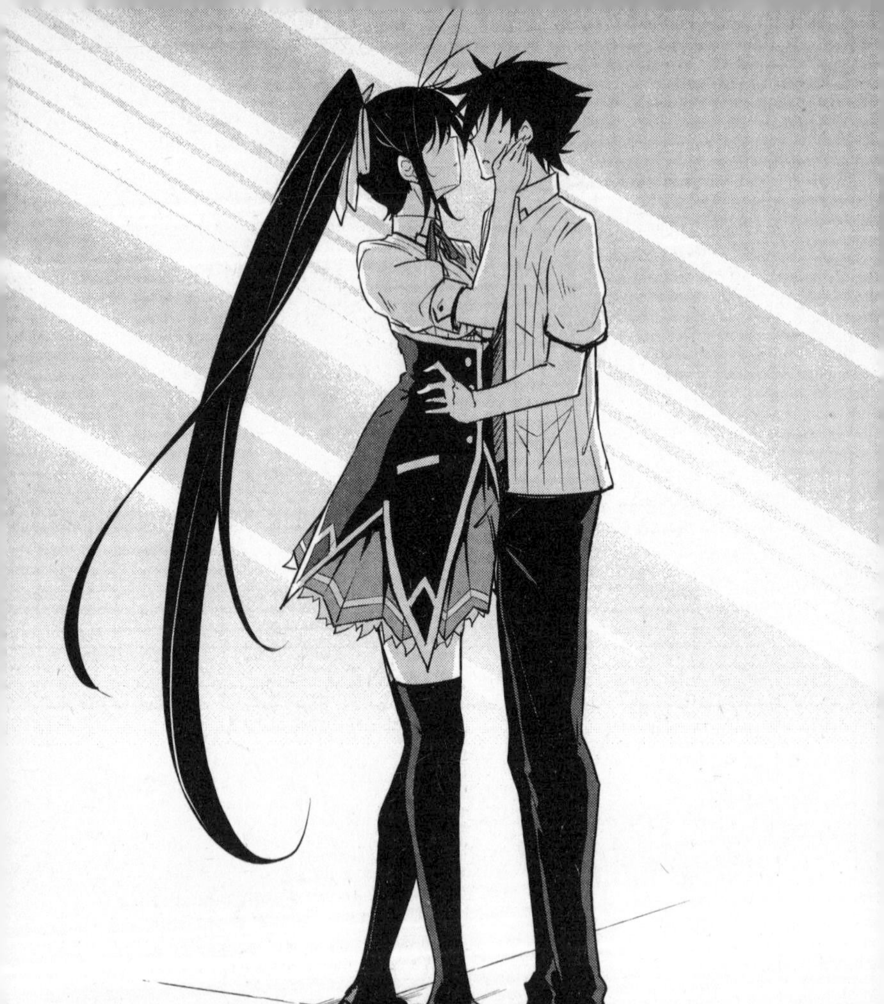
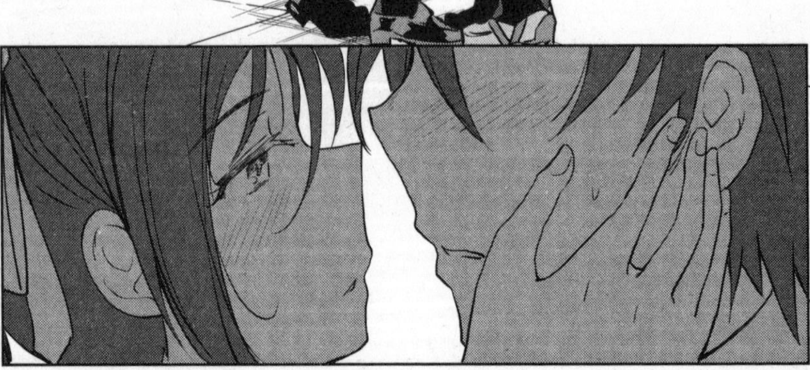

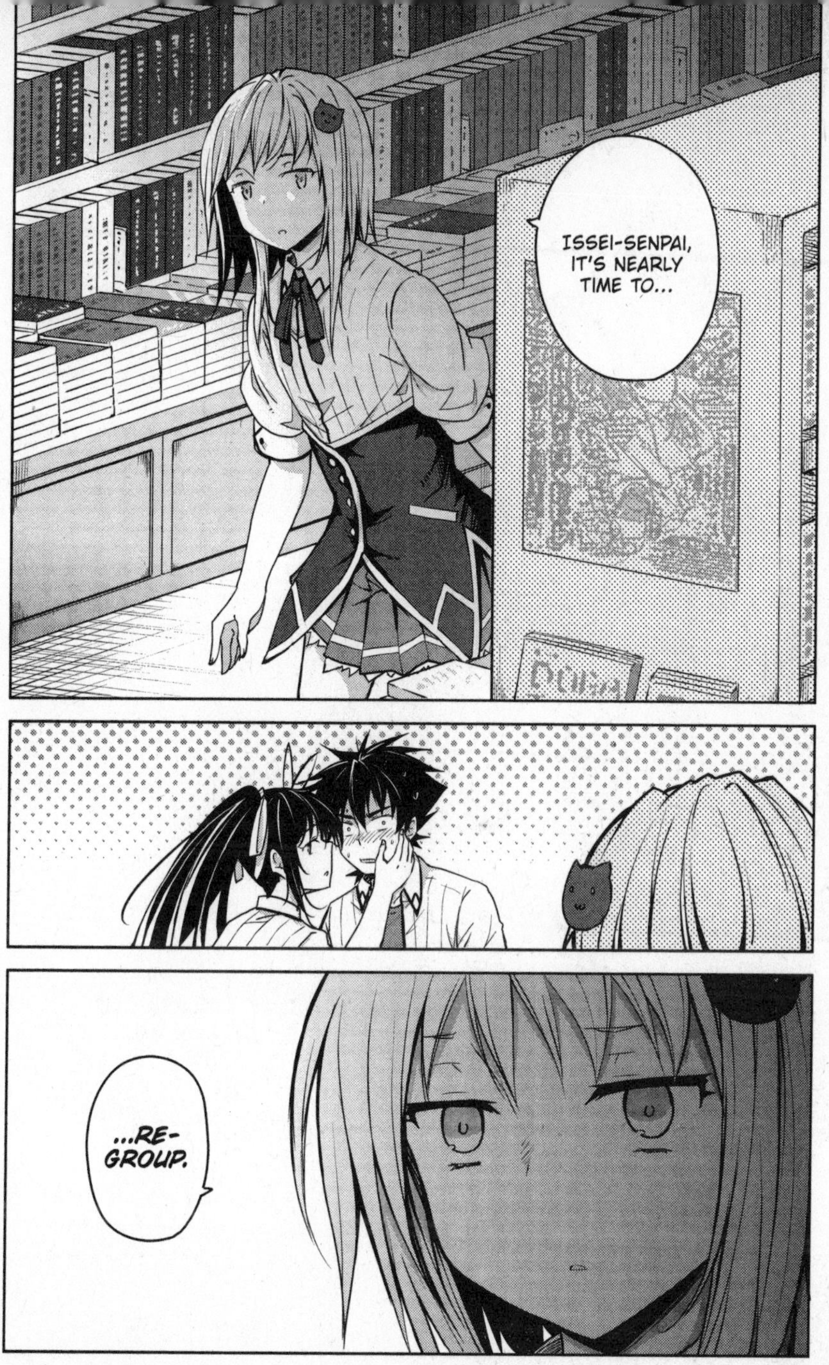
ISSEI-SENPAI, IT'S NEARLY TIME TO...
...RE-GROUP.

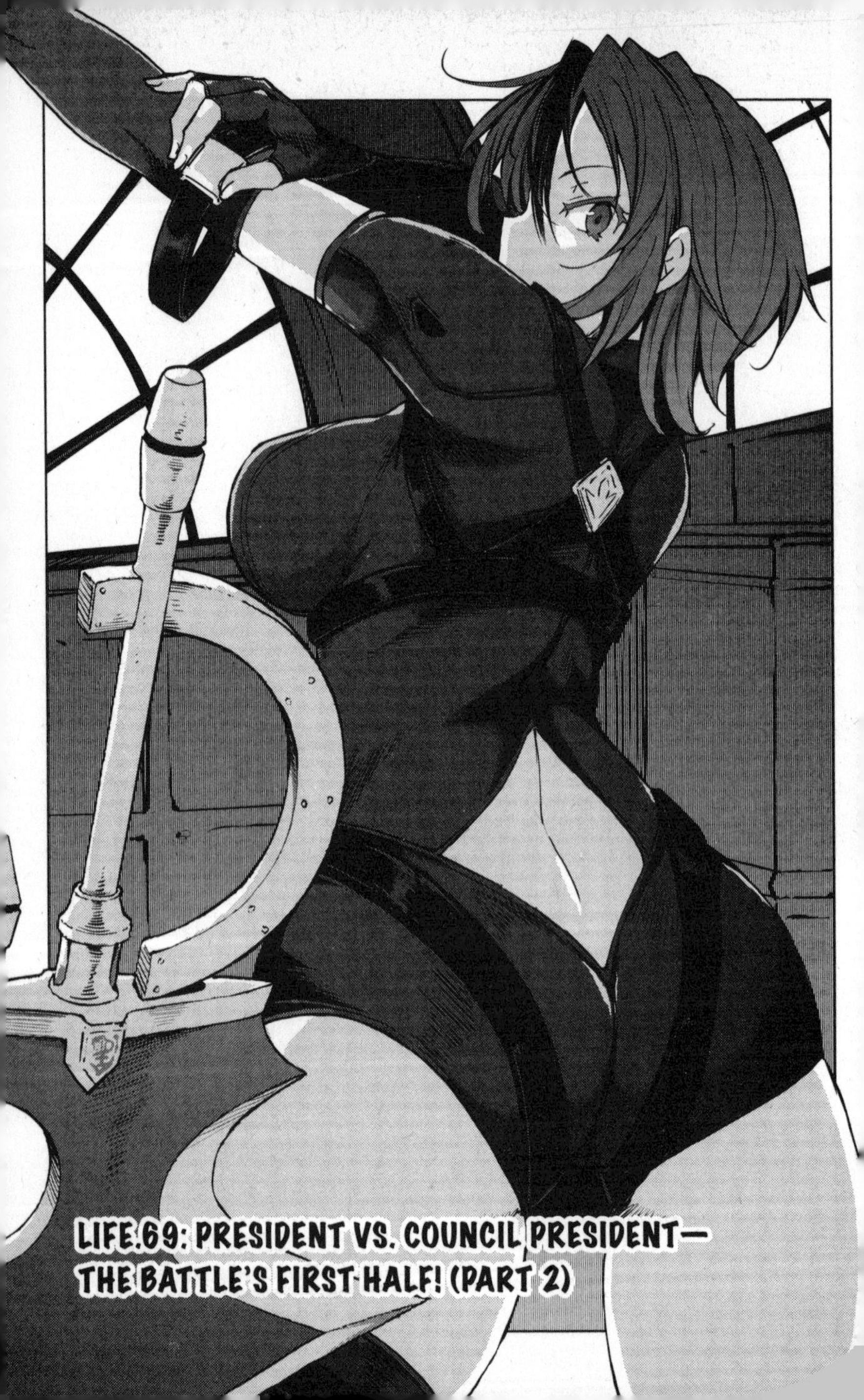
LIFE.69: PRESIDENT VS. COUNCIL PRESIDENT—
THE BATTLE'S FIRST HALF! (PART 2)

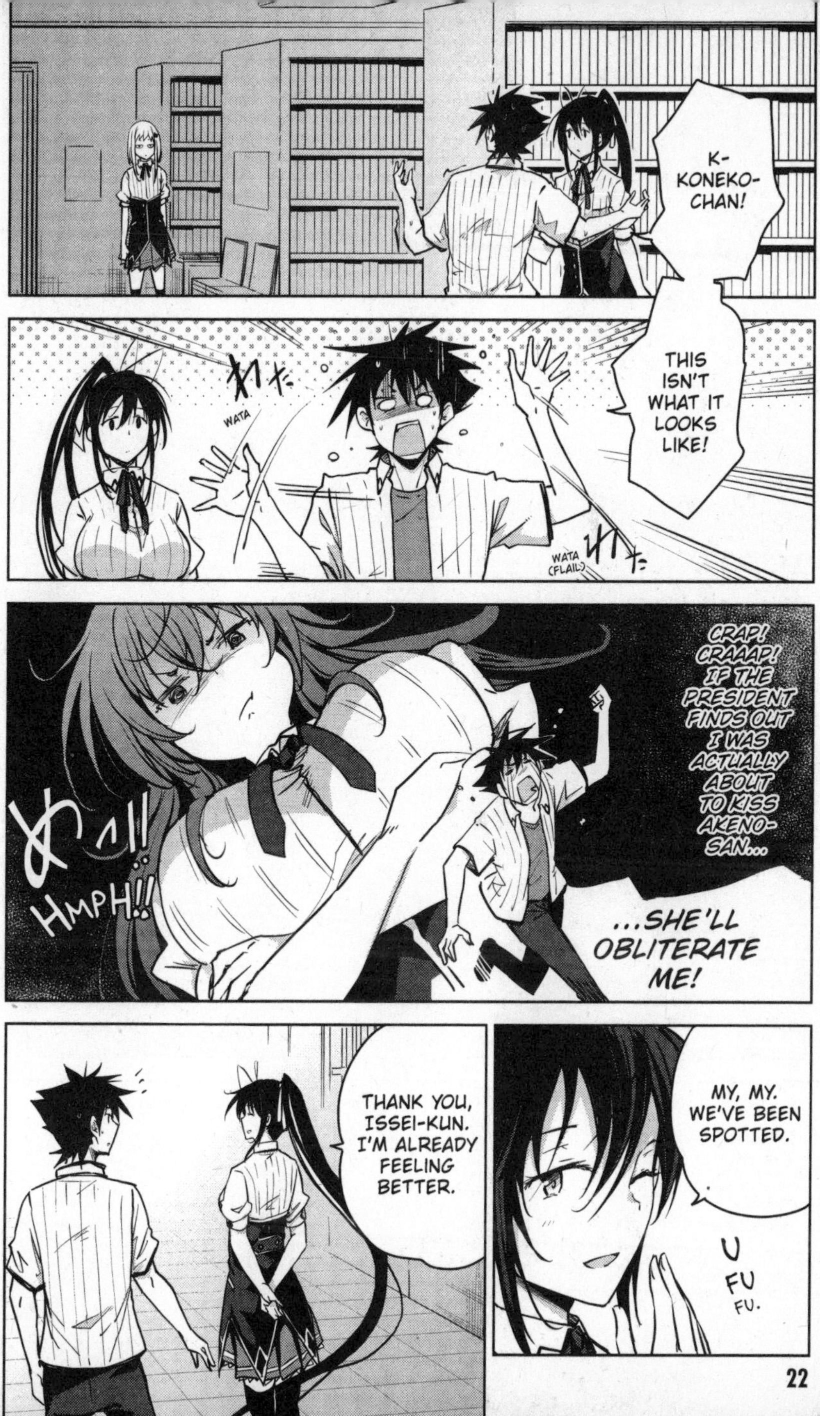
K-KONEKO-CHAN!
THIS ISN'T WHAT IT LOOKS LIKE!
WATA
WATA (FLAIL)
CRAP! CRAAAP! IF THE PRESIDENT FINDS OUT I WAS ACTUALLY ABOUT TO KISS AKENO-SAN...
...SHE'LL OBLITERATE ME!
HMPH!!
MY, MY. WE'VE BEEN SPOTTED.
U FU FU.
THANK YOU, ISSEI-KUN. I'M ALREADY FEELING BETTER.

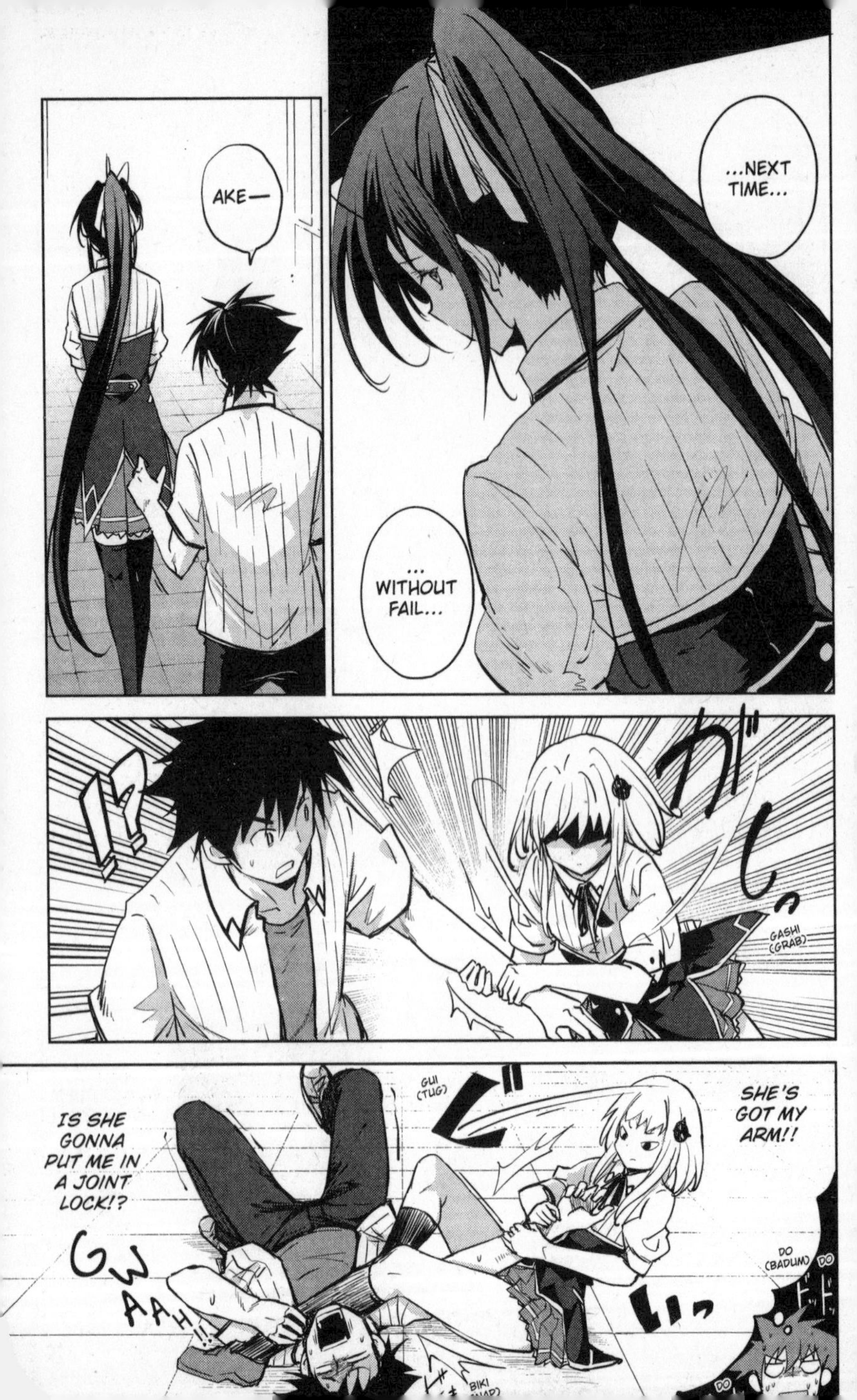
...NEXT TIME...
...WITHOUT FAIL...
AKE—
GASHI (GRAB)
SHE'S GOT MY ARM!!
GUI (TUG)
IS SHE GONNA PUT ME IN A JOINT LOCK!?
DO (BADUM) DO
GWAAH!!
BIKI

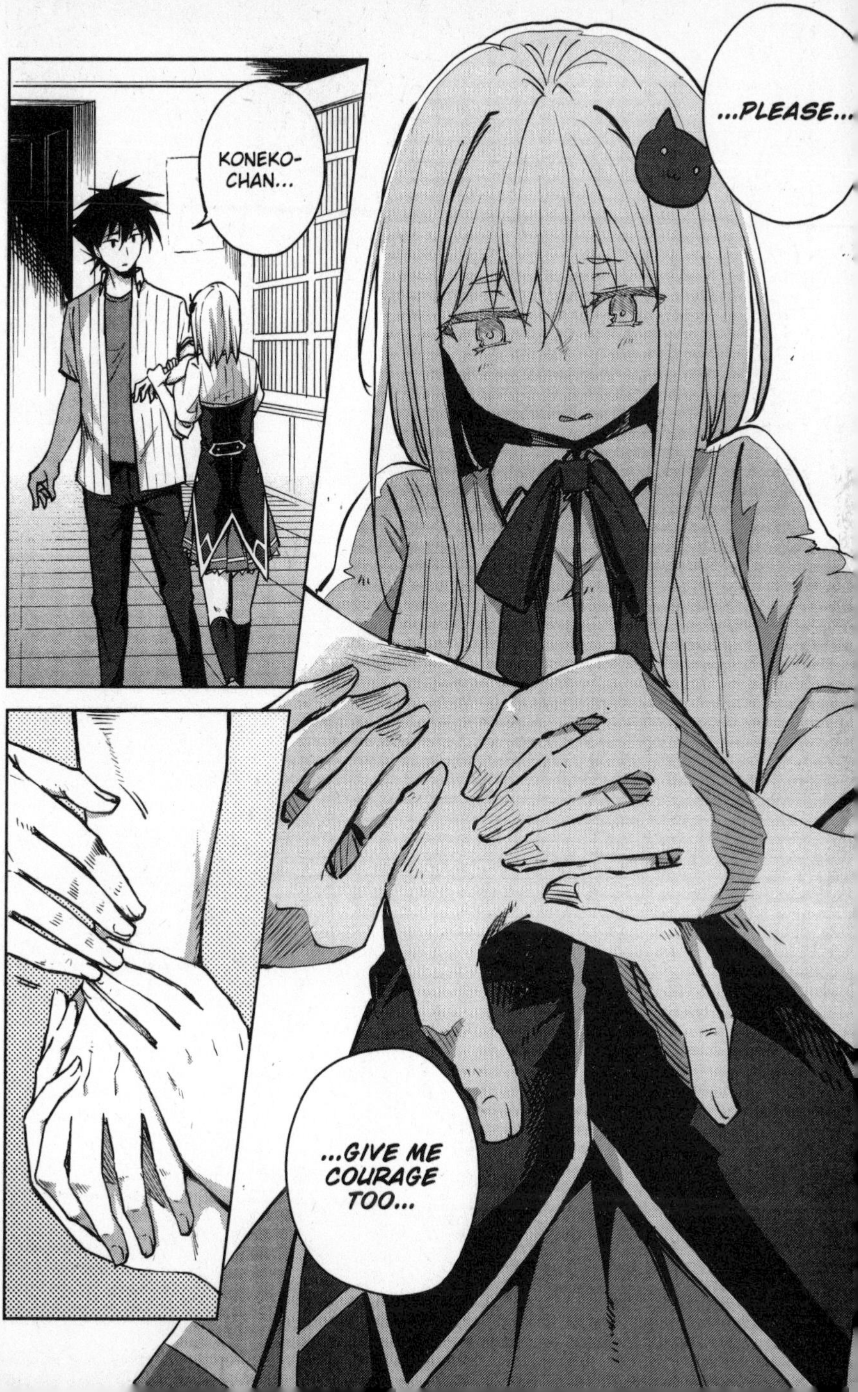
...PLEASE...
...GIVE ME COURAGE TOO...
KONEKO-CHAN...

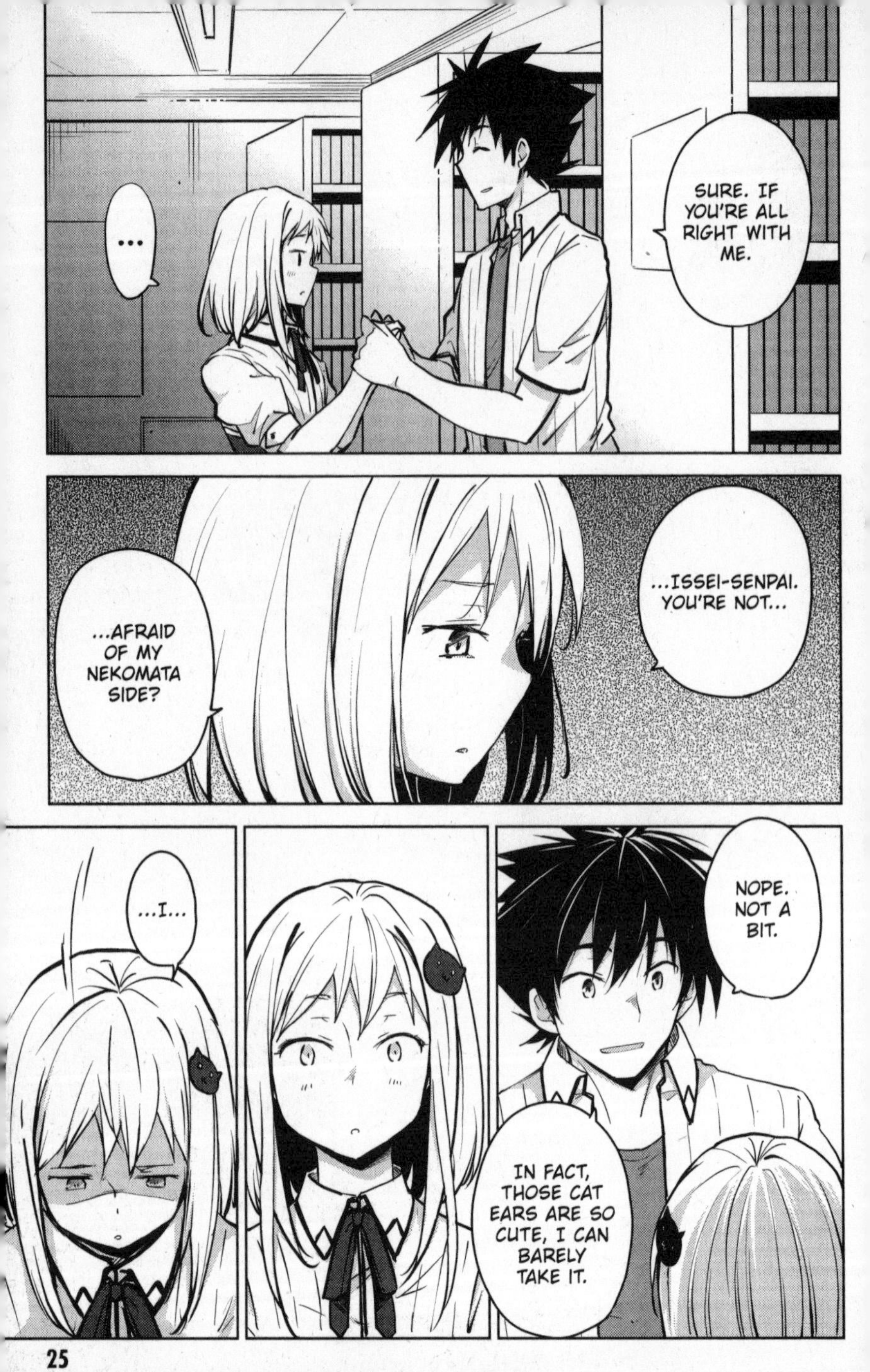
SURE. IF YOU'RE ALL RIGHT WITH ME.
...
...ISSEI-SENPAI. YOU'RE NOT...
...AFRAID OF MY NEKOMATA SIDE?
NOPE. NOT A BIT.
IN FACT, THOSE CAT EARS ARE SO CUTE, I CAN BARELY TAKE IT.
...I...

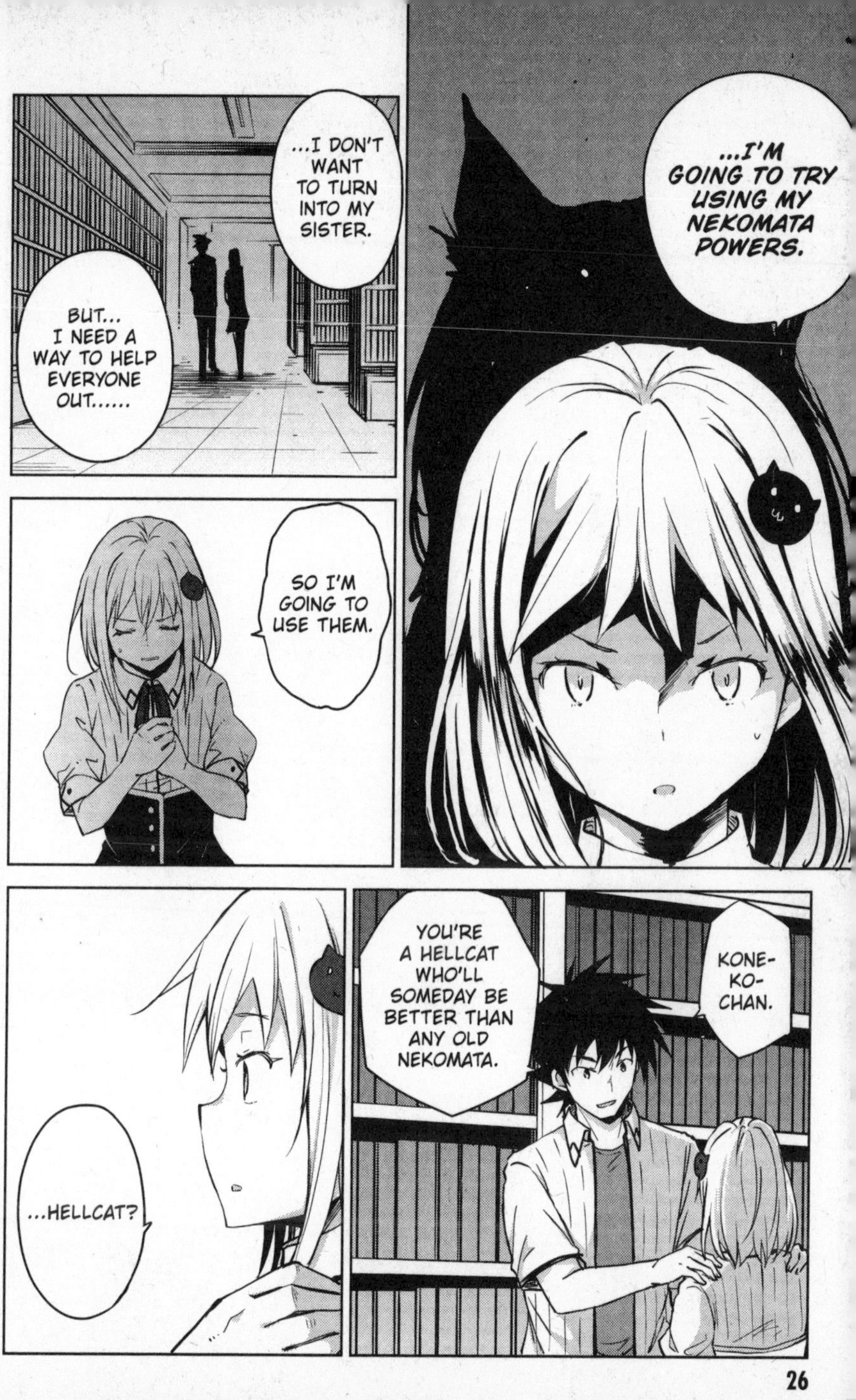
...I'M GOING TO TRY USING MY NEKOMATA POWERS.
...I DON'T WANT TO TURN INTO MY SISTER.
BUT... I NEED A WAY TO HELP EVERYONE OUT......
SO I'M GOING TO USE THEM.
KONE-KO-CHAN.
YOU'RE A HELLCAT WHO'LL SOMEDAY BE BETTER THAN ANY OLD NEKOMATA.
...HELLCAT?

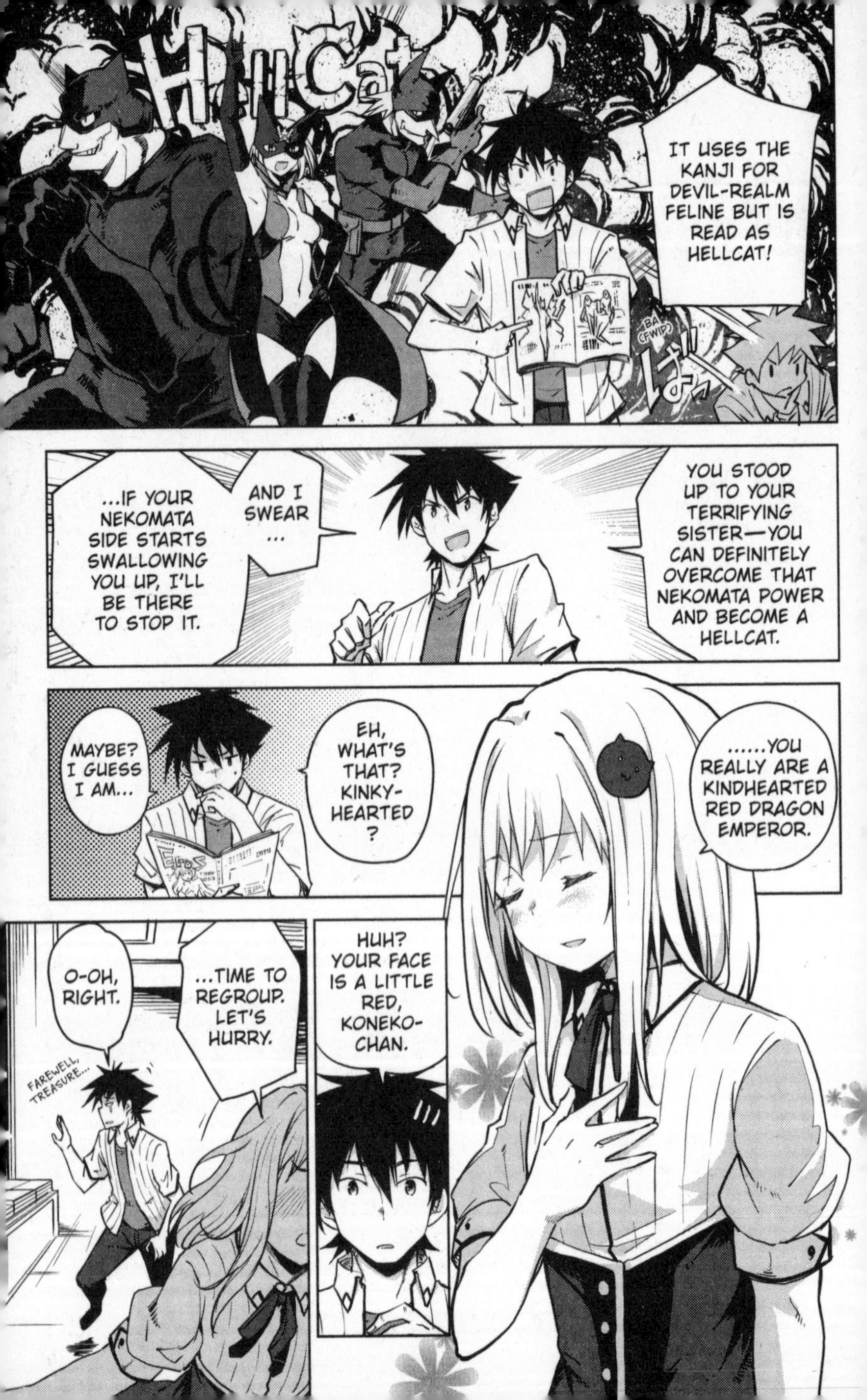
HellCat
IT USES THE KANJI FOR DEVIL-REALM FELINE BUT IS READ AS HELLCAT!
BA (FWIP)
YOU STOOD UP TO YOUR TERRIFYING SISTER—YOU CAN DEFINITELY OVERCOME THAT NEKOMATA POWER AND BECOME A HELLCAT.
AND I SWEAR ...
...IF YOUR NEKOMATA SIDE STARTS SWALLOWING YOU UP, I'LL BE THERE TO STOP IT.
......YOU REALLY ARE A KINDHEARTED RED DRAGON EMPEROR.
EH, WHAT'S THAT? KINKY-HEARTED?
MAYBE? I GUESS I AM...
HUH? YOUR FACE IS A LITTLE RED, KONEKO-CHAN.
...TIME TO REGROUP. LET'S HURRY.
O-OH, RIGHT.
FAREWELL, TREASURE...

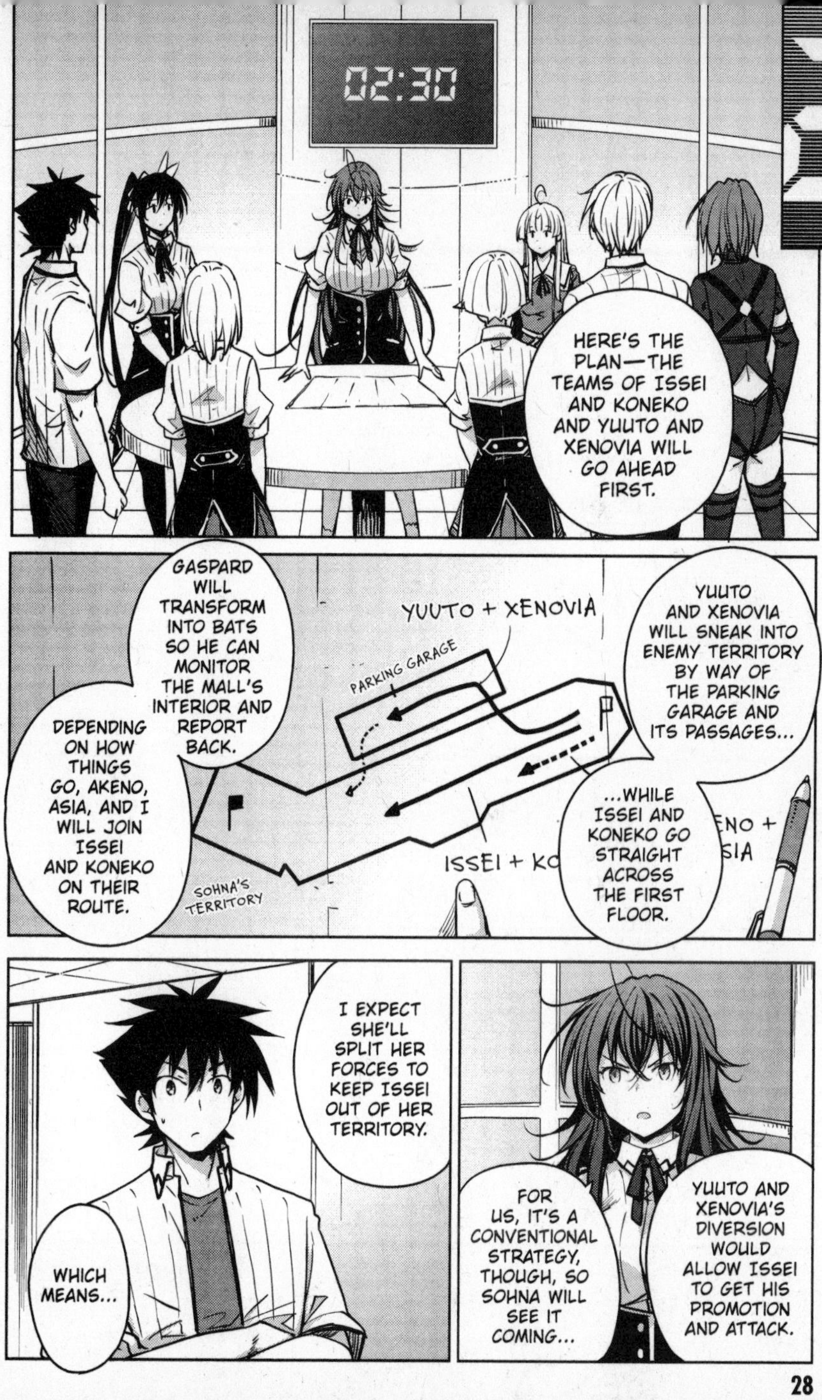
02:30
HERE'S THE PLAN—THE TEAMS OF ISSEI AND KONEKO AND YUUTO AND XENOVIA WILL GO AHEAD FIRST.
YUUTO AND XENOVIA WILL SNEAK INTO ENEMY TERRITORY BY WAY OF THE PARKING GARAGE AND ITS PASSAGES...
...WHILE ISSEI AND KONEKO GO STRAIGHT ACROSS THE FIRST FLOOR.
YUUTO + XENOVIA
PARKING GARAGE
ISSEI + KO
SOHNA'S TERRITORY
GASPARD WILL TRANSFORM INTO BATS SO HE CAN MONITOR THE MALL'S INTERIOR AND REPORT BACK.
DEPENDING ON HOW THINGS GO, AKENO, ASIA, AND I WILL JOIN ISSEI AND KONEKO ON THEIR ROUTE.
YUUTO AND XENOVIA'S DIVERSION WOULD ALLOW ISSEI TO GET HIS PROMOTION AND ATTACK.
FOR US, IT'S A CONVENTIONAL STRATEGY, THOUGH, SO SOHNA WILL SEE IT COMING...
I EXPECT SHE'LL SPLIT HER FORCES TO KEEP ISSEI OUT OF HER TERRITORY.
WHICH MEANS...

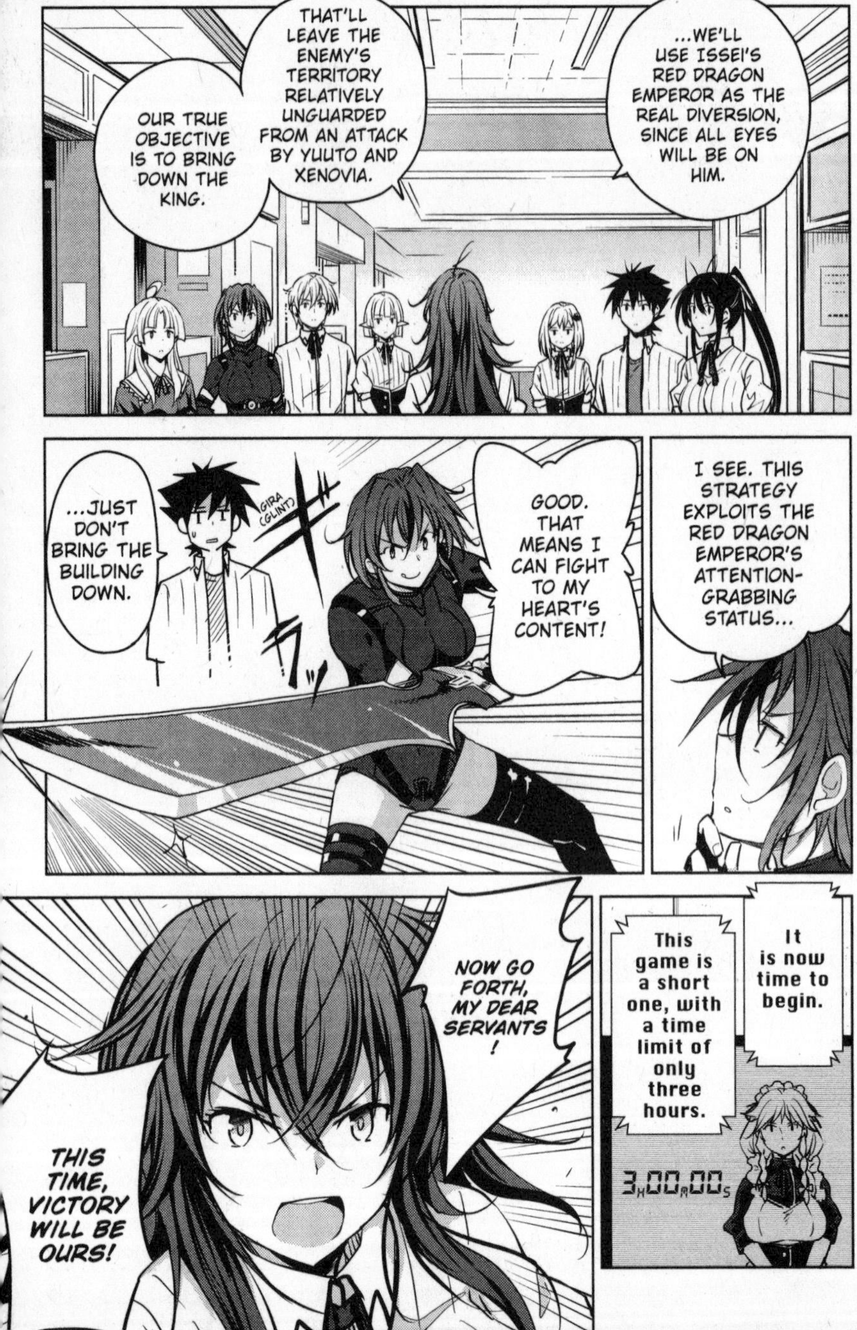
...WE'LL USE ISSEI'S RED DRAGON EMPEROR AS THE REAL DIVERSION, SINCE ALL EYES WILL BE ON HIM.
THAT'LL LEAVE THE ENEMY'S TERRITORY RELATIVELY UNGUARDED FROM AN ATTACK BY YUUTO AND XENOVIA.
OUR TRUE OBJECTIVE IS TO BRING DOWN THE KING.
I SEE. THIS STRATEGY EXPLOITS THE RED DRAGON EMPEROR'S ATTENTION-GRABBING STATUS...
GOOD. THAT MEANS I CAN FIGHT TO MY HEART'S CONTENT!
GIRA (GLINT)
...JUST DON'T BRING THE BUILDING DOWN.
It is now time to begin.
This game is a short one, with a time limit of only three hours.
3H00M00S
NOW GO FORTH, MY DEAR SERVANTS!
THIS TIME, VICTORY WILL BE OURS!

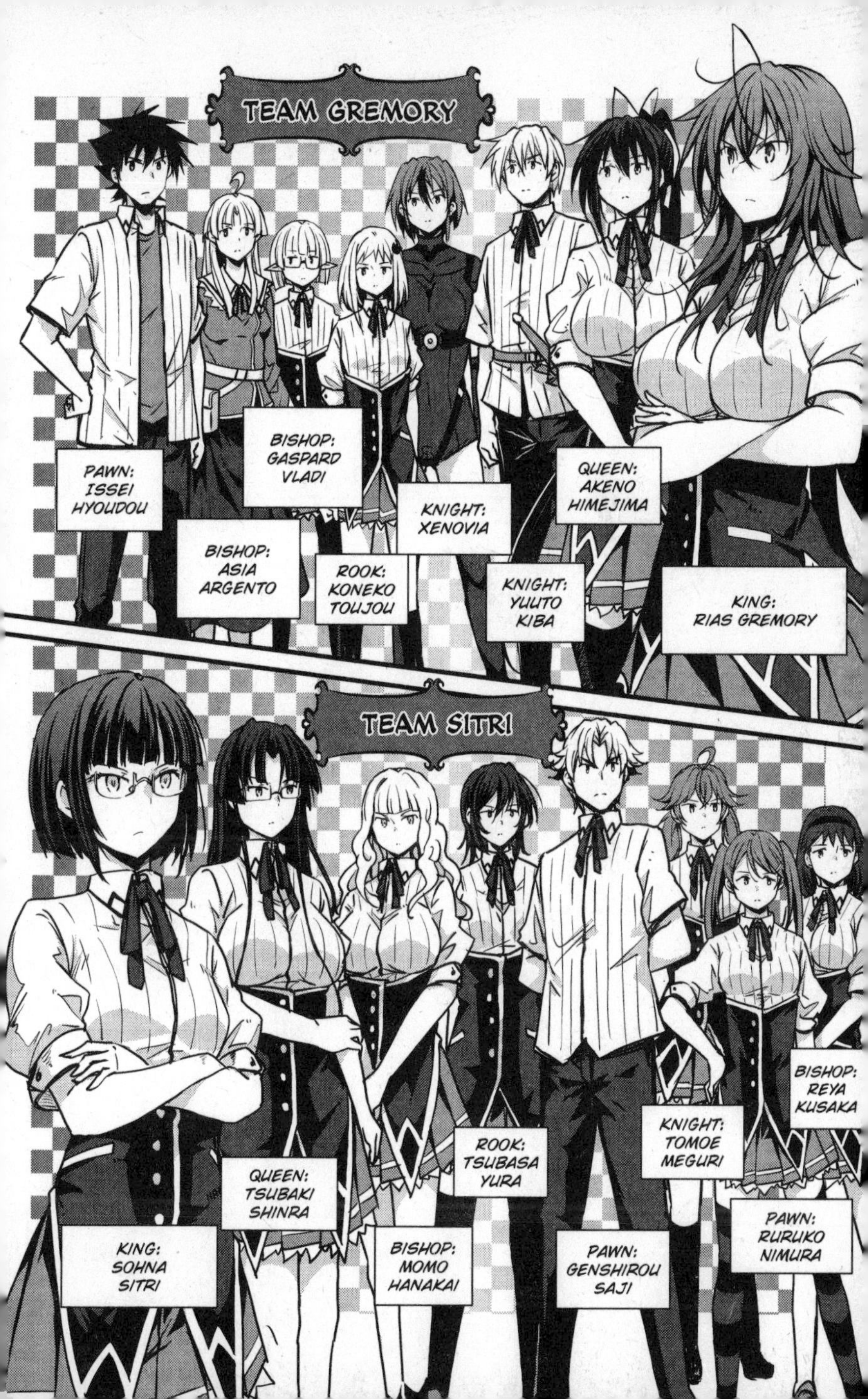
TEAM GREMORY
QUEEN: AKENO HIMEJIMA
KING: RIAS GREMORY
KNIGHT: XENOVIA
KNIGHT: YUUTO KIBA
BISHOP: GASPARD VLADI
ROOK: KONEKO TOUJOU
PAWN: ISSEI HYOUDOU
BISHOP: ASIA ARGENTO
TEAM SITRI
BISHOP: REYA KUSAKA
KNIGHT: TOMOE MEGURI
ROOK: TSUBASA YURA
PAWN: RURUKO NIMURA
PAWN: GENSHIROU SAJI
QUEEN: TSUBAKI SHINRA
BISHOP: MOMO HANAKAI
KING: SOHNA SITRI

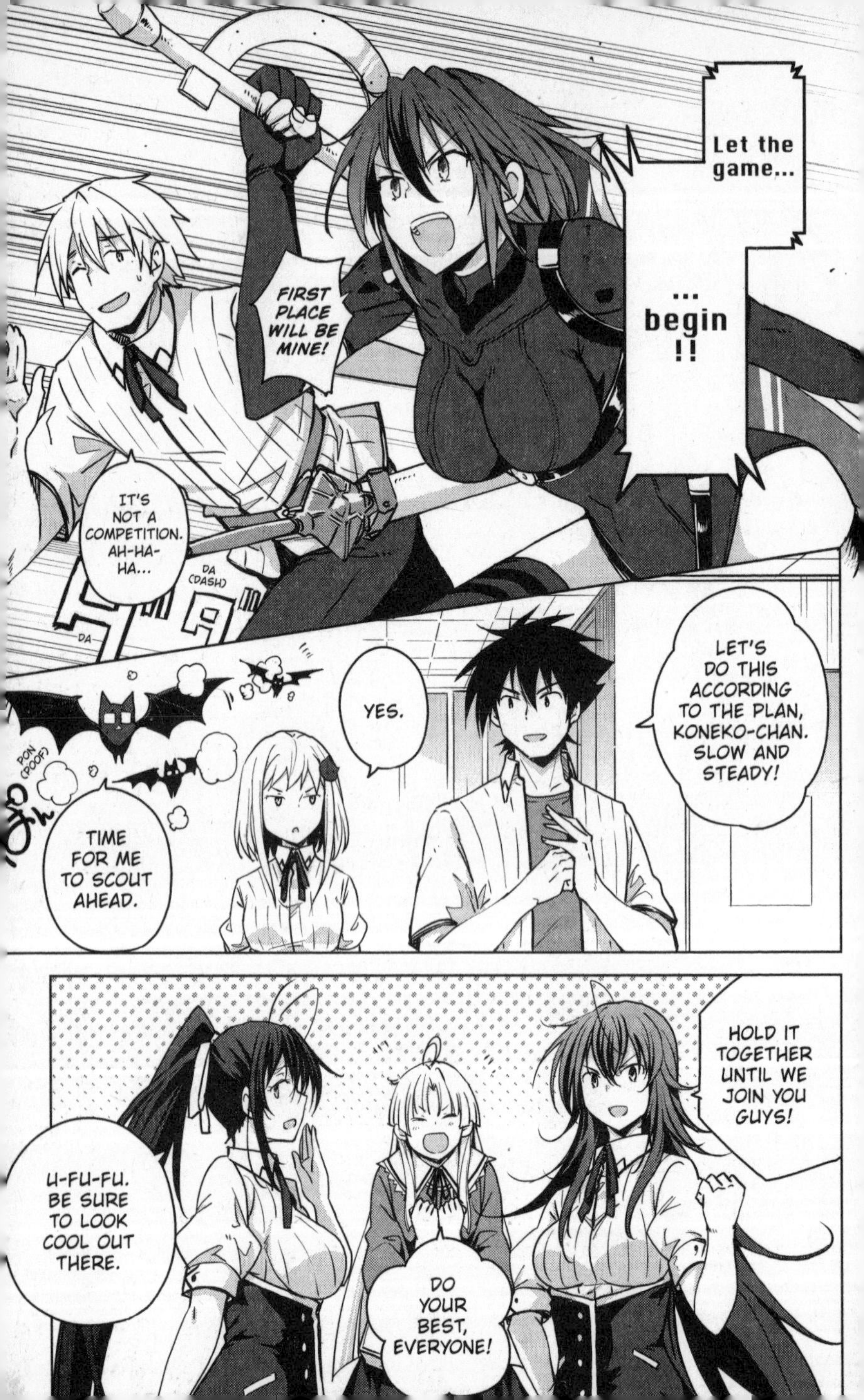
Let the game...
... begin!!
FIRST PLACE WILL BE MINE!
IT'S NOT A COMPETITION. AH-HA-HA...
DA (DASH)
DA
LET'S DO THIS ACCORDING TO THE PLAN, KONEKO-CHAN. SLOW AND STEADY!
YES.
PON (POOF)
TIME FOR ME TO SCOUT AHEAD.
HOLD IT TOGETHER UNTIL WE JOIN YOU GUYS!
DO YOUR BEST, EVERYONE!
U-FU-FU. BE SURE TO LOOK COOL OUT THERE.

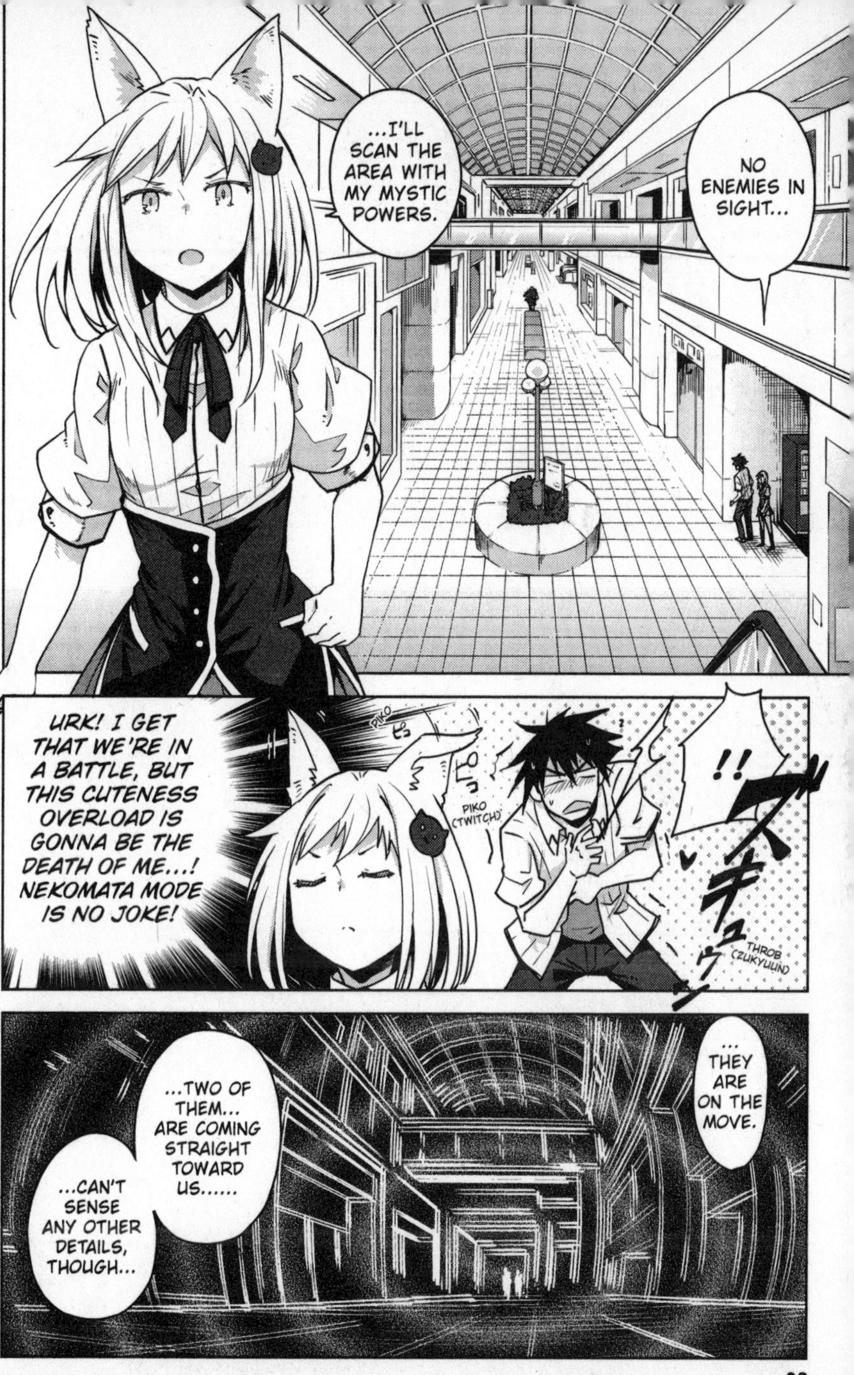
NO ENEMIES IN SIGHT...
...I'LL SCAN THE AREA WITH MY MYSTIC POWERS.
!!
THROB (ZUKYUUN)
PIKO (TWITCH)
PIKO
URK! I GET THAT WE'RE IN A BATTLE, BUT THIS CUTENESS OVERLOAD IS GONNA BE THE DEATH OF ME...! NEKOMATA MODE IS NO JOKE!
...THEY ARE ON THE MOVE.
...TWO OF THEM... ARE COMING STRAIGHT TOWARD US......
...CAN'T SENSE ANY OTHER DETAILS, THOUGH...

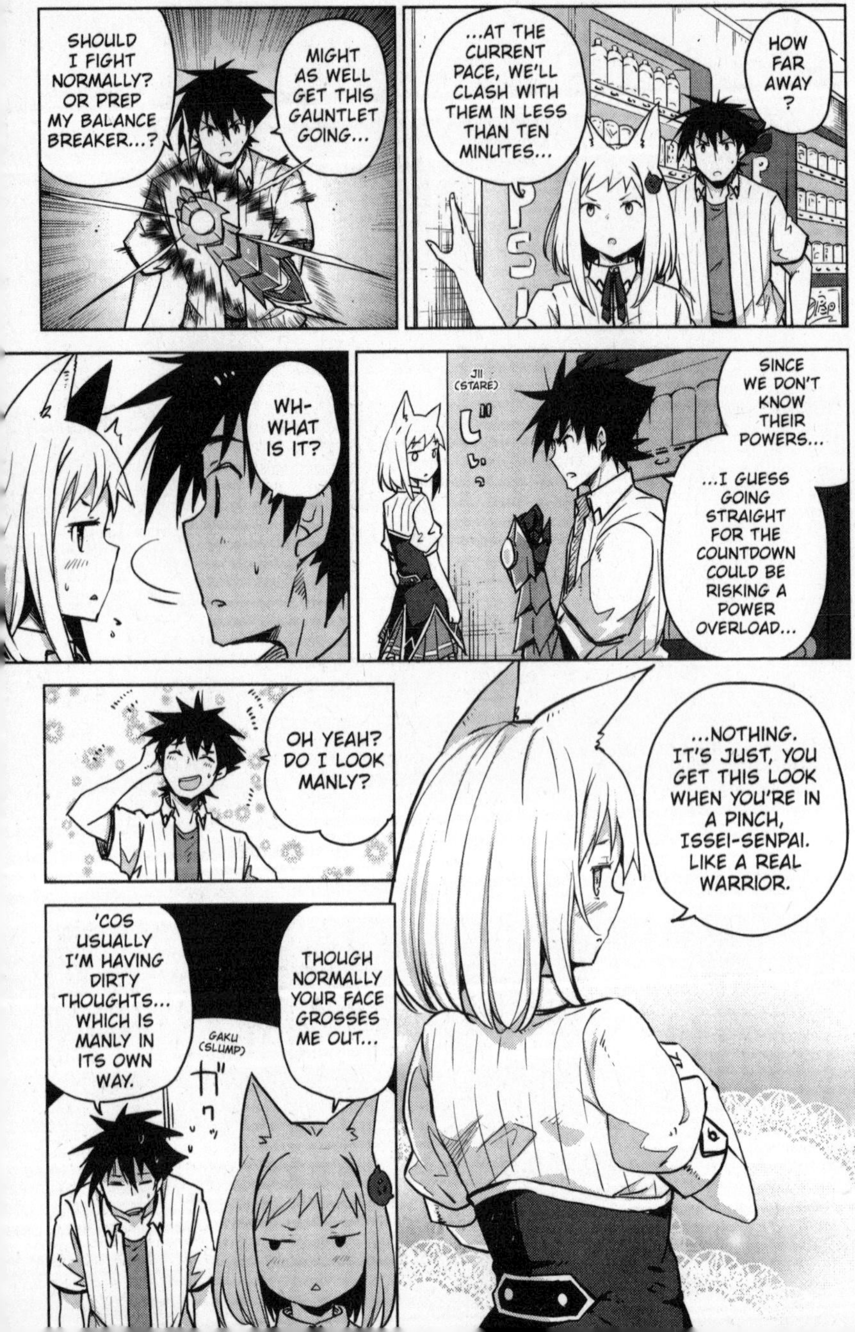
HOW FAR AWAY?
...AT THE CURRENT PACE, WE'LL CLASH WITH THEM IN LESS THAN TEN MINUTES...
MIGHT AS WELL GET THIS GAUNTLET GOING...
SHOULD I FIGHT NORMALLY? OR PREP MY BALANCE BREAKER...?
SINCE WE DON'T KNOW THEIR POWERS...
...I GUESS GOING STRAIGHT FOR THE COUNTDOWN COULD BE RISKING A POWER OVERLOAD...
JII (STARE)
WH-WHAT IS IT?
...NOTHING. IT'S JUST, YOU GET THIS LOOK WHEN YOU'RE IN A PINCH, ISSEI-SENPAI. LIKE A REAL WARRIOR.
OH YEAH? DO I LOOK MANLY?
THOUGH NORMALLY YOUR FACE GROSSES ME OUT...
GAKU (SLUMP)
'COS USUALLY I'M HAVING DIRTY THOUGHTS... WHICH IS MANLY IN ITS OWN WAY.

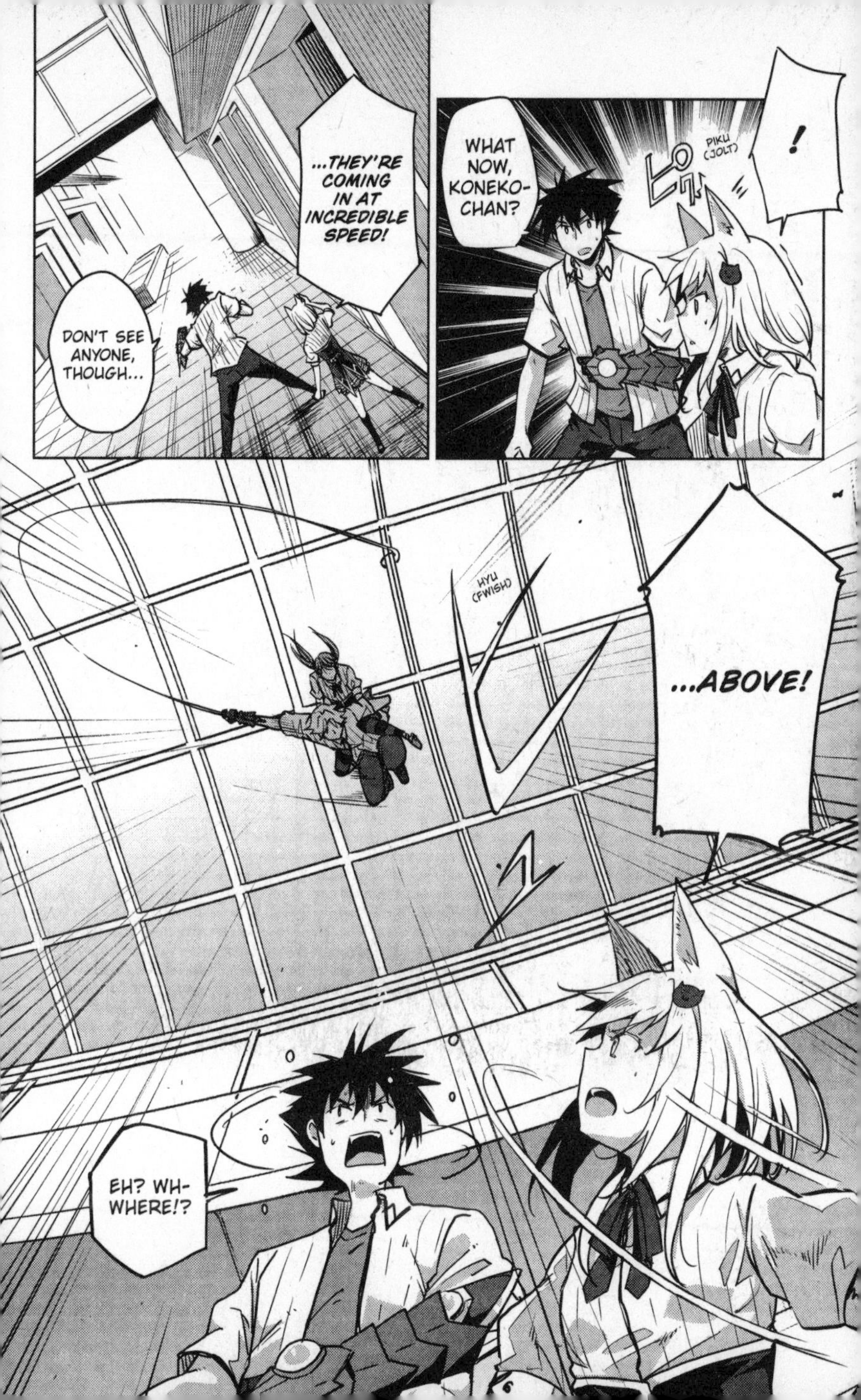
!
PIKU (JOLT)
WHAT NOW, KONEKO-CHAN?
...THEY'RE COMING IN AT INCREDIBLE SPEED!
DON'T SEE ANYONE, THOUGH...
...ABOVE!
HYU (FWISH)
EH? WH-WHERE!?

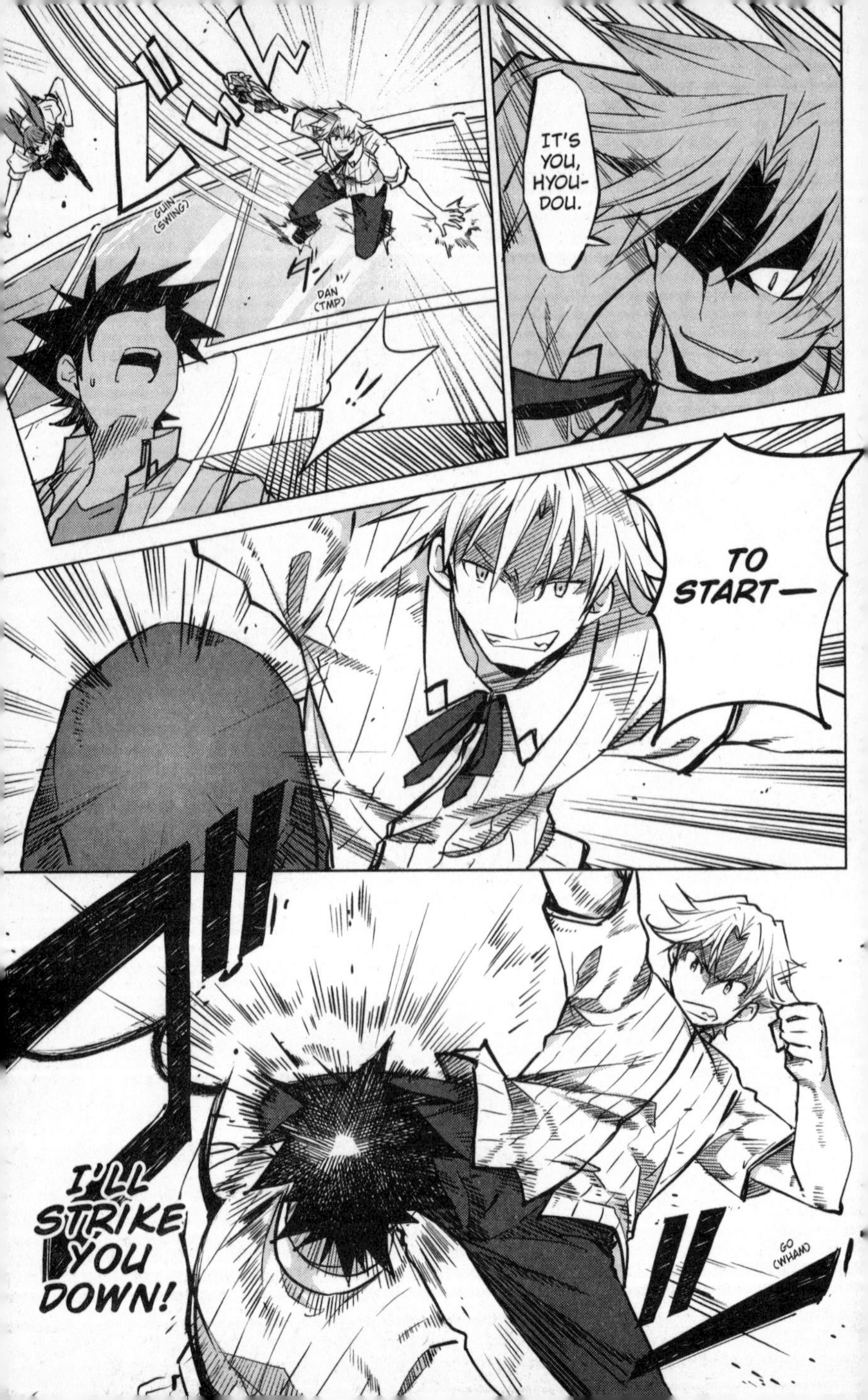

IT'S YOU, HYOU-DOU.
GUIN (SWING)
DAN (TMP)
TO START—
I'LL STRIKE YOU DOWN!
GO (WHAM)

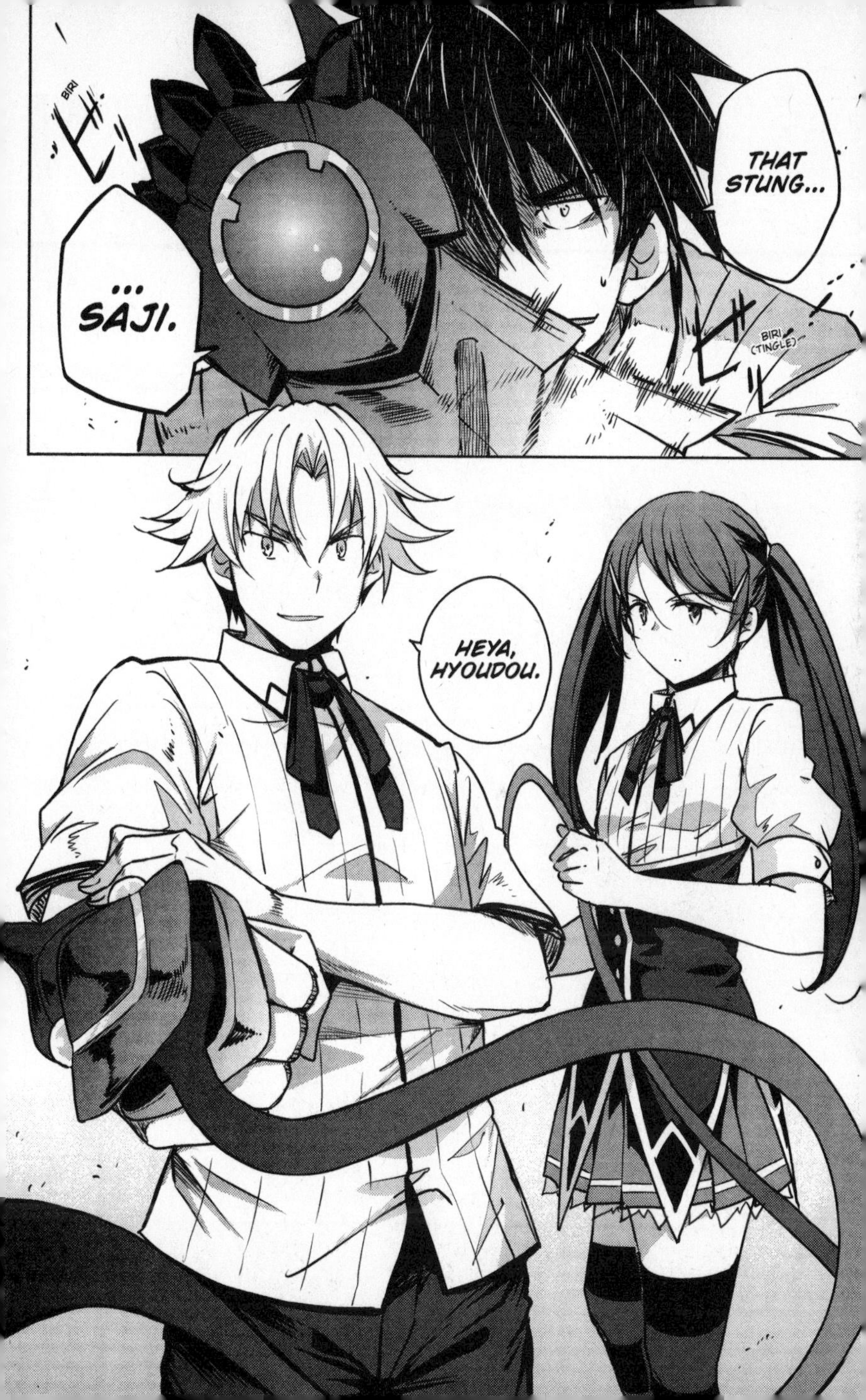
THAT STUNG...
BIRI (TINGLE)
BIRI
...SÄJI.
HEYA, HYOUDOU.

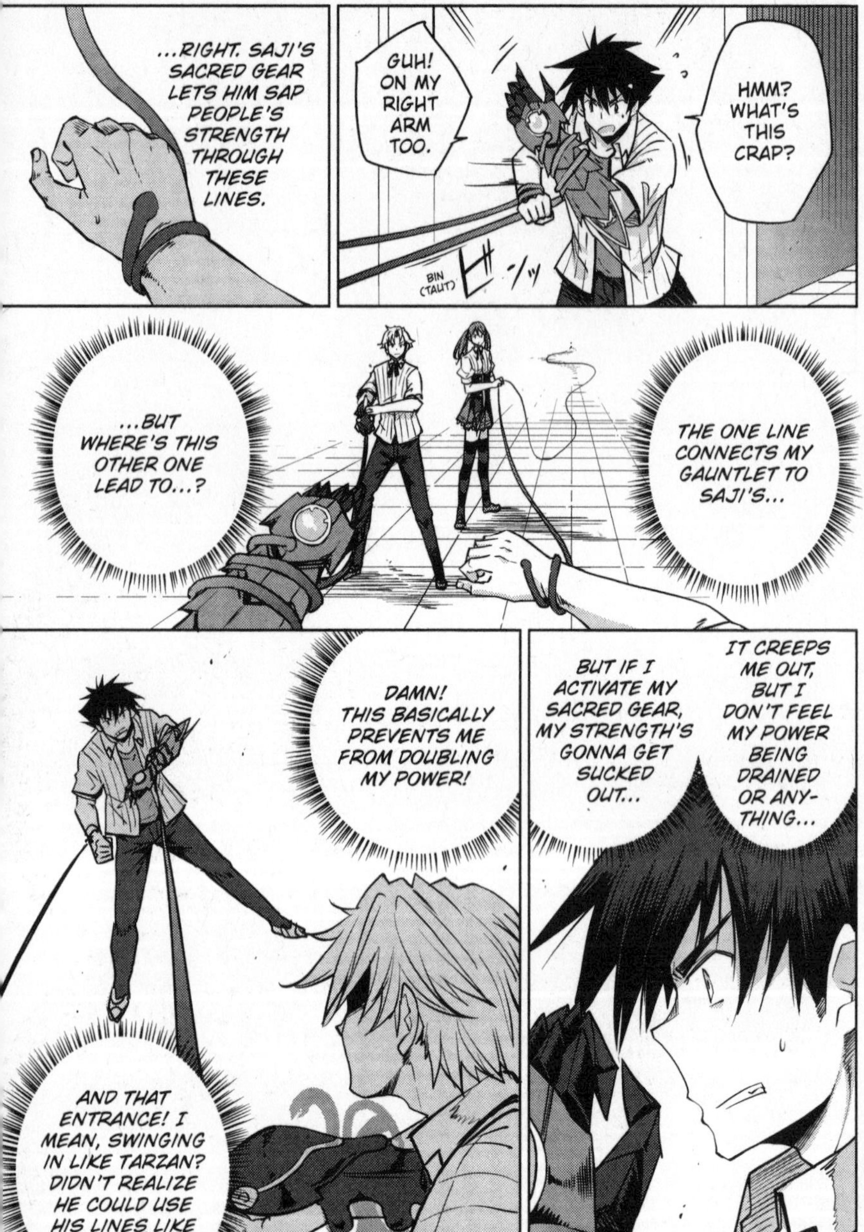
HMM? WHAT'S THIS CRAP?
GUH! ON MY RIGHT ARM TOO.
BIN (TAUT)
...RIGHT. SAJI'S SACRED GEAR LETS HIM SAP PEOPLE'S STRENGTH THROUGH THESE LINES.
THE ONE LINE CONNECTS MY GAUNTLET TO SAJI'S...
...BUT WHERE'S THIS OTHER ONE LEAD TO...?
IT CREEPS ME OUT, BUT I DON'T FEEL MY POWER BEING DRAINED OR ANY-THING...
BUT IF I ACTIVATE MY SACRED GEAR, MY STRENGTH'S GONNA GET SUCKED OUT...
DAMN! THIS BASICALLY PREVENTS ME FROM DOUBLING MY POWER!
AND THAT ENTRANCE! I MEAN, SWINGING IN LIKE TARZAN? DIDN'T REALIZE HE COULD USE HIS LINES LIKE THAT!

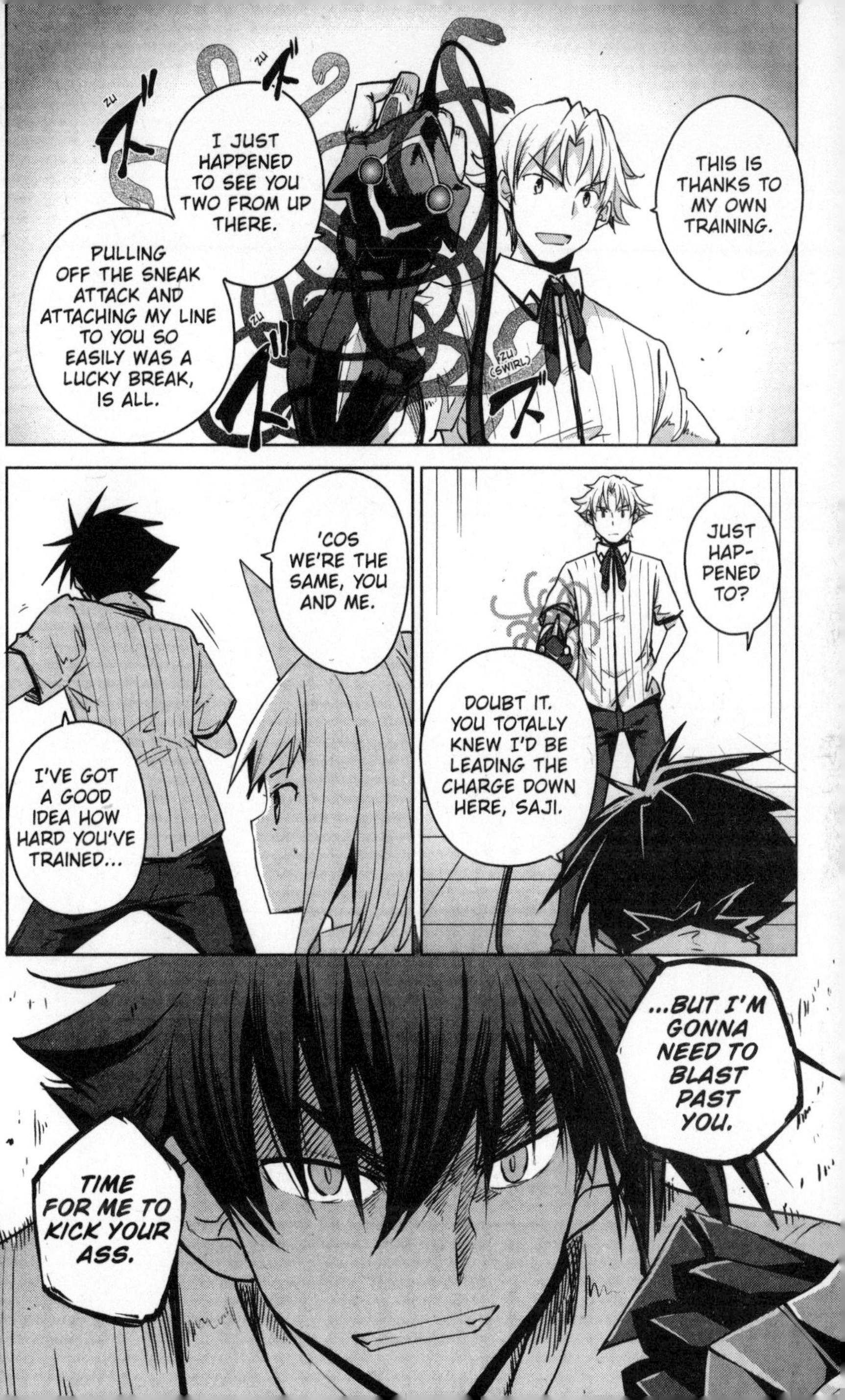
THIS IS THANKS TO MY OWN TRAINING.
ZU
ZU
I JUST HAPPENED TO SEE YOU TWO FROM UP THERE.
PULLING OFF THE SNEAK ATTACK AND ATTACHING MY LINE TO YOU SO EASILY WAS A LUCKY BREAK, IS ALL.
ZU
ZU (SWIRL)
JUST HAP-PENED TO?
DOUBT IT. YOU TOTALLY KNEW I'D BE LEADING THE CHARGE DOWN HERE, SAJI.
'COS WE'RE THE SAME, YOU AND ME.
I'VE GOT A GOOD IDEA HOW HARD YOU'VE TRAINED...
...BUT I'M GONNA NEED TO BLAST PAST YOU.
TIME FOR ME TO KICK YOUR ASS.

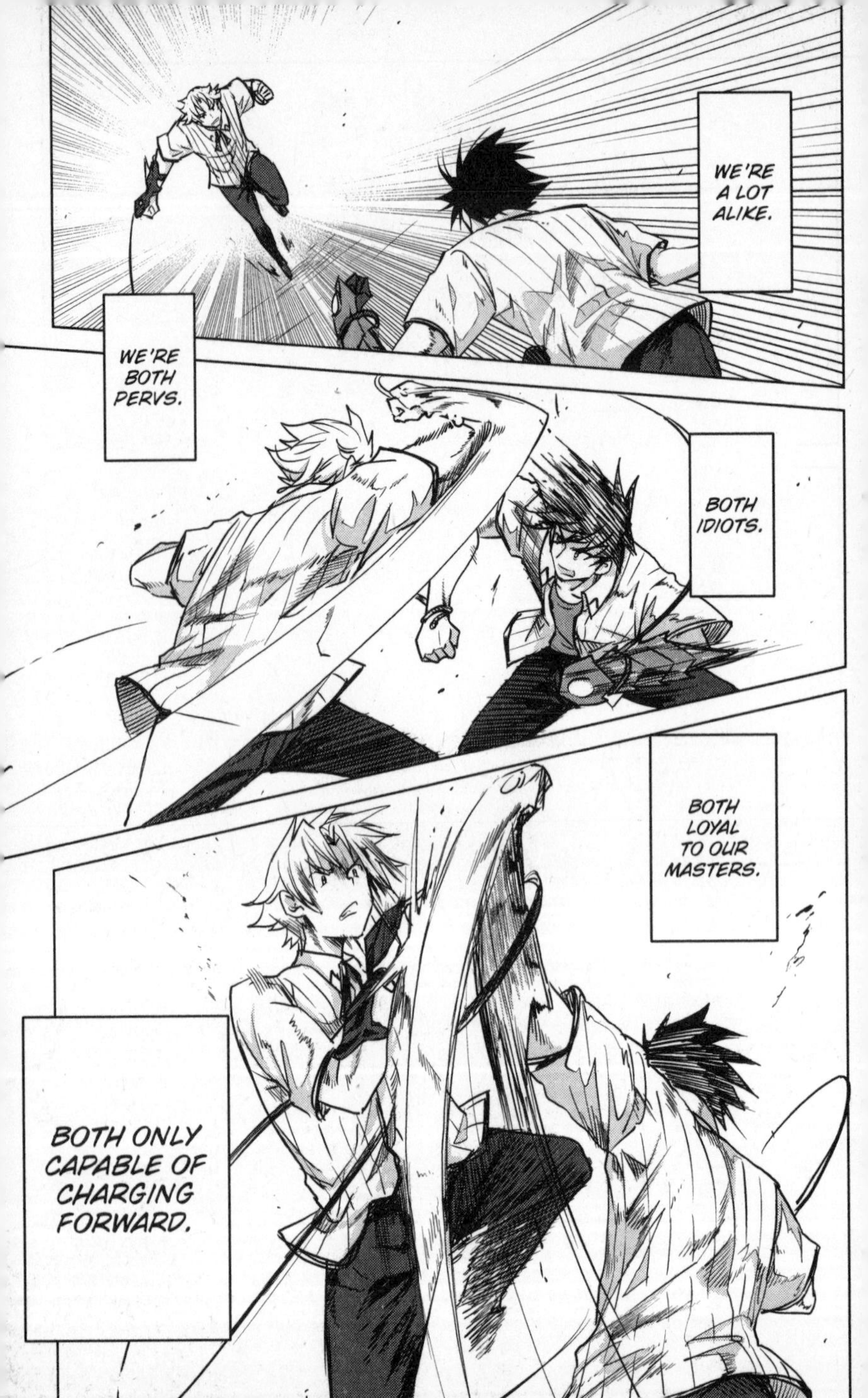
WE'RE A LOT ALIKE.
WE'RE BOTH PERVS.
BOTH IDIOTS.
BOTH LOYAL TO OUR MASTERS.
BOTH ONLY CAPABLE OF CHARGING FORWARD.

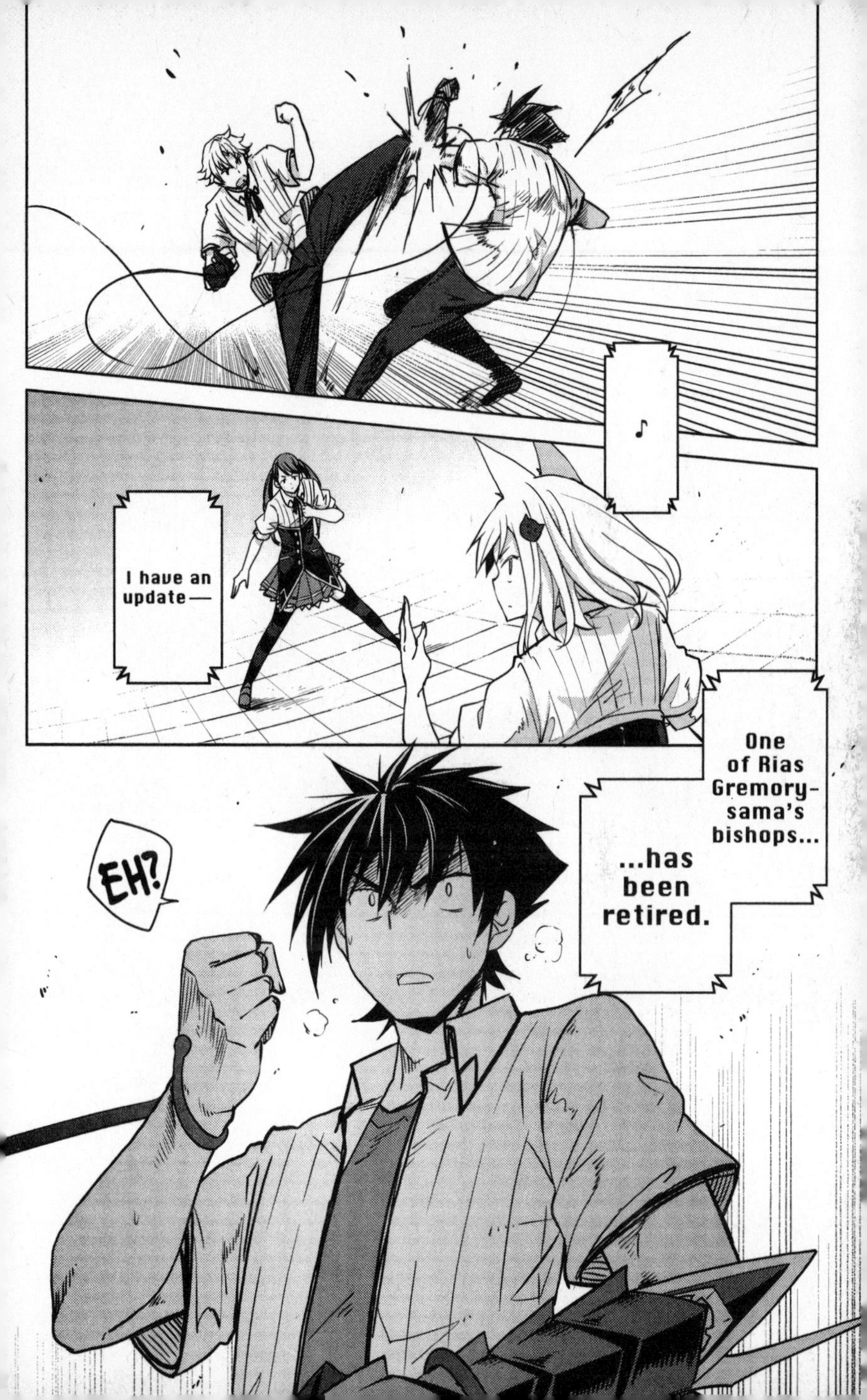
♪
I have an update—
One of Rias Gremory-sama's bishops...
...has been retired.
EH?

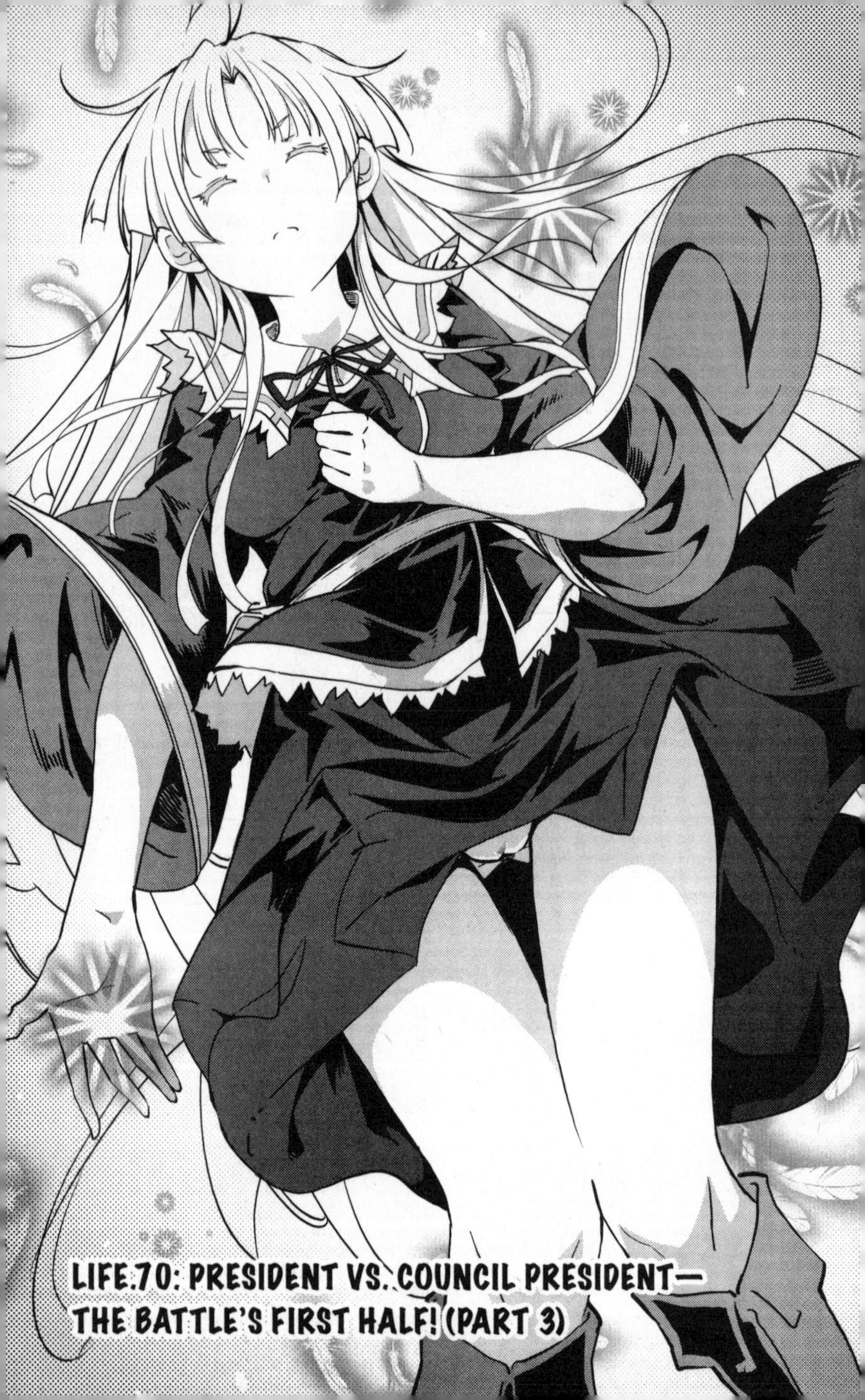

LIFE.70: PRESIDENT VS. COUNCIL PRESIDENT—THE BATTLE'S FIRST HALF! (PART 3)

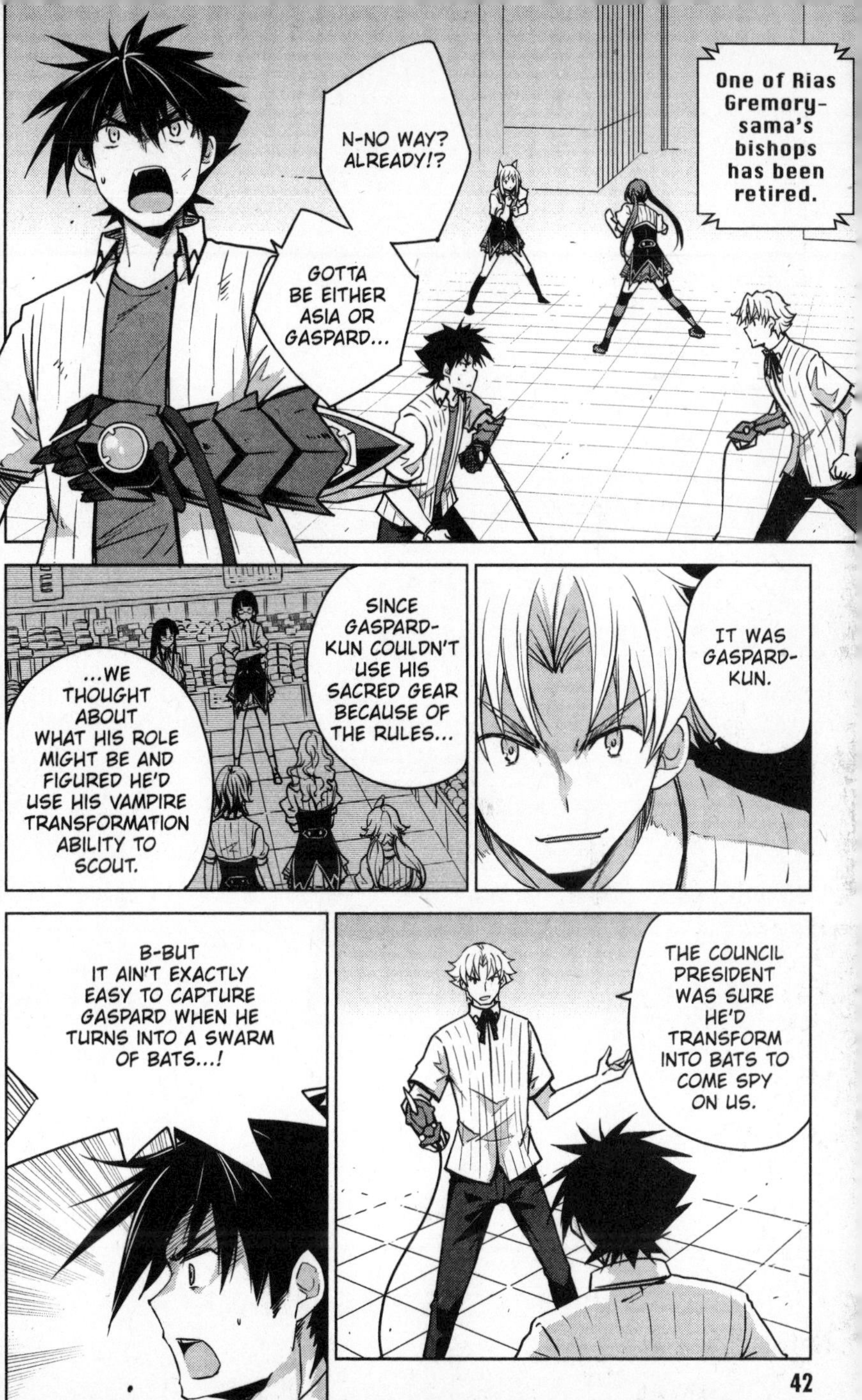
One of Rias Gremory-sama's bishops has been retired.
N-NO WAY? ALREADY!?
GOTTA BE EITHER ASIA OR GASPARD...
IT WAS GASPARD-KUN.
SINCE GASPARD-KUN COULDN'T USE HIS SACRED GEAR BECAUSE OF THE RULES...
...WE THOUGHT ABOUT WHAT HIS ROLE MIGHT BE AND FIGURED HE'D USE HIS VAMPIRE TRANSFORMATION ABILITY TO SCOUT.
THE COUNCIL PRESIDENT WAS SURE HE'D TRANSFORM INTO BATS TO COME SPY ON US.
B-BUT IT AIN'T EXACTLY EASY TO CAPTURE GASPARD WHEN HE TURNS INTO A SWARM OF BATS...!

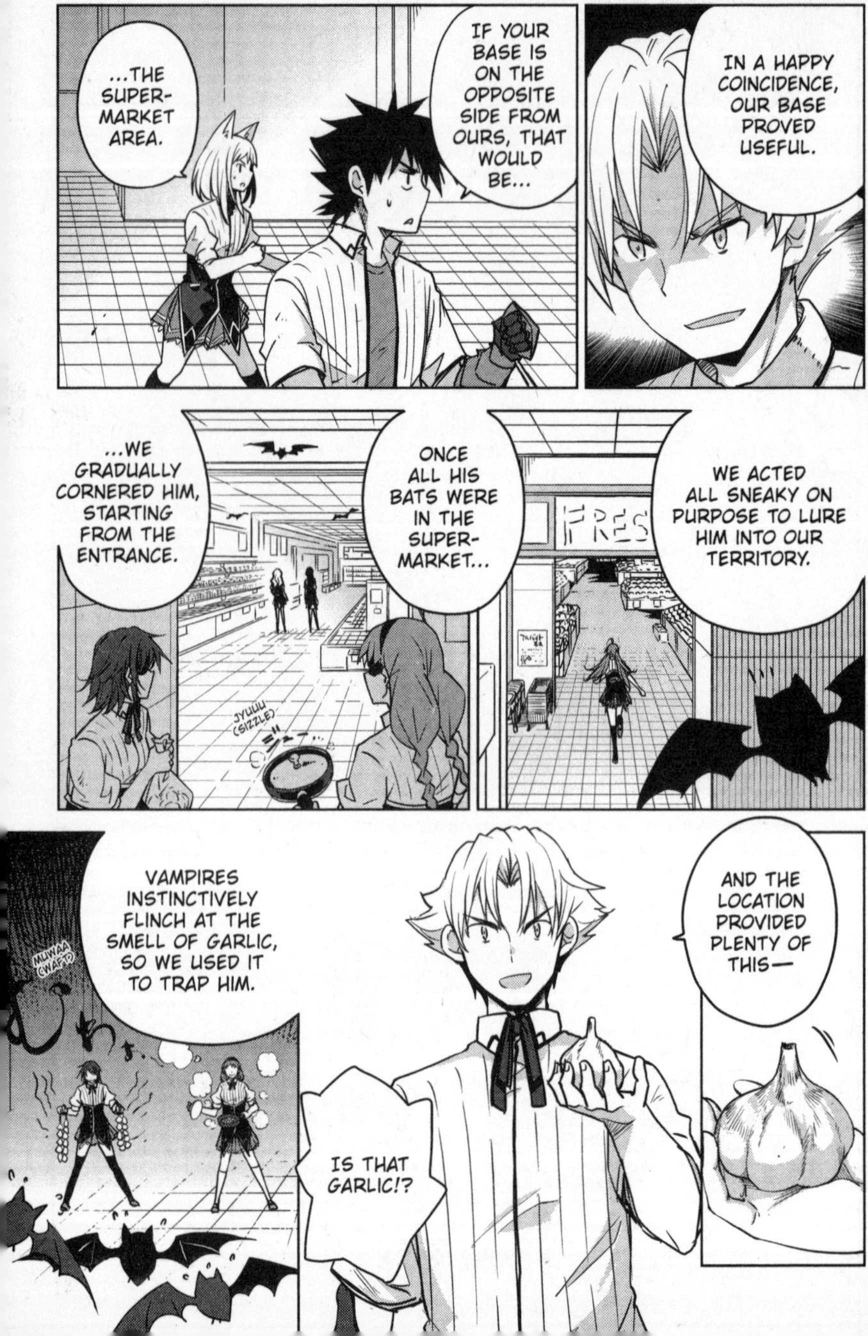
IN A HAPPY COINCIDENCE, OUR BASE PROVED USEFUL.
IF YOUR BASE IS ON THE OPPOSITE SIDE FROM OURS, THAT WOULD BE...
...THE SUPER-MARKET AREA.
WE ACTED ALL SNEAKY ON PURPOSE TO LURE HIM INTO OUR TERRITORY.
ONCE ALL HIS BATS WERE IN THE SUPER-MARKET...
...WE GRADUALLY CORNERED HIM, STARTING FROM THE ENTRANCE.
JYUUUU (SIZZLE)
AND THE LOCATION PROVIDED PLENTY OF THIS—
VAMPIRES INSTINCTIVELY FLINCH AT THE SMELL OF GARLIC, SO WE USED IT TO TRAP HIM.
MUWAA (WAFT)
IS THAT GARLIC!?

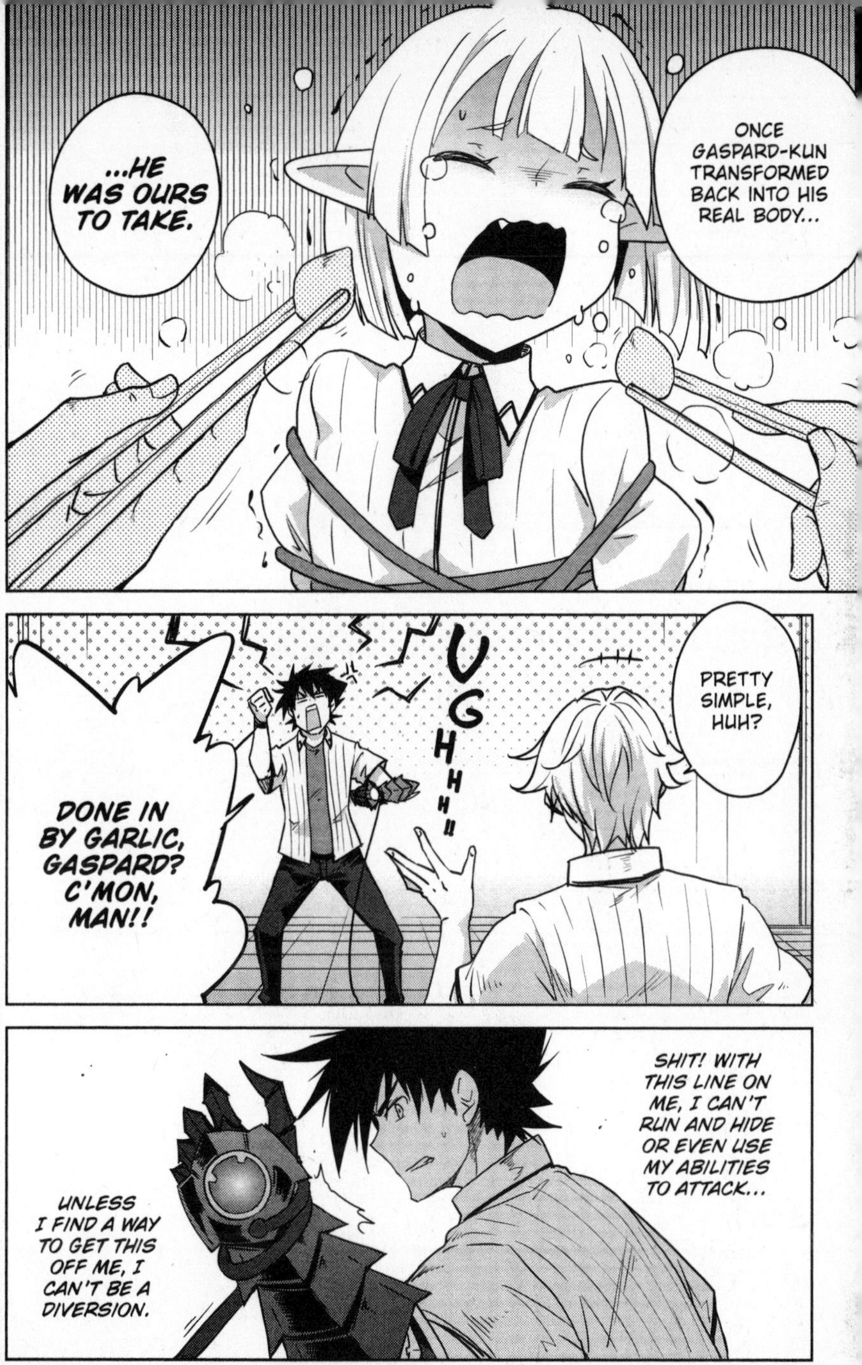
ONCE GASPARD-KUN TRANSFORMED BACK INTO HIS REAL BODY...
...HE WAS OURS TO TAKE.
PRETTY SIMPLE, HUH?
UGHHH!!
DONE IN BY GARLIC, GASPARD? C'MON, MAN!!
SHIT! WITH THIS LINE ON ME, I CAN'T RUN AND HIDE OR EVEN USE MY ABILITIES TO ATTACK...
UNLESS I FIND A WAY TO GET THIS OFF ME, I CAN'T BE A DIVERSION.

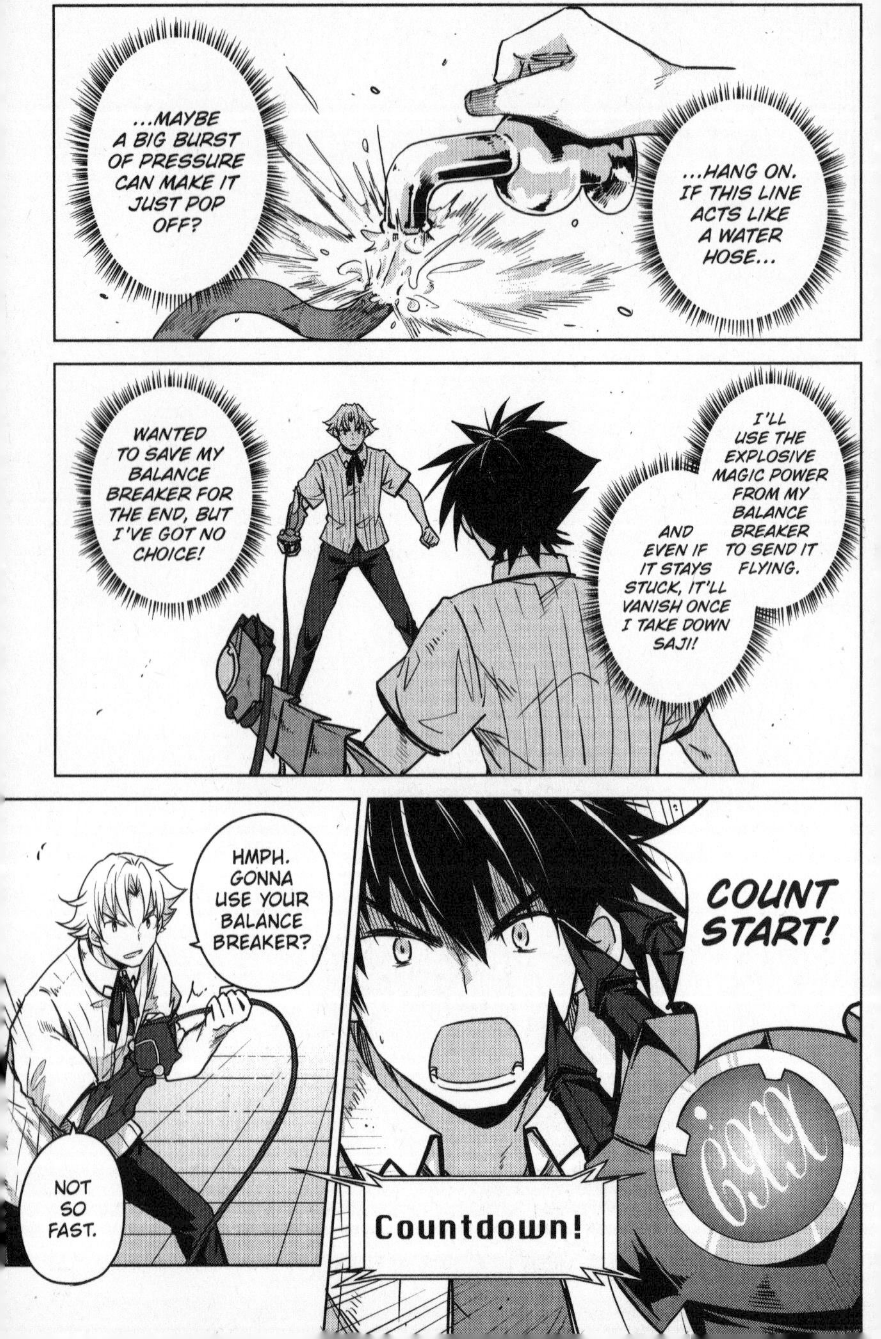
...HANG ON. IF THIS LINE ACTS LIKE A WATER HOSE...
...MAYBE A BIG BURST OF PRESSURE CAN MAKE IT JUST POP OFF?
I'LL USE THE EXPLOSIVE MAGIC POWER FROM MY BALANCE BREAKER TO SEND IT FLYING.
AND EVEN IF IT STAYS STUCK, IT'LL VANISH ONCE I TAKE DOWN SAJI!
WANTED TO SAVE MY BALANCE BREAKER FOR THE END, BUT I'VE GOT NO CHOICE!
COUNT START!
Countdown!
HMPH. GONNA USE YOUR BALANCE BREAKER?
NOT SO FAST.

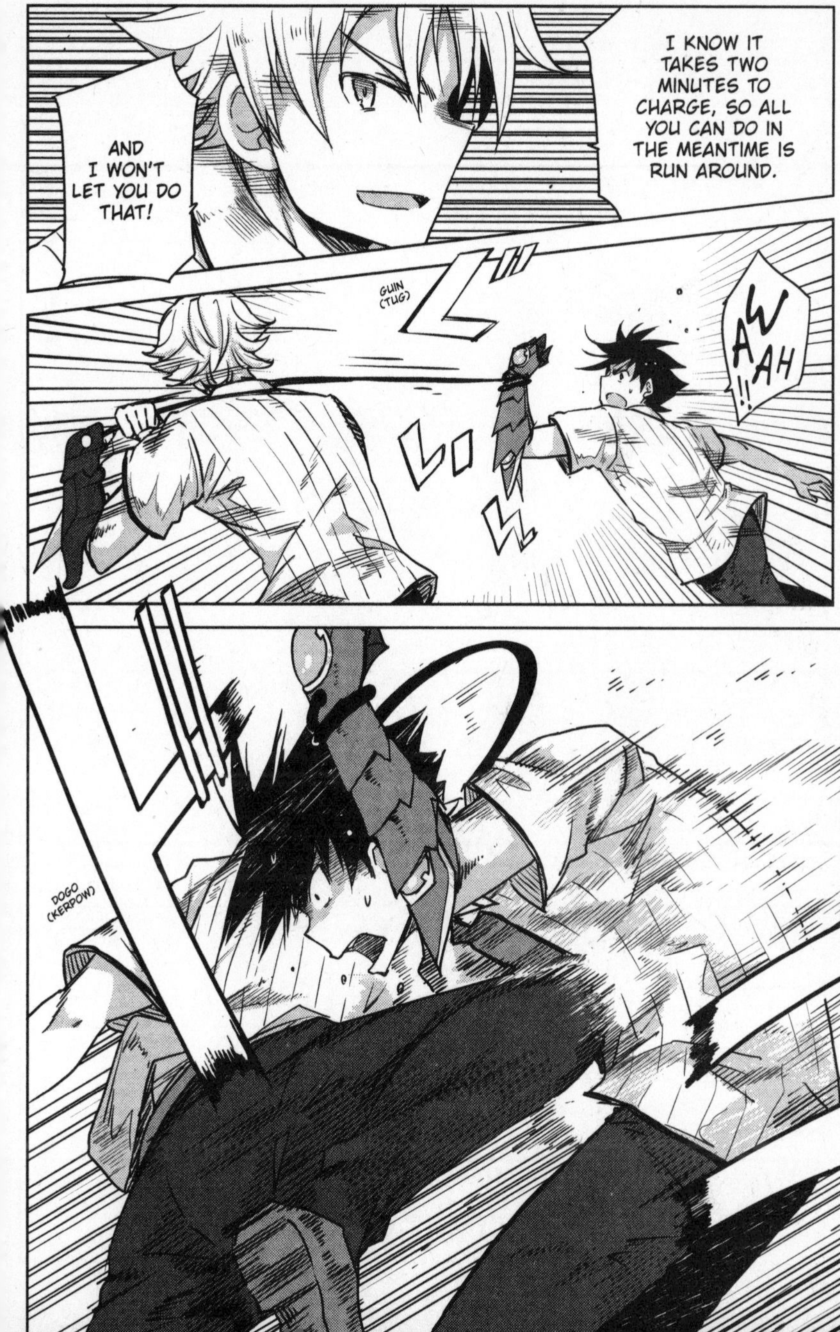
I KNOW IT TAKES TWO MINUTES TO CHARGE, SO ALL YOU CAN DO IN THE MEANTIME IS RUN AROUND.
AND I WON'T LET YOU DO THAT!
WAAH!!
GUIN (TUG)
DOGO (KERPOW)

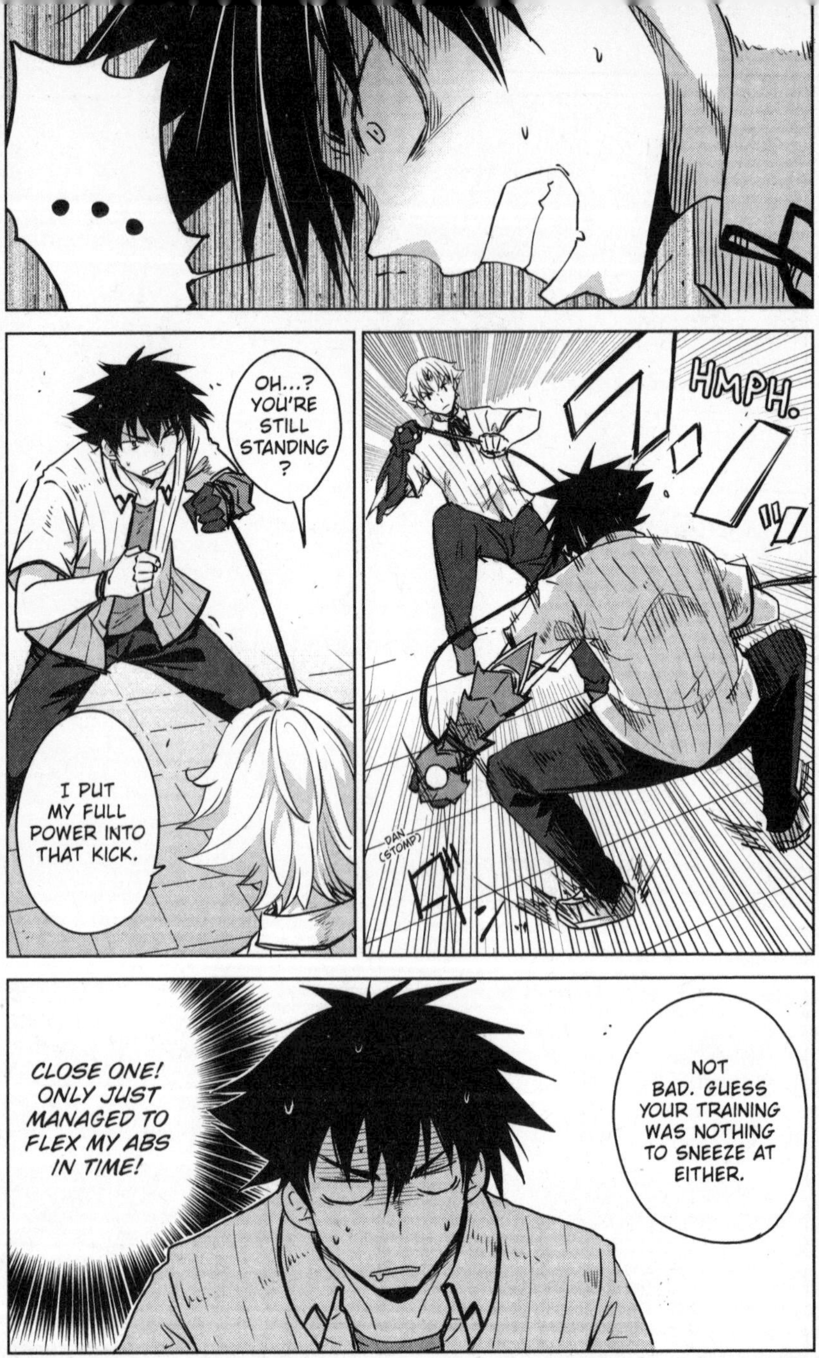
. . .
HMPH.
DAN (STOMP)
OH...? YOU'RE STILL STANDING?
I PUT MY FULL POWER INTO THAT KICK.
NOT BAD. GUESS YOUR TRAINING WAS NOTHING TO SNEEZE AT EITHER.
CLOSE ONE! ONLY JUST MANAGED TO FLEX MY ABS IN TIME!

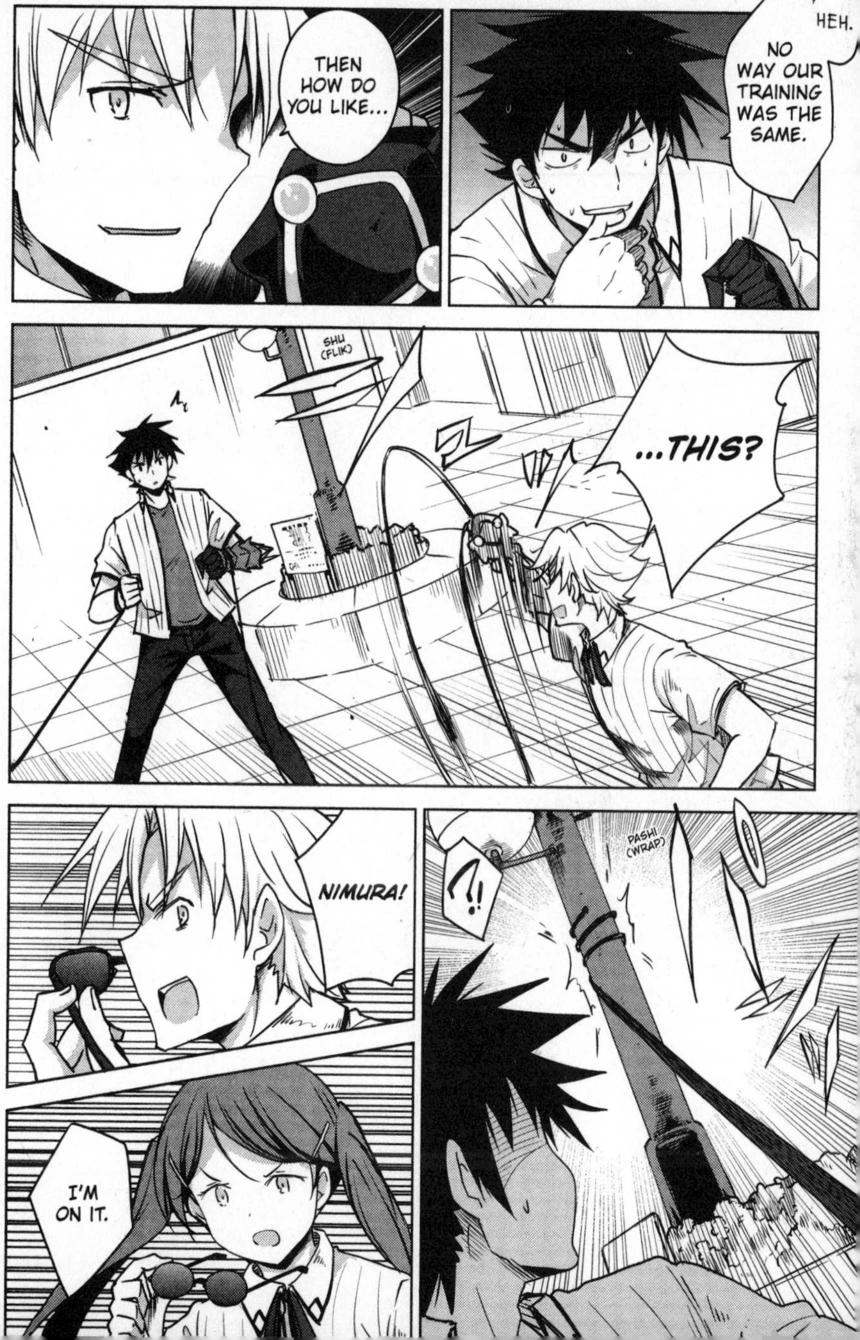
HEH.
NO WAY OUR TRAINING WAS THE SAME.
THEN HOW DO YOU LIKE...
...THIS?
SHU (FLIK)
PASHI (WRAP)
!!
NIMURA!
I'M ON IT.

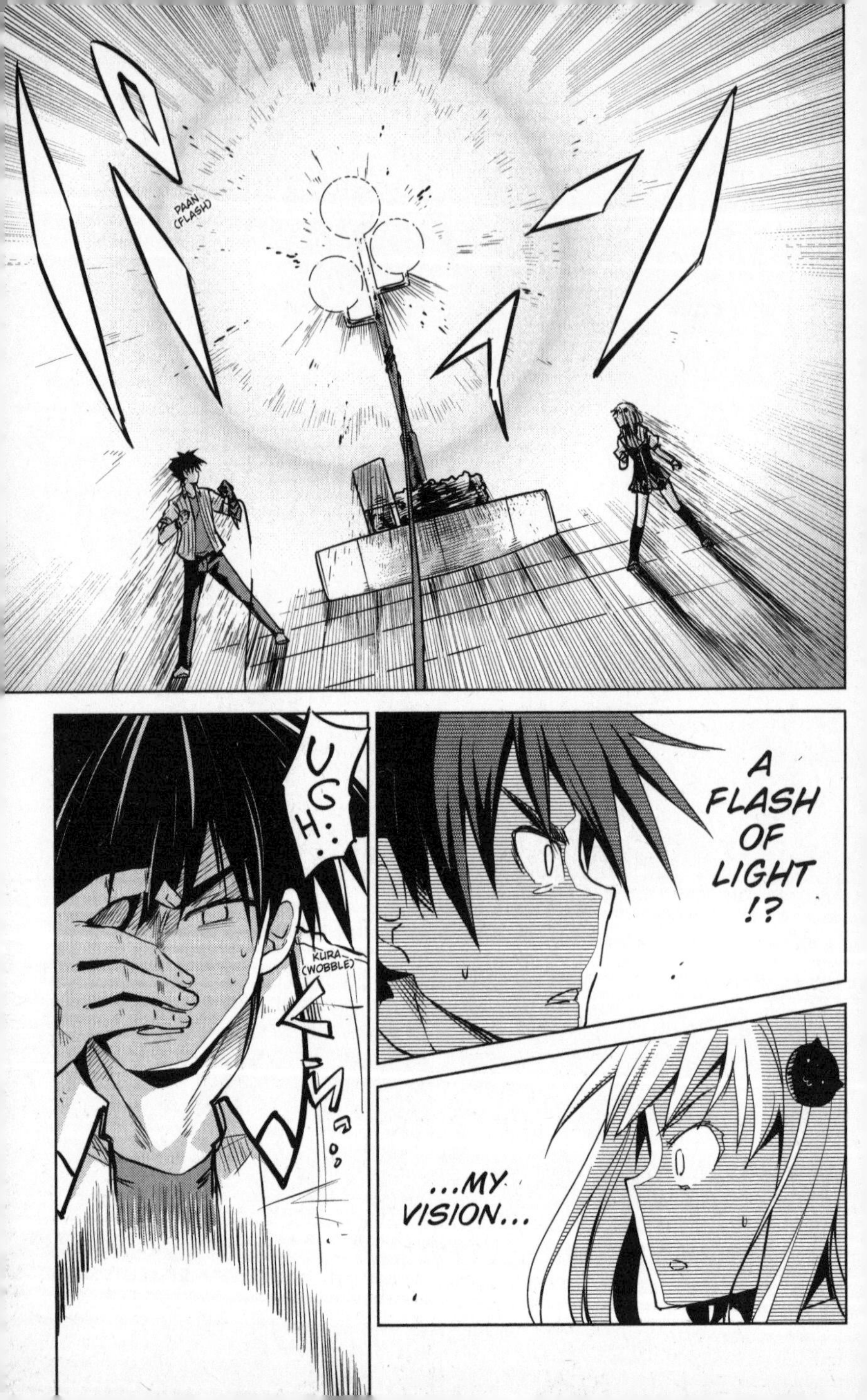
PAAN (FLASH)
A FLASH OF LIGHT!?
...MY VISION...
UGH...
KURA (WOBBLE)

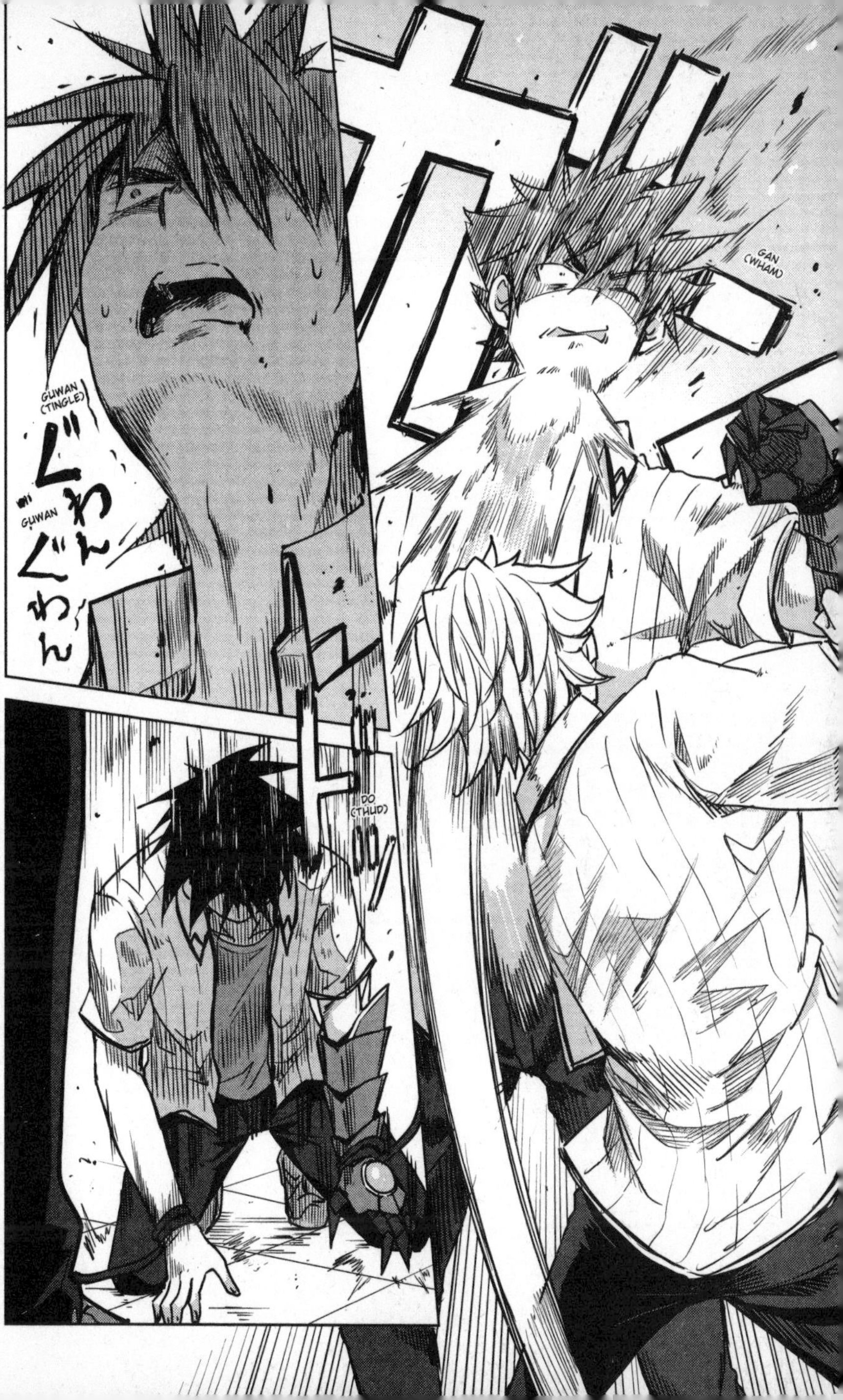
GAN (WHAM)
GUWAN (TINGLE)
ぐわん
GUWAN
ぐわん
DO (THUD)

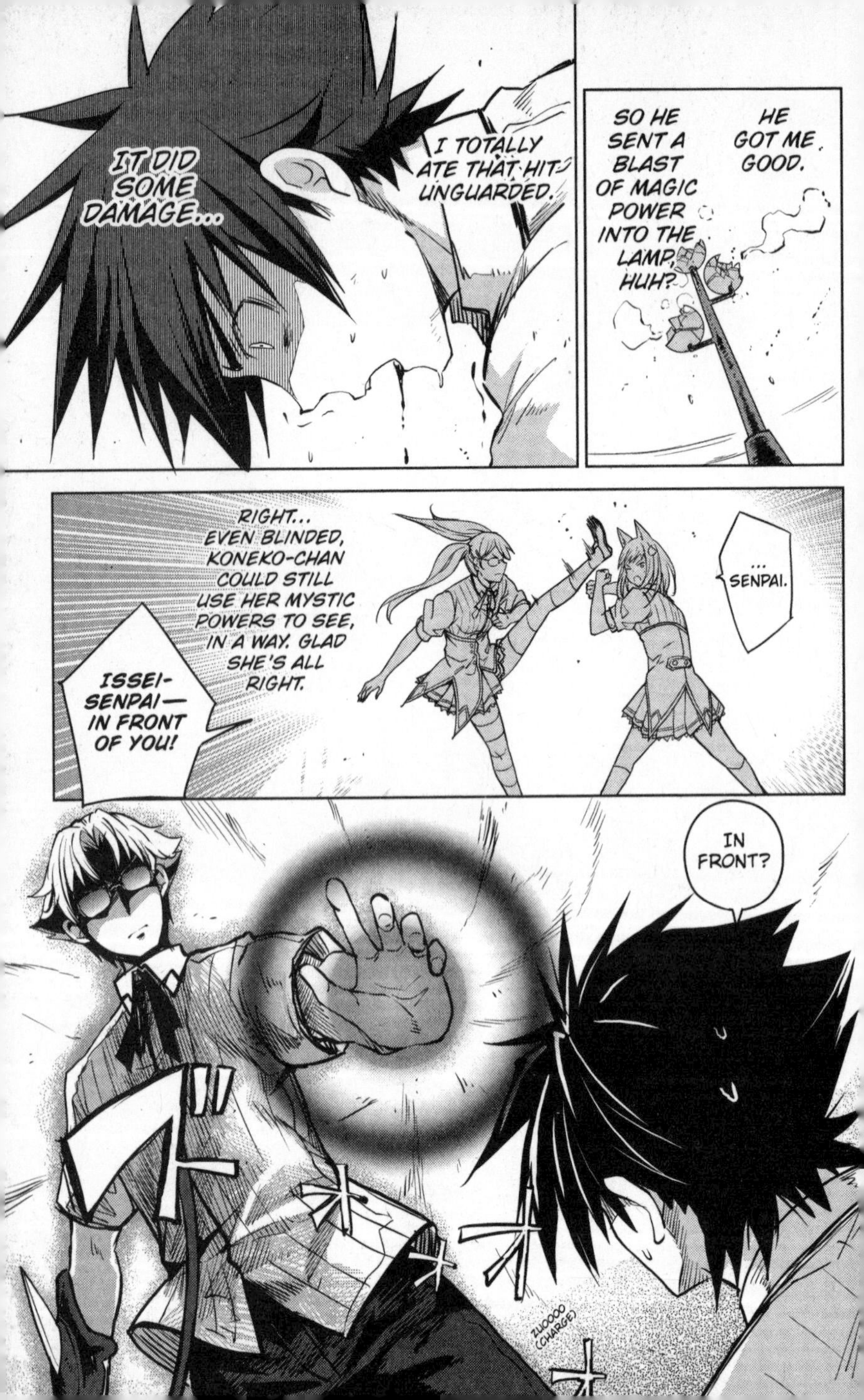

HE GOT ME GOOD.
SO HE SENT A BLAST OF MAGIC POWER INTO THE LAMP, HUH?
I TOTALLY ATE THAT HIT UNGUARDED.
IT DID SOME DAMAGE...
...SENPAI.
RIGHT... EVEN BLINDED, KONEKO-CHAN COULD STILL USE HER MYSTIC POWERS TO SEE, IN A WAY. GLAD SHE'S ALL RIGHT.
ISSEI-SENPAI—IN FRONT OF YOU!
IN FRONT?
ZUOOOO (CHARGE)

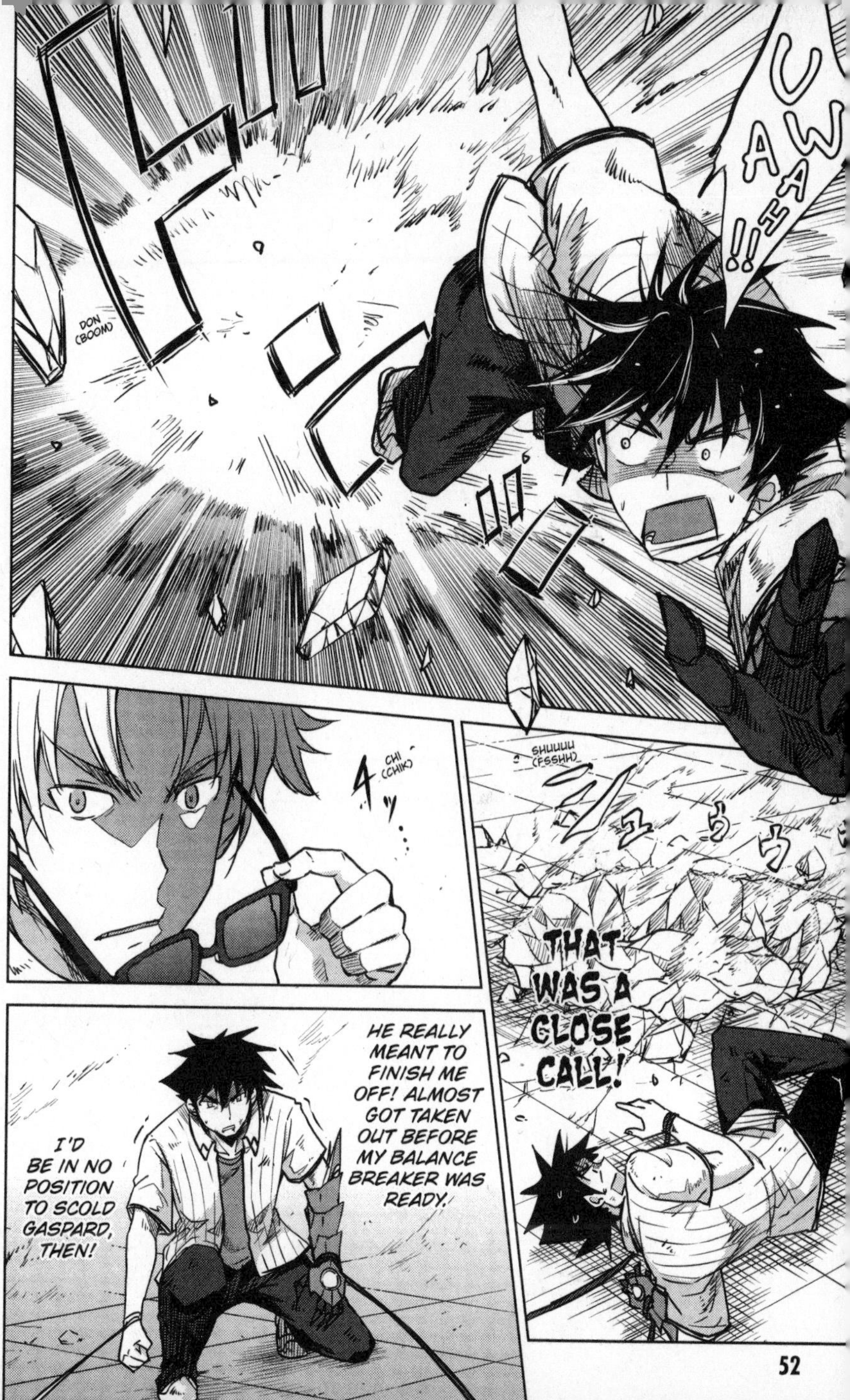
UWAAH!!
DON (BOOM)
SHUUUU (FSSHH)
THAT WAS A CLOSE CALL!
CHI (CHIK)
HE REALLY MEANT TO FINISH ME OFF! ALMOST GOT TAKEN OUT BEFORE MY BALANCE BREAKER WAS READY.
I'D BE IN NO POSITION TO SCOLD GASPARD, THEN!

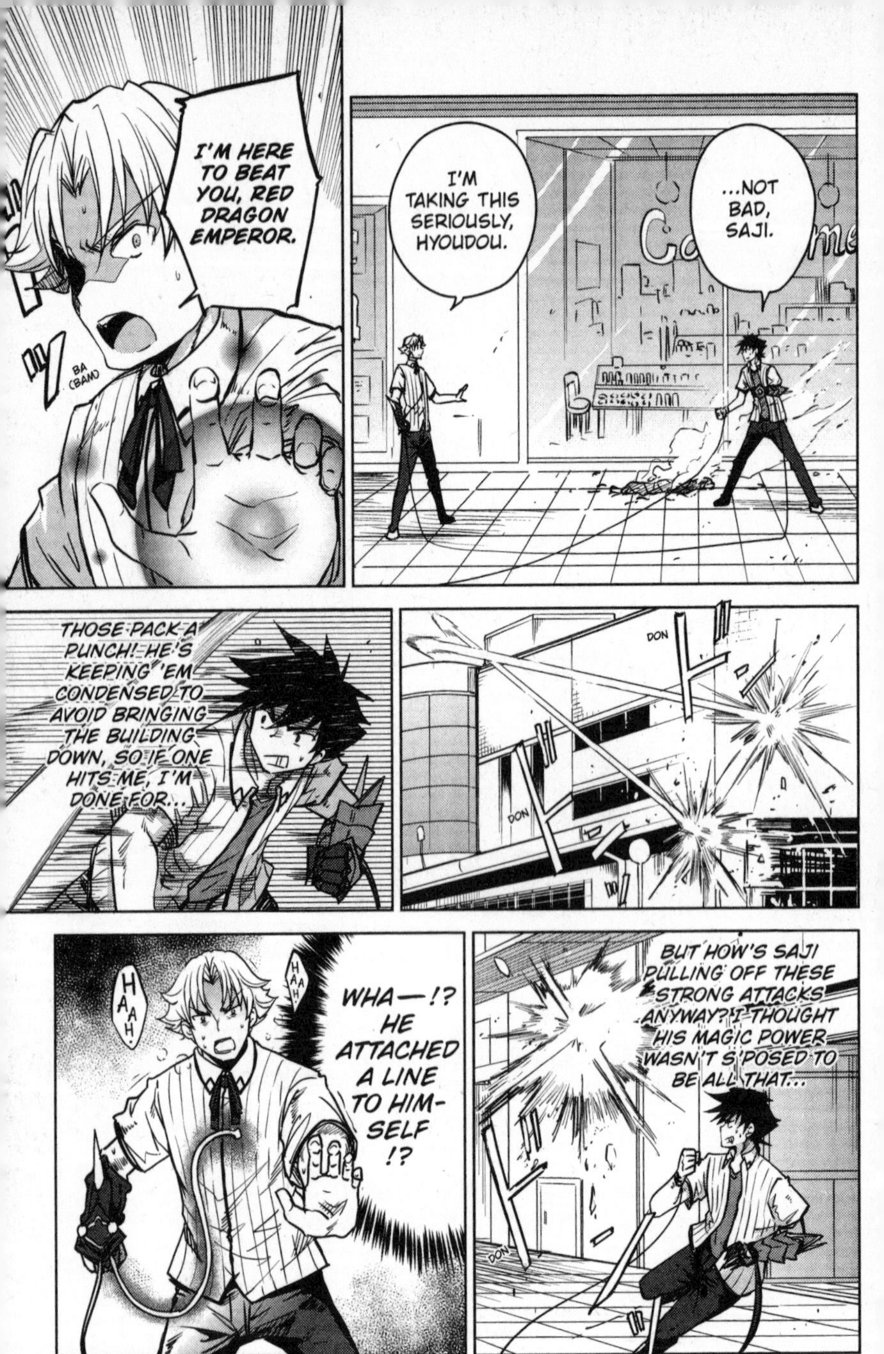
...NOT BAD, SAJI.
I'M TAKING THIS SERIOUSLY, HYOUDOU.
I'M HERE TO BEAT YOU, RED DRAGON EMPEROR.
BA (BAM)
DON
DON
THOSE PACK A PUNCH! HE'S KEEPING 'EM CONDENSED TO AVOID BRINGING THE BUILDING DOWN, SO IF ONE HITS ME, I'M DONE FOR...
BUT HOW'S SAJI PULLING OFF THESE STRONG ATTACKS ANYWAY? I THOUGHT HIS MAGIC POWER WASN'T S'POSED TO BE ALL THAT...
DON
HAAH
HAAH
WHA—!? HE ATTACHED A LINE TO HIM-SELF !?

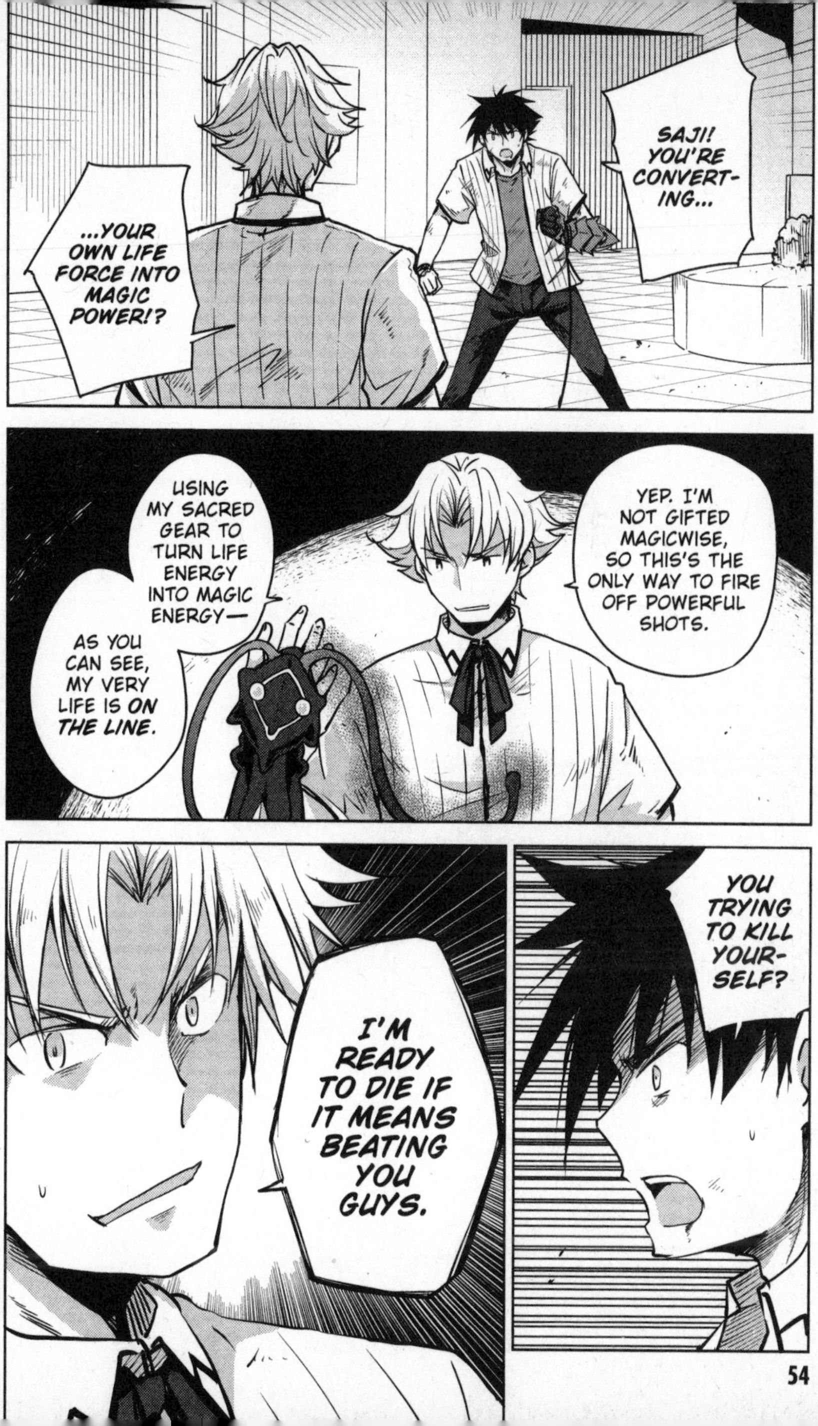
SAJI! YOU'RE CONVERTING...
...YOUR OWN LIFE FORCE INTO MAGIC POWER!?
YEP. I'M NOT GIFTED MAGICWISE, SO THIS'S THE ONLY WAY TO FIRE OFF POWERFUL SHOTS.
USING MY SACRED GEAR TO TURN LIFE ENERGY INTO MAGIC ENERGY—
AS YOU CAN SEE, MY VERY LIFE IS ON THE LINE.
YOU TRYING TO KILL YOURSELF?
I'M READY TO DIE IF IT MEANS BEATING YOU GUYS.

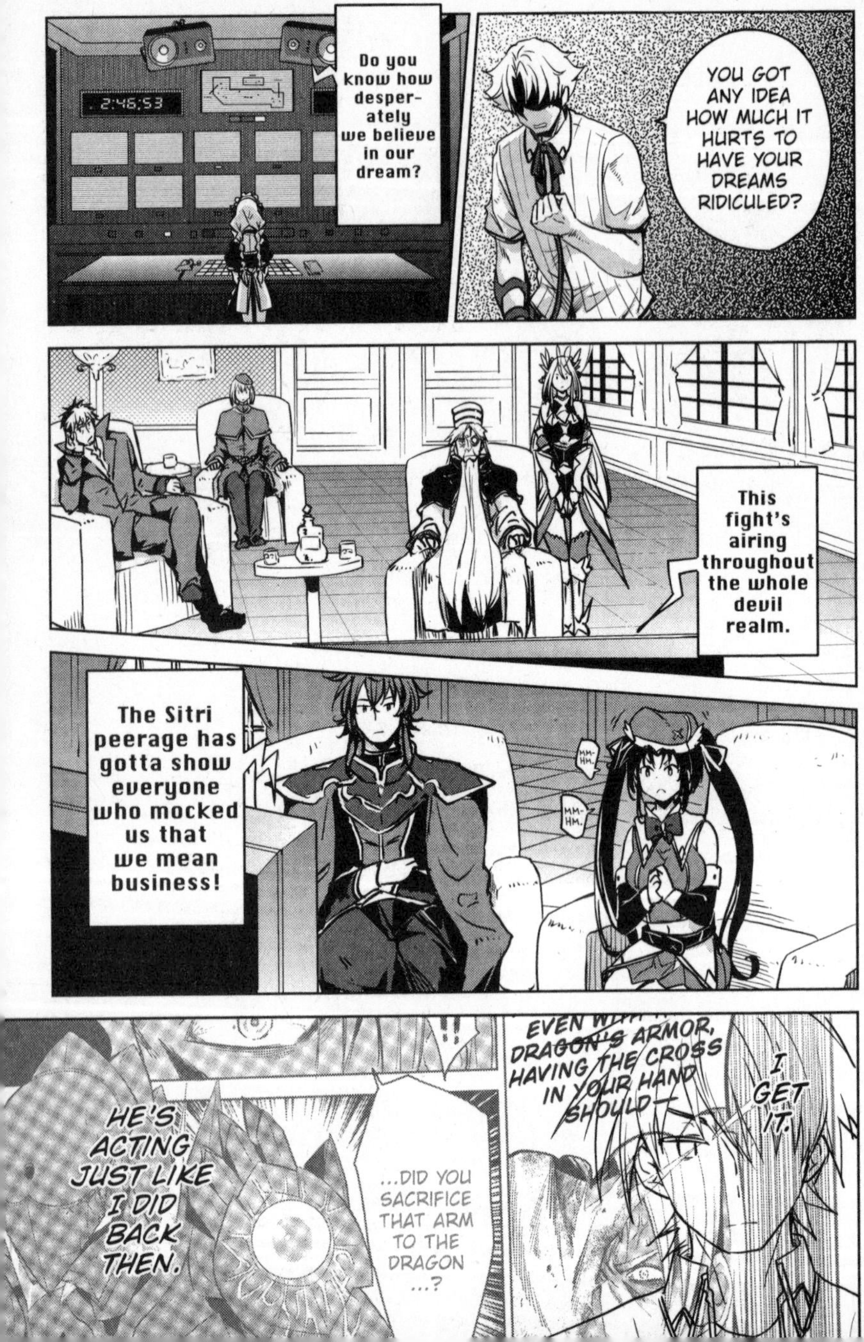
YOU GOT ANY IDEA HOW MUCH IT HURTS TO HAVE YOUR DREAMS RIDICULED?
Do you know how desperately we believe in our dream?
2:46:53
This fight's airing throughout the whole devil realm.
The Sitri peerage has gotta show everyone who mocked us that we mean business!
MM-HM.
MM-HM.
EVEN WITH DRAGON'S ARMOR, HAVING THE CROSS IN YOUR HAND SHOULD—
I GET IT.
...DID YOU SACRIFICE THAT ARM TO THE DRAGON ...?
HE'S ACTING JUST LIKE I DID BACK THEN.

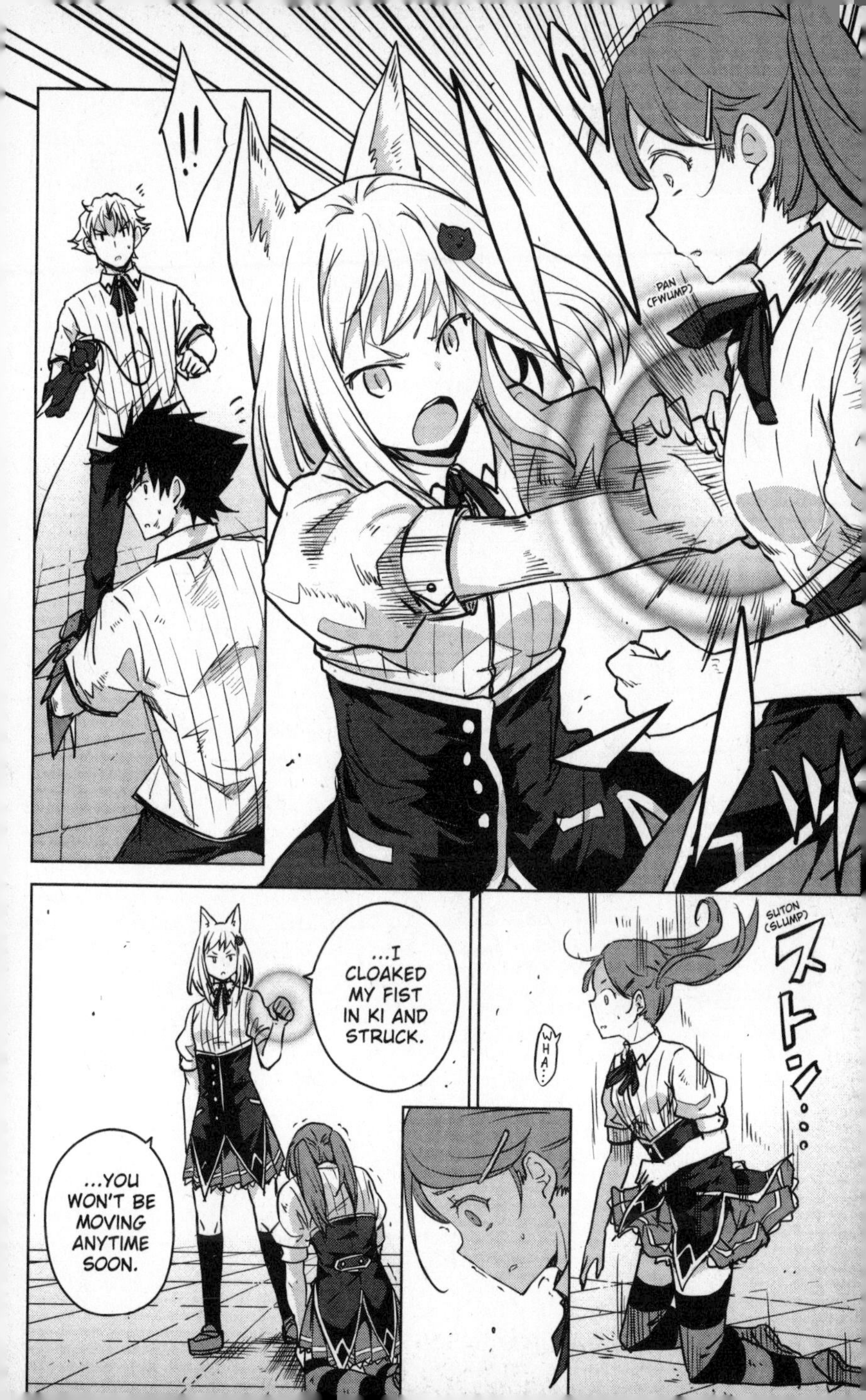
PAN (FWUMP)
!!
SUTON (SLUMP)
WHA...
...I CLOAKED MY FIST IN KI AND STRUCK.
...YOU WON'T BE MOVING ANYTIME SOON.

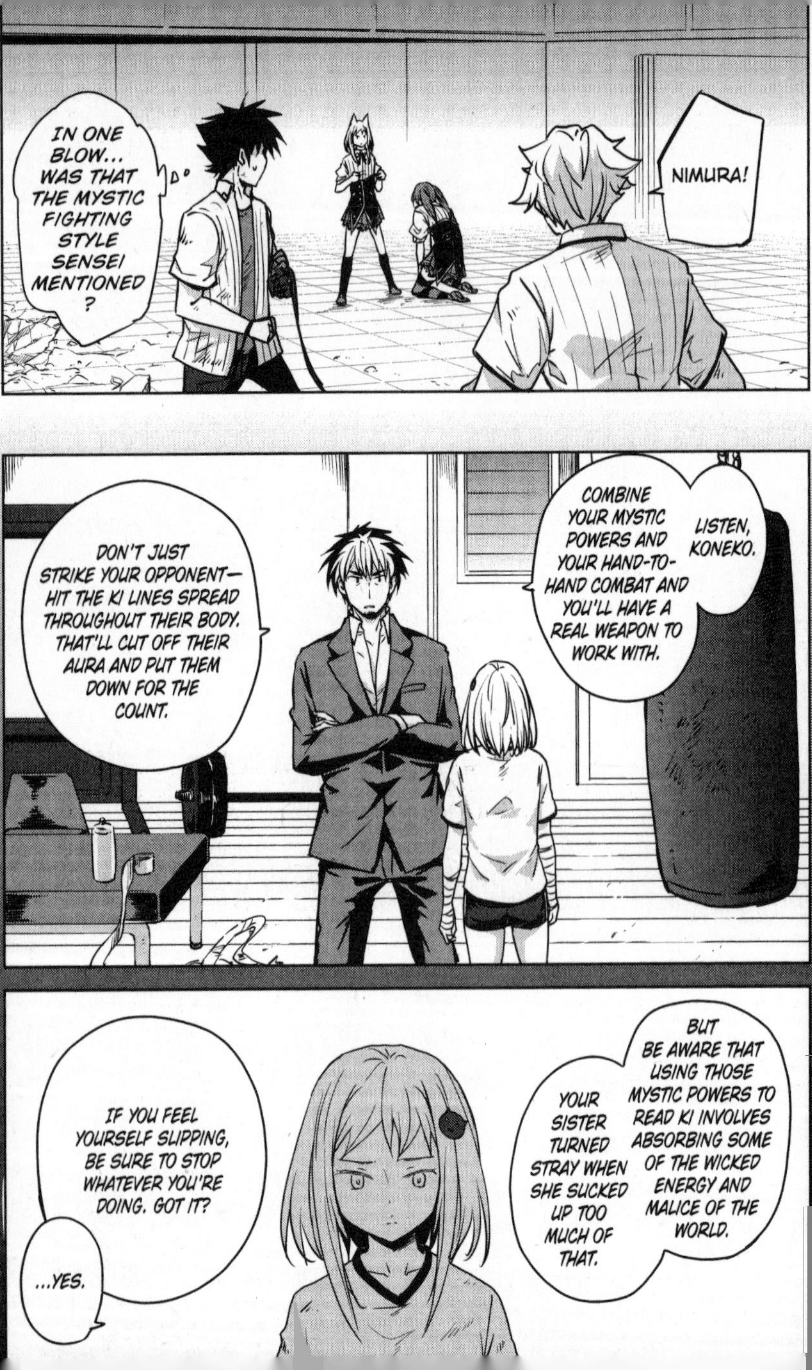
NIMURA!
IN ONE BLOW... WAS THAT THE MYSTIC FIGHTING STYLE SENSEI MENTIONED?
LISTEN, KONEKO.
COMBINE YOUR MYSTIC POWERS AND YOUR HAND-TO-HAND COMBAT AND YOU'LL HAVE A REAL WEAPON TO WORK WITH.
DON'T JUST STRIKE YOUR OPPONENT—HIT THE KI LINES SPREAD THROUGHOUT THEIR BODY. THAT'LL CUT OFF THEIR AURA AND PUT THEM DOWN FOR THE COUNT.
BUT BE AWARE THAT USING THOSE MYSTIC POWERS TO READ KI INVOLVES ABSORBING SOME OF THE WICKED ENERGY AND MALICE OF THE WORLD.
YOUR SISTER TURNED STRAY WHEN SHE SUCKED UP TOO MUCH OF THAT.
IF YOU FEEL YOURSELF SLIPPING, BE SURE TO STOP WHATEVER YOU'RE DOING. GOT IT?
...YES.

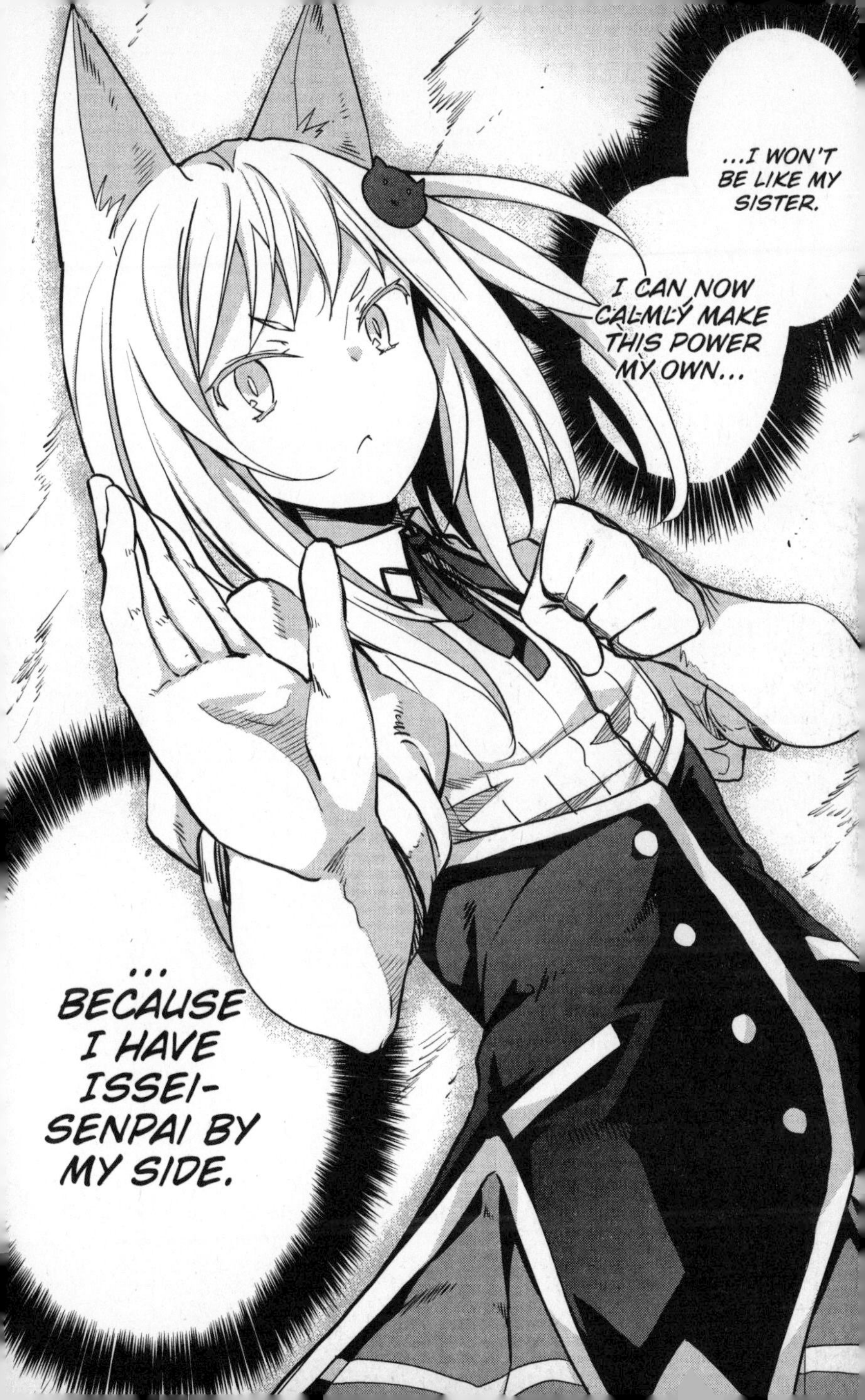
...I WON'T BE LIKE MY SISTER.
I CAN NOW CALMLY MAKE THIS POWER MY OWN...
...BECAUSE I HAVE ISSEI-SENPAI BY MY SIDE.

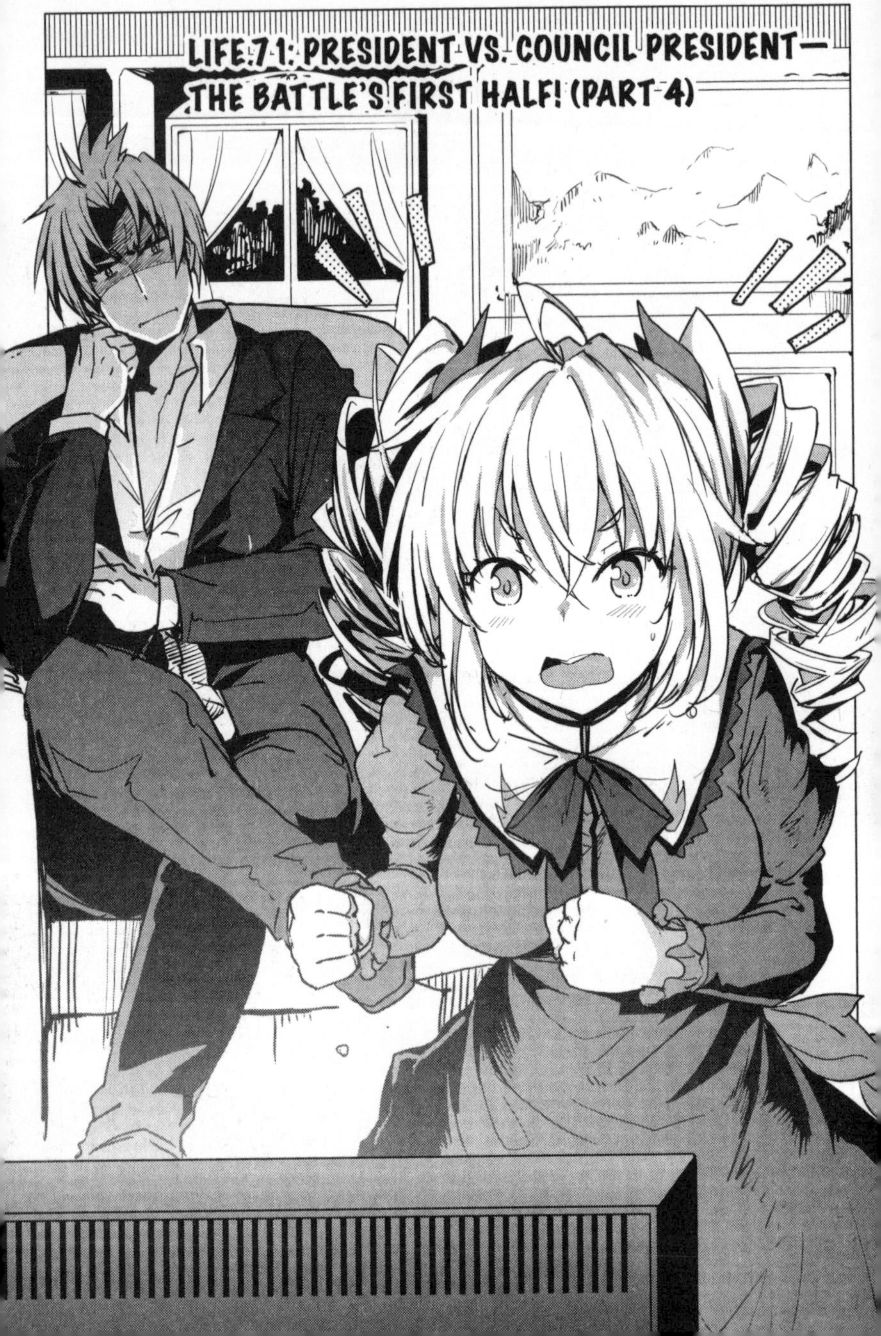
LIFE 71: PRESIDENT VS. COUNCIL PRESIDENT—
THE BATTLE'S FIRST HALF! (PART 4)

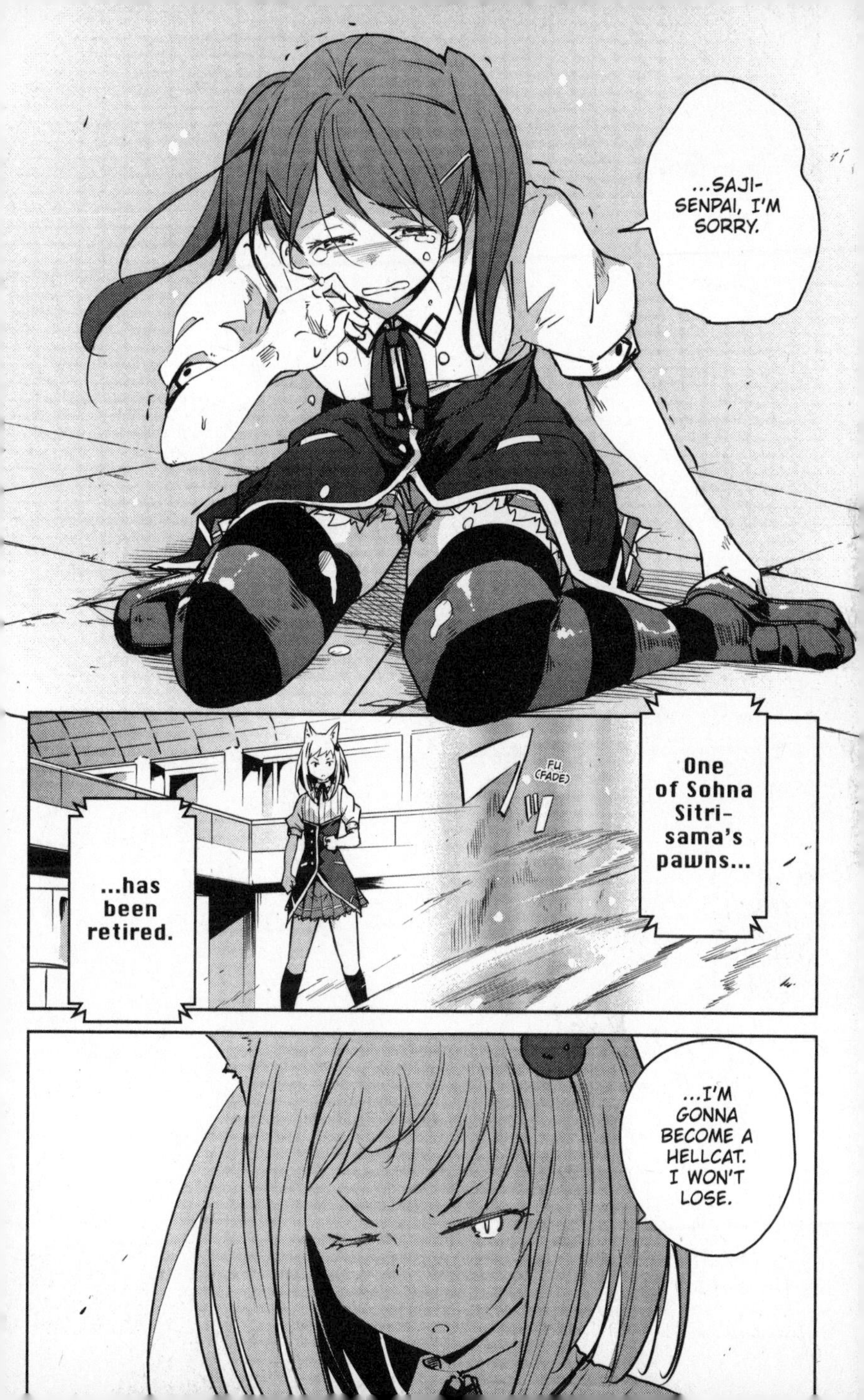
...SAJI-SENPAI, I'M SORRY.
FU (FADE)
One of Sohna Sitri-sama's pawns...
...has been retired.
...I'M GONNA BECOME A HELLCAT. I WON'T LOSE.

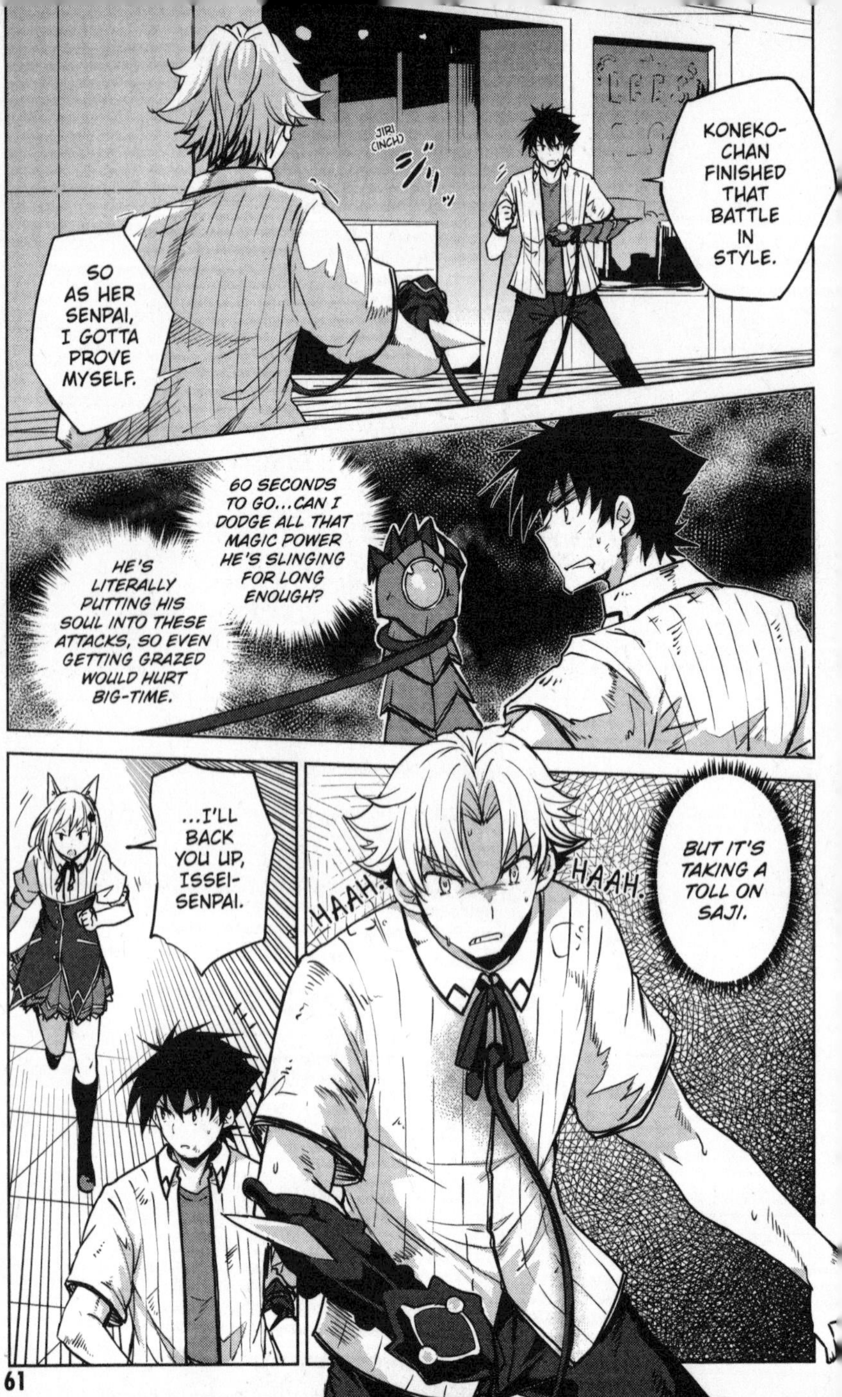

KONEKO-CHAN FINISHED THAT BATTLE IN STYLE.
JIRI (INCH)
SO AS HER SENPAI, I GOTTA PROVE MYSELF.
60 SECONDS TO GO...CAN I DODGE ALL THAT MAGIC POWER HE'S SLINGING FOR LONG ENOUGH?
HE'S LITERALLY PUTTING HIS SOUL INTO THESE ATTACKS, SO EVEN GETTING GRAZED WOULD HURT BIG-TIME.
BUT IT'S TAKING A TOLL ON SAJI.
HAAH.
HAAH.
...I'LL BACK YOU UP, ISSEI-SENPAI.

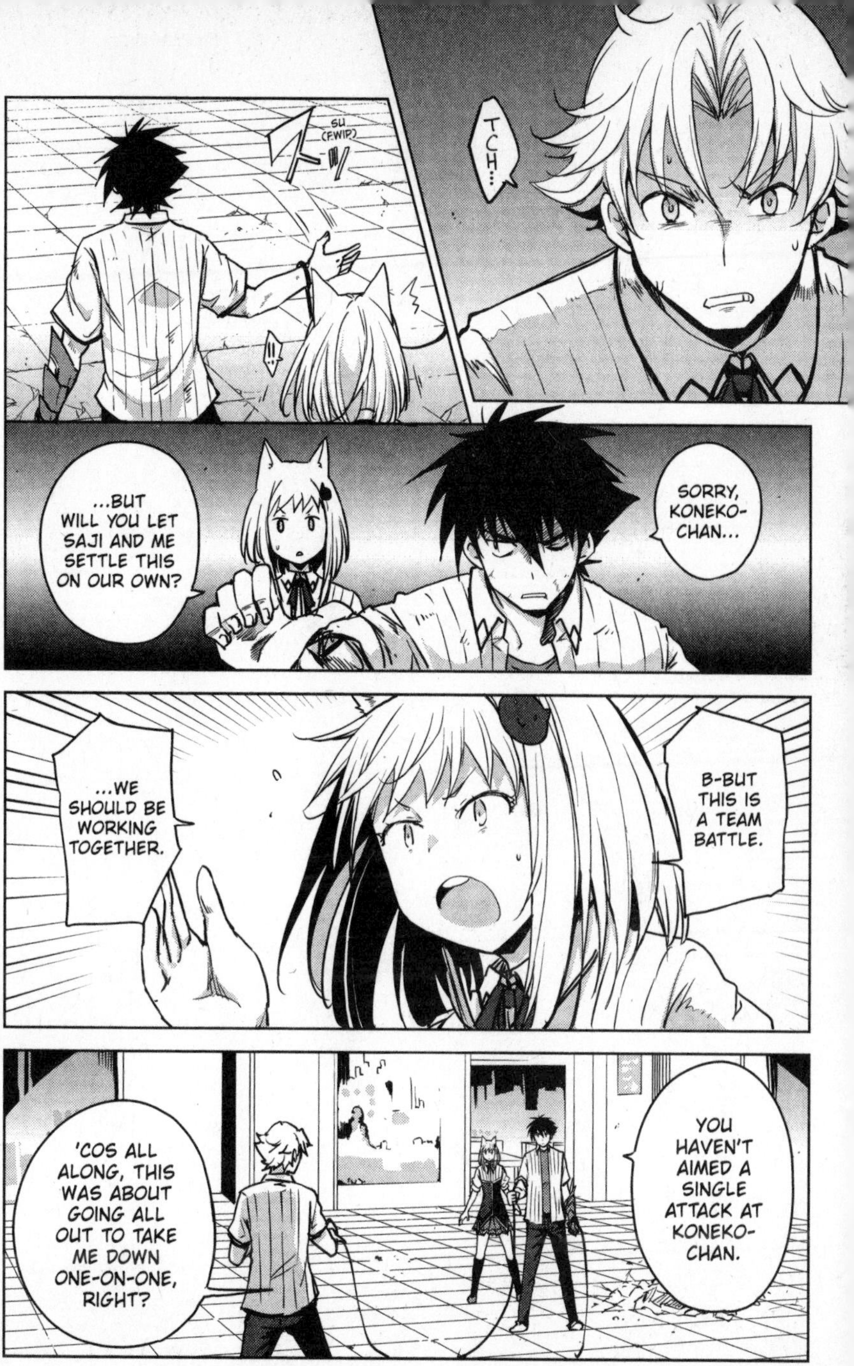
TCH...
SU (F.WIP)
!!
SORRY, KONEKO-CHAN...
...BUT WILL YOU LET SAJI AND ME SETTLE THIS ON OUR OWN?
B-BUT THIS IS A TEAM BATTLE.
...WE SHOULD BE WORKING TOGETHER.
YOU HAVEN'T AIMED A SINGLE ATTACK AT KONEKO-CHAN.
'COS ALL ALONG, THIS WAS ABOUT GOING ALL OUT TO TAKE ME DOWN ONE-ON-ONE, RIGHT?

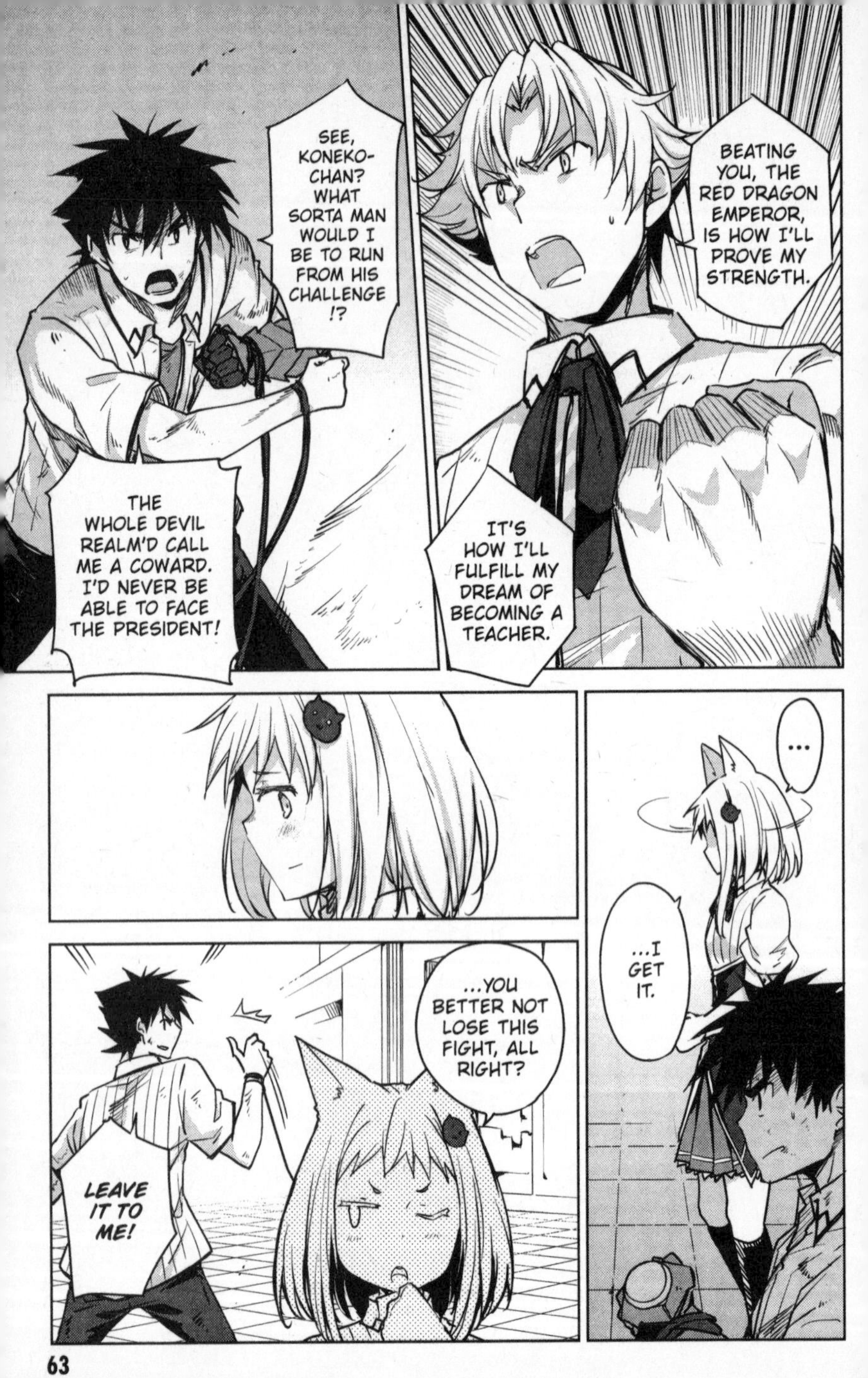
BEATING YOU, THE RED DRAGON EMPEROR, IS HOW I'LL PROVE MY STRENGTH.
IT'S HOW I'LL FULFILL MY DREAM OF BECOMING A TEACHER.
SEE, KONEKO-CHAN? WHAT SORTA MAN WOULD I BE TO RUN FROM HIS CHALLENGE!?
THE WHOLE DEVIL REALM'D CALL ME A COWARD. I'D NEVER BE ABLE TO FACE THE PRESIDENT!
...
...I GET IT.
...YOU BETTER NOT LOSE THIS FIGHT, ALL RIGHT?
LEAVE IT TO ME!

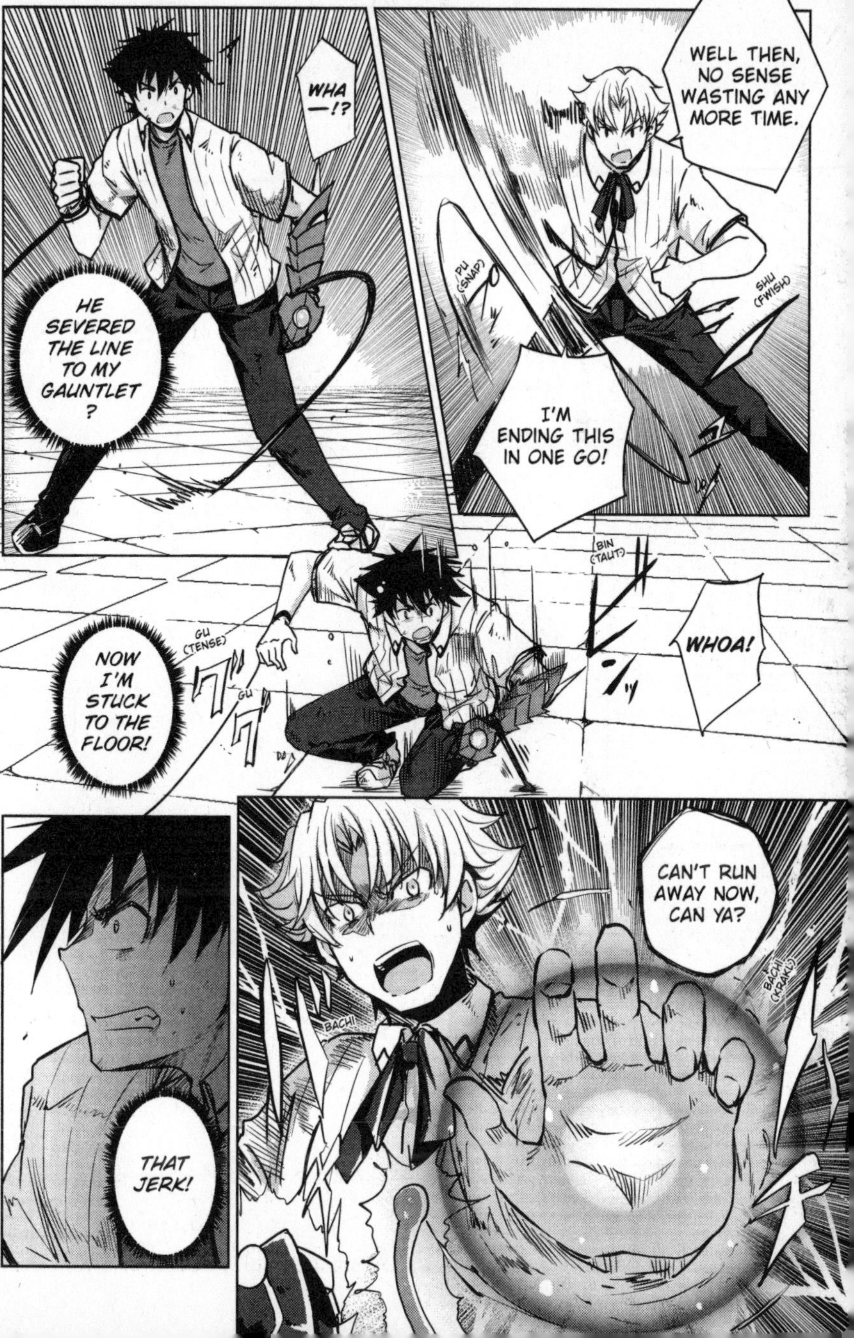
WELL THEN, NO SENSE WASTING ANY MORE TIME.
PU (SNAP)
SHU (FWISH)
I'M ENDING THIS IN ONE GO!
WHA—!?
HE SEVERED THE LINE TO MY GAUNTLET?
BIN (TAUT)
WHOA!
GU (TENSE)
NOW I'M STUCK TO THE FLOOR!
GU
CAN'T RUN AWAY NOW, CAN YA?
BACHI (KRAKL)
BACHI
THAT JERK!

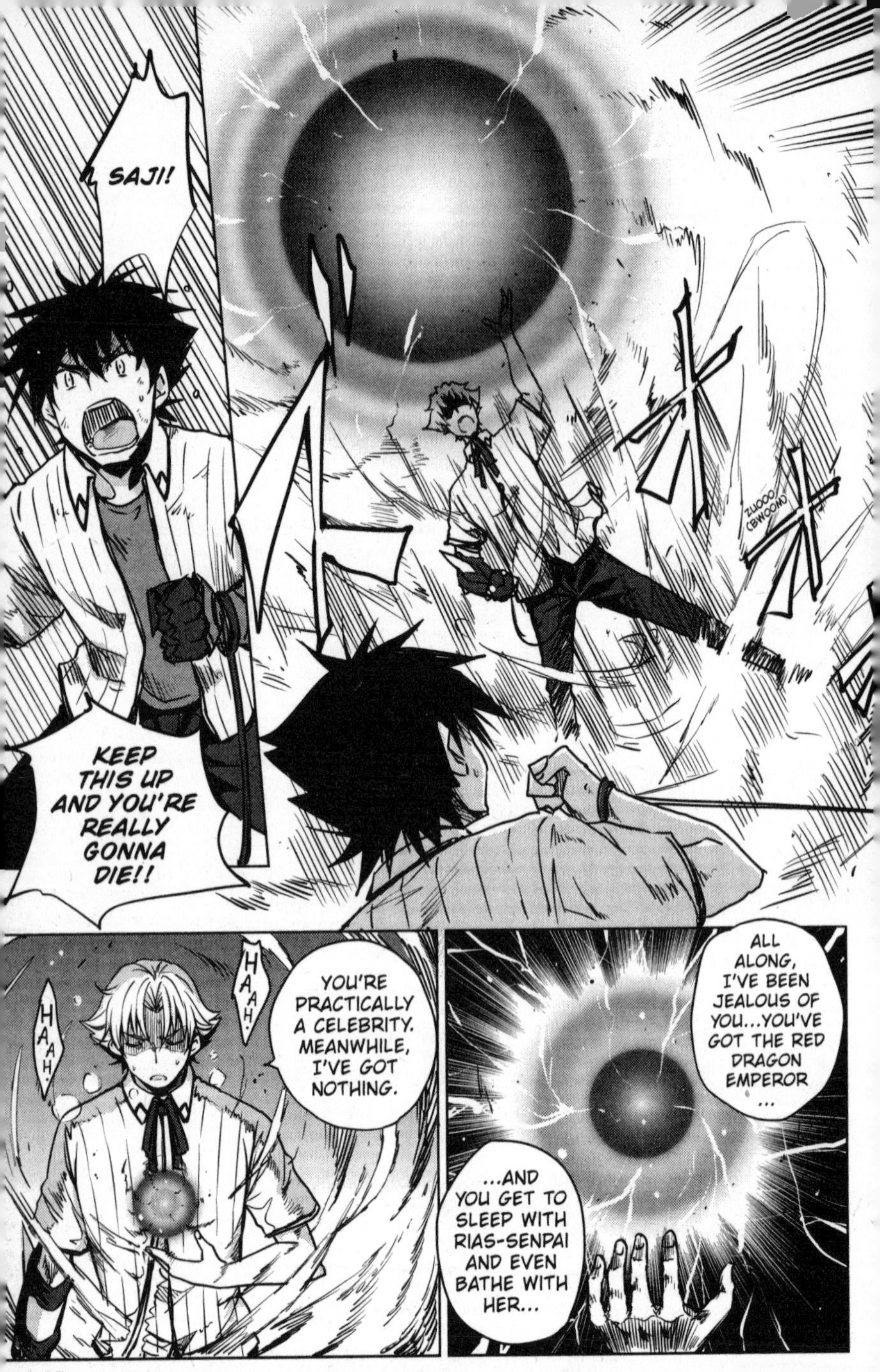
SAJI!
ZUOOO (BWOOM)
KEEP THIS UP AND YOU'RE REALLY GONNA DIE!!
ALL ALONG, I'VE BEEN JEALOUS OF YOU...YOU'VE GOT THE RED DRAGON EMPEROR...
...AND YOU GET TO SLEEP WITH RIAS-SENPAI AND EVEN BATHE WITH HER...
HAAH.
HAAH.
YOU'RE PRACTICALLY A CELEBRITY. MEANWHILE, I'VE GOT NOTHING.

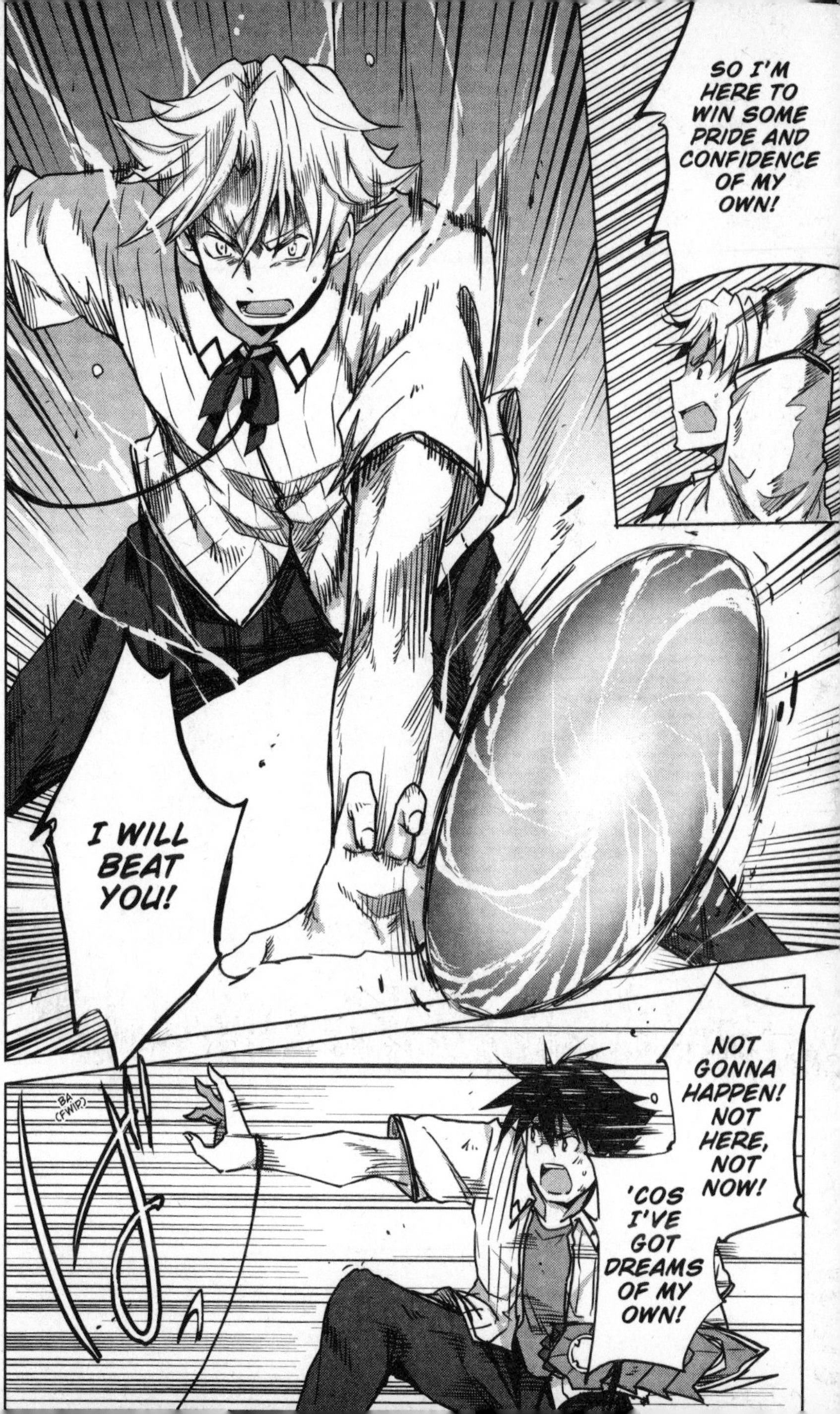
SO I'M HERE TO WIN SOME PRIDE AND CONFIDENCE OF MY OWN!
I WILL BEAT YOU!
NOT GONNA HAPPEN! NOT HERE, NOT NOW!
'COS I'VE GOT DREAMS OF MY OWN!
BA (FWIP)

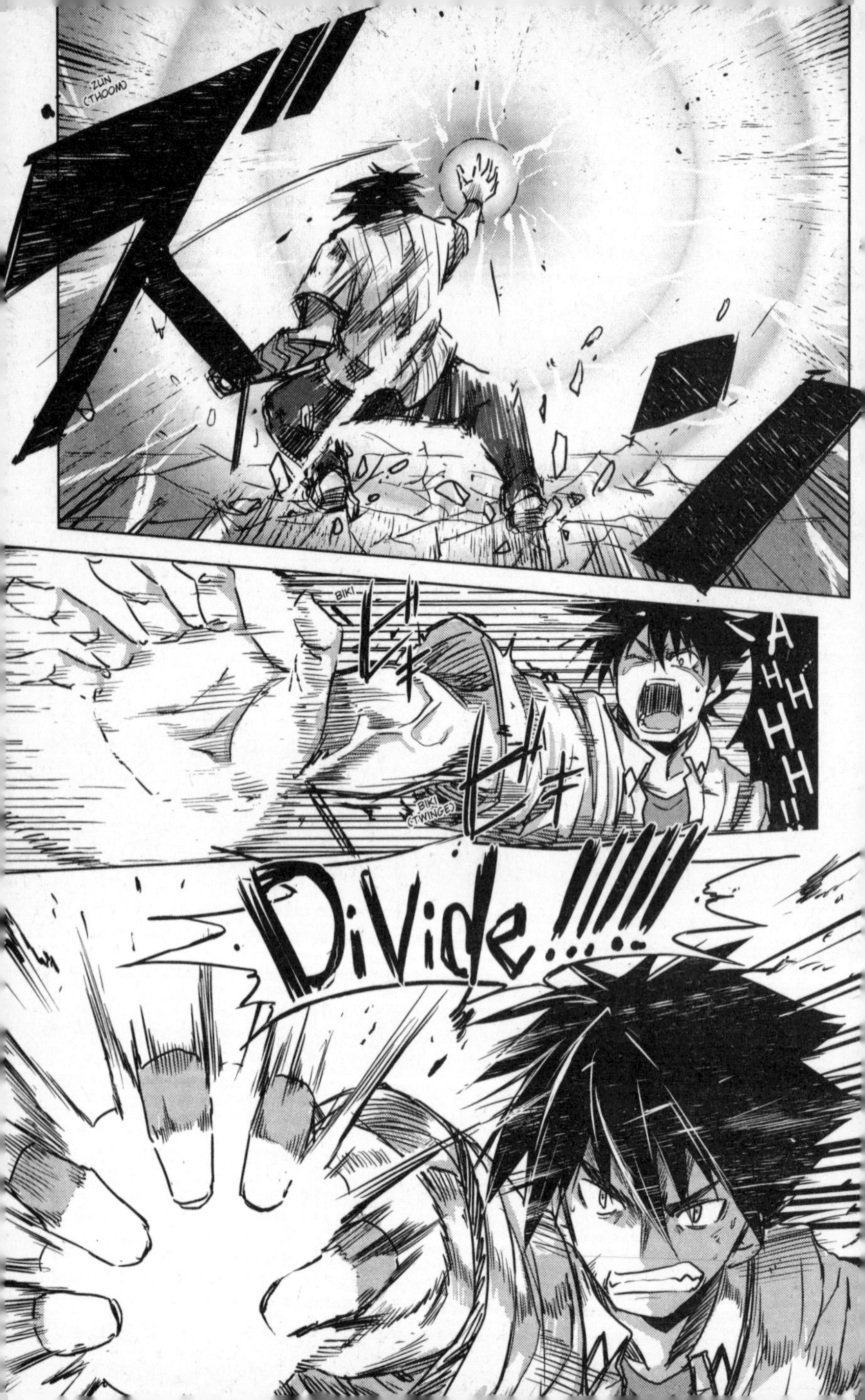
ZUN (THOOM)
BIKI
BIKI (TWINGE)
AHHHH!!
DiVide!!!!!

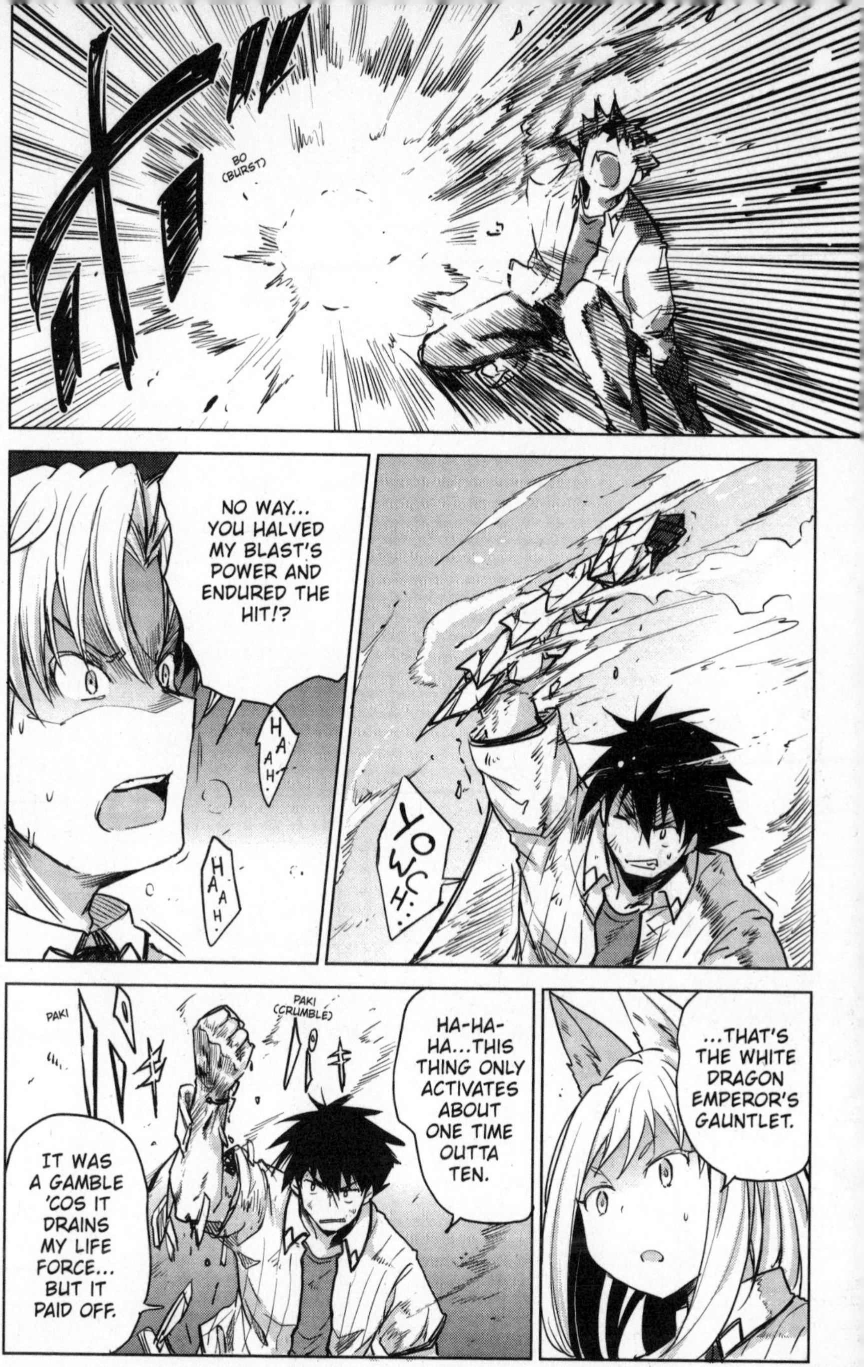
BO (BURST)
YOWCH...
NO WAY... YOU HALVED MY BLAST'S POWER AND ENDURED THE HIT!?
HAAH...
HAAH.
...THAT'S THE WHITE DRAGON EMPEROR'S GAUNTLET.
PAKI (CRUMBLE)
HA-HA-HA...THIS THING ONLY ACTIVATES ABOUT ONE TIME OUTTA TEN.
PAKI
IT WAS A GAMBLE 'COS IT DRAINS MY LIFE FORCE... BUT IT PAID OFF.

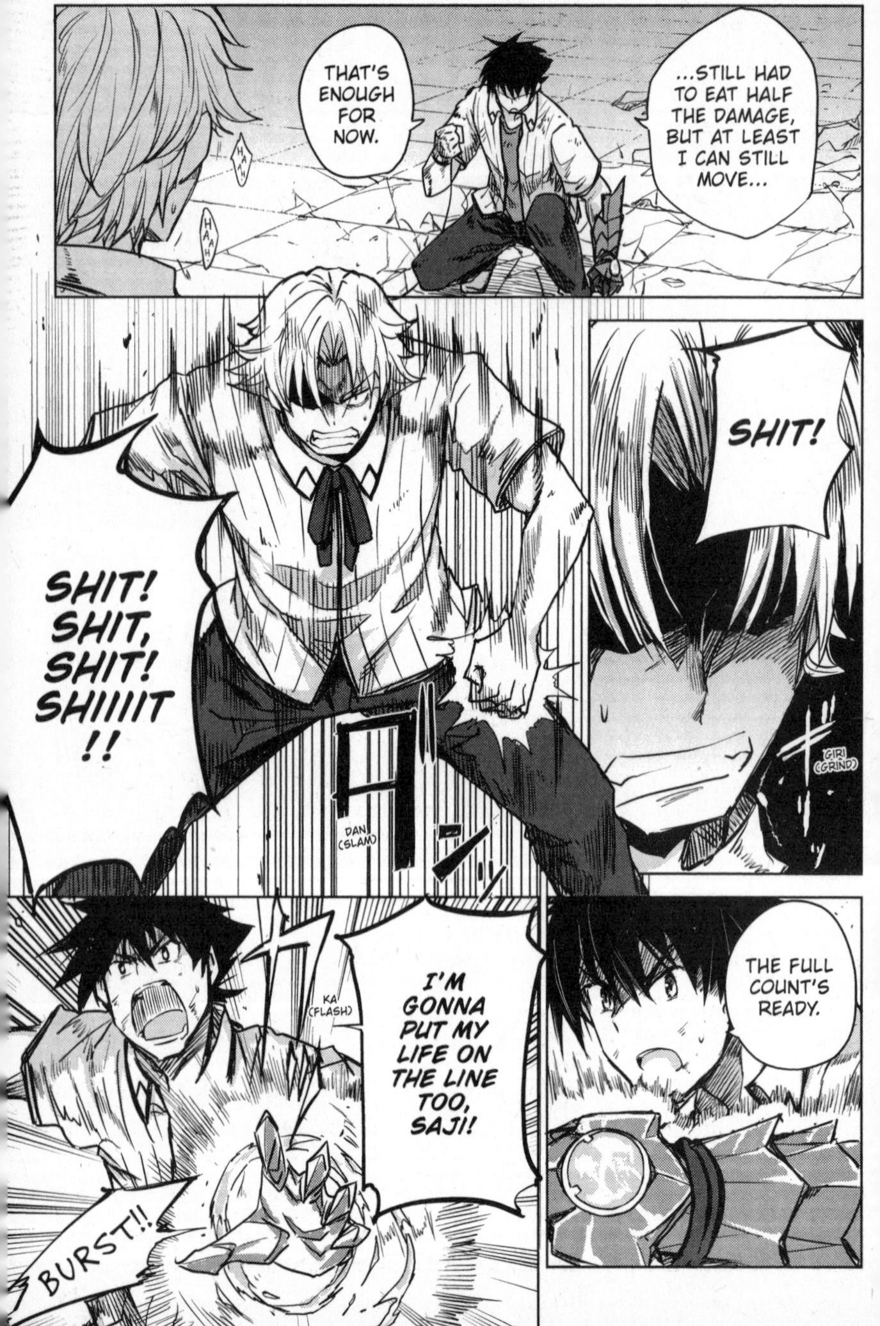
...STILL HAD TO EAT HALF THE DAMAGE, BUT AT LEAST I CAN STILL MOVE...
THAT'S ENOUGH FOR NOW.
SHIT!
GIRI (GRIND)
SHIT! SHIT, SHIT! SHIIIIT!!
DAN (SLAM)
THE FULL COUNT'S READY.
I'M GONNA PUT MY LIFE ON THE LINE TOO, SAJI!
KA (FLASH)
BURST!!

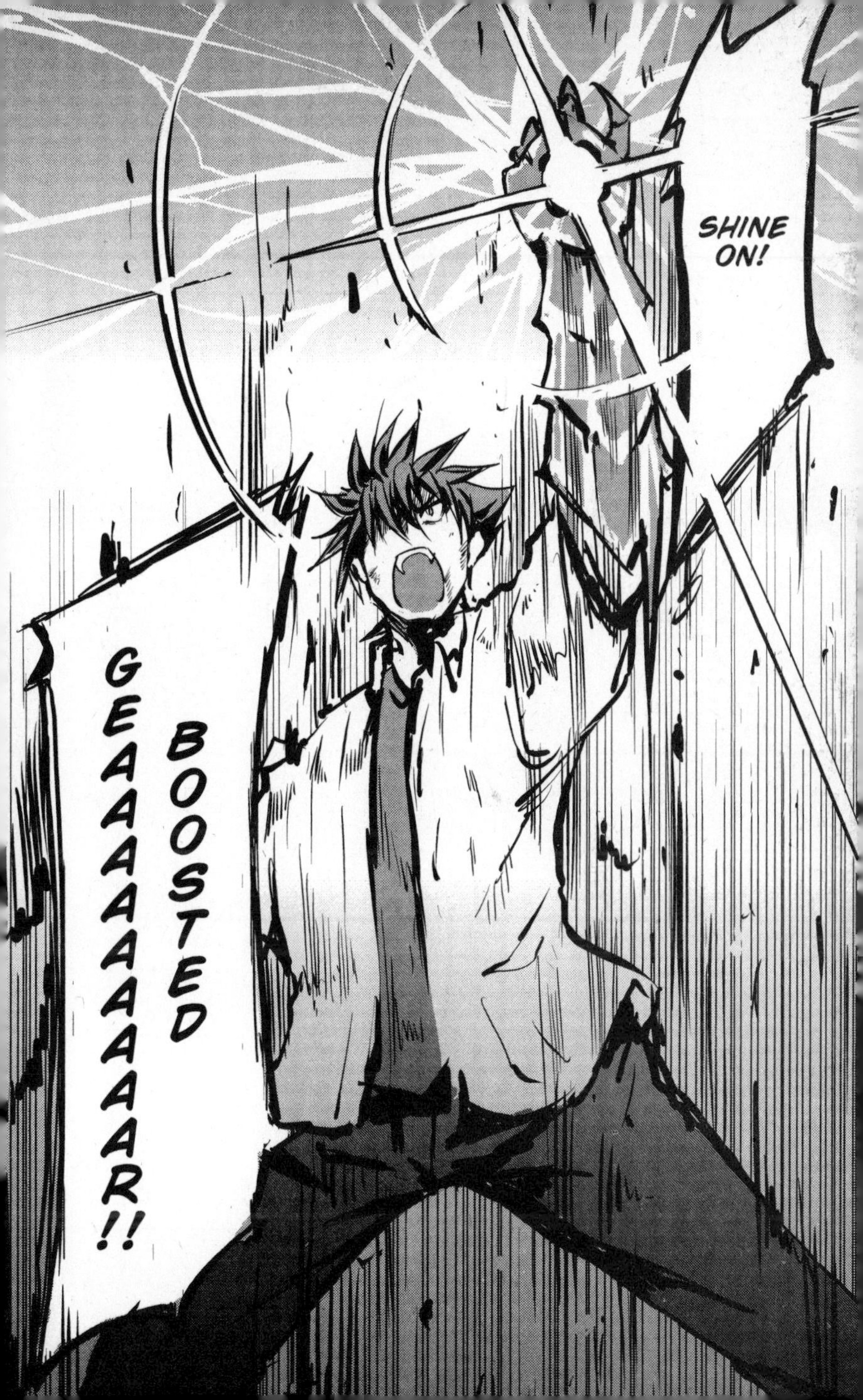
SHINE ON!
BOOSTED
GEAAAAAAAAAR!!

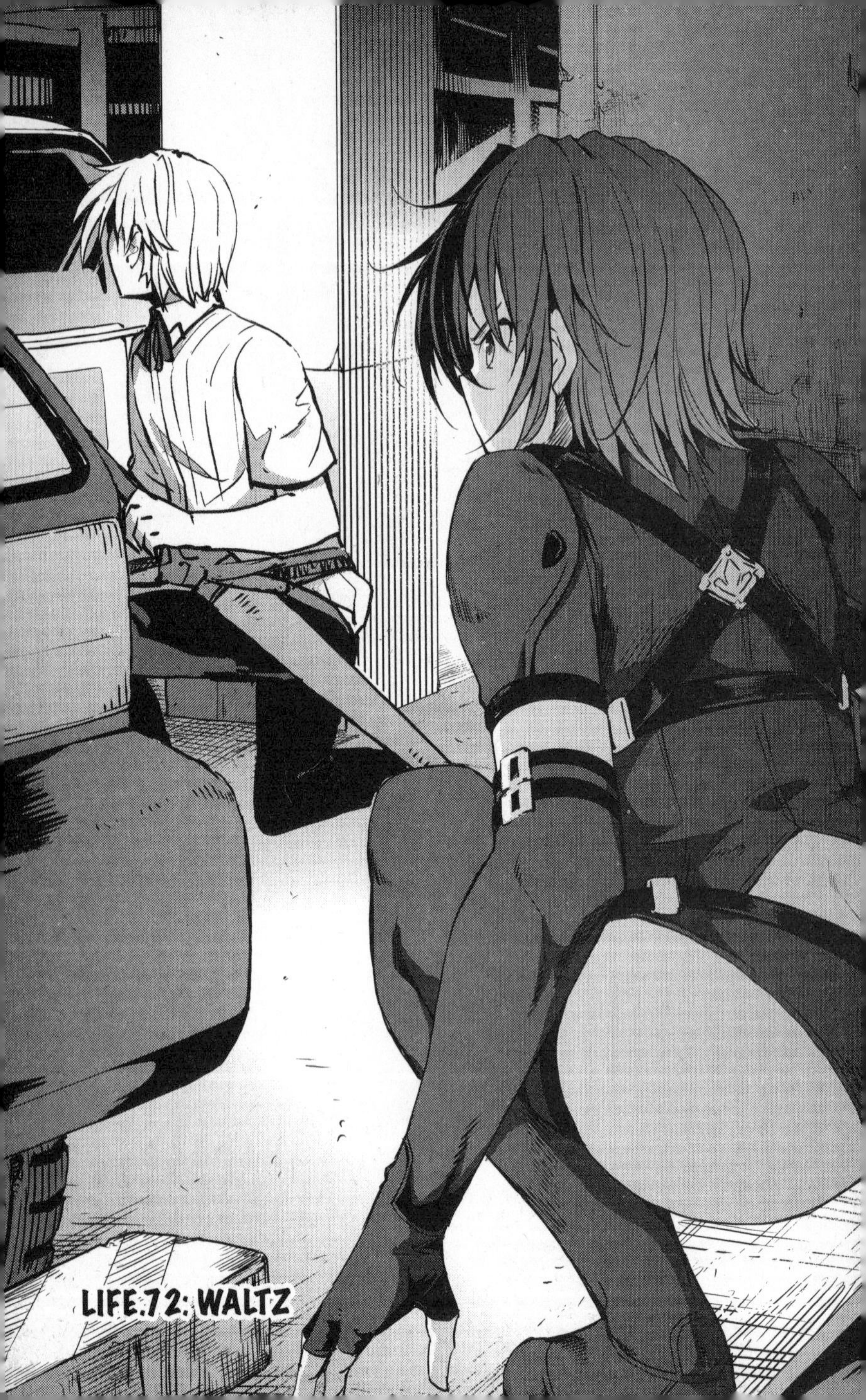
LIFE.72: WALTZ

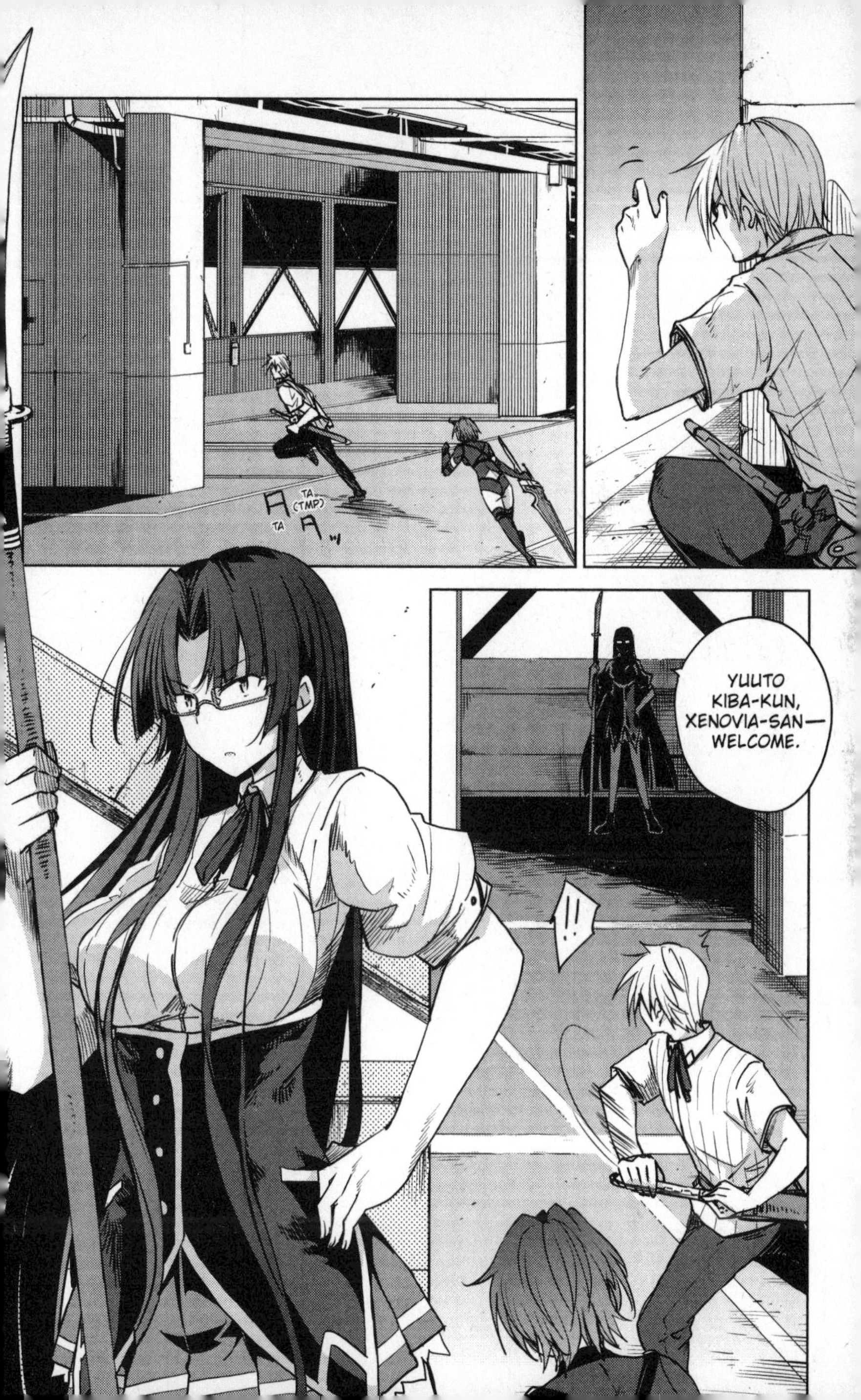
TA (TMP)
TA
YUUTO KIBA-KUN, XENOVIA-SAN— WELCOME.
!!

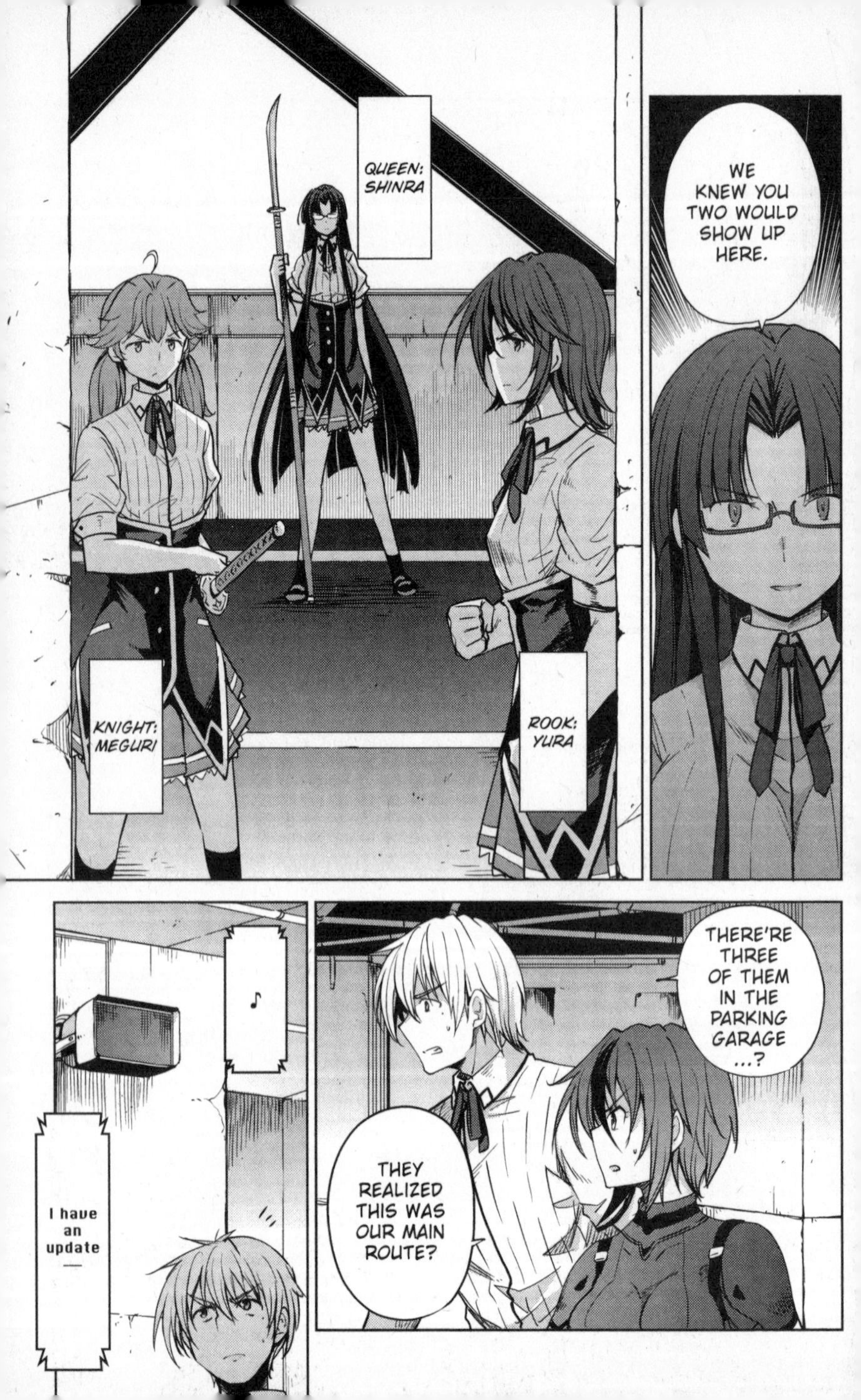
WE KNEW YOU TWO WOULD SHOW UP HERE.
QUEEN: SHINRA
ROOK: YURA
KNIGHT: MEGURI
THERE'RE THREE OF THEM IN THE PARKING GARAGE ...?
THEY REALIZED THIS WAS OUR MAIN ROUTE?
♪
I have an update —

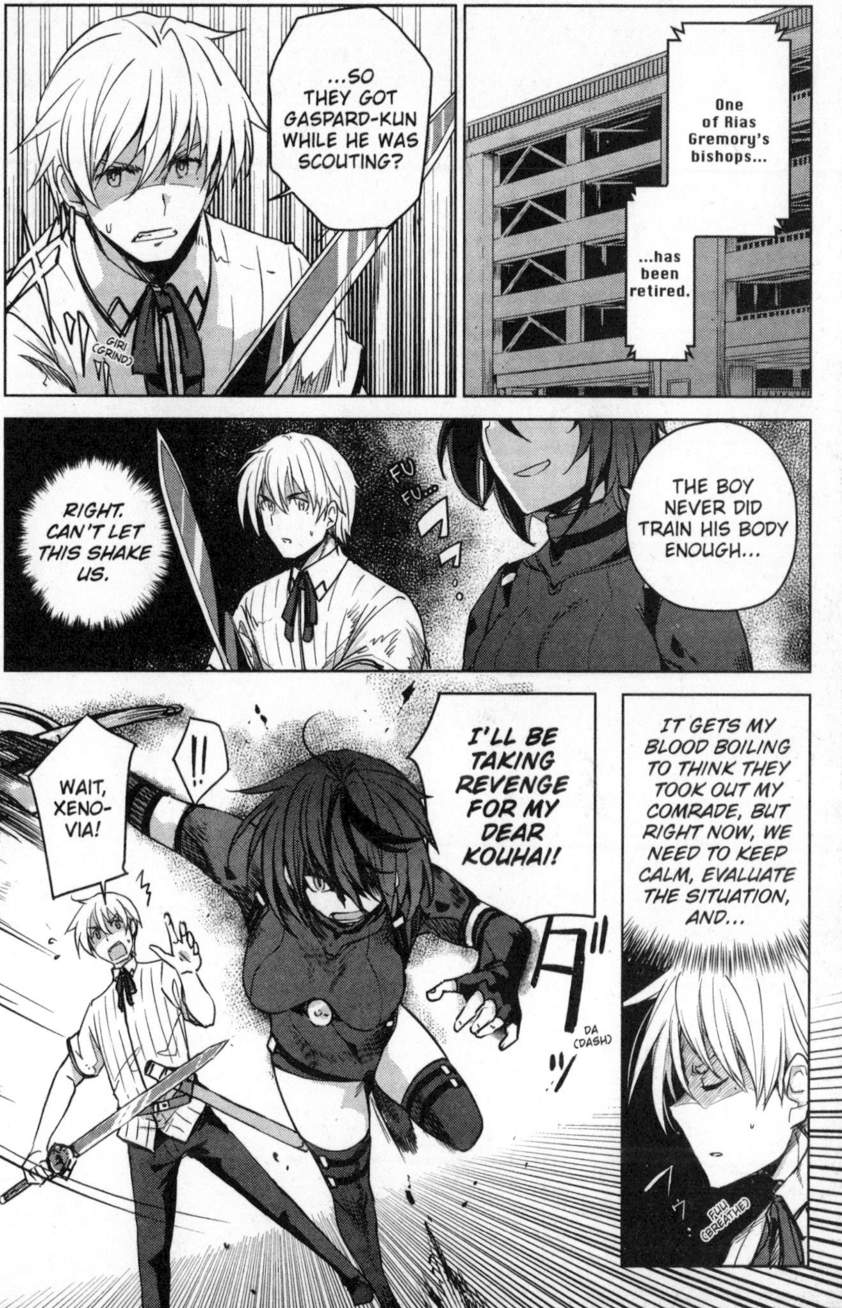
One of Rias Gremory's bishops...
...has been retired.
...SO THEY GOT GASPARD-KUN WHILE HE WAS SCOUTING?
GIRI (GRIND)
THE BOY NEVER DID TRAIN HIS BODY ENOUGH...
FU FU...
RIGHT. CAN'T LET THIS SHAKE US.
IT GETS MY BLOOD BOILING TO THINK THEY TOOK OUT MY COMRADE, BUT RIGHT NOW, WE NEED TO KEEP CALM, EVALUATE THE SITUATION, AND...
FUU (BREATHE)
I'LL BE TAKING REVENGE FOR MY DEAR KOUHAI!
DA (DASH)
!!
WAIT, XENO-VIA!

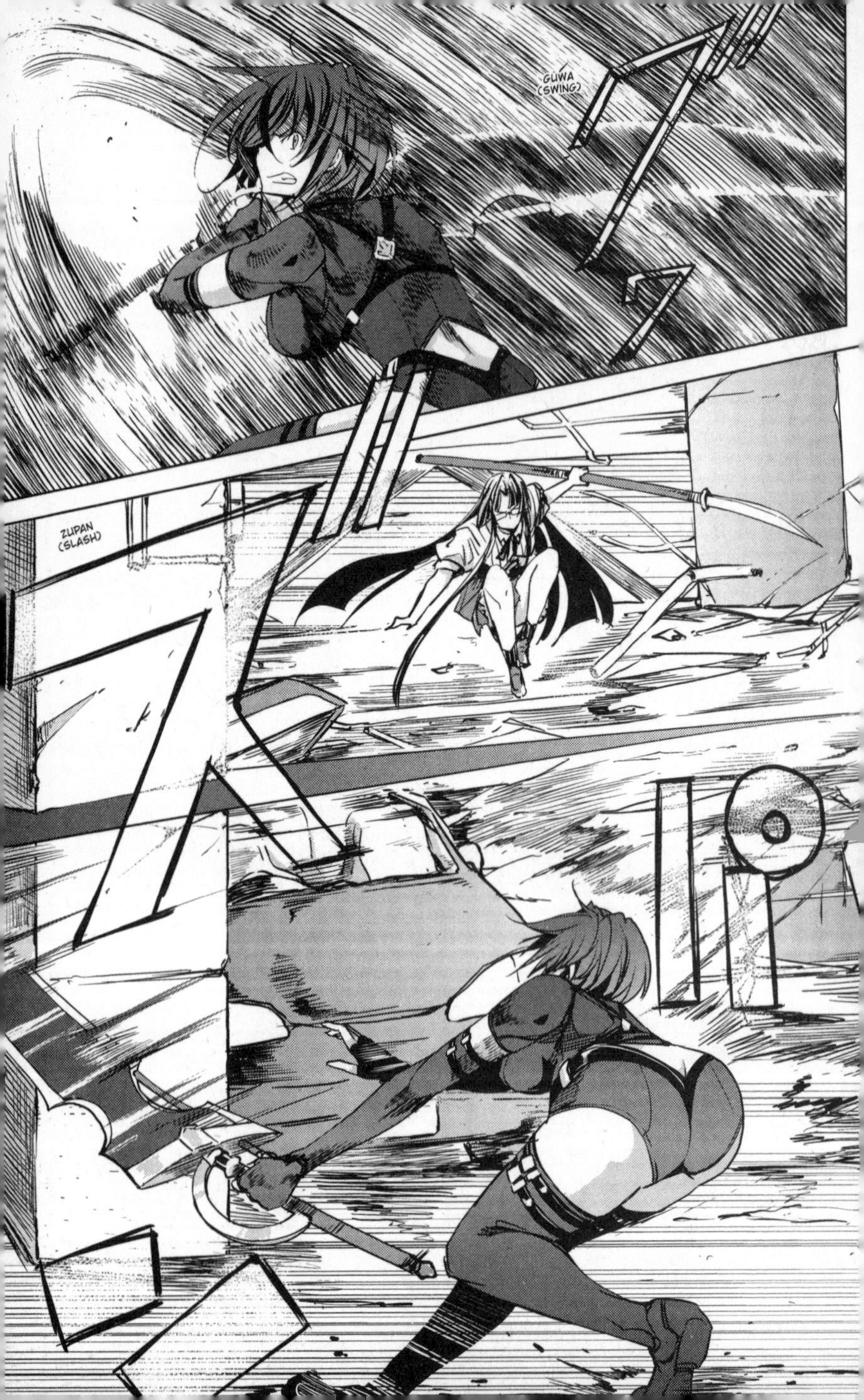
GUWA
(SWING)
ZUPAN
(SLASH)

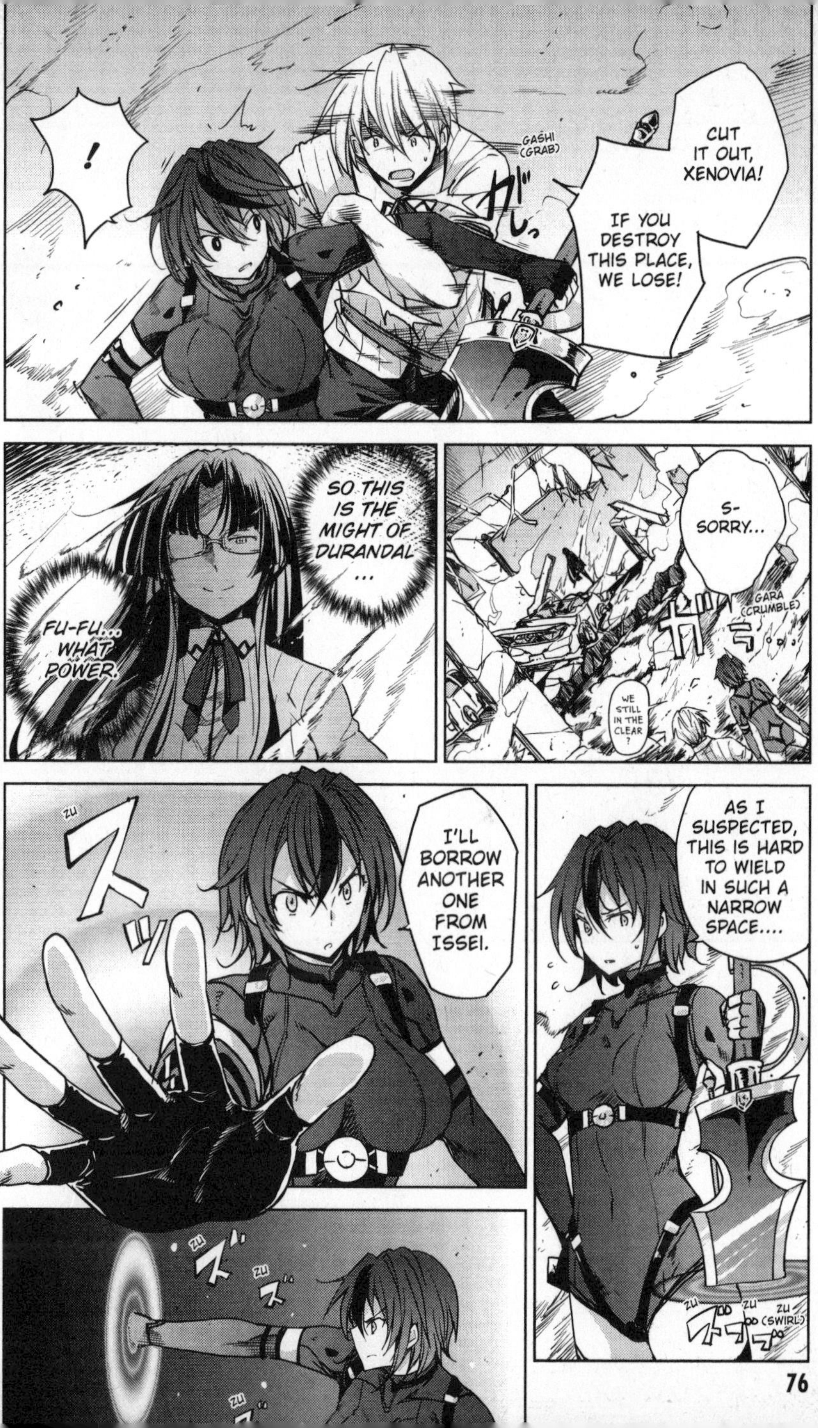
CUT IT OUT, XENOVIA!
IF YOU DESTROY THIS PLACE, WE LOSE!
GASHI (GRAB)
!
S-SORRY...
GARA (CRUMBLE)
WE STILL IN THE CLEAR?
SO THIS IS THE MIGHT OF DURANDAL...
FU-FU... WHAT POWER.
AS I SUSPECTED, THIS IS HARD TO WIELD IN SUCH A NARROW SPACE....
ZU ZU ZU (SWIRL)
ZU
I'LL BORROW ANOTHER ONE FROM ISSEI.
ZU
ZU
ZU

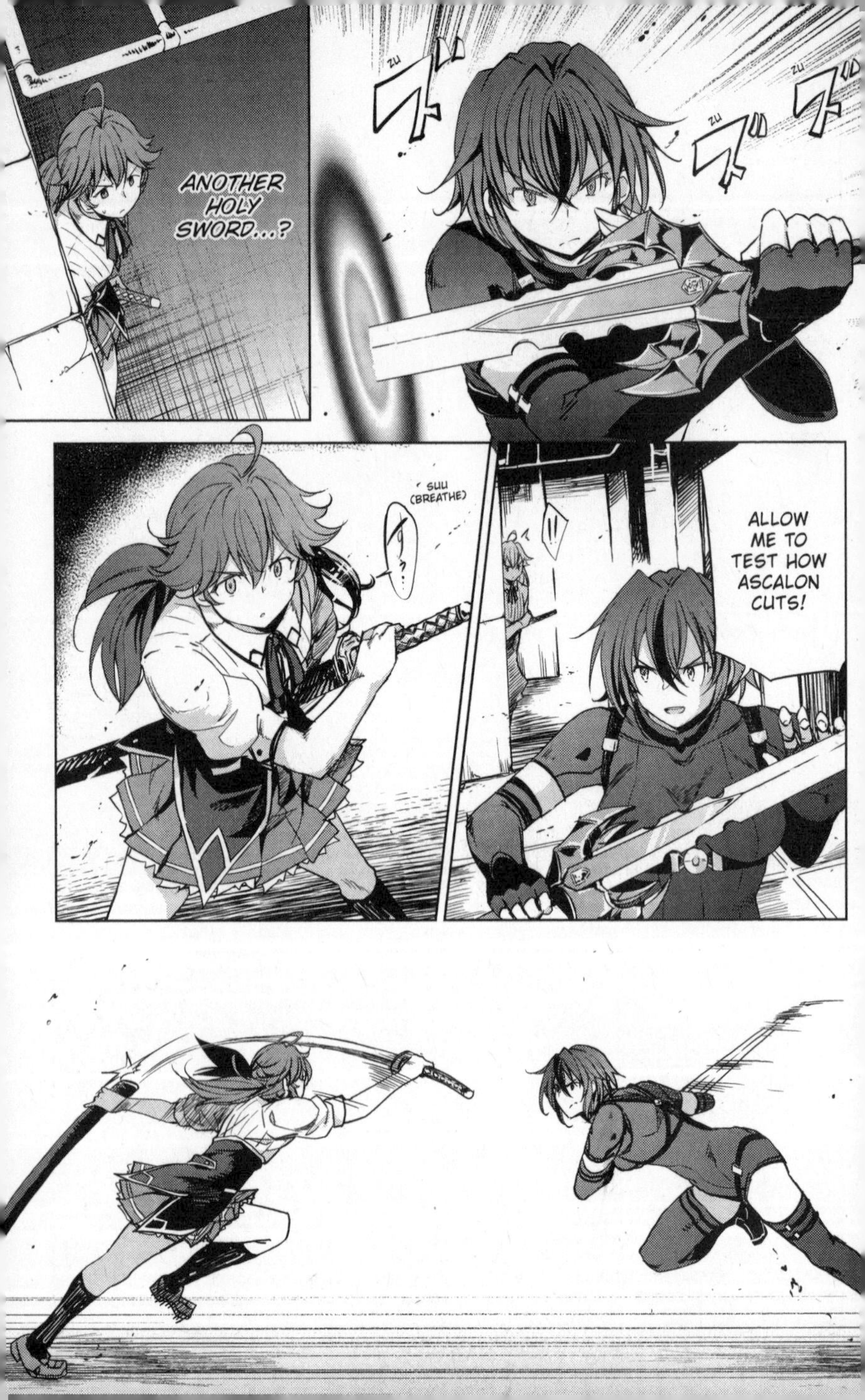
ZU
ZU
ZU
ANOTHER HOLY SWORD...?
ALLOW ME TO TEST HOW ASCALON CUTS!
SUU (BREATHE)

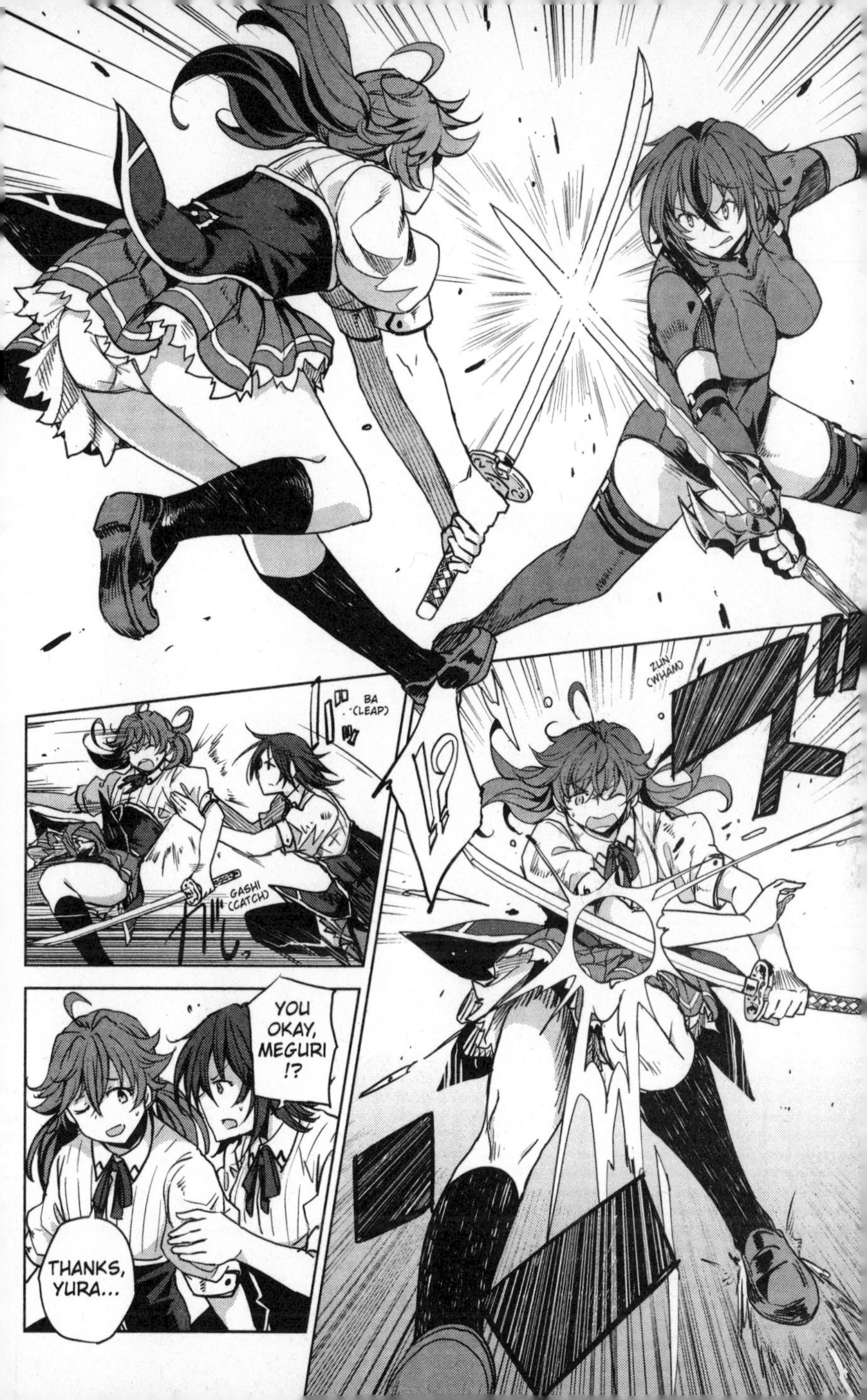
ZUN (WHAM)
!?
BA (LEAP)
GASHI (CATCH)
YOU OKAY, MEGURI !?
THANKS, YURA...

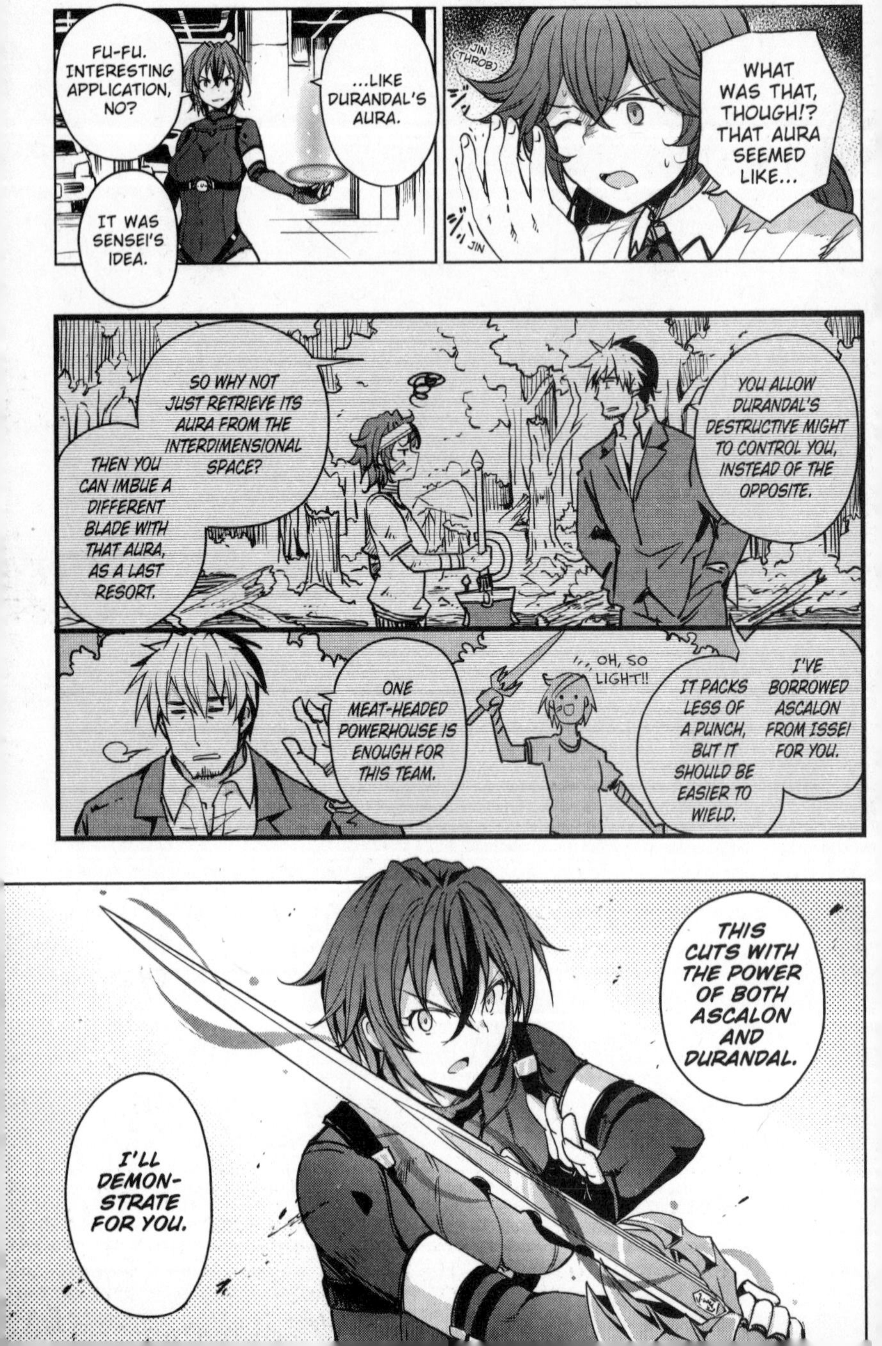
JIN (THROB)
JIN
WHAT WAS THAT, THOUGH!? THAT AURA SEEMED LIKE...
...LIKE DURANDAL'S AURA.
FU-FU. INTERESTING APPLICATION, NO?
IT WAS SENSEI'S IDEA.
YOU ALLOW DURANDAL'S DESTRUCTIVE MIGHT TO CONTROL YOU, INSTEAD OF THE OPPOSITE.
SO WHY NOT JUST RETRIEVE ITS AURA FROM THE INTERDIMENSIONAL SPACE?
THEN YOU CAN IMBUE A DIFFERENT BLADE WITH THAT AURA, AS A LAST RESORT.
I'VE BORROWED ASCALON FROM ISSEI FOR YOU.
IT PACKS LESS OF A PUNCH, BUT IT SHOULD BE EASIER TO WIELD.
OH, SO LIGHT!!
ONE MEAT-HEADED POWERHOUSE IS ENOUGH FOR THIS TEAM.
THIS CUTS WITH THE POWER OF BOTH ASCALON AND DURANDAL.
I'LL DEMON-STRATE FOR YOU.

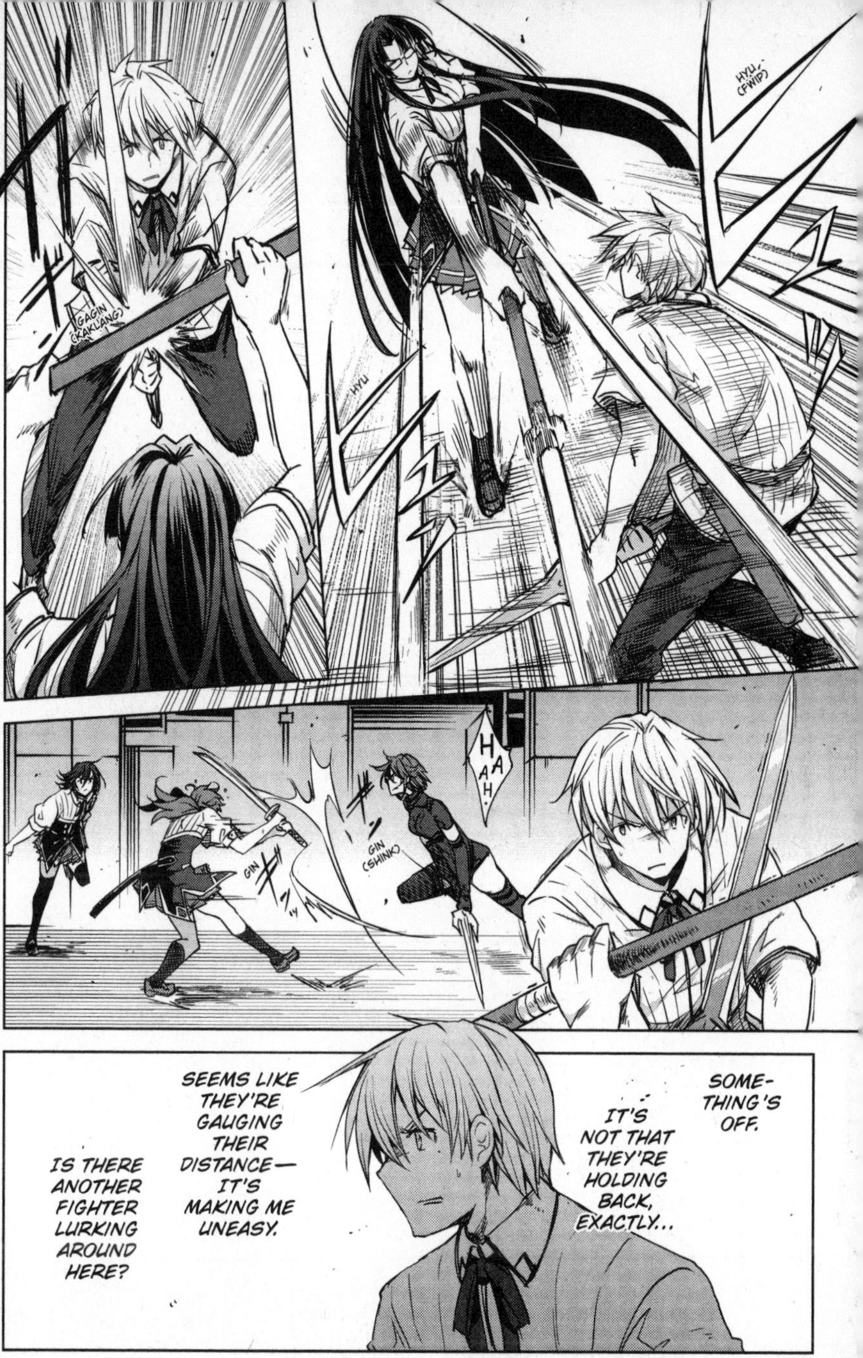
HYU (FWIP)
HYU
GAGIN (KAKLANG)
HAAH...
GIN (SHINK)
GIN
SOMETHING'S OFF.
IT'S NOT THAT THEY'RE HOLDING BACK, EXACTLY...
SEEMS LIKE THEY'RE GAUGING THEIR DISTANCE—IT'S MAKING ME UNEASY.
IS THERE ANOTHER FIGHTER LURKING AROUND HERE?

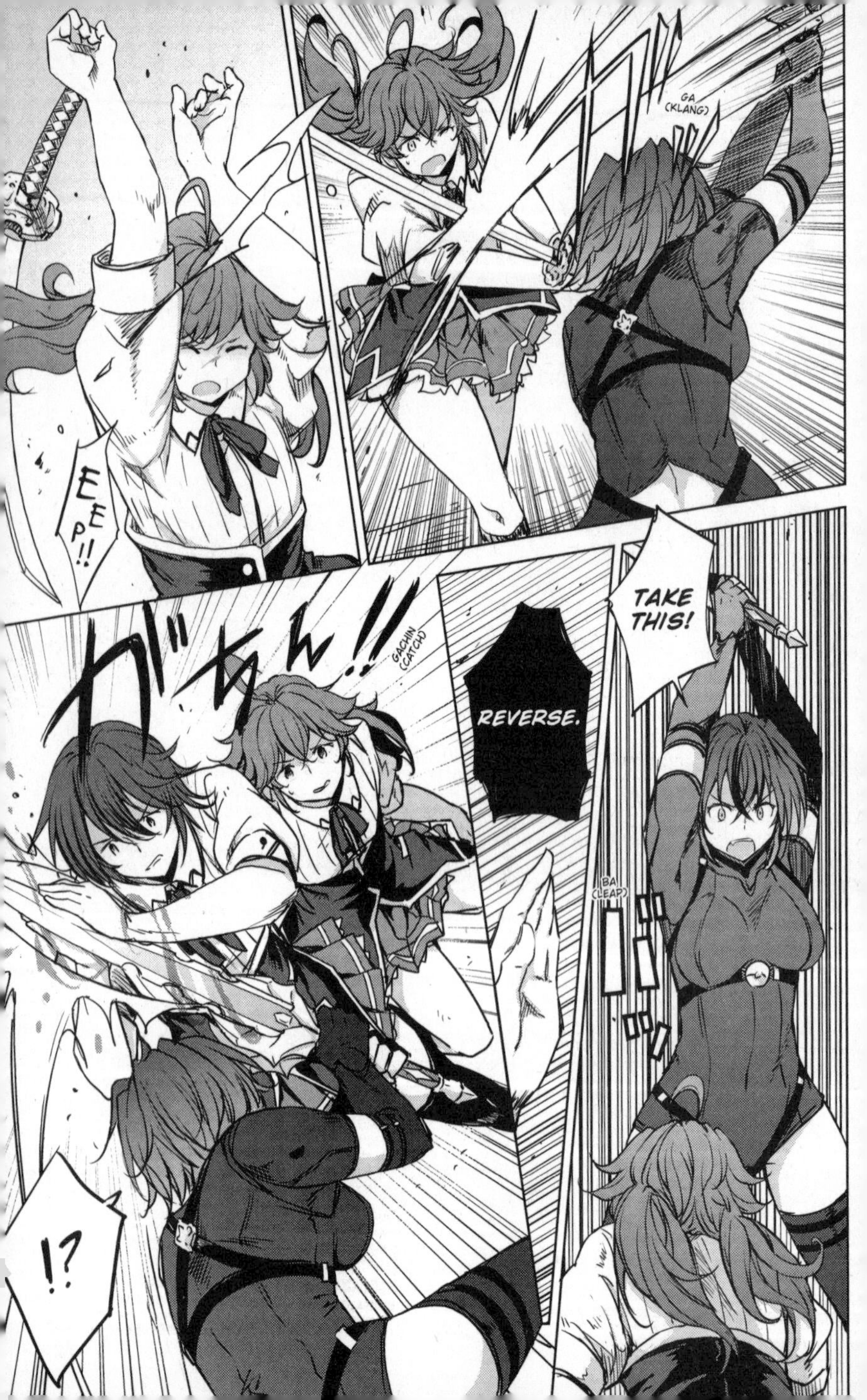
GA (KLANG)
EEP!!
TAKE THIS!
BA (LEAP)
REVERSE.
ガちん!!
GACHIN (CATCH)
!?

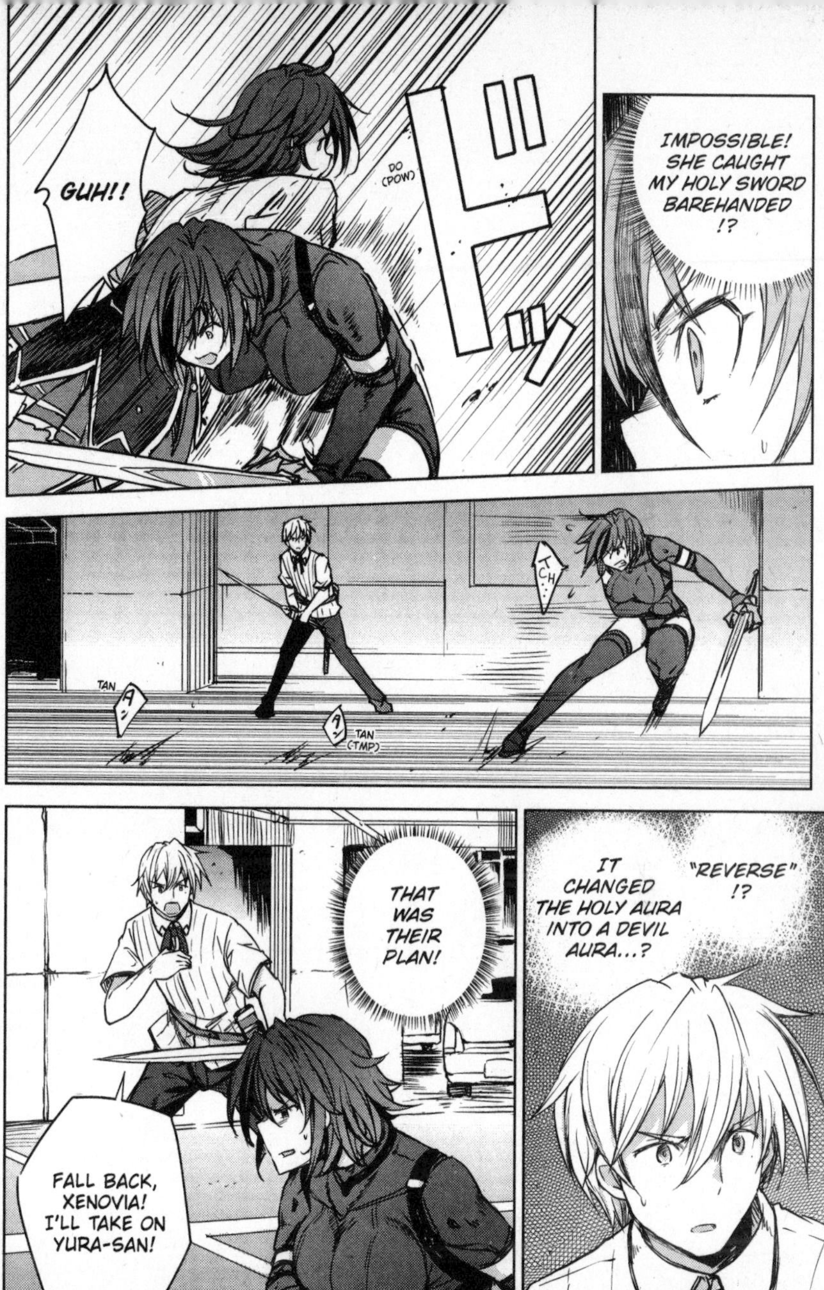
IMPOSSIBLE! SHE CAUGHT MY HOLY SWORD BAREHANDED !?
DO (POW)
GUH!!
TCH...
TAN (TMP)
TAN
"REVERSE" !?
IT CHANGED THE HOLY AURA INTO A DEVIL AURA...?
THAT WAS THEIR PLAN!
FALL BACK, XENOVIA! I'LL TAKE ON YURA-SAN!

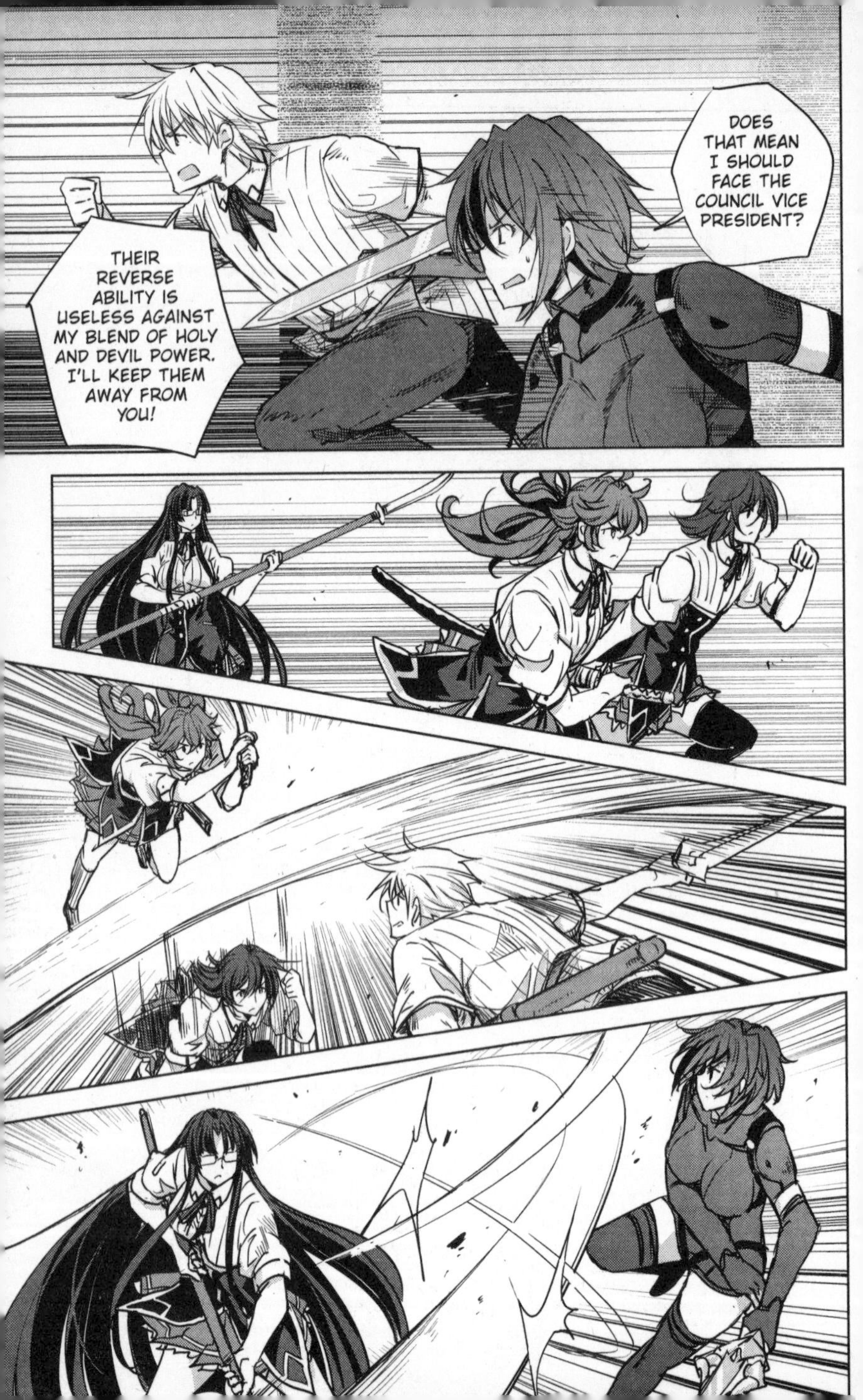
DOES THAT MEAN I SHOULD FACE THE COUNCIL VICE PRESIDENT?
THEIR REVERSE ABILITY IS USELESS AGAINST MY BLEND OF HOLY AND DEVIL POWER. I'LL KEEP THEM AWAY FROM YOU!

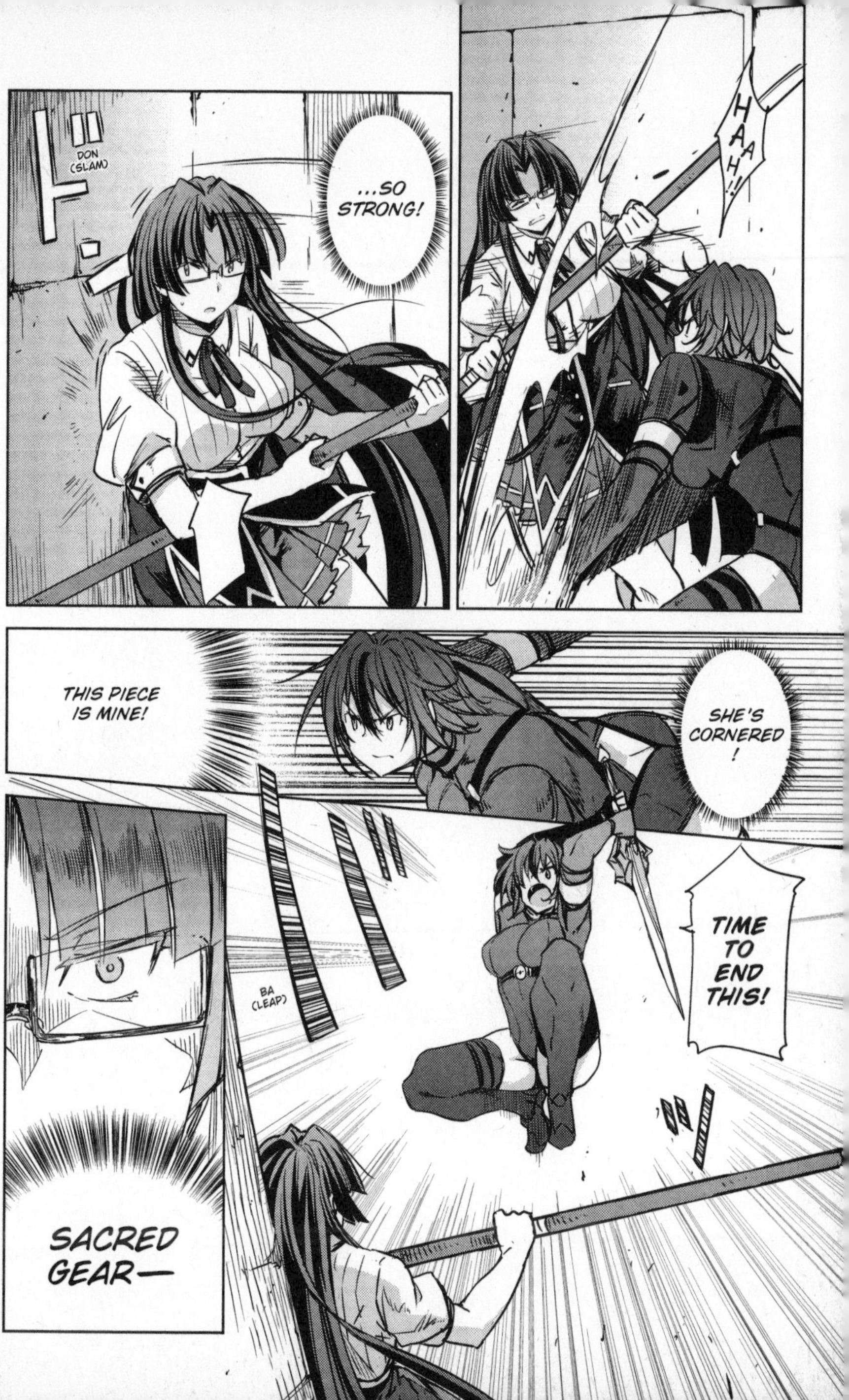
HAAH!!
DON (SLAM)
...SO STRONG!
SHE'S CORNERED!
THIS PIECE IS MINE!
TIME TO END THIS!
BA (LEAP)
SACRED GEAR—

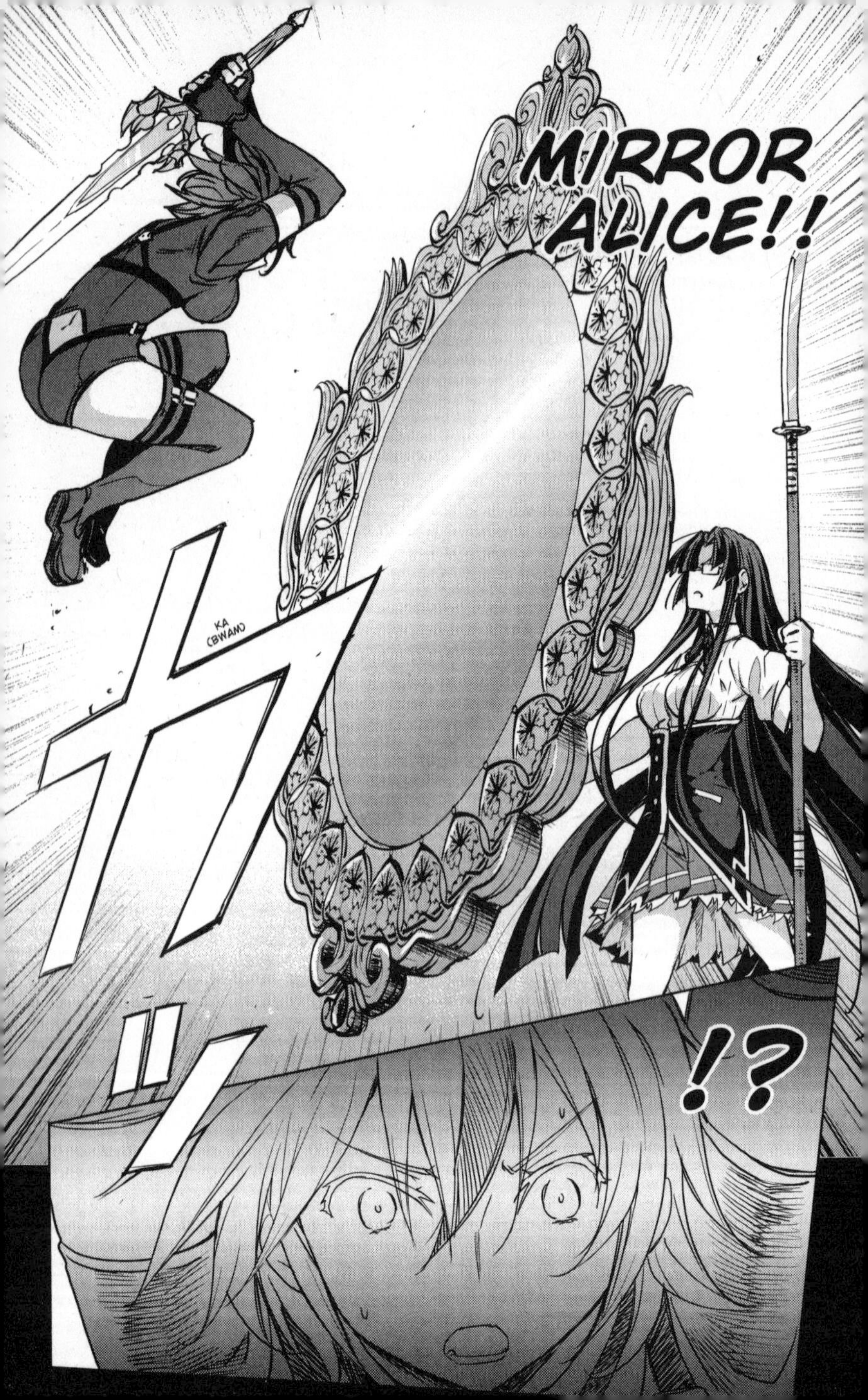
MIRROR ALICE!!
KA (BWAM)
!?

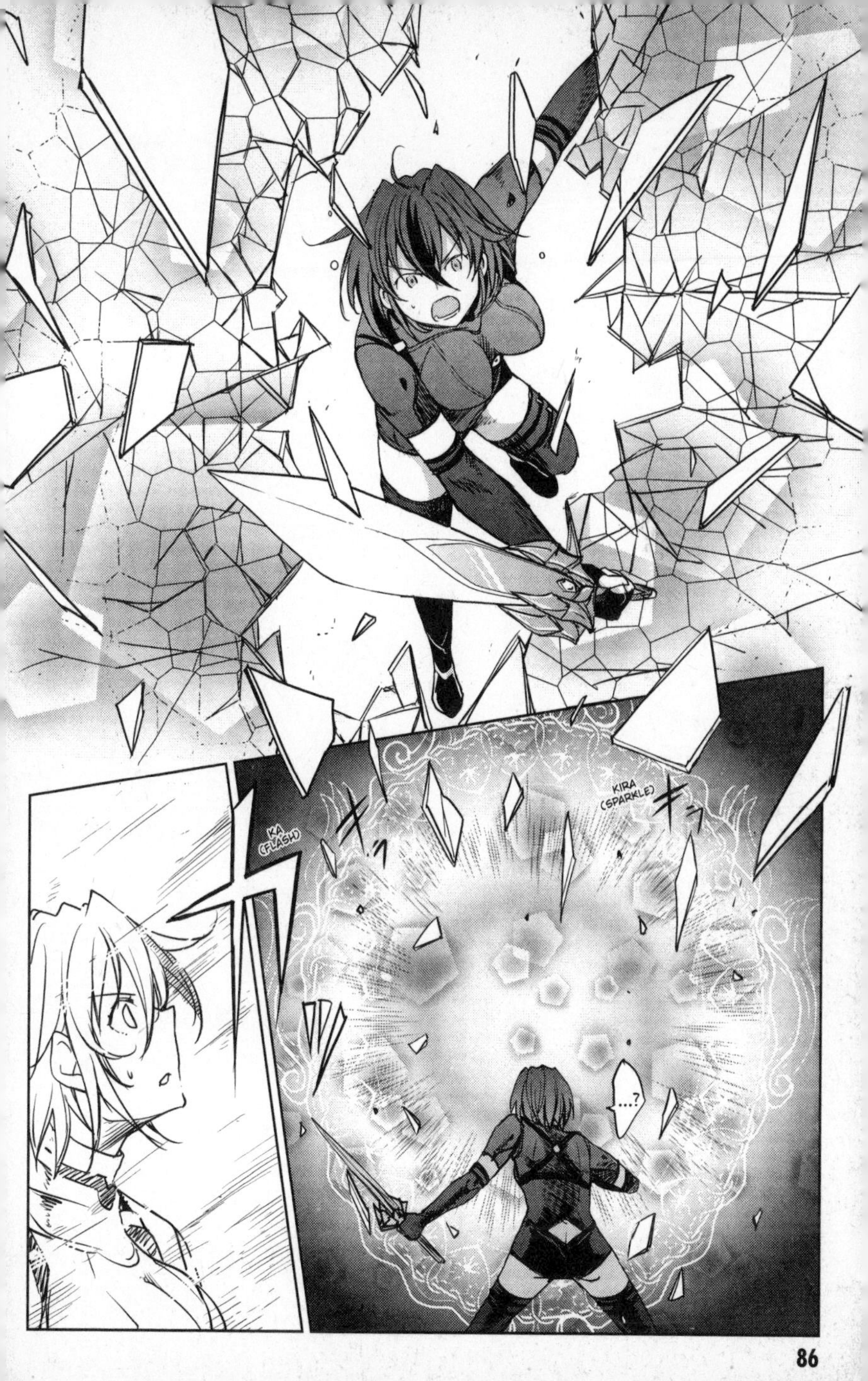
KIRA (SPARKLE)
KA (FLASH)
...?

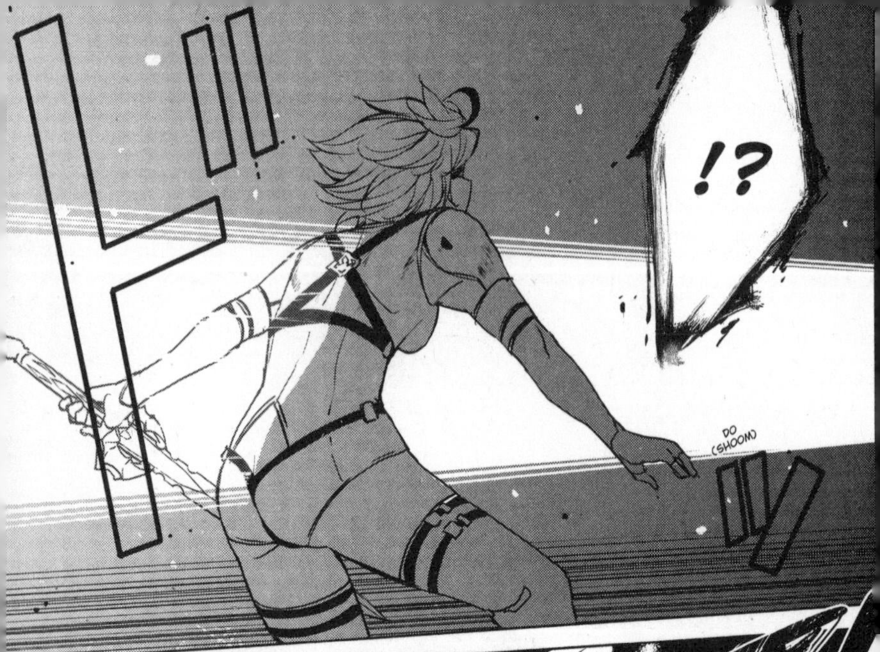
!?
DO
(SHOOM)
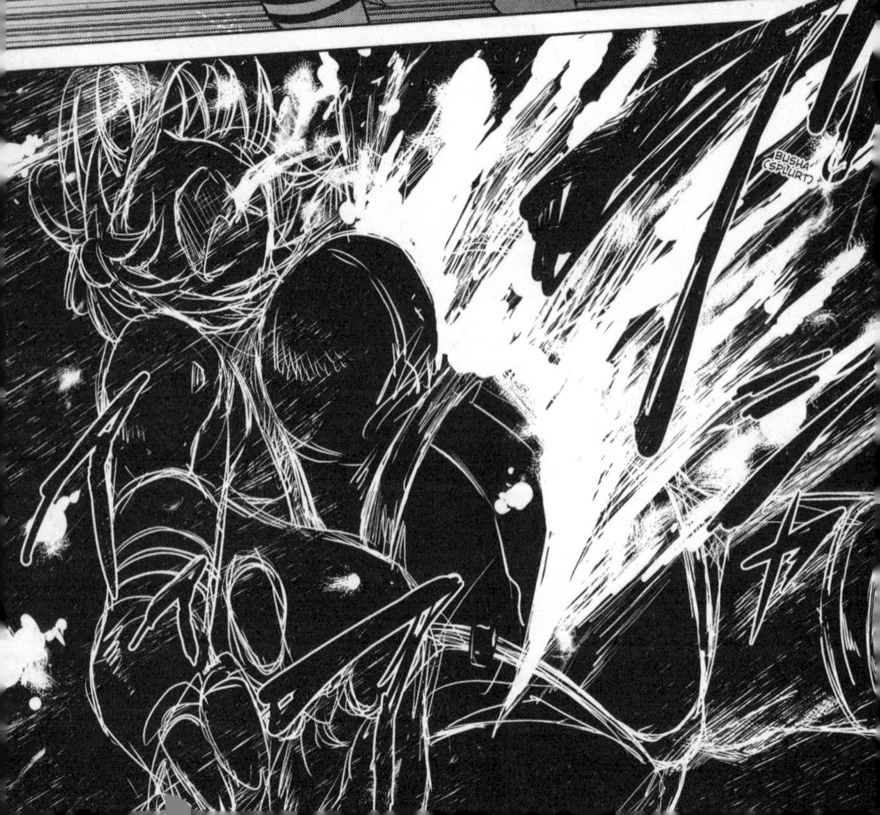
BUSHA
(SPLURT)

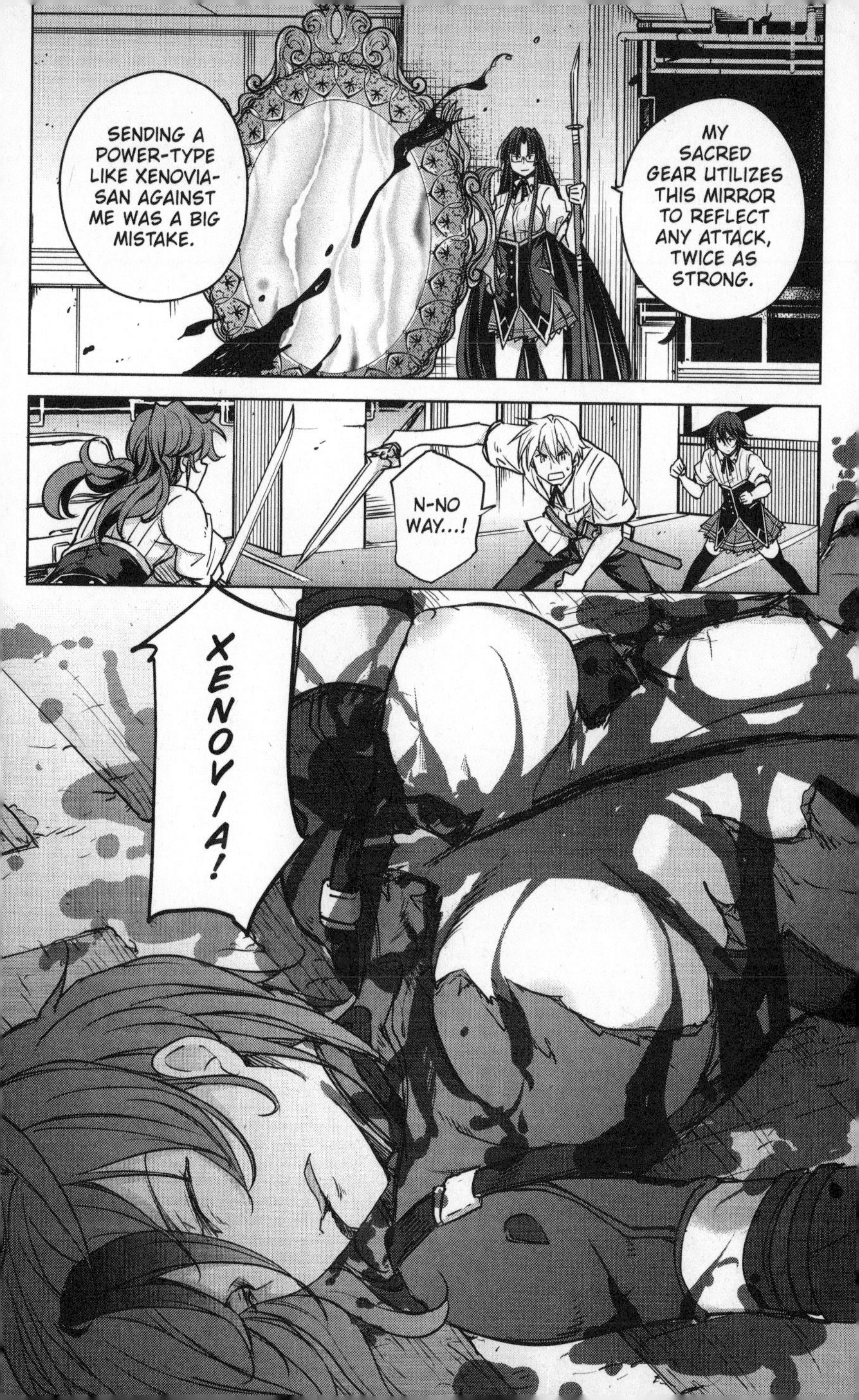
MY SACRED GEAR UTILIZES THIS MIRROR TO REFLECT ANY ATTACK, TWICE AS STRONG.
SENDING A POWER-TYPE LIKE XENOVIA-SAN AGAINST ME WAS A BIG MISTAKE.
N-NO WAY...!
XENOVIA!

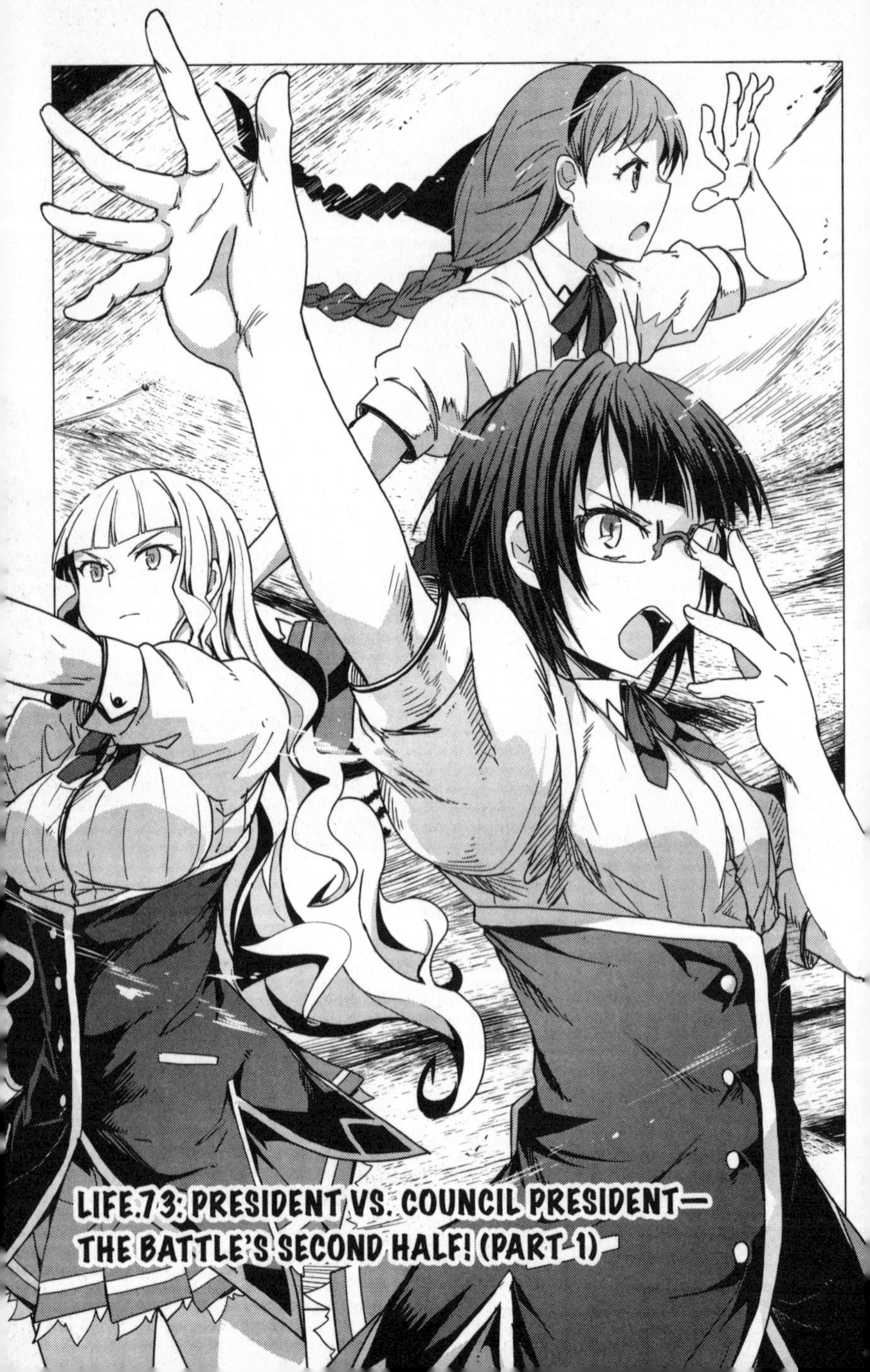
LIFE.73: PRESIDENT VS. COUNCIL PRESIDENT—
THE BATTLE'S SECOND HALF! (PART 1)

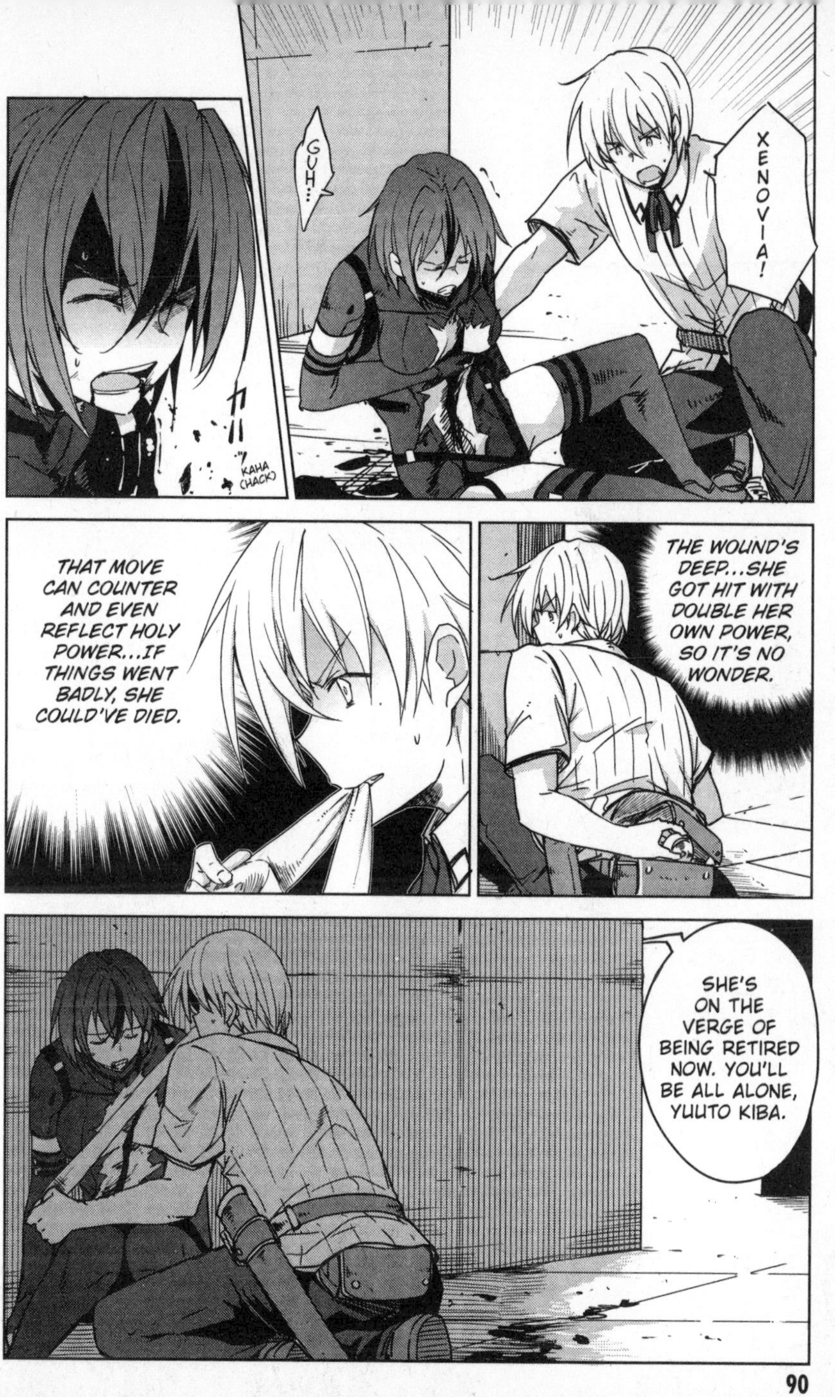
XENOVIA!
GUH...
KAHA (HACK)
THE WOUND'S DEEP...SHE GOT HIT WITH DOUBLE HER OWN POWER, SO IT'S NO WONDER.
THAT MOVE CAN COUNTER AND EVEN REFLECT HOLY POWER...IF THINGS WENT BADLY, SHE COULD'VE DIED.
SHE'S ON THE VERGE OF BEING RETIRED NOW. YOU'LL BE ALL ALONE, YUUTO KIBA.

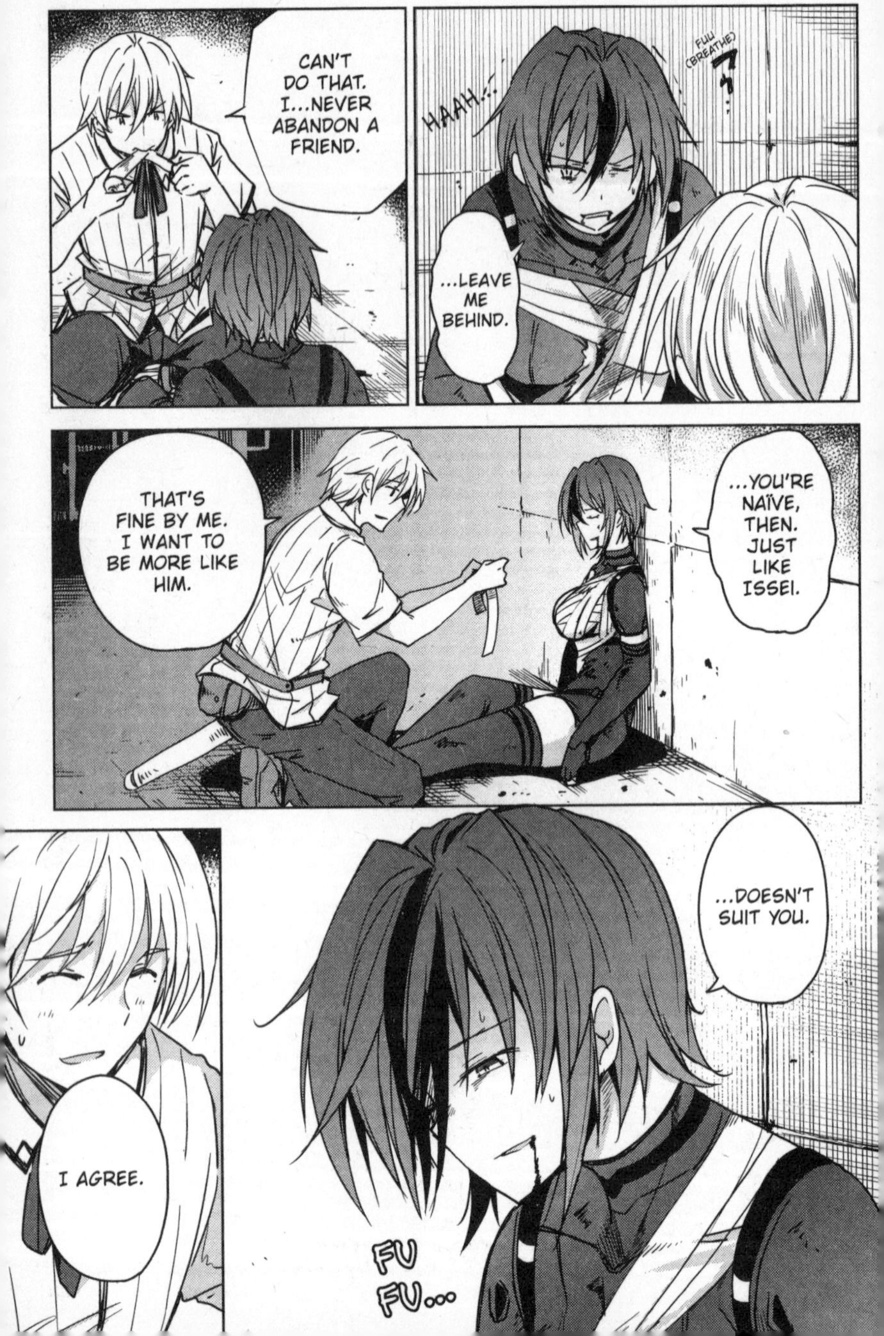
FUU (BREATHE)
HAAH...
...LEAVE ME BEHIND.
CAN'T DO THAT. I...NEVER ABANDON A FRIEND.
...YOU'RE NAÏVE, THEN. JUST LIKE ISSEI.
THAT'S FINE BY ME. I WANT TO BE MORE LIKE HIM.
...DOESN'T SUIT YOU.
FU FU...
I AGREE.

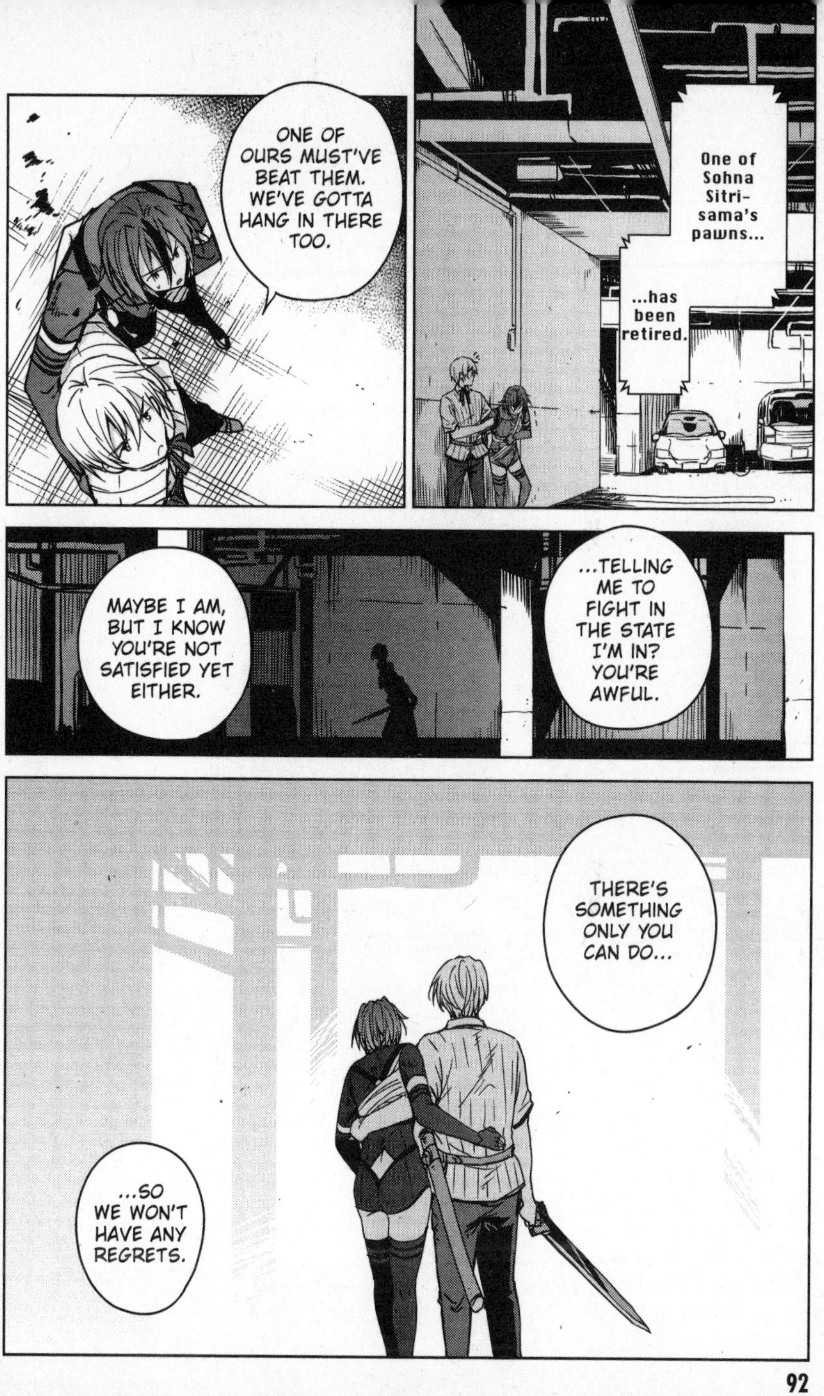
One of Sohna Sitri-sama's pawns...
...has been retired.
ONE OF OURS MUST'VE BEAT THEM. WE'VE GOTTA HANG IN THERE TOO.
...TELLING ME TO FIGHT IN THE STATE I'M IN? YOU'RE AWFUL.
MAYBE I AM, BUT I KNOW YOU'RE NOT SATISFIED YET EITHER.
THERE'S SOMETHING ONLY YOU CAN DO...
...SO WE WON'T HAVE ANY REGRETS.

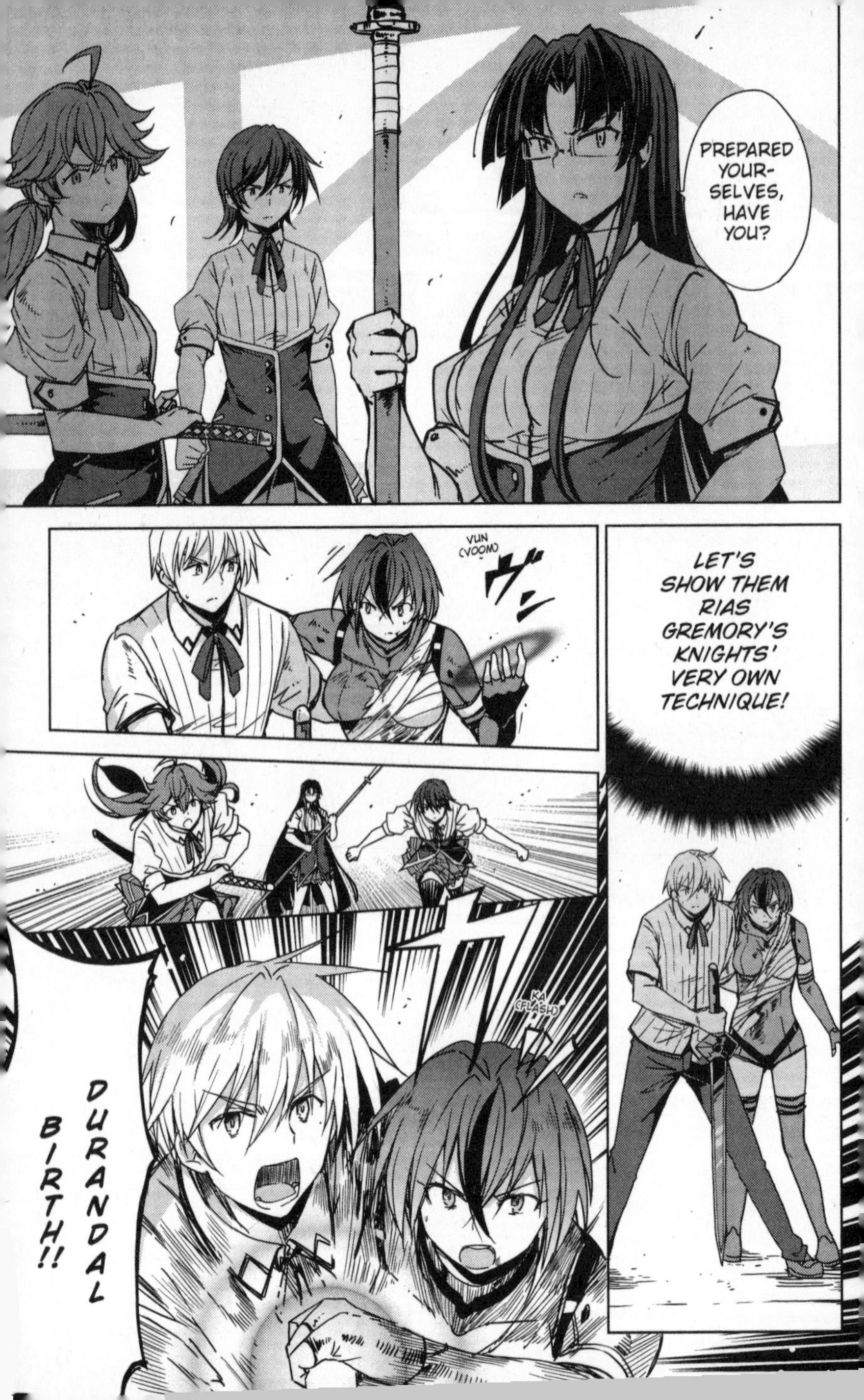
PREPARED YOUR-SELVES, HAVE YOU?
LET'S SHOW THEM RIAS GREMORY'S KNIGHTS' VERY OWN TECHNIQUE!
VUN (VOOM)
KA (FLASH)
DURANDAL BIRTH!!

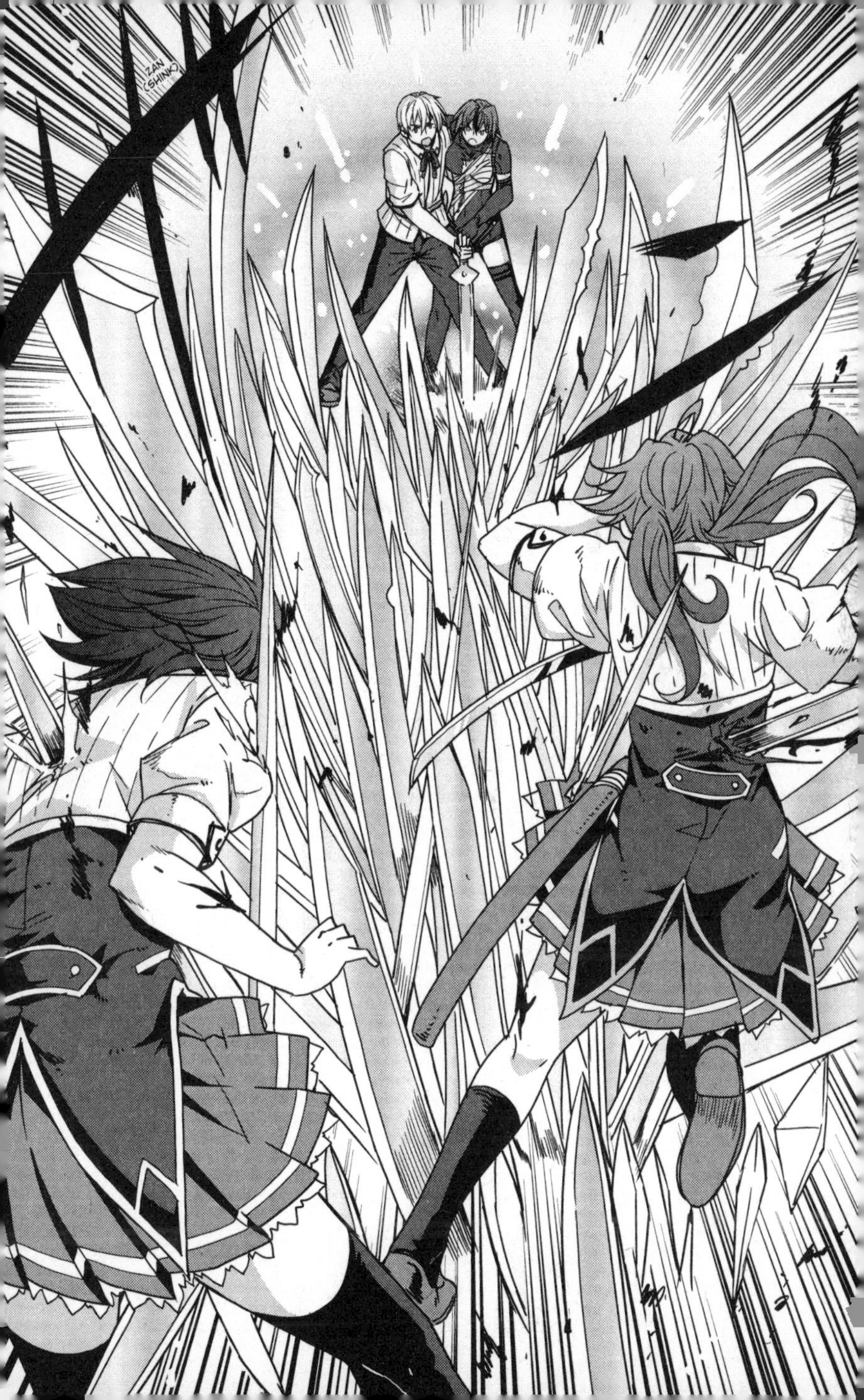
ZAN (SHINK)

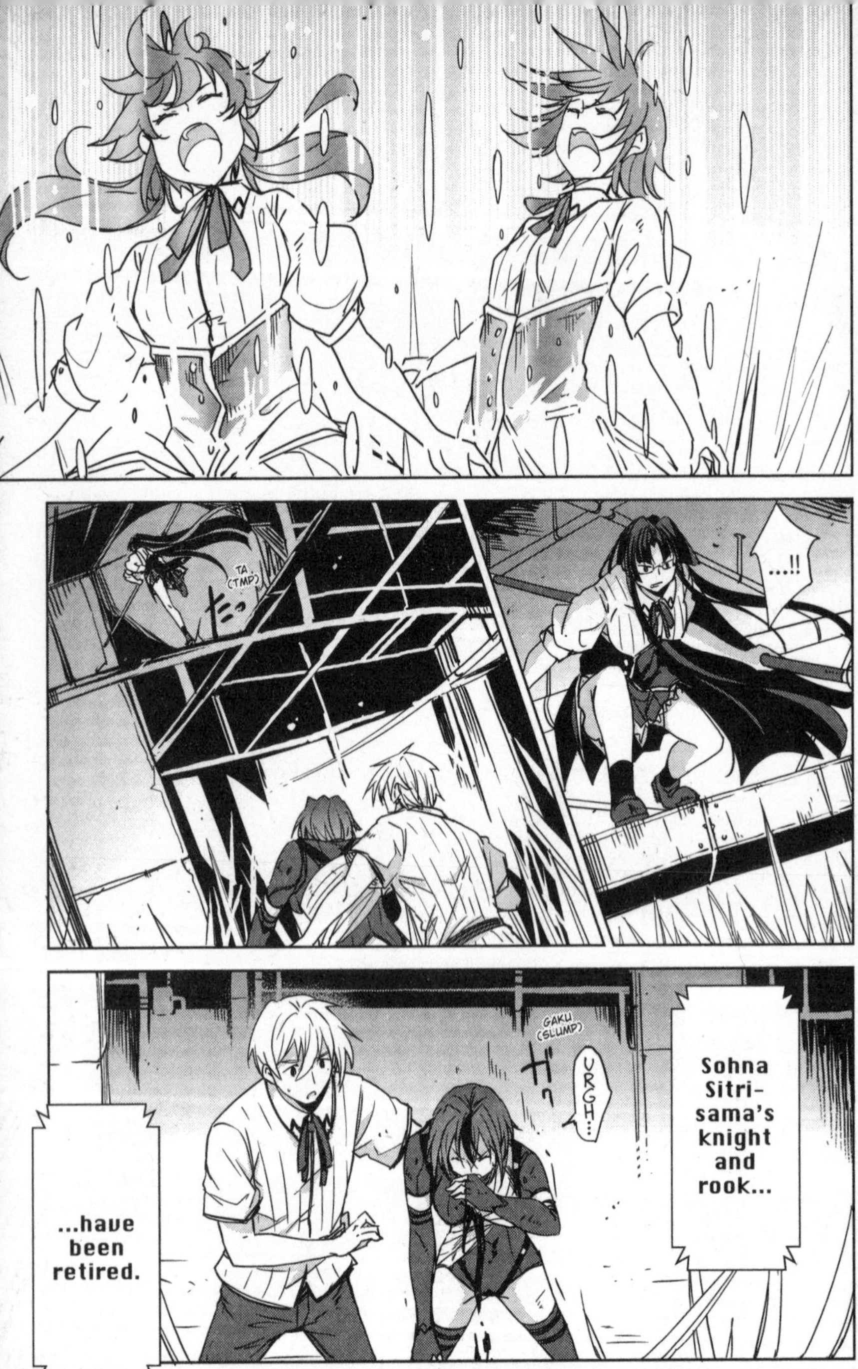
...!!
TA (TMP)
Sohna Sitri-sama's knight and rook...
URGH...
GAKU (SLUMP)
...have been retired.

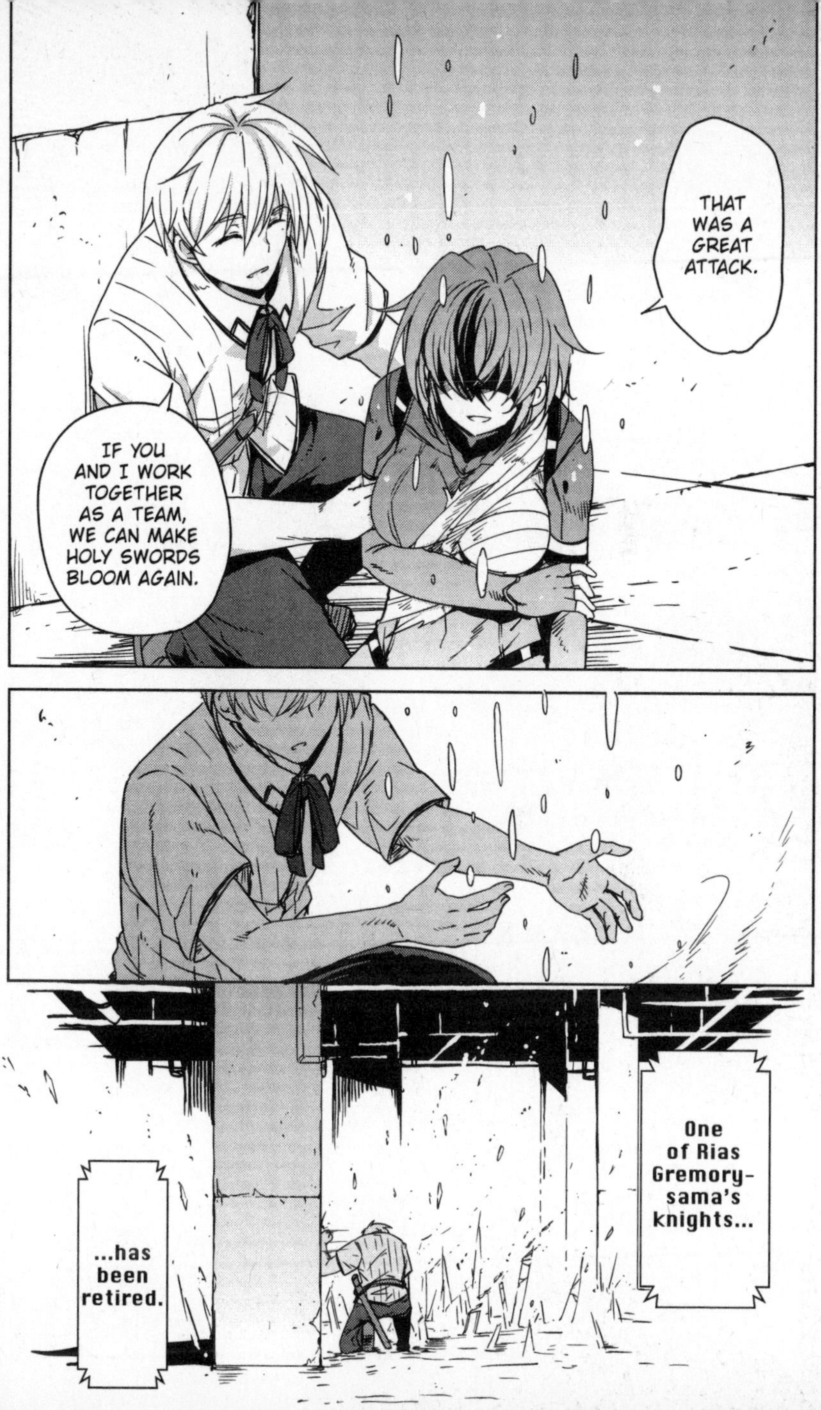
THAT WAS A GREAT ATTACK.
IF YOU AND I WORK TOGETHER AS A TEAM, WE CAN MAKE HOLY SWORDS BLOOM AGAIN.
One of Rias Gremory-sama's knights...
...has been retired.

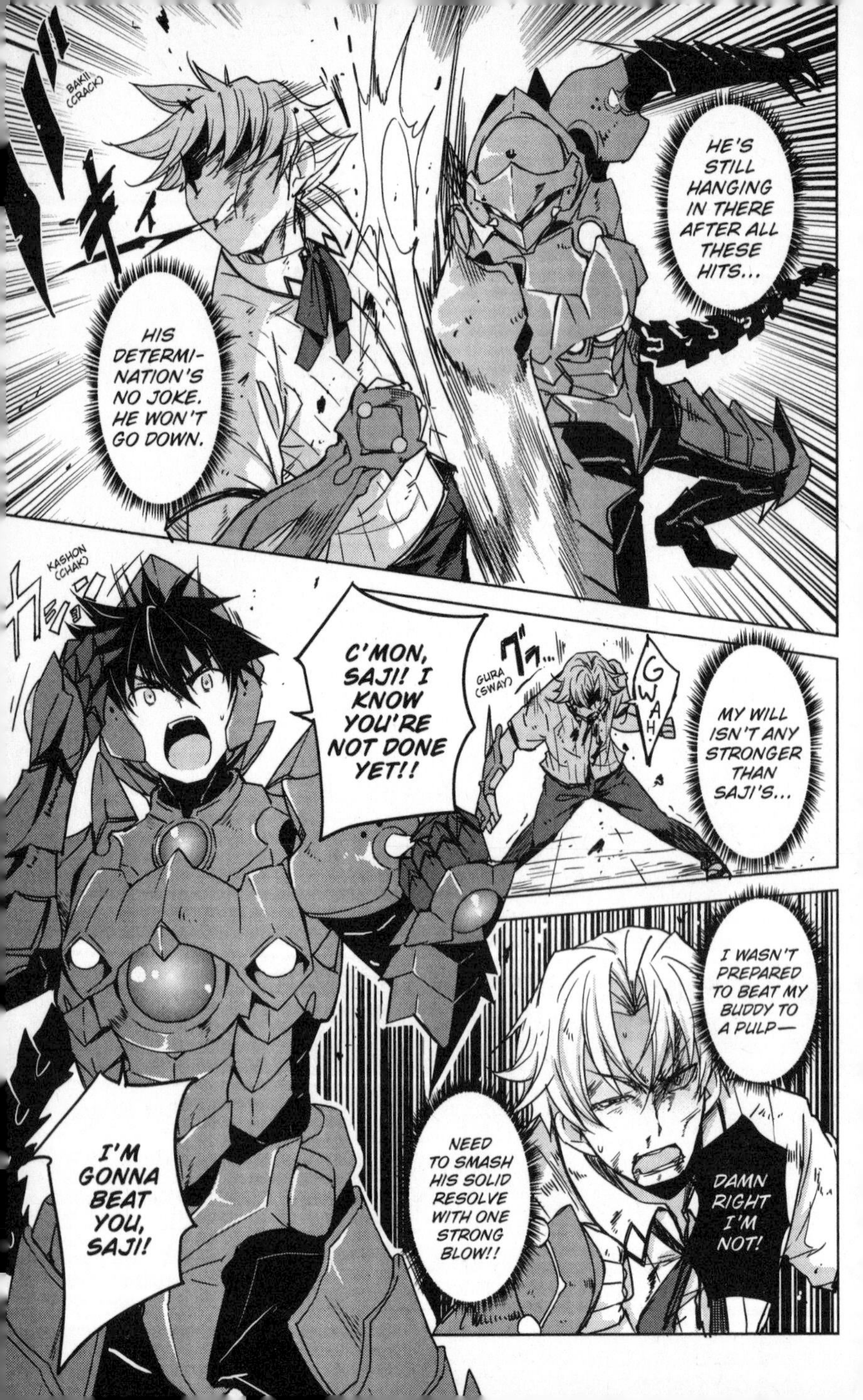
HE'S STILL HANGING IN THERE AFTER ALL THESE HITS...
BAKII (CRACK)
HIS DETERMINATION'S NO JOKE. HE WON'T GO DOWN.
MY WILL ISN'T ANY STRONGER THAN SAJI'S...
GWAH!
GURA (SWAY)
C'MON, SAJI! I KNOW YOU'RE NOT DONE YET!!
KASHON (CHAK)
I WASN'T PREPARED TO BEAT MY BUDDY TO A PULP—
DAMN RIGHT I'M NOT!
NEED TO SMASH HIS SOLID RESOLVE WITH ONE STRONG BLOW!!
I'M GONNA BEAT YOU, SAJI!

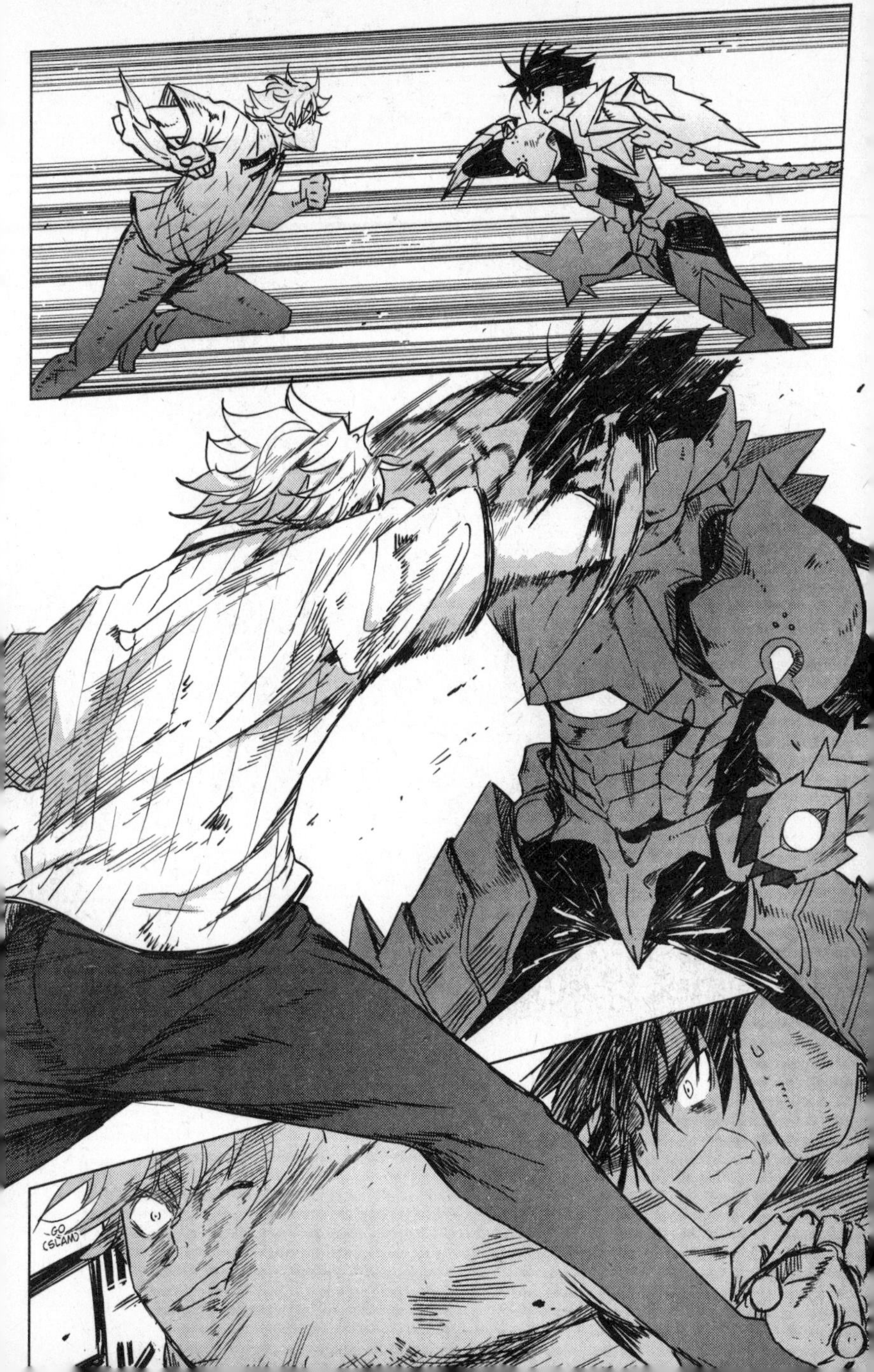
GO
(SLAM)

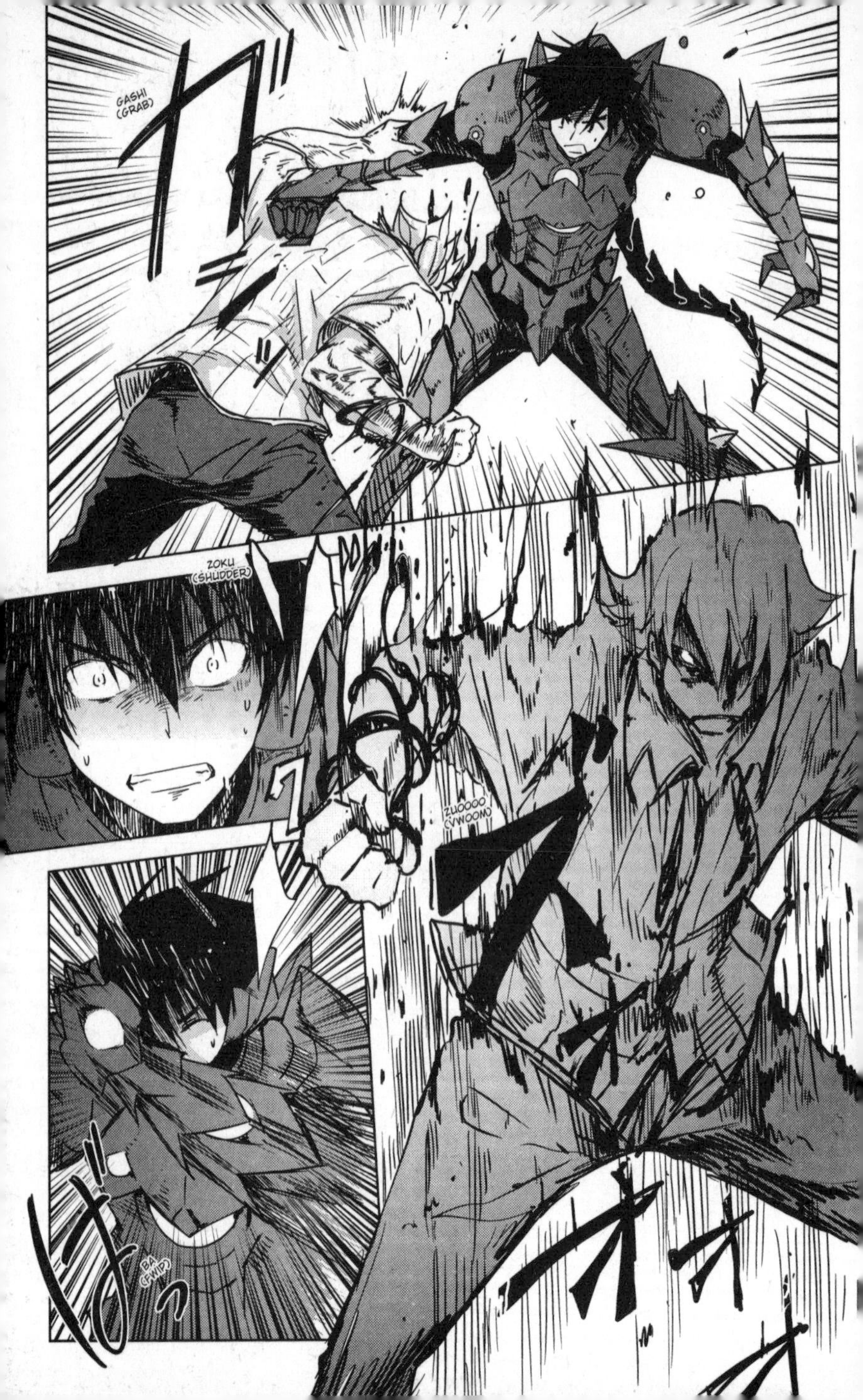
GASHI (GRAB)
ZUOOOO (VWOOM)
ZOKU (SHUDDER)
BA (FWIP)

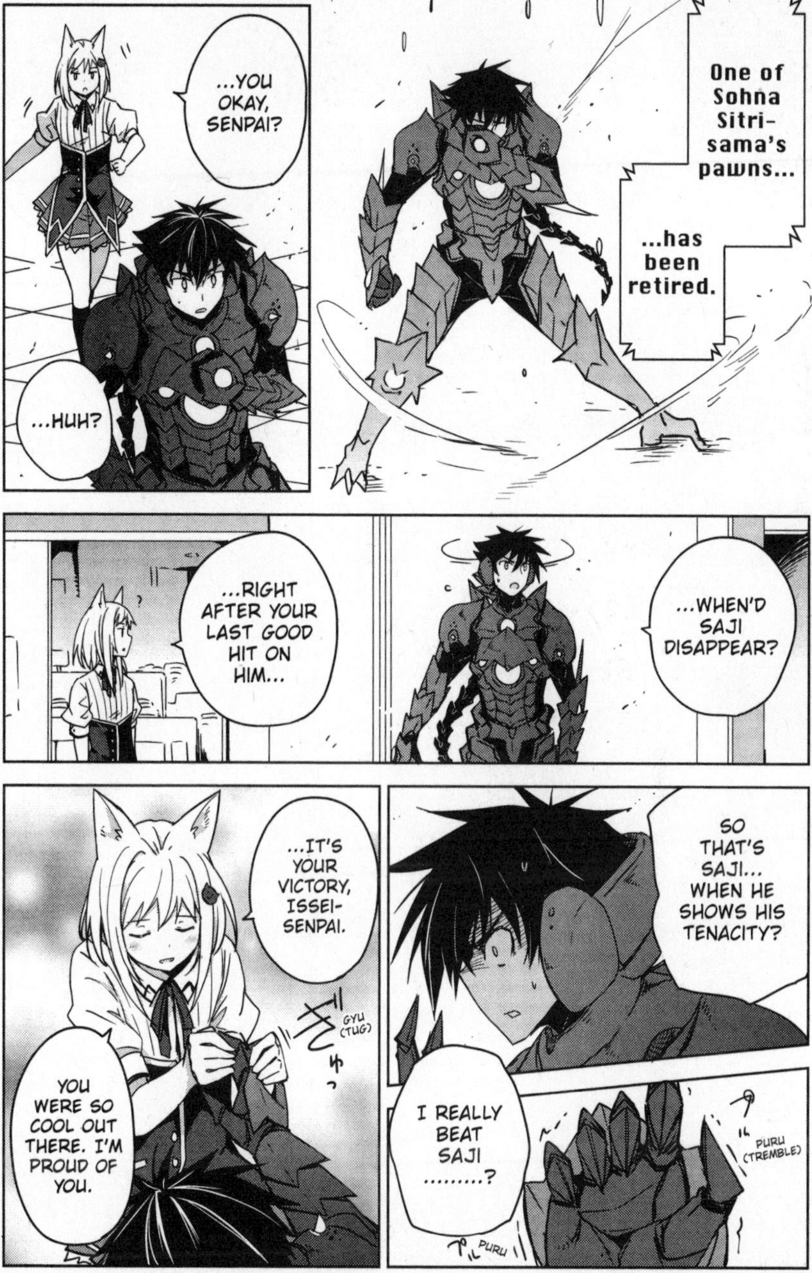
One of Sohna Sitri-sama's pawns...
...has been retired.
...YOU OKAY, SENPAI?
...HUH?
...WHEN'D SAJI DISAPPEAR?
...RIGHT AFTER YOUR LAST GOOD HIT ON HIM...
SO THAT'S SAJI... WHEN HE SHOWS HIS TENACITY?
I REALLY BEAT SAJI ....?
PURU (TREMBLE)
PURU
...IT'S YOUR VICTORY, ISSEI-SENPAI.
GYU (TUG)
YOU WERE SO COOL OUT THERE. I'M PROUD OF YOU.

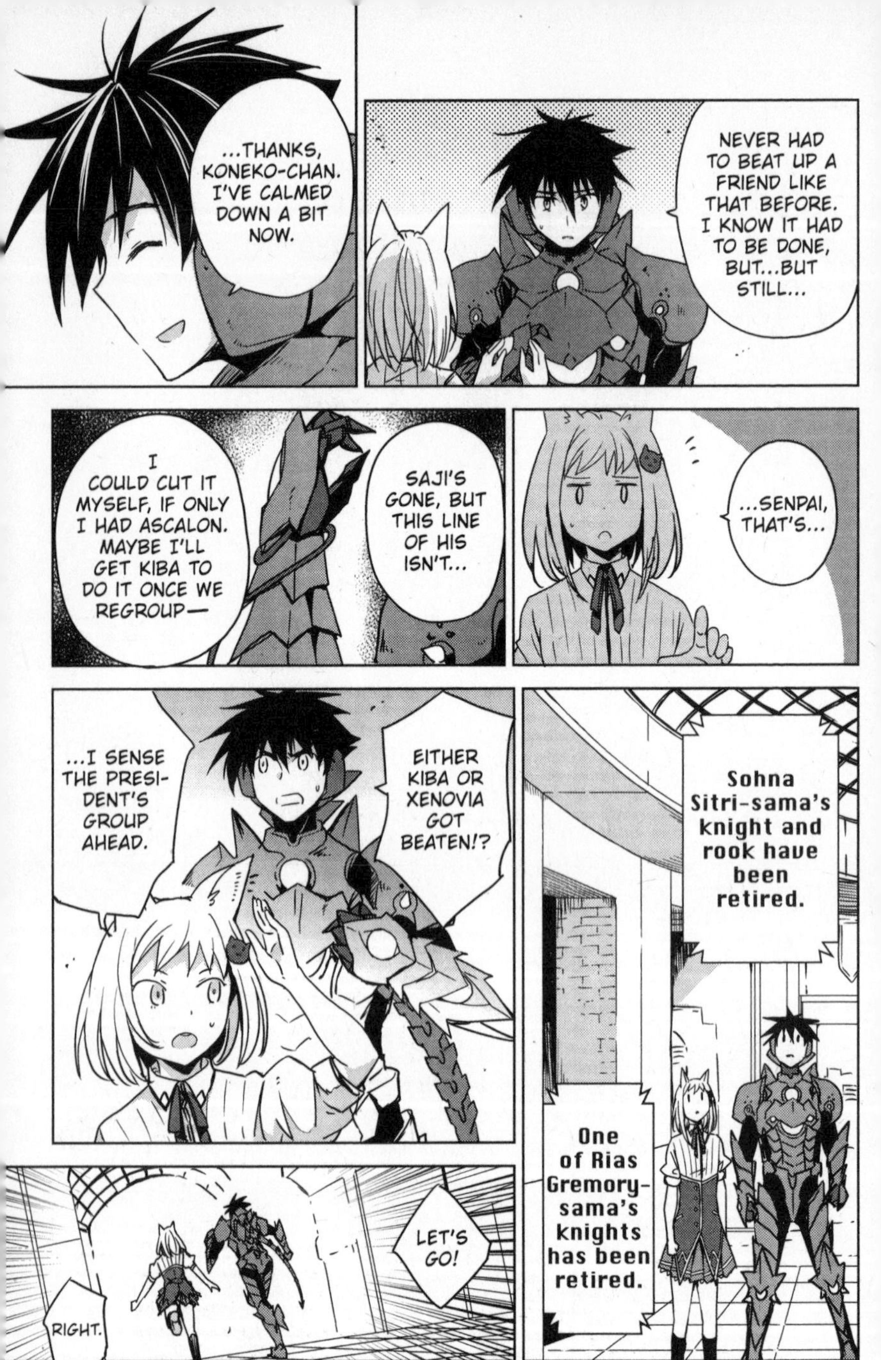
NEVER HAD TO BEAT UP A FRIEND LIKE THAT BEFORE. I KNOW IT HAD TO BE DONE, BUT...BUT STILL...
...THANKS, KONEKO-CHAN. I'VE CALMED DOWN A BIT NOW.
...SENPAI, THAT'S...
SAJI'S GONE, BUT THIS LINE OF HIS ISN'T...
I COULD CUT IT MYSELF, IF ONLY I HAD ASCALON. MAYBE I'LL GET KIBA TO DO IT ONCE WE REGROUP—
Sohna Sitri-sama's knight and rook have been retired.
One of Rias Gremory-sama's knights has been retired.
EITHER KIBA OR XENOVIA GOT BEATEN!?
...I SENSE THE PRESIDENT'S GROUP AHEAD.
LET'S GO!
RIGHT.

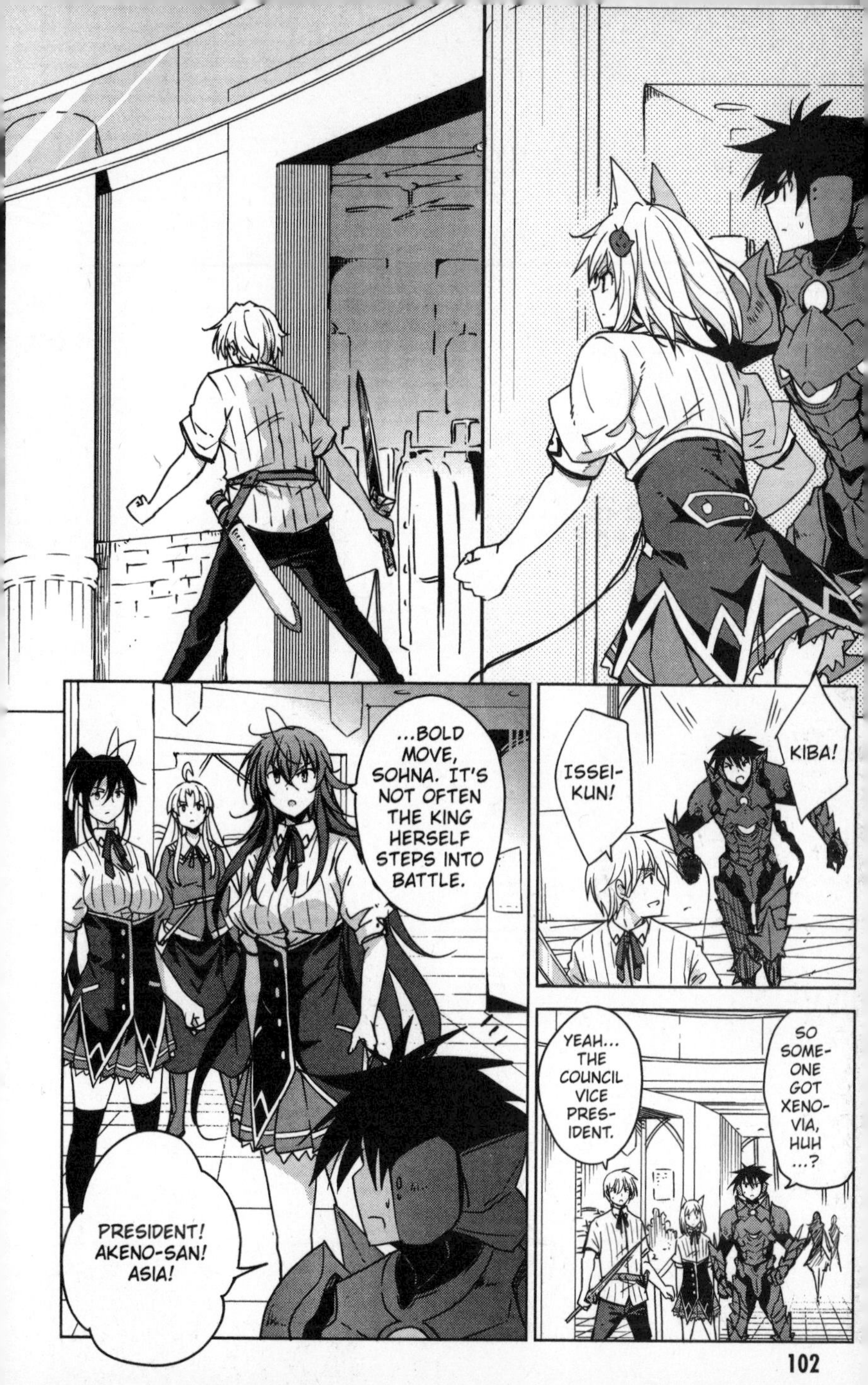
KIBA!
ISSEI-KUN!
SO SOMEONE GOT XENOVIA, HUH...?
YEAH... THE COUNCIL VICE PRESIDENT.
...BOLD MOVE, SOHNA. IT'S NOT OFTEN THE KING HERSELF STEPS INTO BATTLE.
PRESIDENT! AKENO-SAN! ASIA!

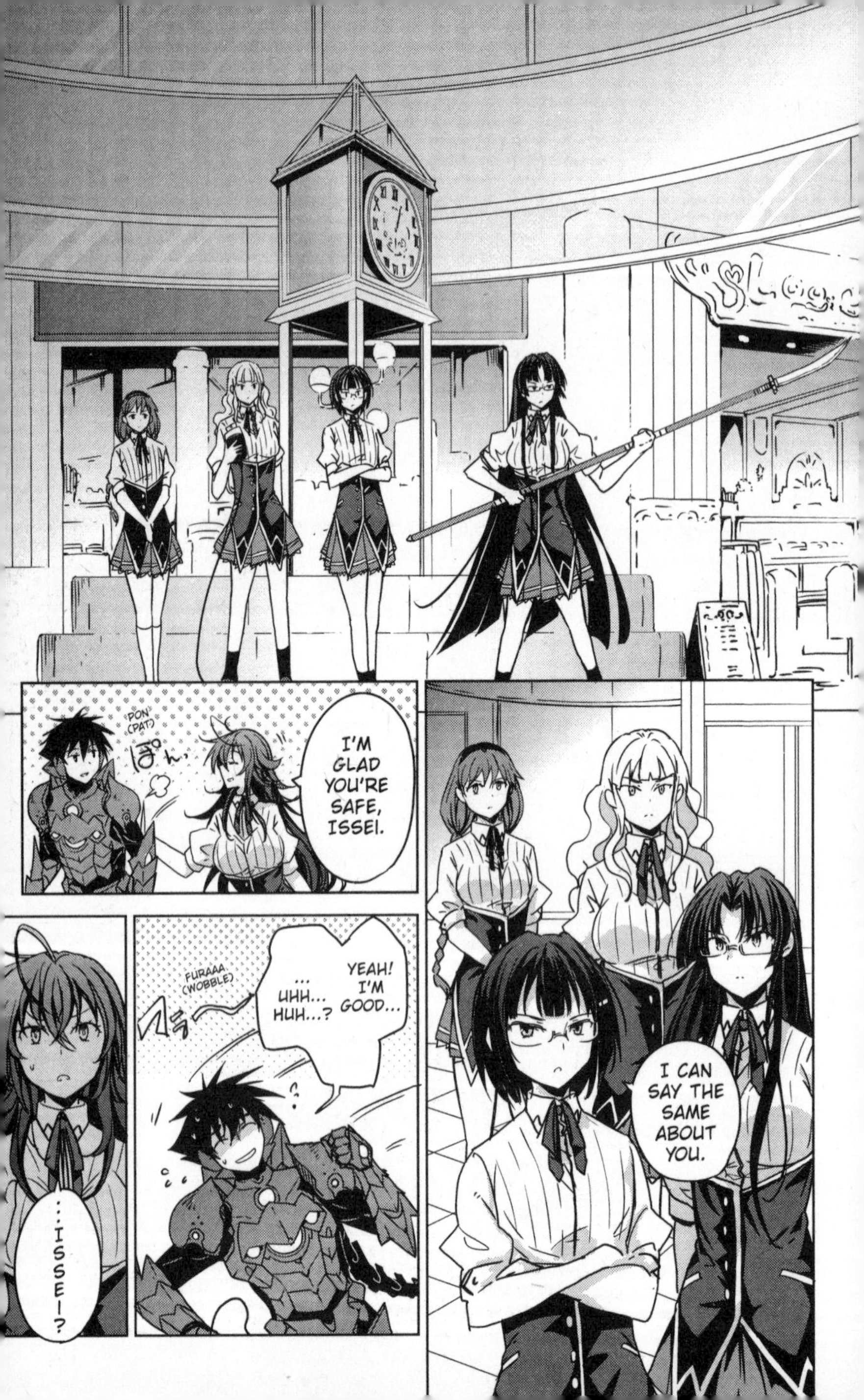
I CAN SAY THE SAME ABOUT YOU.
PON (PAT)
I'M GLAD YOU'RE SAFE, ISSEI.
YEAH! I'M GOOD...
... UHH... HUH...?
FURAAA (WOBBLE)
...ISSEI!?

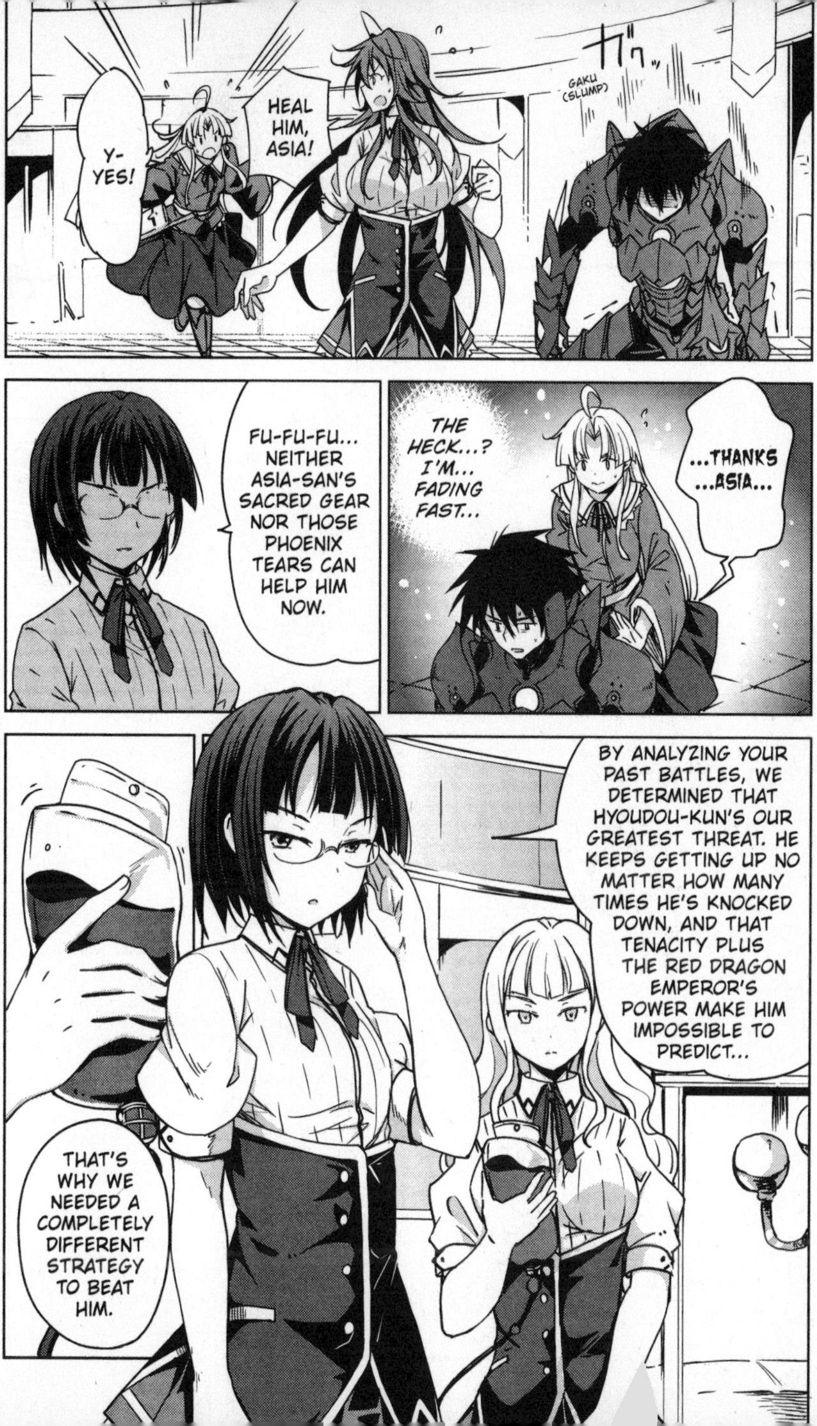
ガクッ
GAKU (SLUMP)
HEAL HIM, ASIA!
Y-YES!
...THANKS ...ASIA...
THE HECK...? I'M... FADING FAST...
FU-FU-FU... NEITHER ASIA-SAN'S SACRED GEAR NOR THOSE PHOENIX TEARS CAN HELP HIM NOW.
BY ANALYZING YOUR PAST BATTLES, WE DETERMINED THAT HYOUDOU-KUN'S OUR GREATEST THREAT. HE KEEPS GETTING UP NO MATTER HOW MANY TIMES HE'S KNOCKED DOWN, AND THAT TENACITY PLUS THE RED DRAGON EMPEROR'S POWER MAKE HIM IMPOSSIBLE TO PREDICT...
THAT'S WHY WE NEEDED A COMPLETELY DIFFERENT STRATEGY TO BEAT HIM.

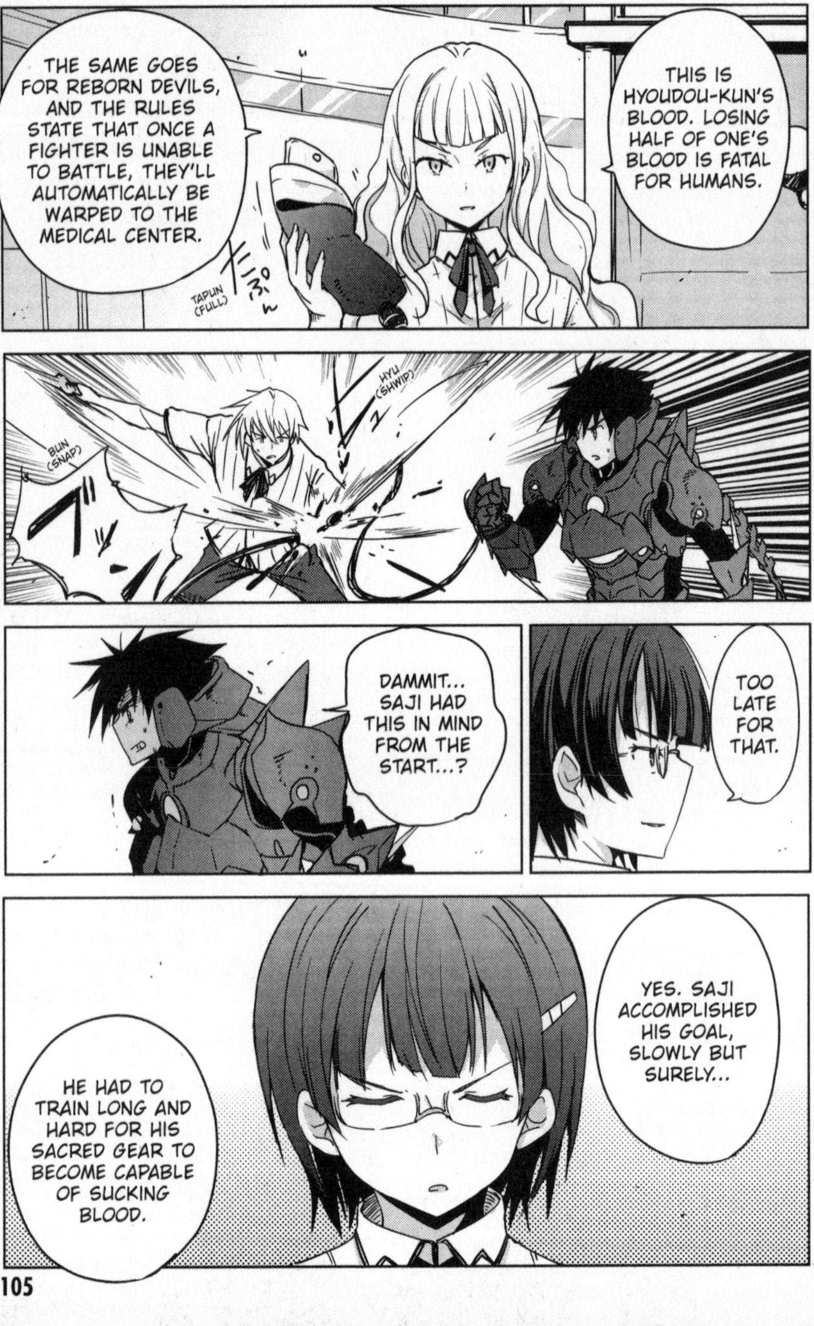
THIS IS HYOUDOU-KUN'S BLOOD. LOSING HALF OF ONE'S BLOOD IS FATAL FOR HUMANS.
THE SAME GOES FOR REBORN DEVILS, AND THE RULES STATE THAT ONCE A FIGHTER IS UNABLE TO BATTLE, THEY'LL AUTOMATICALLY BE WARPED TO THE MEDICAL CENTER.
TAPUN (FULL)
HYU (SHWIP)
BUN (SNAP)
TOO LATE FOR THAT.
DAMMIT... SAJI HAD THIS IN MIND FROM THE START...?
YES. SAJI ACCOMPLISHED HIS GOAL, SLOWLY BUT SURELY...
HE HAD TO TRAIN LONG AND HARD FOR HIS SACRED GEAR TO BECOME CAPABLE OF SUCKING BLOOD.

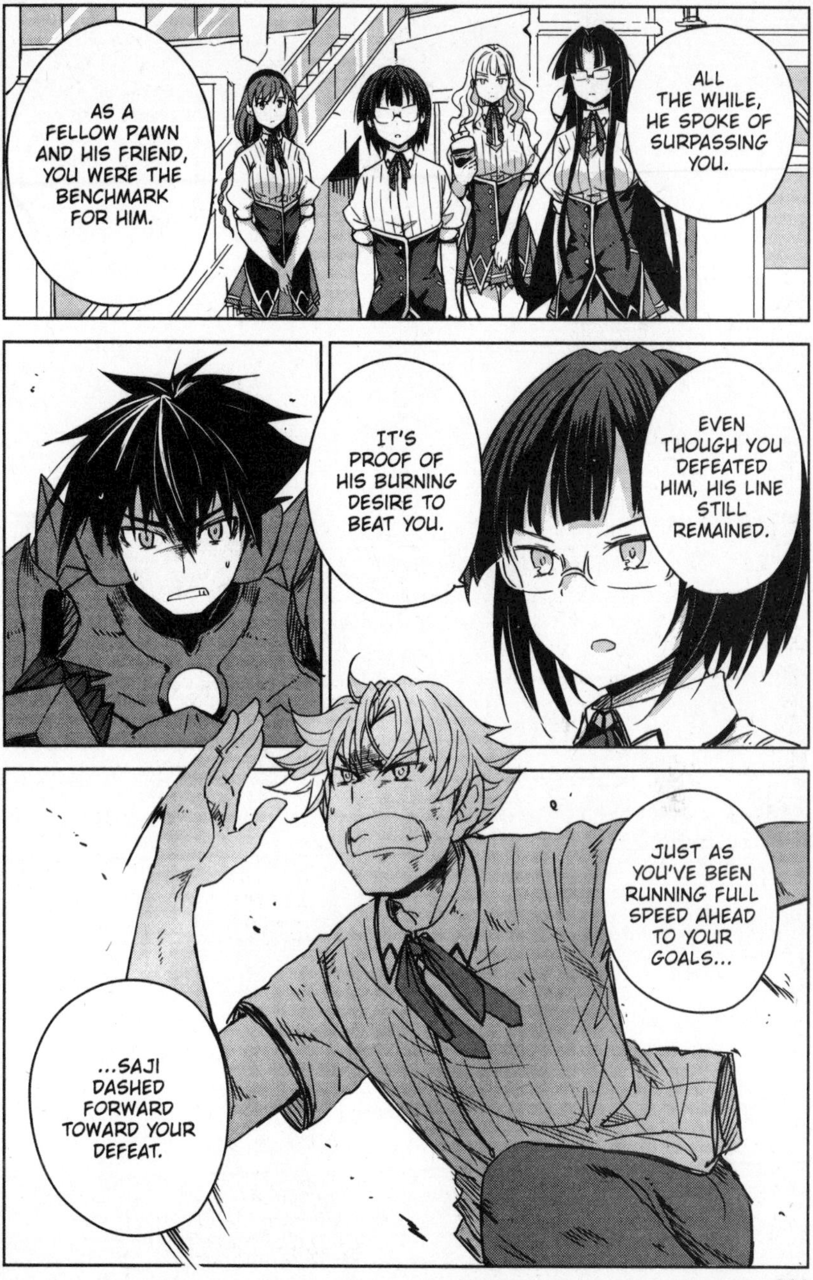
ALL THE WHILE, HE SPOKE OF SURPASSING YOU.
AS A FELLOW PAWN AND HIS FRIEND, YOU WERE THE BENCHMARK FOR HIM.
EVEN THOUGH YOU DEFEATED HIM, HIS LINE STILL REMAINED.
IT'S PROOF OF HIS BURNING DESIRE TO BEAT YOU.
JUST AS YOU'VE BEEN RUNNING FULL SPEED AHEAD TO YOUR GOALS...
...SAJI DASHED FORWARD TOWARD YOUR DEFEAT.

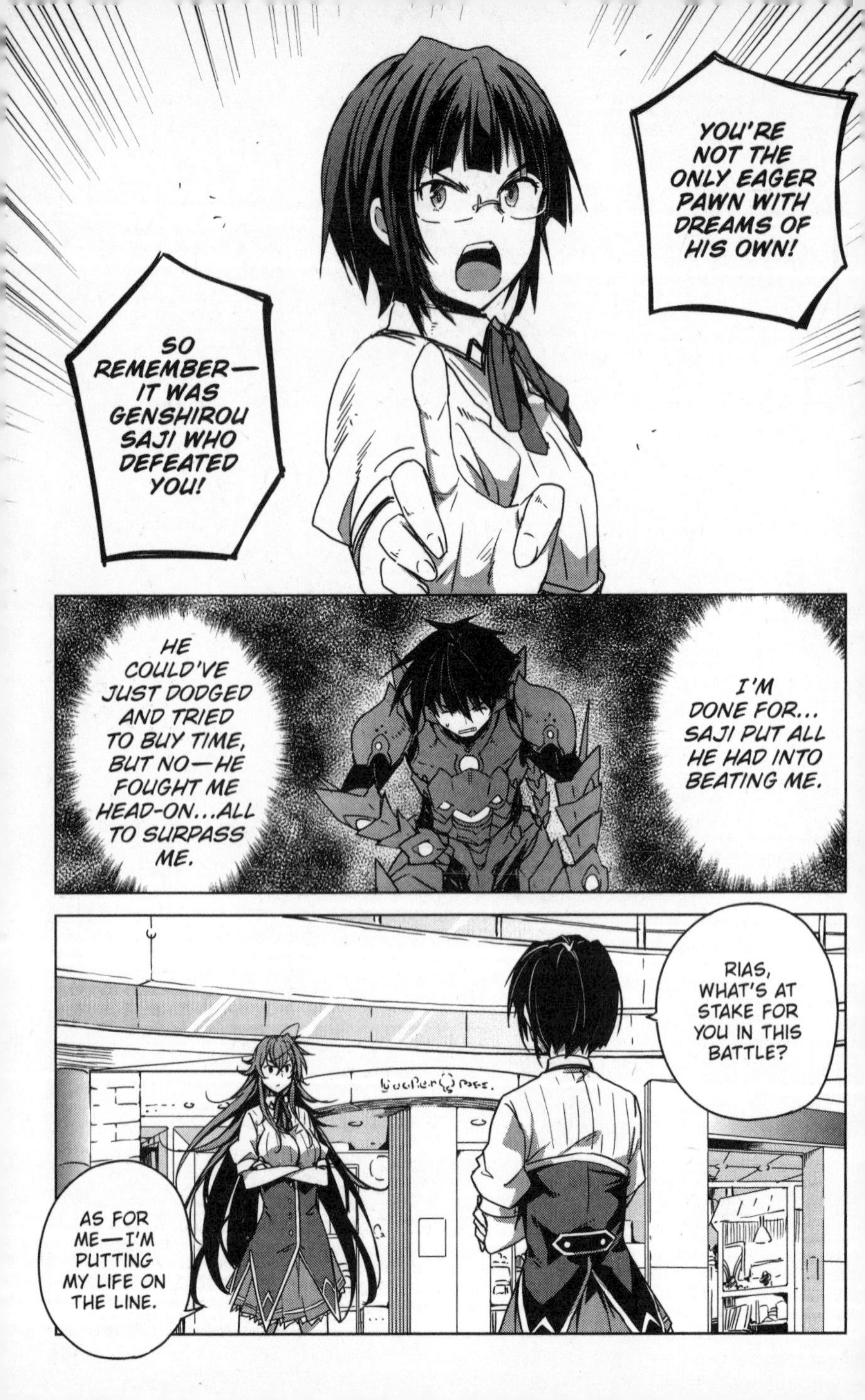
YOU'RE NOT THE ONLY EAGER PAWN WITH DREAMS OF HIS OWN!
SO REMEMBER—IT WAS GENSHIROU SAJI WHO DEFEATED YOU!
I'M DONE FOR... SAJI PUT ALL HE HAD INTO BEATING ME.
HE COULD'VE JUST DODGED AND TRIED TO BUY TIME, BUT NO—HE FOUGHT ME HEAD-ON...ALL TO SURPASS ME.
RIAS, WHAT'S AT STAKE FOR YOU IN THIS BATTLE?
AS FOR ME—I'M PUTTING MY LIFE ON THE LINE.

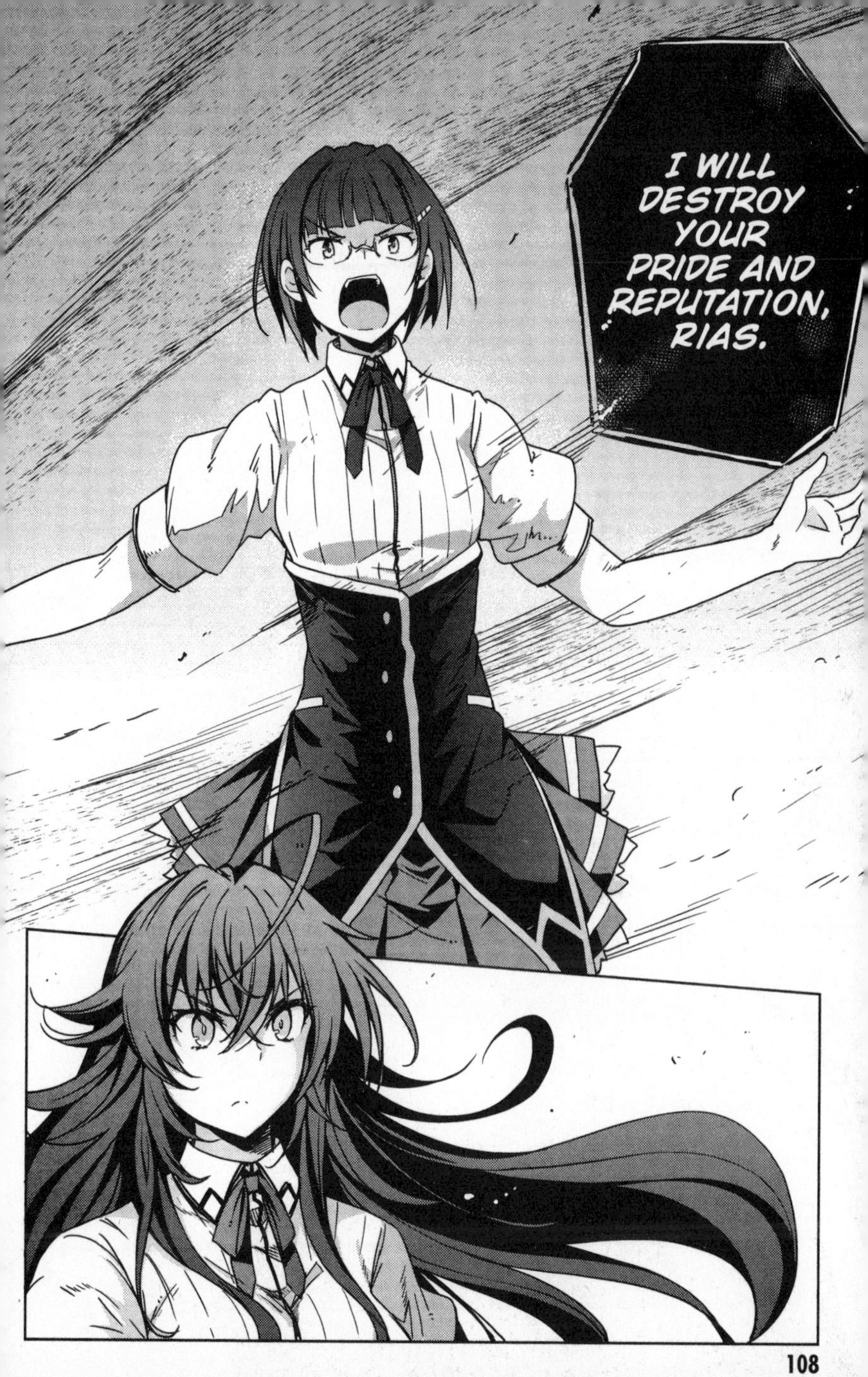
I WILL DESTROY YOUR PRIDE AND REPUTATION, RIAS.

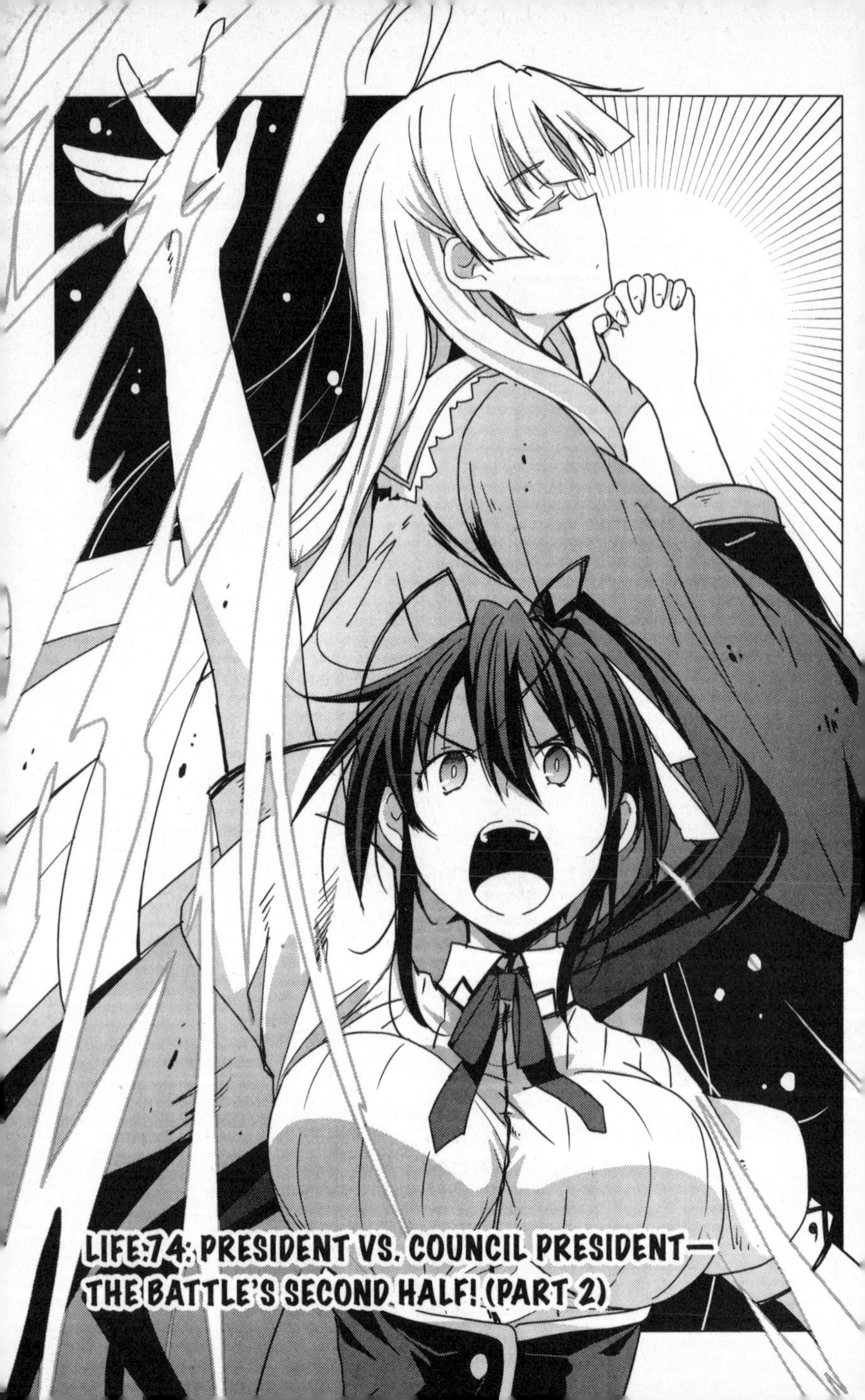
LIFE.74: PRESIDENT VS. COUNCIL PRESIDENT—
THE BATTLE'S SECOND HALF! (PART 2)

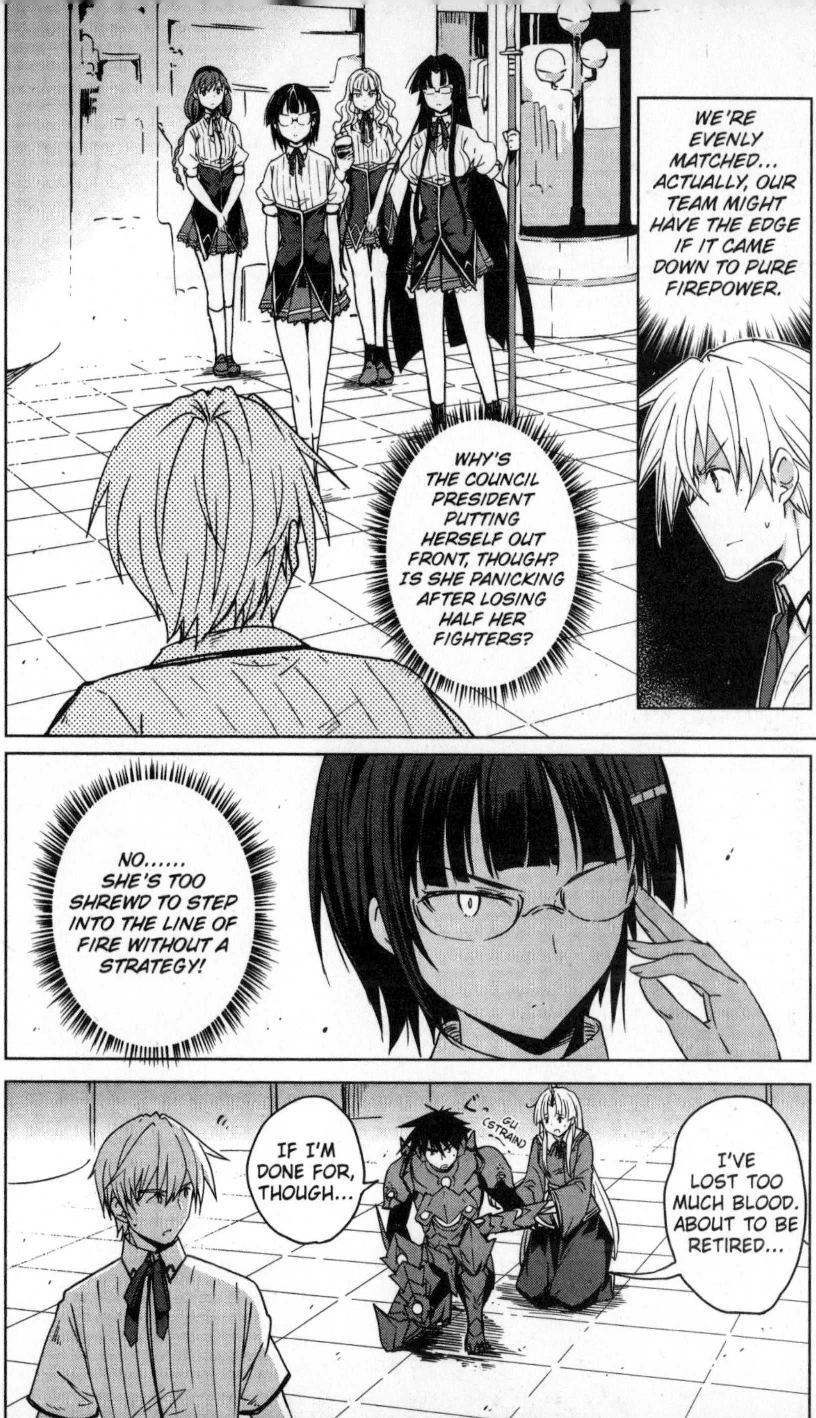
WE'RE EVENLY MATCHED... ACTUALLY, OUR TEAM MIGHT HAVE THE EDGE IF IT CAME DOWN TO PURE FIREPOWER.
WHY'S THE COUNCIL PRESIDENT PUTTING HERSELF OUT FRONT, THOUGH? IS SHE PANICKING AFTER LOSING HALF HER FIGHTERS?
NO...... SHE'S TOO SHREWD TO STEP INTO THE LINE OF FIRE WITHOUT A STRATEGY!
I'VE LOST TOO MUCH BLOOD. ABOUT TO BE RETIRED...
GU (STRAIN)
IF I'M DONE FOR, THOUGH...

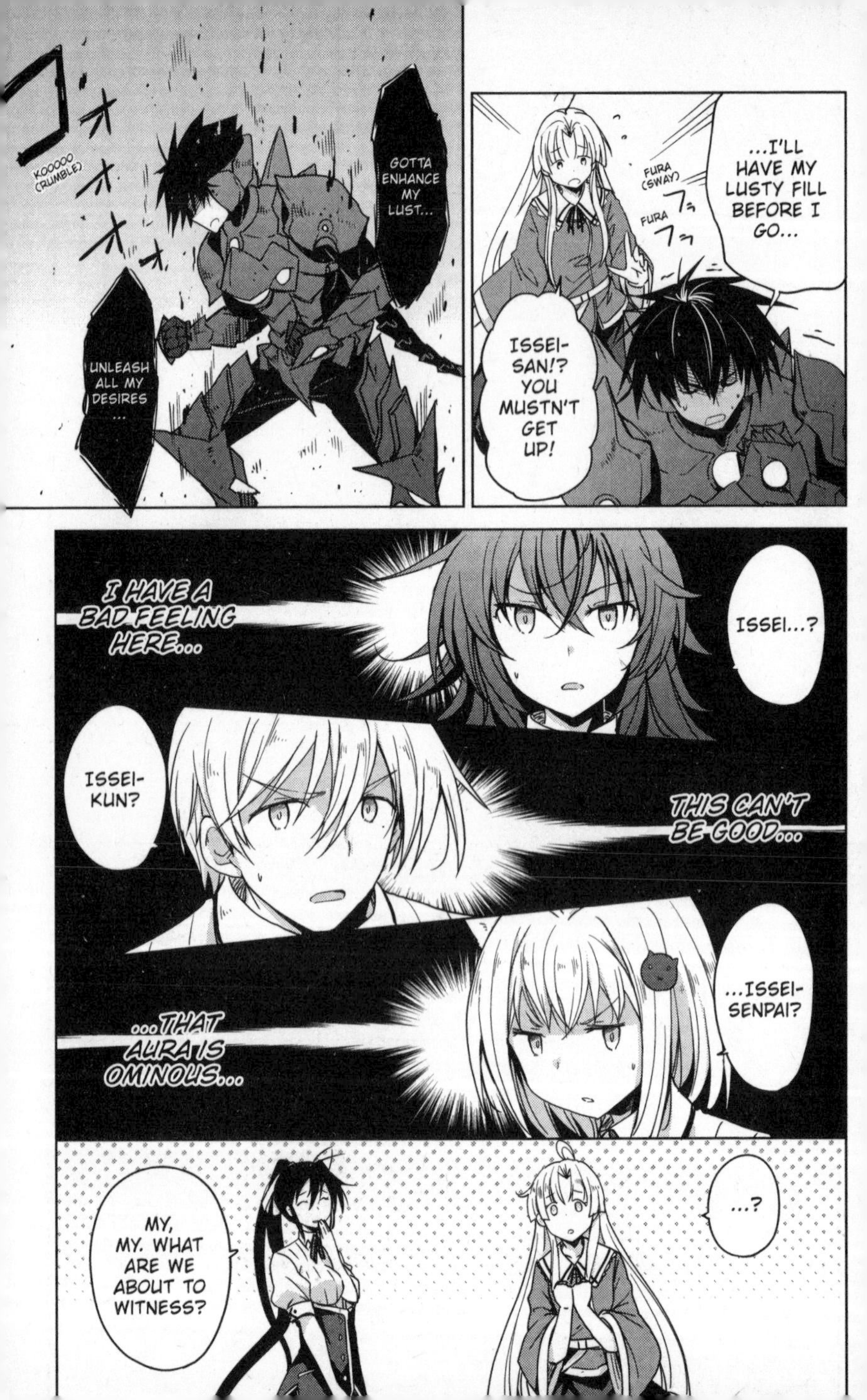
...I'LL HAVE MY LUSTY FILL BEFORE I GO...
FURA (SWAY)
FURA
ISSEI-SAN!? YOU MUSTN'T GET UP!
KOOOOO (RUMBLE)
GOTTA ENHANCE MY LUST...
UNLEASH ALL MY DESIRES...
ISSEI...?
I HAVE A BAD FEELING HERE...
THIS CAN'T BE GOOD...
ISSEI-KUN?
...ISSEI-SENPAI?
...THAT AURA IS OMINOUS...
...?
MY, MY. WHAT ARE WE ABOUT TO WITNESS?

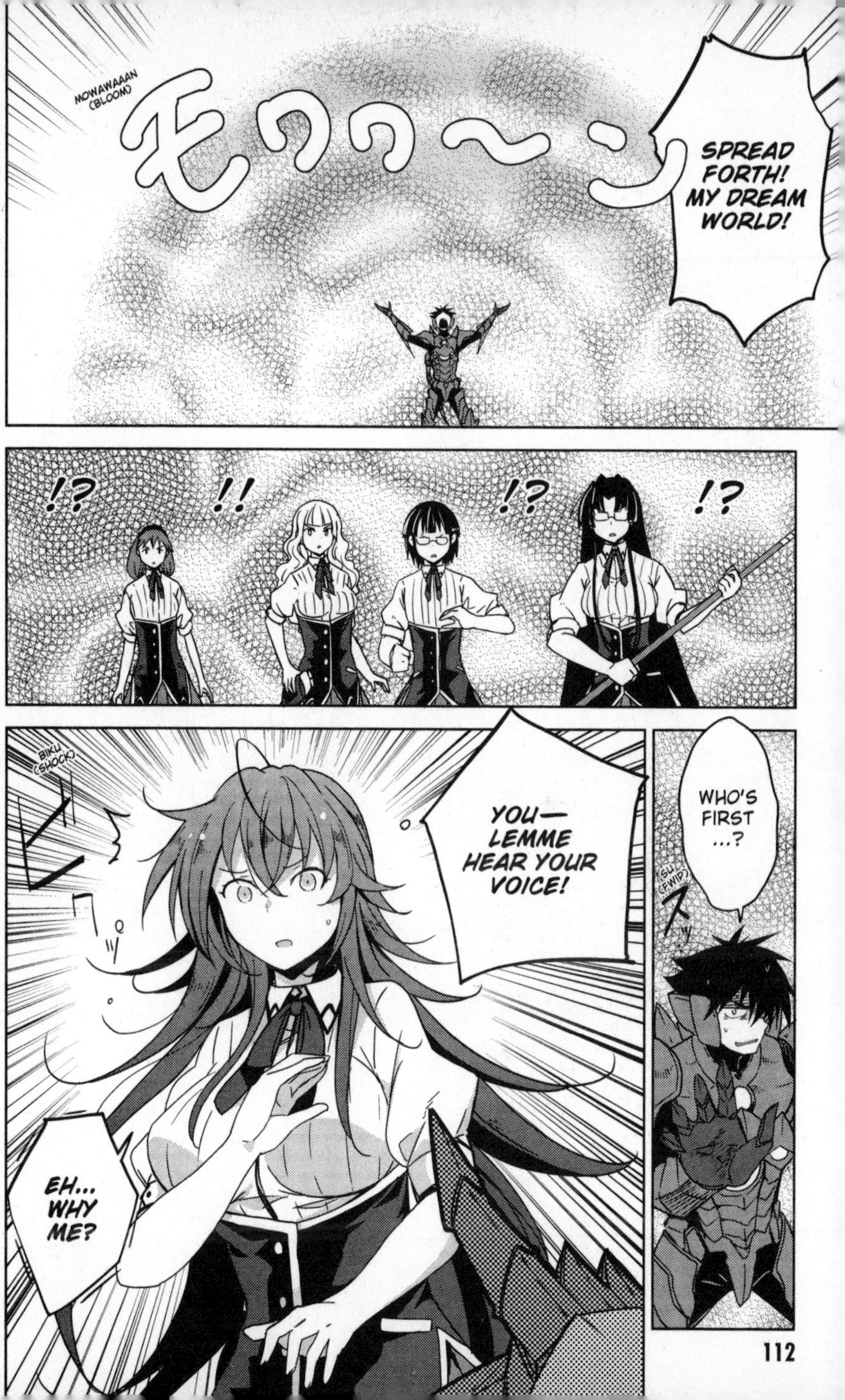
MOWAWAAAN (BLOOM)
SPREAD FORTH! MY DREAM WORLD!
!?
!?
!!
!?
WHO'S FIRST ...?
SU (FWIP)
YOU— LEMME HEAR YOUR VOICE!
BIKU (SHOCK)
EH... WHY ME?

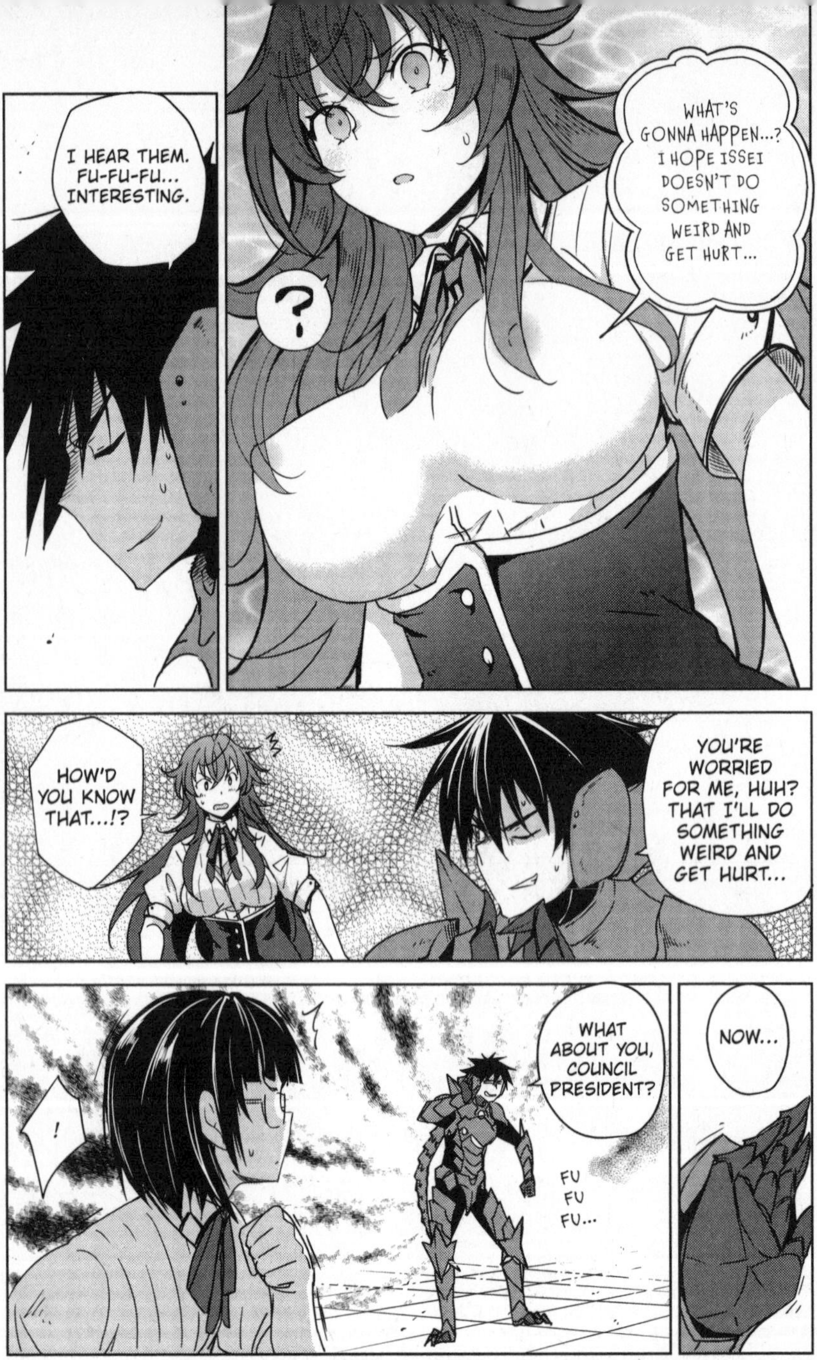
WHAT'S GONNA HAPPEN...? I HOPE ISSEI DOESN'T DO SOMETHING WEIRD AND GET HURT...
?
I HEAR THEM. FU-FU-FU... INTERESTING.
YOU'RE WORRIED FOR ME, HUH? THAT I'LL DO SOMETHING WEIRD AND GET HURT...
HOW'D YOU KNOW THAT...!?
NOW...
WHAT ABOUT YOU, COUNCIL PRESIDENT?
FU FU FU...
!

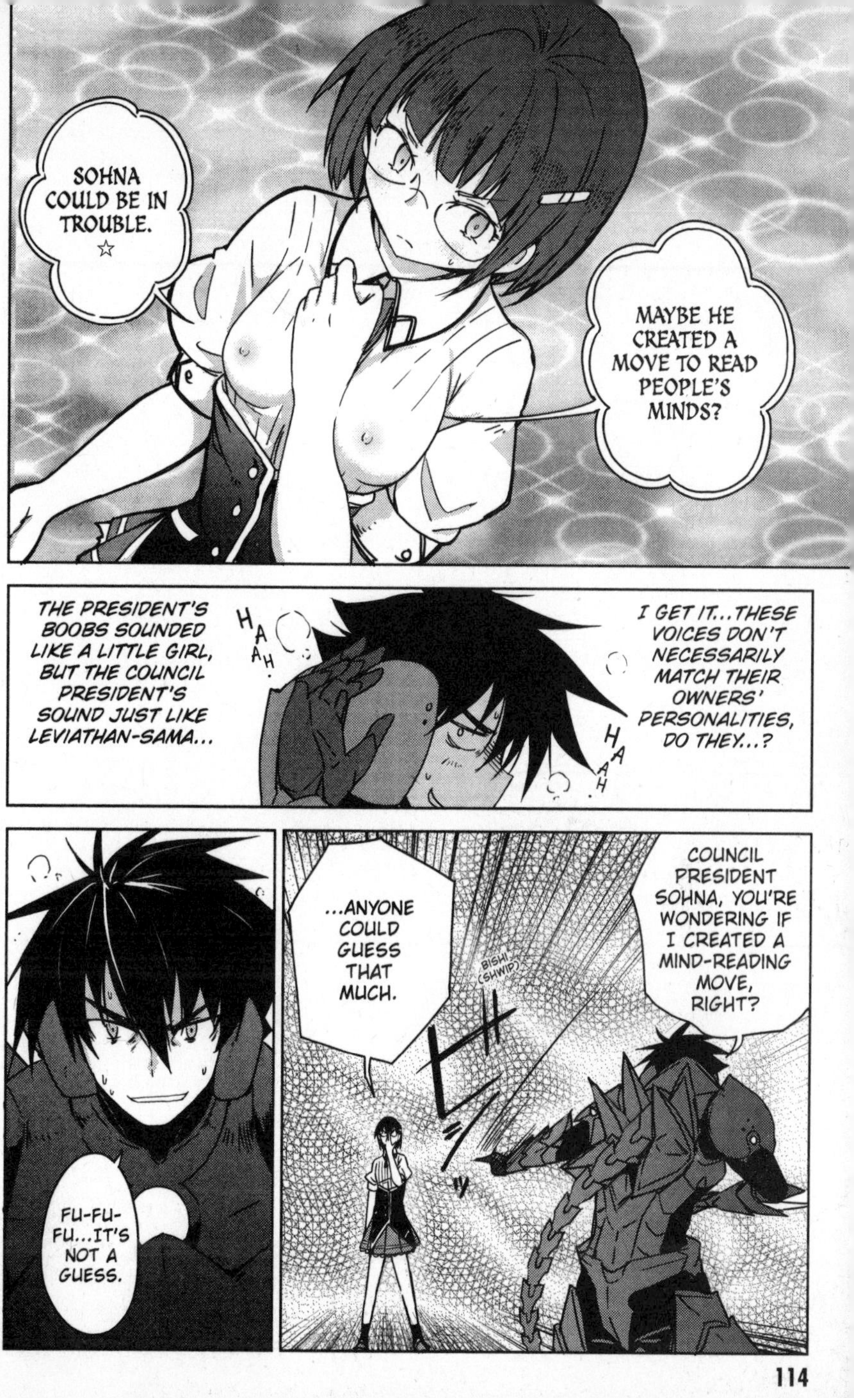
MAYBE HE CREATED A MOVE TO READ PEOPLE'S MINDS?
SOHNA COULD BE IN TROUBLE. ☆
I GET IT...THESE VOICES DON'T NECESSARILY MATCH THEIR OWNERS' PERSONALITIES, DO THEY...?
HAAH
THE PRESIDENT'S BOOBS SOUNDED LIKE A LITTLE GIRL, BUT THE COUNCIL PRESIDENT'S SOUND JUST LIKE LEVIATHAN-SAMA...
HAAH!
COUNCIL PRESIDENT SOHNA, YOU'RE WONDERING IF I CREATED A MIND-READING MOVE, RIGHT?
BISHI (SHWIP)
...ANYONE COULD GUESS THAT MUCH.
FU-FU-FU...IT'S NOT A GUESS.

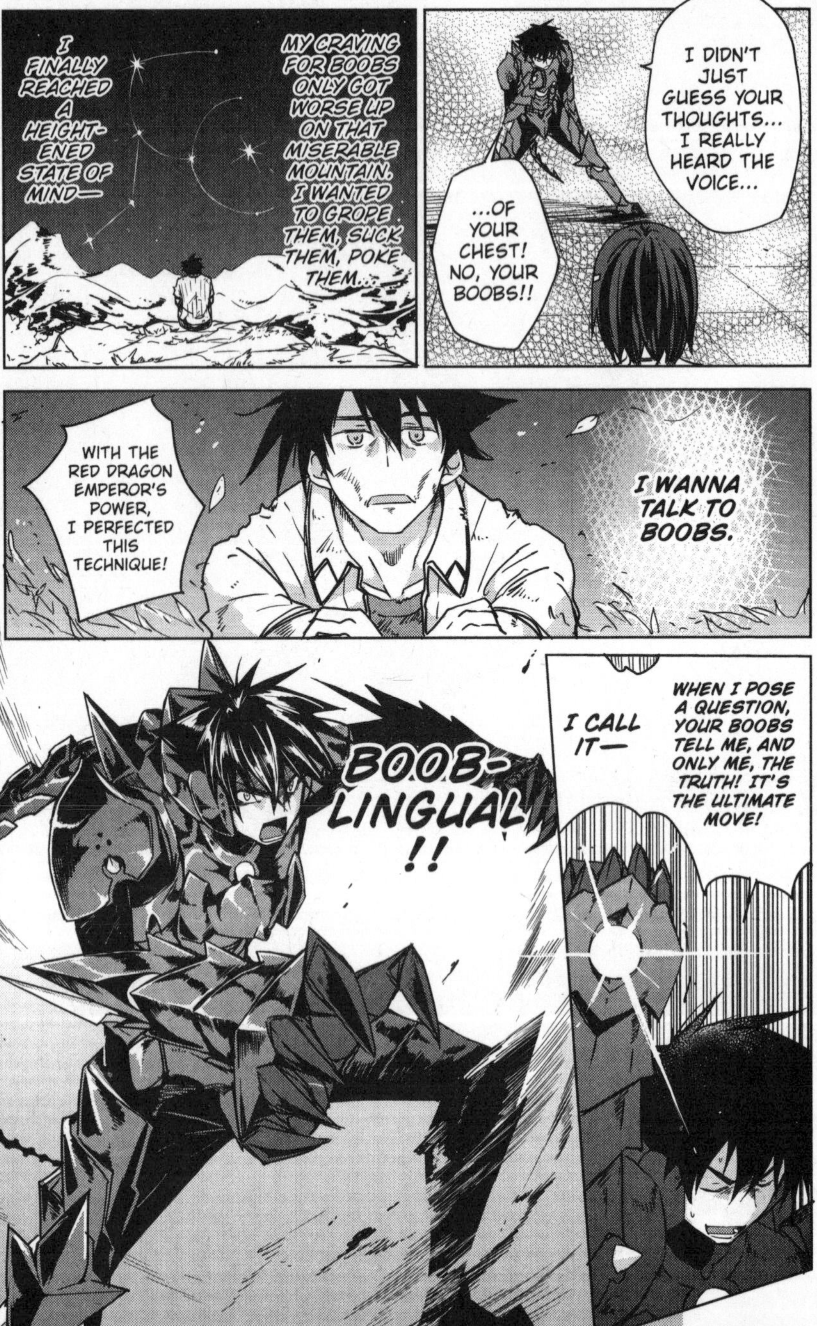
I DIDN'T JUST GUESS YOUR THOUGHTS... I REALLY HEARD THE VOICE...
...OF YOUR CHEST! NO, YOUR BOOBS!!
MY CRAVING FOR BOOBS ONLY GOT WORSE UP ON THAT MISERABLE MOUNTAIN. I WANTED TO GROPE THEM, SUCK THEM, POKE THEM...
I FINALLY REACHED A HEIGHT-ENED STATE OF MIND—
I WANNA TALK TO BOOBS.
WITH THE RED DRAGON EMPEROR'S POWER, I PERFECTED THIS TECHNIQUE!
WHEN I POSE A QUESTION, YOUR BOOBS TELL ME, AND ONLY ME, THE TRUTH! IT'S THE ULTIMATE MOVE!
I CALL IT—
BOOB-LINGUAL!!

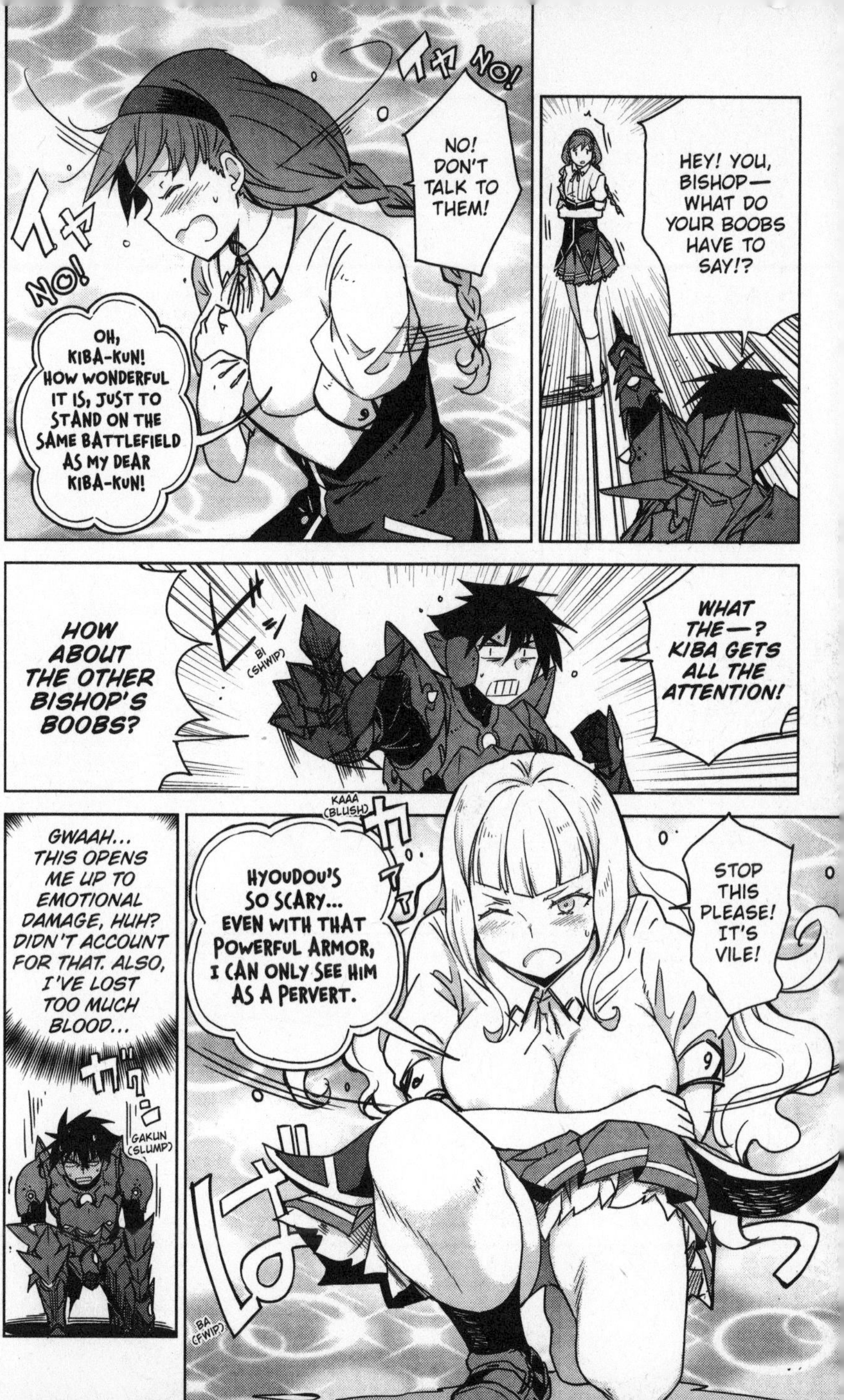
HEY! YOU, BISHOP—WHAT DO YOUR BOOBS HAVE TO SAY!?
NO!
NO! DON'T TALK TO THEM!
NO!
OH, KIBA-KUN! HOW WONDERFUL IT IS, JUST TO STAND ON THE SAME BATTLEFIELD AS MY DEAR KIBA-KUN!
WHAT THE—? KIBA GETS ALL THE ATTENTION!
BI (SHWIP)
HOW ABOUT THE OTHER BISHOP'S BOOBS?
STOP THIS PLEASE! IT'S VILE!
KAAA (BLUSH)
HYOUDOU'S SO SCARY... EVEN WITH THAT POWERFUL ARMOR, I CAN ONLY SEE HIM AS A PERVERT.
BA (FWIP)
GWAAH... THIS OPENS ME UP TO EMOTIONAL DAMAGE, HUH? DIDN'T ACCOUNT FOR THAT. ALSO, I'VE LOST TOO MUCH BLOOD...
GAKUN (SLUMP)

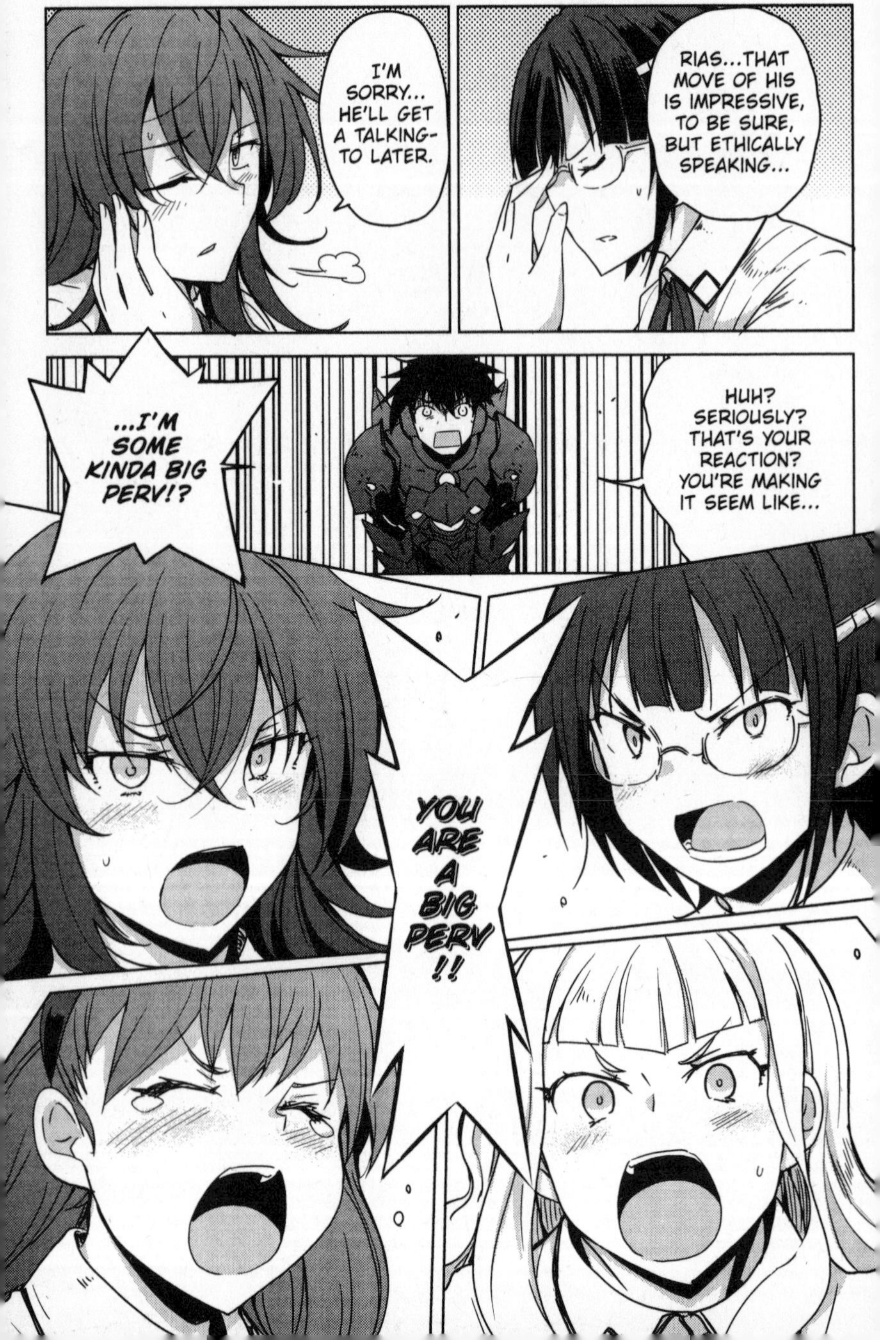
RIAS...THAT MOVE OF HIS IS IMPRESSIVE, TO BE SURE, BUT ETHICALLY SPEAKING...
I'M SORRY... HE'LL GET A TALKING-TO LATER.
HUH? SERIOUSLY? THAT'S YOUR REACTION? YOU'RE MAKING IT SEEM LIKE...
...I'M SOME KINDA BIG PERV!?
YOU ARE A BIG PERV!!

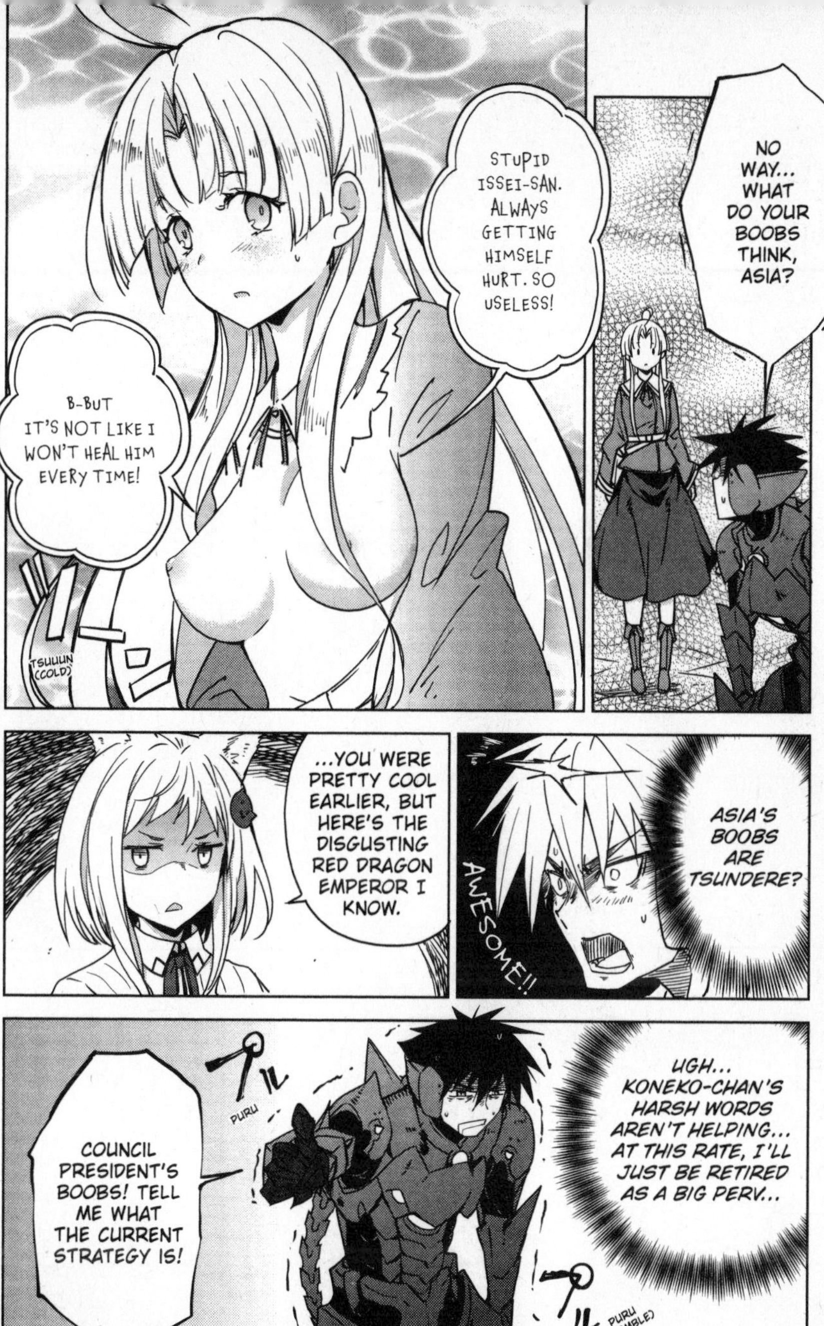
NO WAY... WHAT DO YOUR BOOBS THINK, ASIA?
STUPID ISSEI-SAN. ALWAYS GETTING HIMSELF HURT. SO USELESS!
B-BUT IT'S NOT LIKE I WON'T HEAL HIM EVERY TIME!
TSUUUN (COLD)
ASIA'S BOOBS ARE TSUNDERE?
AWESOME!!
...YOU WERE PRETTY COOL EARLIER, BUT HERE'S THE DISGUSTING RED DRAGON EMPEROR I KNOW.
UGH... KONEKO-CHAN'S HARSH WORDS AREN'T HELPING... AT THIS RATE, I'LL JUST BE RETIRED AS A BIG PERV...
PURU
COUNCIL PRESIDENT'S BOOBS! TELL ME WHAT THE CURRENT STRATEGY IS!
PURU (TREMBLE)

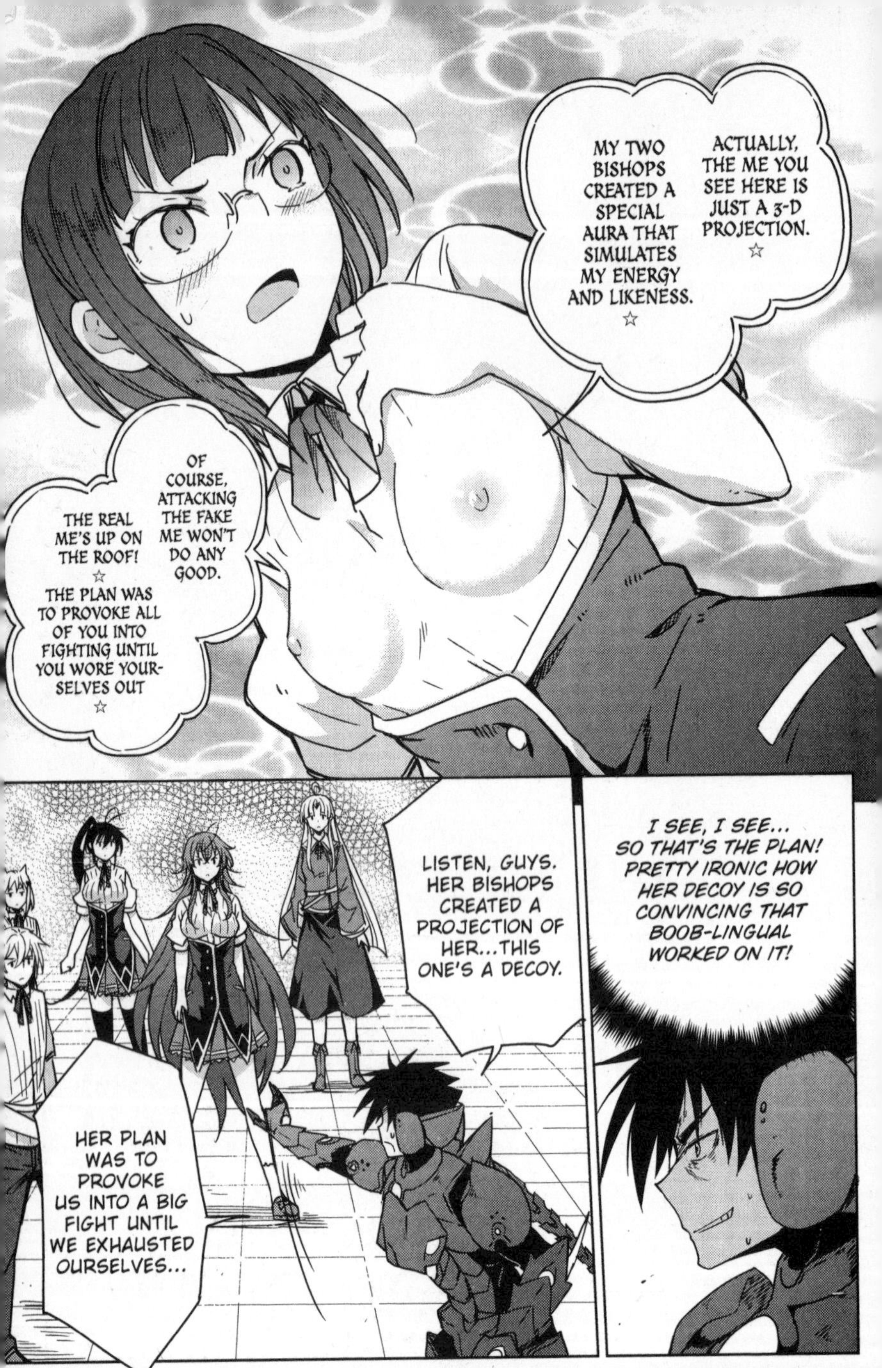
ACTUALLY, THE ME YOU SEE HERE IS JUST A 3-D PROJECTION. ☆
MY TWO BISHOPS CREATED A SPECIAL AURA THAT SIMULATES MY ENERGY AND LIKENESS. ☆
OF COURSE, ATTACKING THE FAKE ME WON'T DO ANY GOOD.
THE REAL ME'S UP ON THE ROOF! ☆
THE PLAN WAS TO PROVOKE ALL OF YOU INTO FIGHTING UNTIL YOU WORE YOUR-SELVES OUT ☆
I SEE, I SEE... SO THAT'S THE PLAN! PRETTY IRONIC HOW HER DECOY IS SO CONVINCING THAT BOOB-LINGUAL WORKED ON IT!
LISTEN, GUYS. HER BISHOPS CREATED A PROJECTION OF HER...THIS ONE'S A DECOY.
HER PLAN WAS TO PROVOKE US INTO A BIG FIGHT UNTIL WE EXHAUSTED OURSELVES...

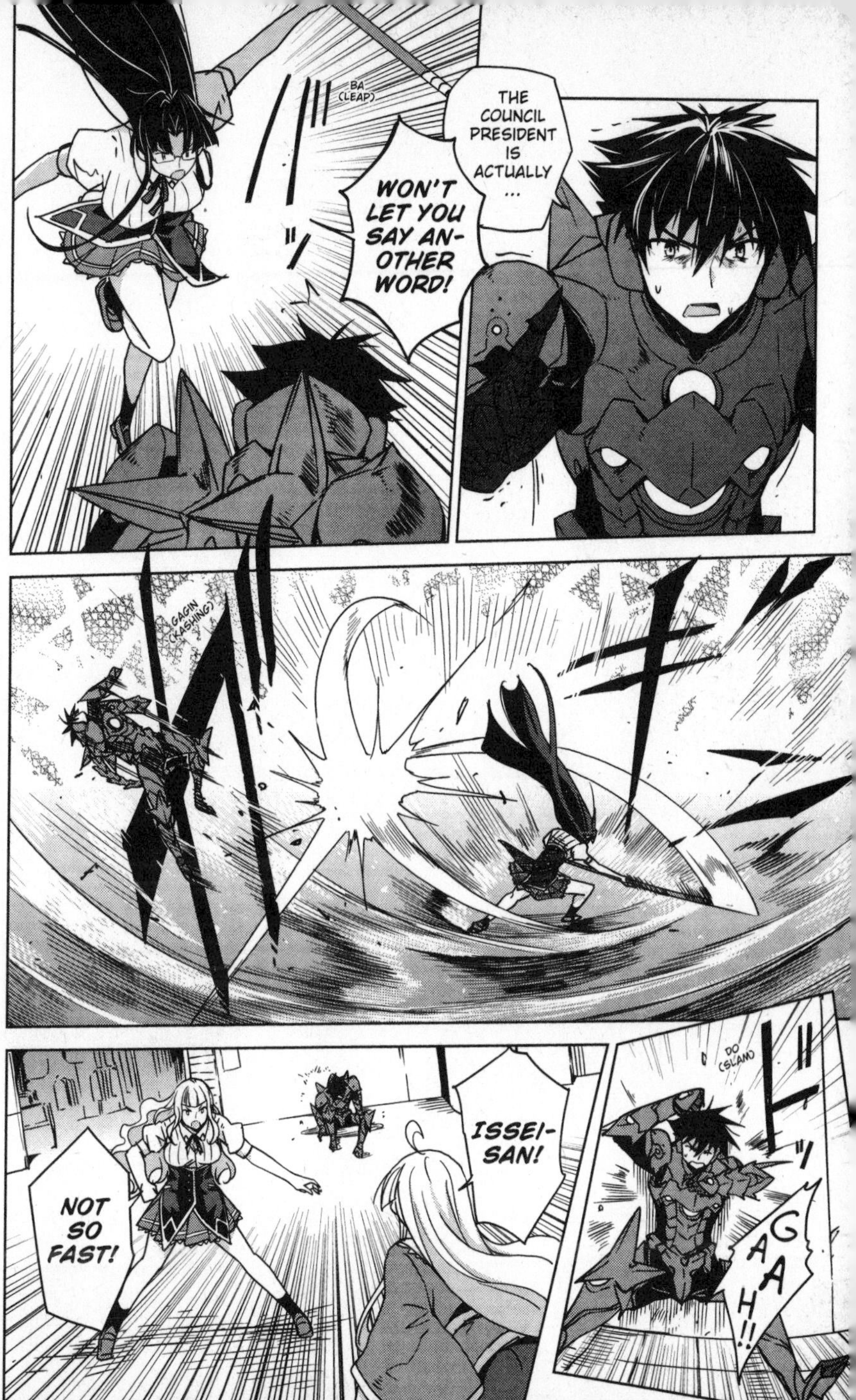
THE COUNCIL PRESIDENT IS ACTUALLY ...
BA (LEAP)
WON'T LET YOU SAY AN-OTHER WORD!
GAGIN (KASHING)
DO (SLAM)
GAAH!!
ISSEI-SAN!
NOT SO FAST!

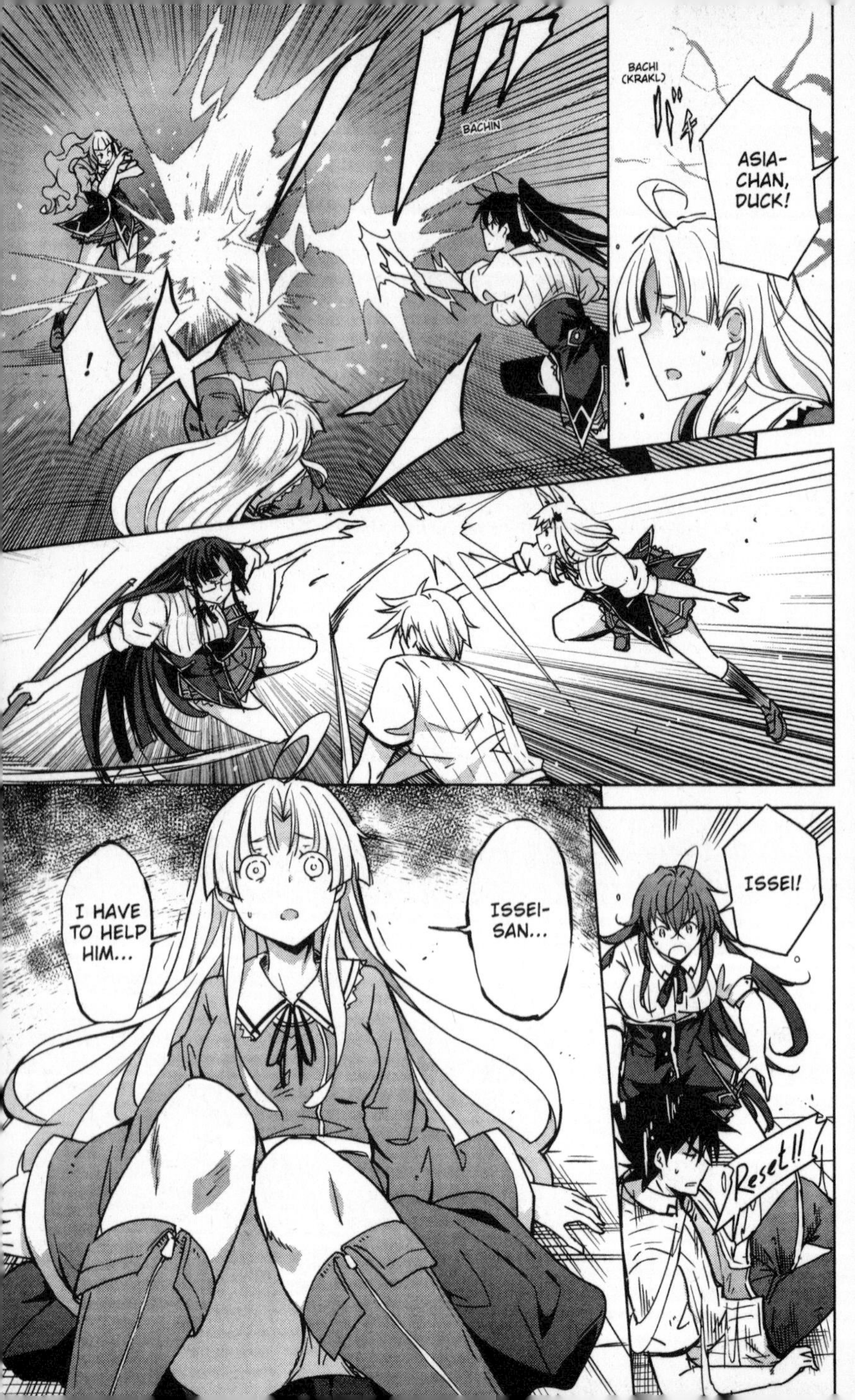
BACHI (KRAKL)
ASIA-CHAN, DUCK!
!
BACHIN
!
ISSEI!
Reset!!
ISSEI-SAN...
I HAVE TO HELP HIM...

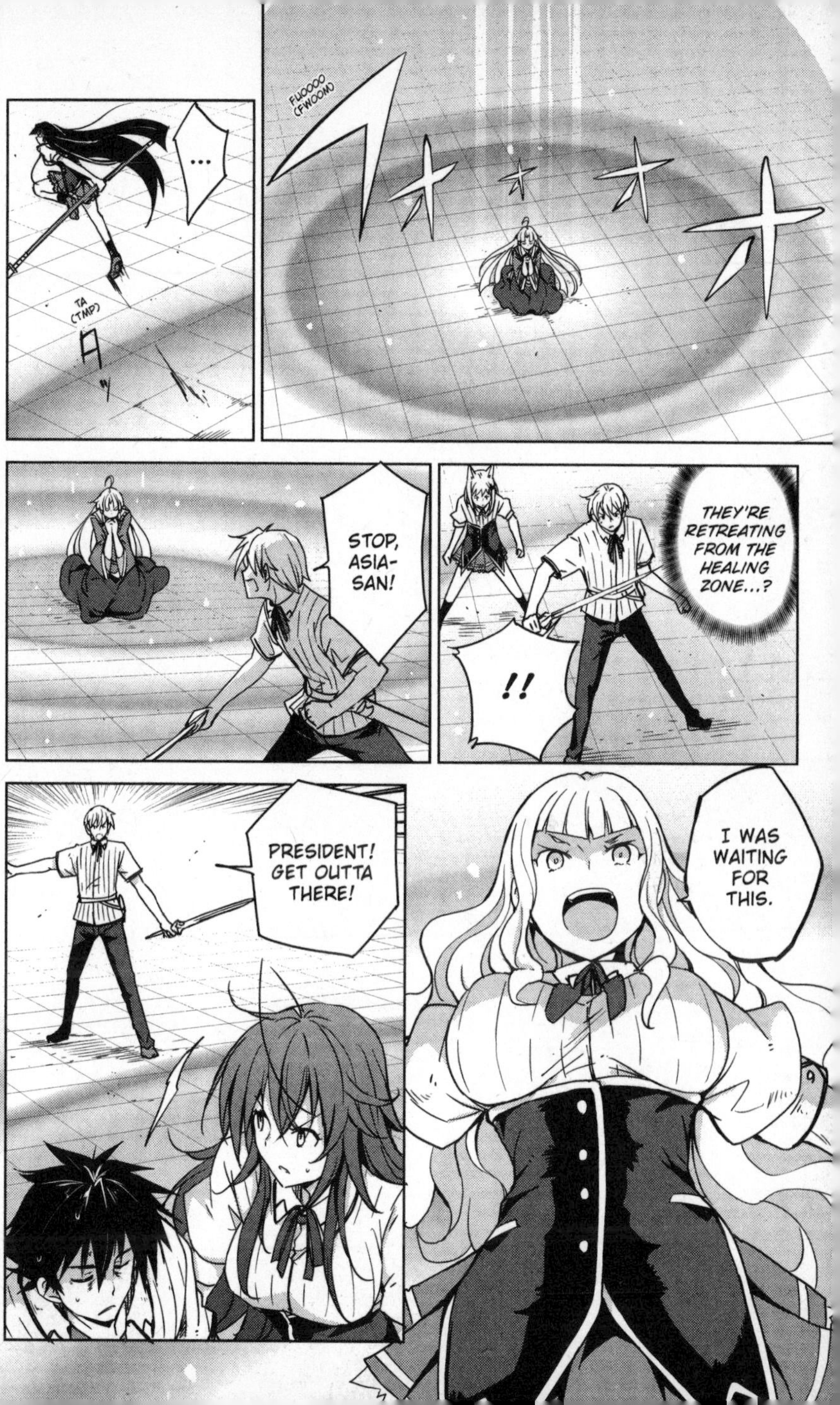
FUOOOO (FWOOOM)
...
TA (TMP)
THEY'RE RETREATING FROM THE HEALING ZONE...?
!!
STOP, ASIA-SAN!
I WAS WAITING FOR THIS.
PRESIDENT! GET OUTTA THERE!

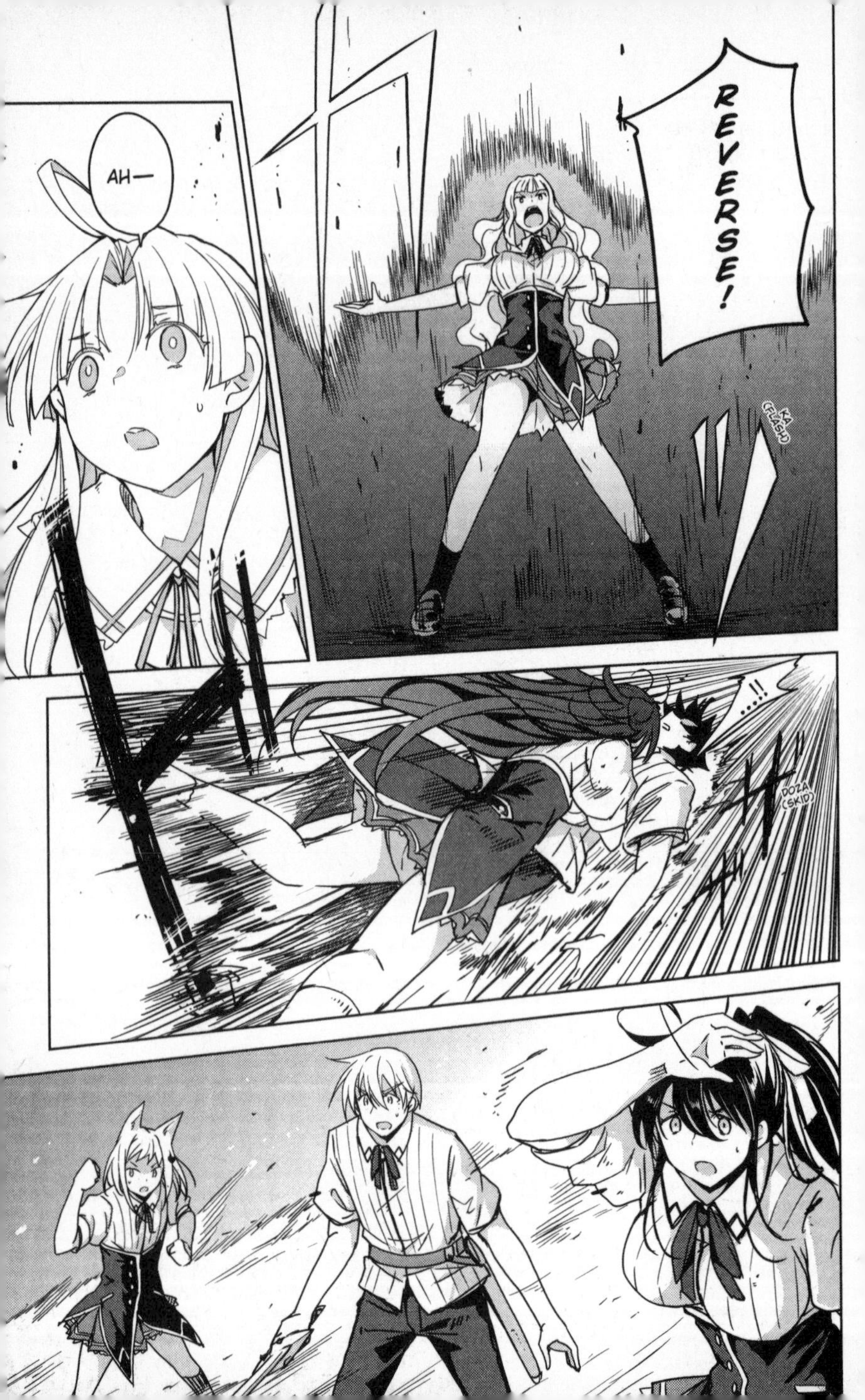
REVERSE!
KA (FLASH)
AH—
...!!
DOZA (SKID)

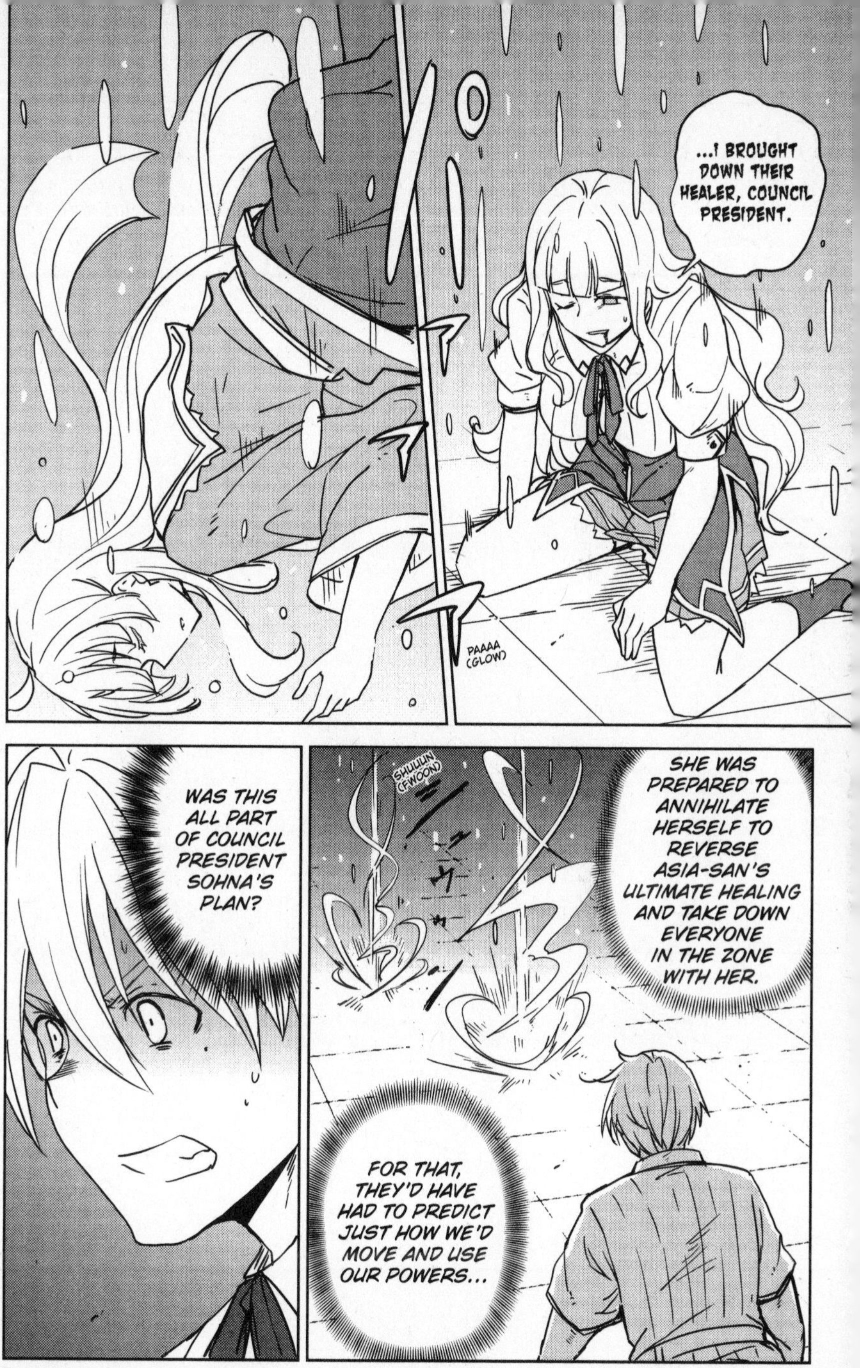
...I BROUGHT DOWN THEIR HEALER, COUNCIL PRESIDENT.
PAAAA (GLOW)
SHUULUN (FWOON)
SHE WAS PREPARED TO ANNIHILATE HERSELF TO REVERSE ASIA-SAN'S ULTIMATE HEALING AND TAKE DOWN EVERYONE IN THE ZONE WITH HER.
FOR THAT, THEY'D HAVE HAD TO PREDICT JUST HOW WE'D MOVE AND USE OUR POWERS...
WAS THIS ALL PART OF COUNCIL PRESIDENT SOHNA'S PLAN?

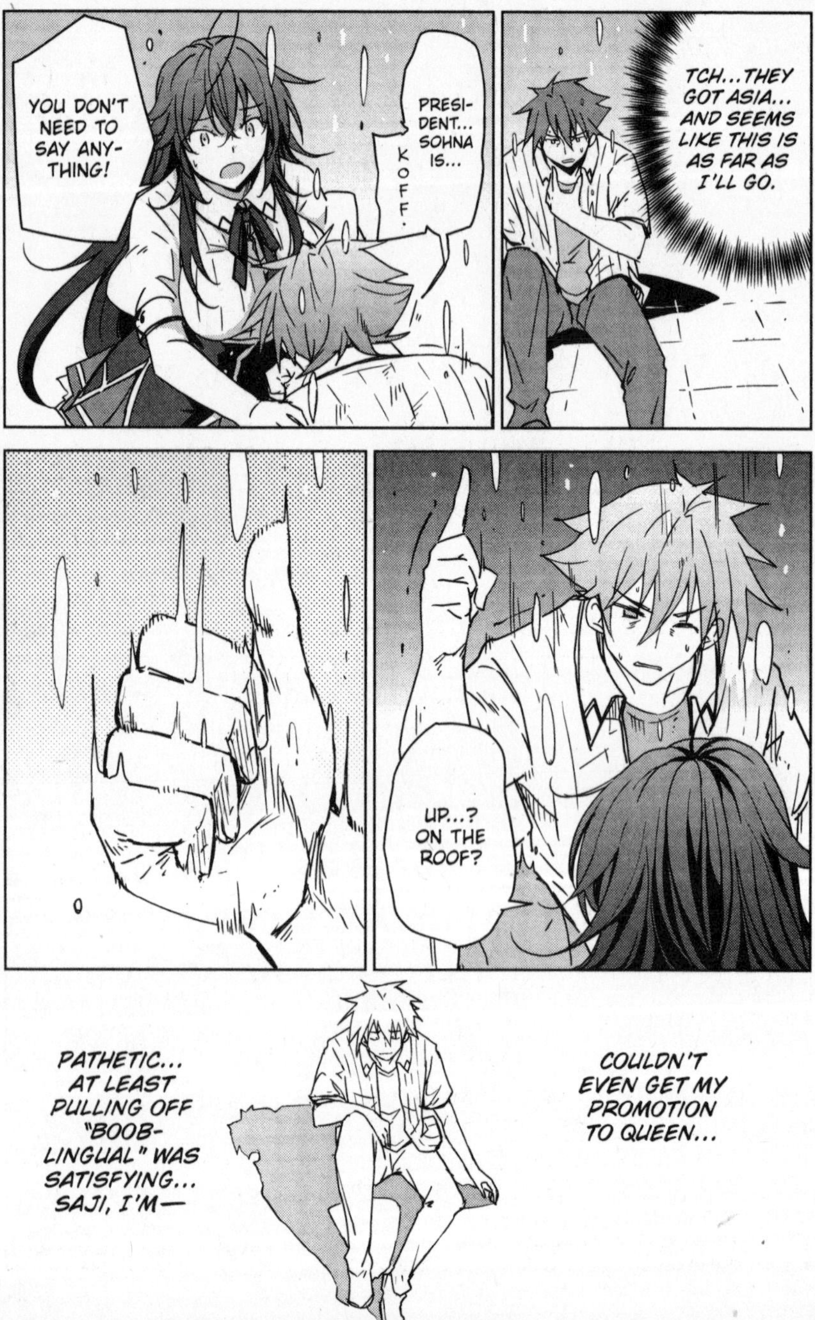
TCH...THEY GOT ASIA... AND SEEMS LIKE THIS IS AS FAR AS I'LL GO.
PRESIDENT... SOHNA IS...
KOFF.
YOU DON'T NEED TO SAY ANYTHING!
UP...? ON THE ROOF?
COULDN'T EVEN GET MY PROMOTION TO QUEEN...
PATHETIC... AT LEAST PULLING OFF "BOOB-LINGUAL" WAS SATISFYING... SAJI, I'M—

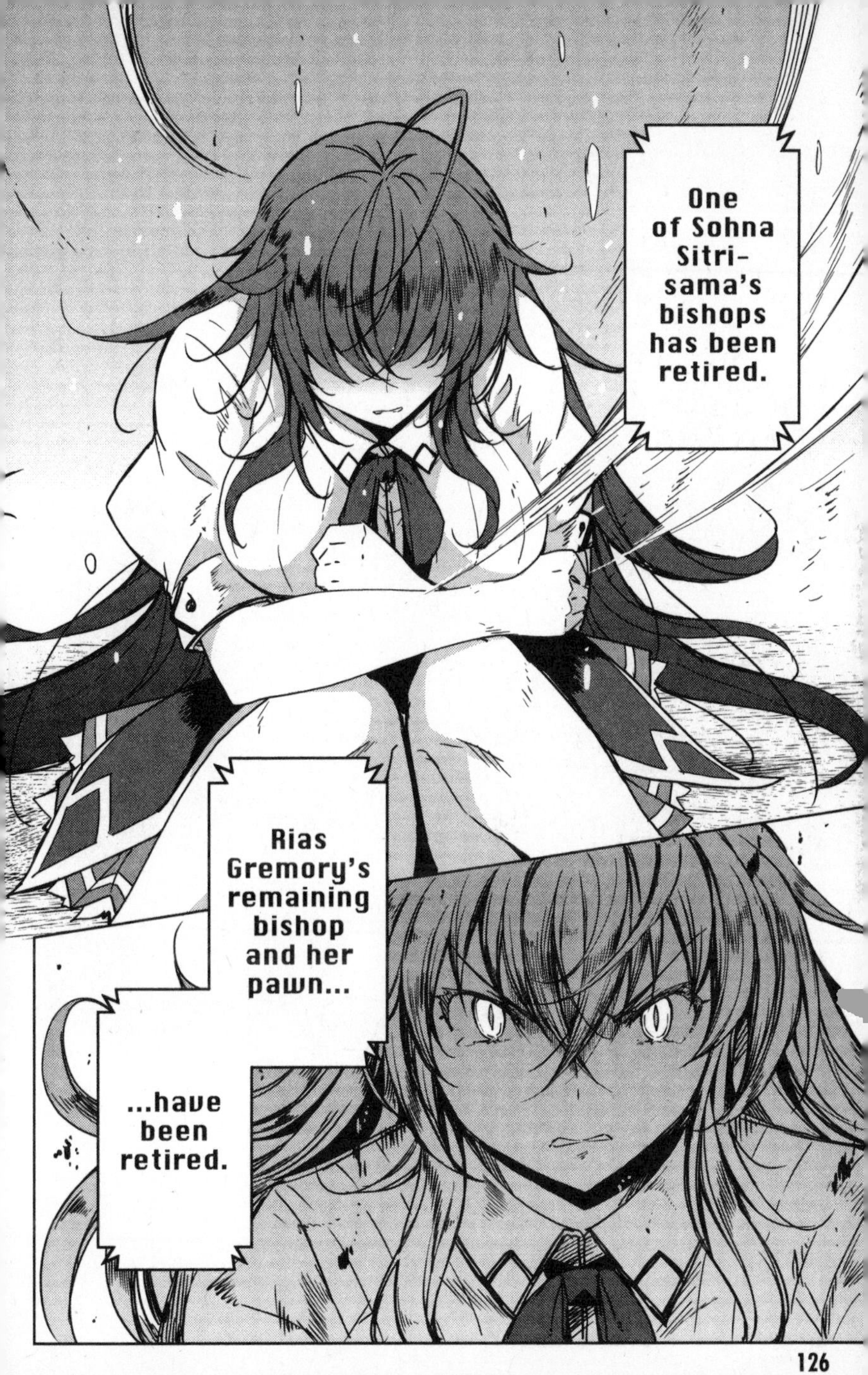
One of Sohna Sitri-sama's bishops has been retired.
Rias Gremory's remaining bishop and her pawn...
...have been retired.

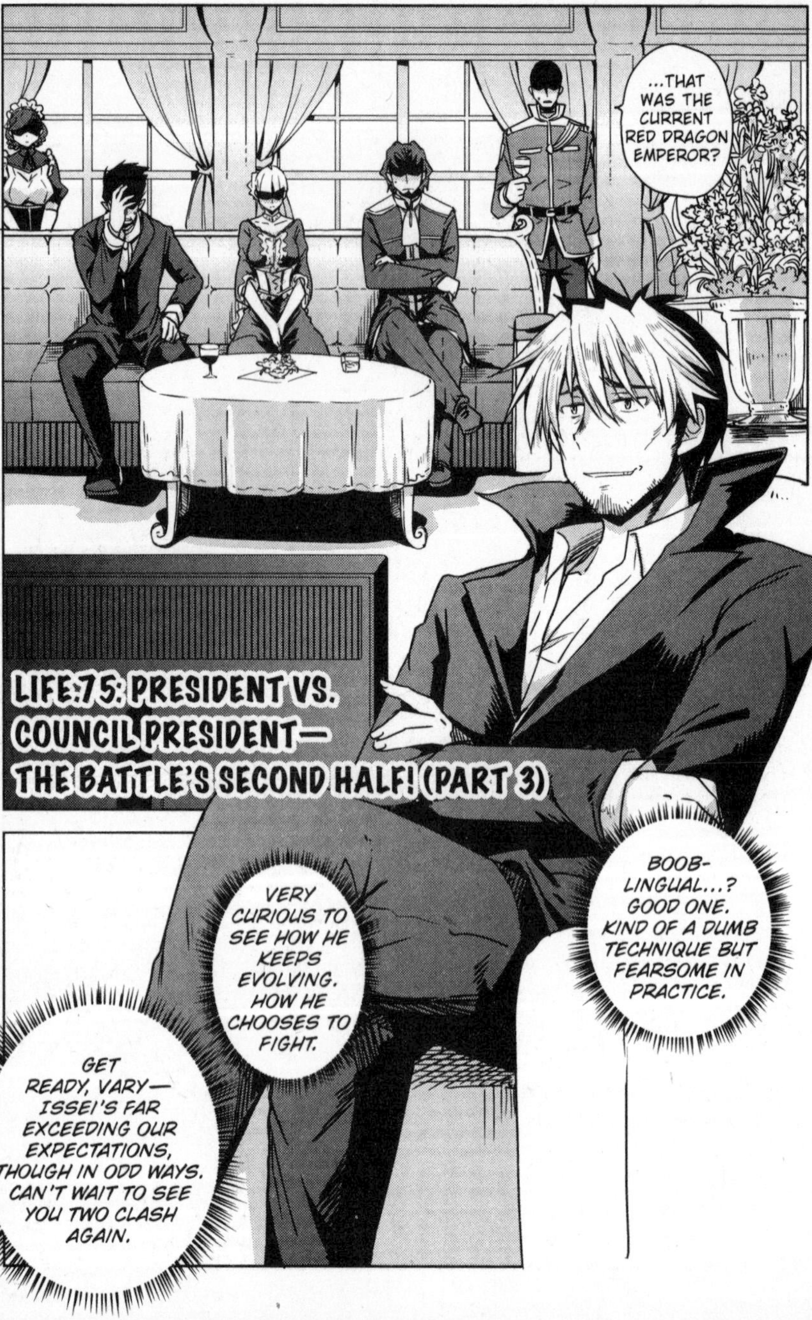
...THAT WAS THE CURRENT RED DRAGON EMPEROR?
LIFE.75: PRESIDENT VS. COUNCIL PRESIDENT— THE BATTLE'S SECOND HALF! (PART 3)
BOOB-LINGUAL...? GOOD ONE. KIND OF A DUMB TECHNIQUE BUT FEARSOME IN PRACTICE.
VERY CURIOUS TO SEE HOW HE KEEPS EVOLVING. HOW HE CHOOSES TO FIGHT.
GET READY, VARY— ISSEI'S FAR EXCEEDING OUR EXPECTATIONS, THOUGH IN ODD WAYS. CAN'T WAIT TO SEE YOU TWO CLASH AGAIN.

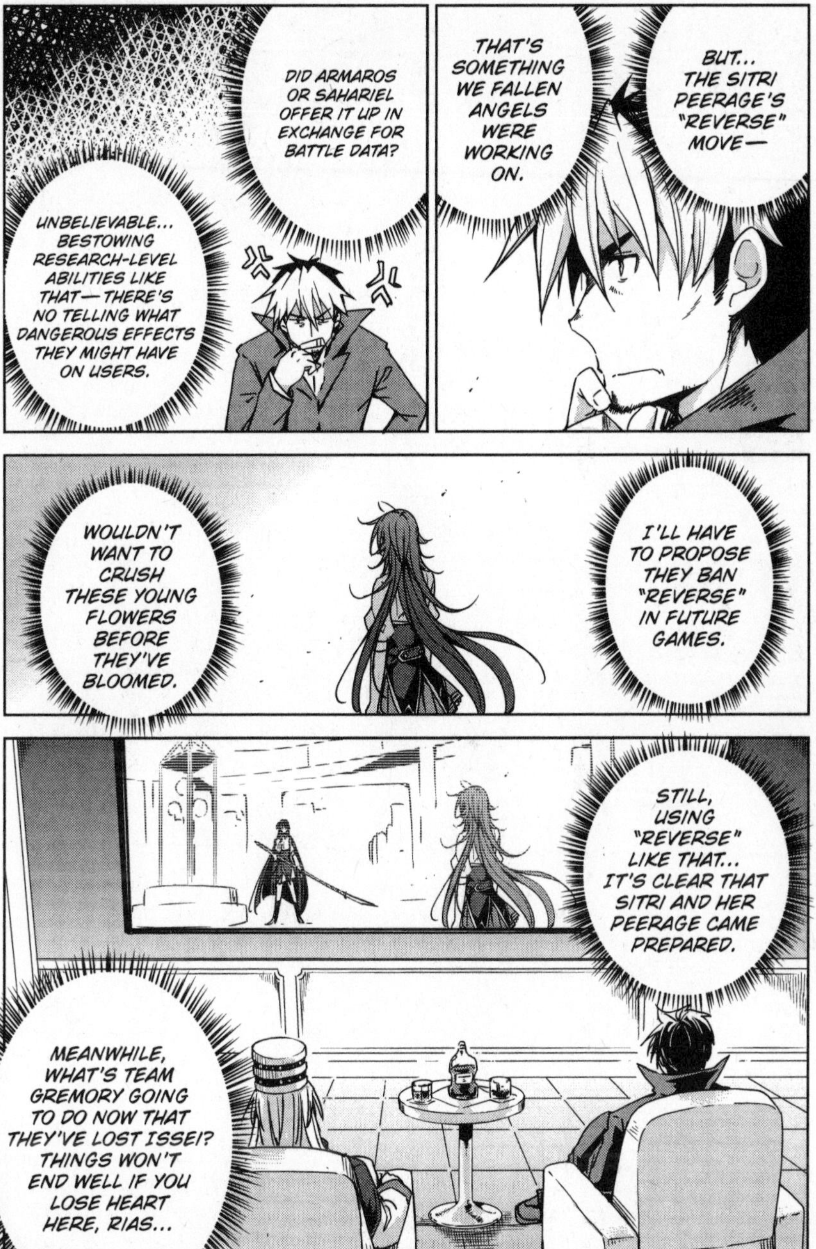
BUT... THE SITRI PEERAGE'S "REVERSE" MOVE—
THAT'S SOMETHING WE FALLEN ANGELS WERE WORKING ON.
DID ARMAROS OR SAHARIEL OFFER IT UP IN EXCHANGE FOR BATTLE DATA?
UNBELIEVABLE... BESTOWING RESEARCH-LEVEL ABILITIES LIKE THAT—THERE'S NO TELLING WHAT DANGEROUS EFFECTS THEY MIGHT HAVE ON USERS.
I'LL HAVE TO PROPOSE THEY BAN "REVERSE" IN FUTURE GAMES.
WOULDN'T WANT TO CRUSH THESE YOUNG FLOWERS BEFORE THEY'VE BLOOMED.
STILL, USING "REVERSE" LIKE THAT... IT'S CLEAR THAT SITRI AND HER PEERAGE CAME PREPARED.
MEANWHILE, WHAT'S TEAM GREMORY GOING TO DO NOW THAT THEY'VE LOST ISSEI? THINGS WON'T END WELL IF YOU LOSE HEART HERE, RIAS...

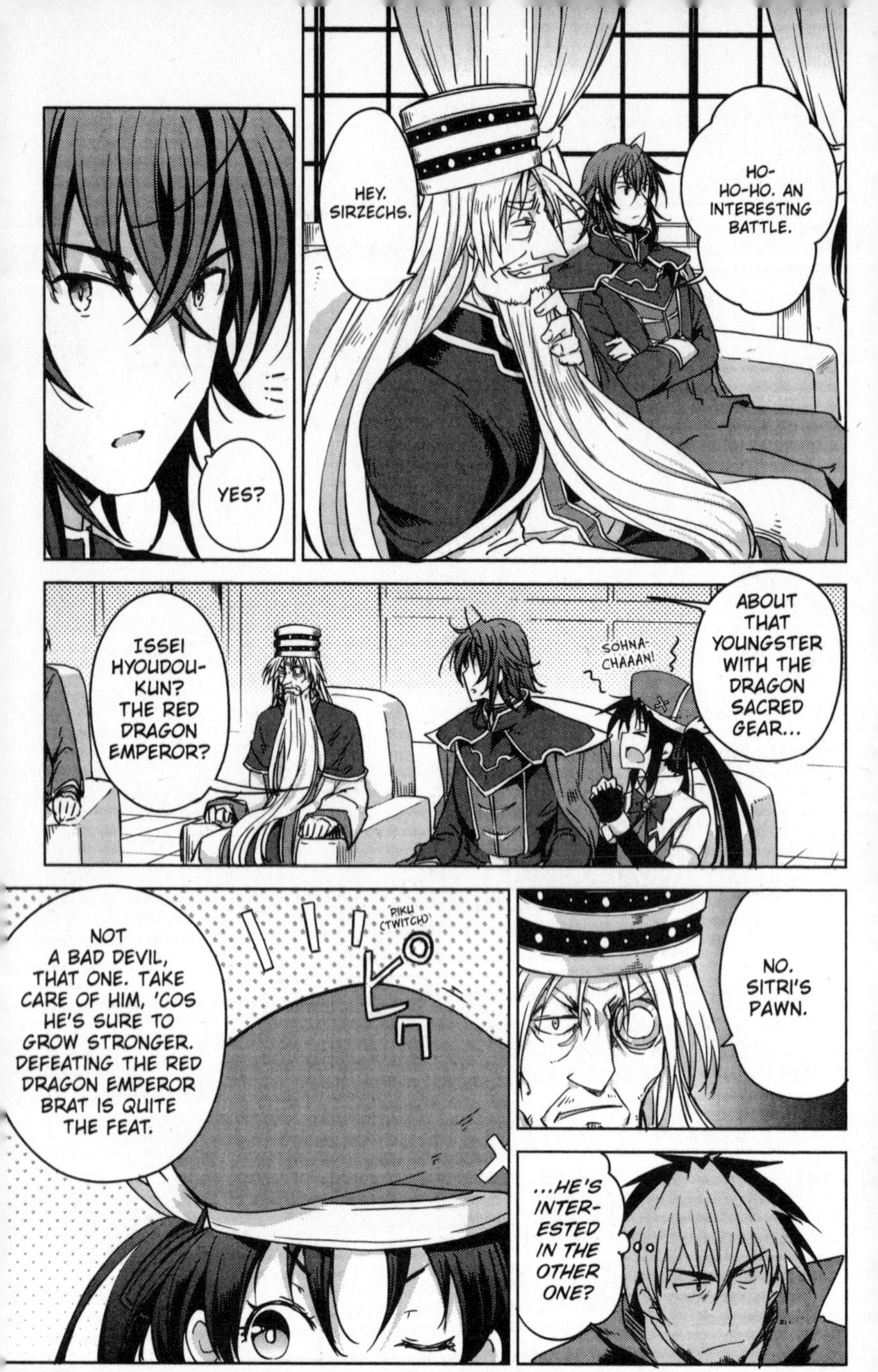
HO-HO-HO. AN INTERESTING BATTLE.
HEY. SIRZECHS.
YES?
ABOUT THAT YOUNGSTER WITH THE DRAGON SACRED GEAR...
SOHNA-CHAAAN!
ISSEI HYOUDOU-KUN? THE RED DRAGON EMPEROR?
NO. SITRI'S PAWN.
...HE'S INTER-ESTED IN THE OTHER ONE?
PIKU (TWITCH)
NOT A BAD DEVIL, THAT ONE. TAKE CARE OF HIM, 'COS HE'S SURE TO GROW STRONGER. DEFEATING THE RED DRAGON EMPEROR BRAT IS QUITE THE FEAT.

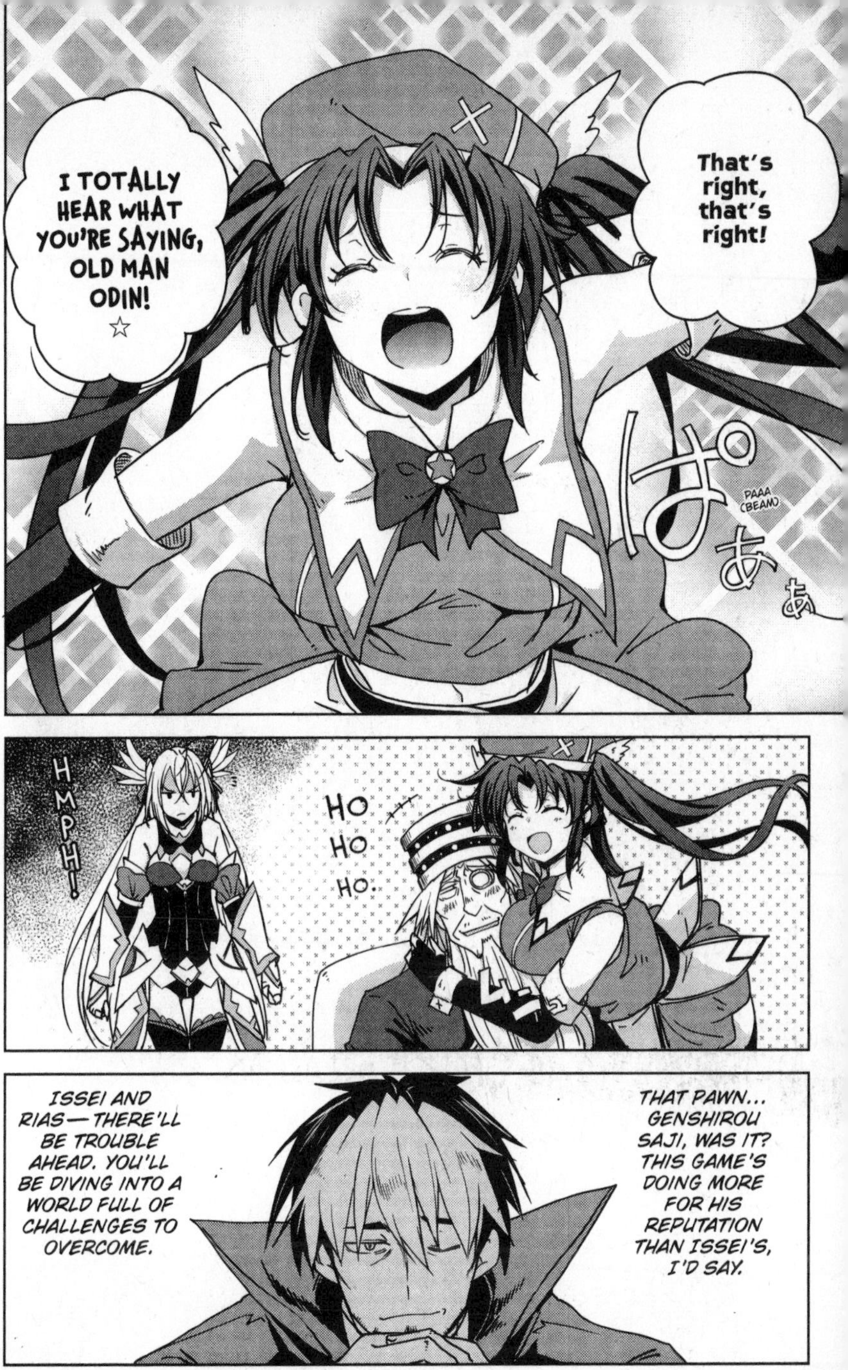
That's right, that's right!
I TOTALLY HEAR WHAT YOU'RE SAYING, OLD MAN ODIN! ☆
ぱあぁ
PAAA (BEAM)
HO HO HO.
HMPH!
THAT PAWN... GENSHIROU SAJI, WAS IT? THIS GAME'S DOING MORE FOR HIS REPUTATION THAN ISSEI'S, I'D SAY.
ISSEI AND RIAS—THERE'LL BE TROUBLE AHEAD. YOU'LL BE DIVING INTO A WORLD FULL OF CHALLENGES TO OVERCOME.

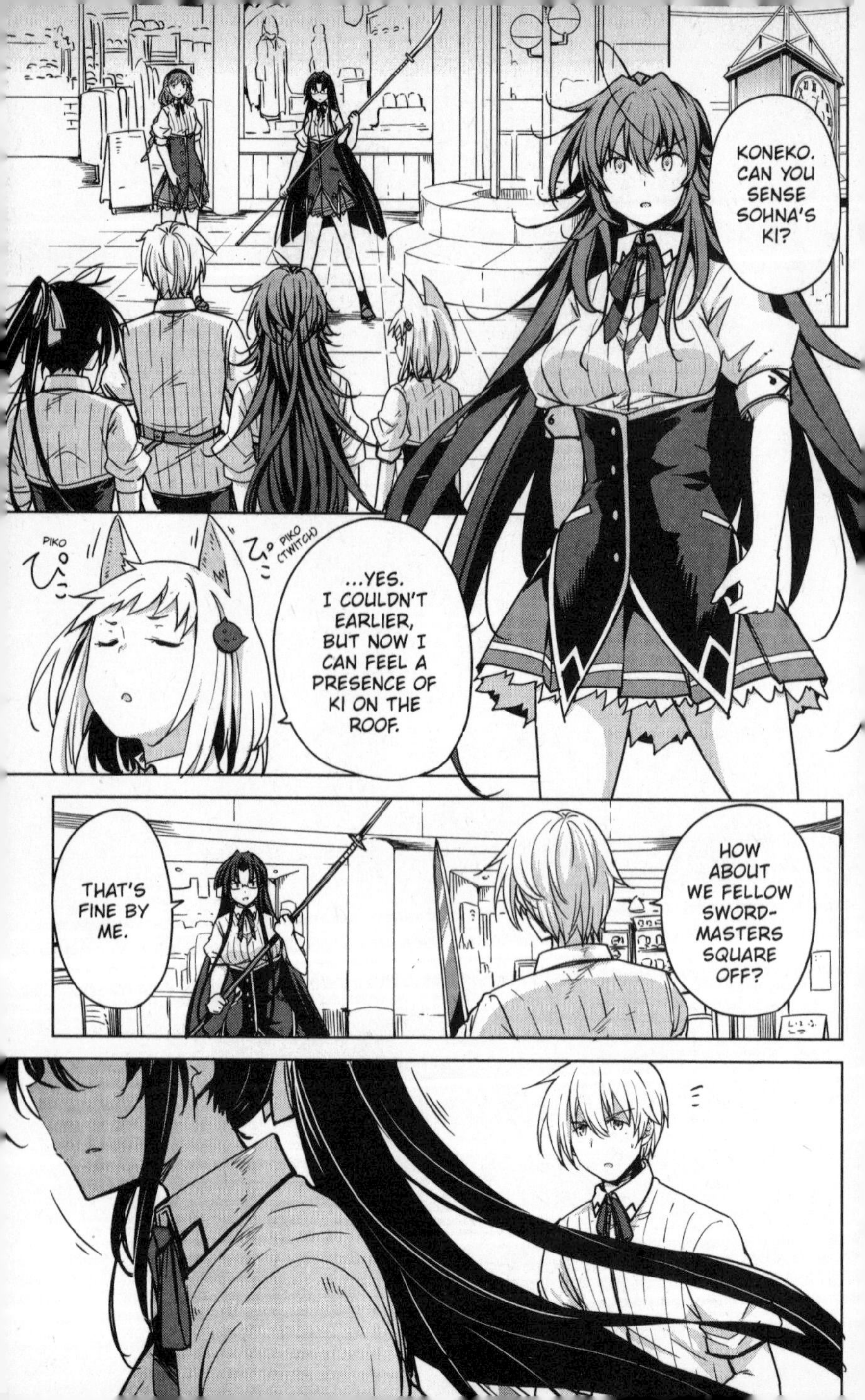
KONEKO. CAN YOU SENSE SOHNA'S KI?
PIKO (TWITCH)
...YES. I COULDN'T EARLIER, BUT NOW I CAN FEEL A PRESENCE OF KI ON THE ROOF.
PIKO
HOW ABOUT WE FELLOW SWORD-MASTERS SQUARE OFF?
THAT'S FINE BY ME.

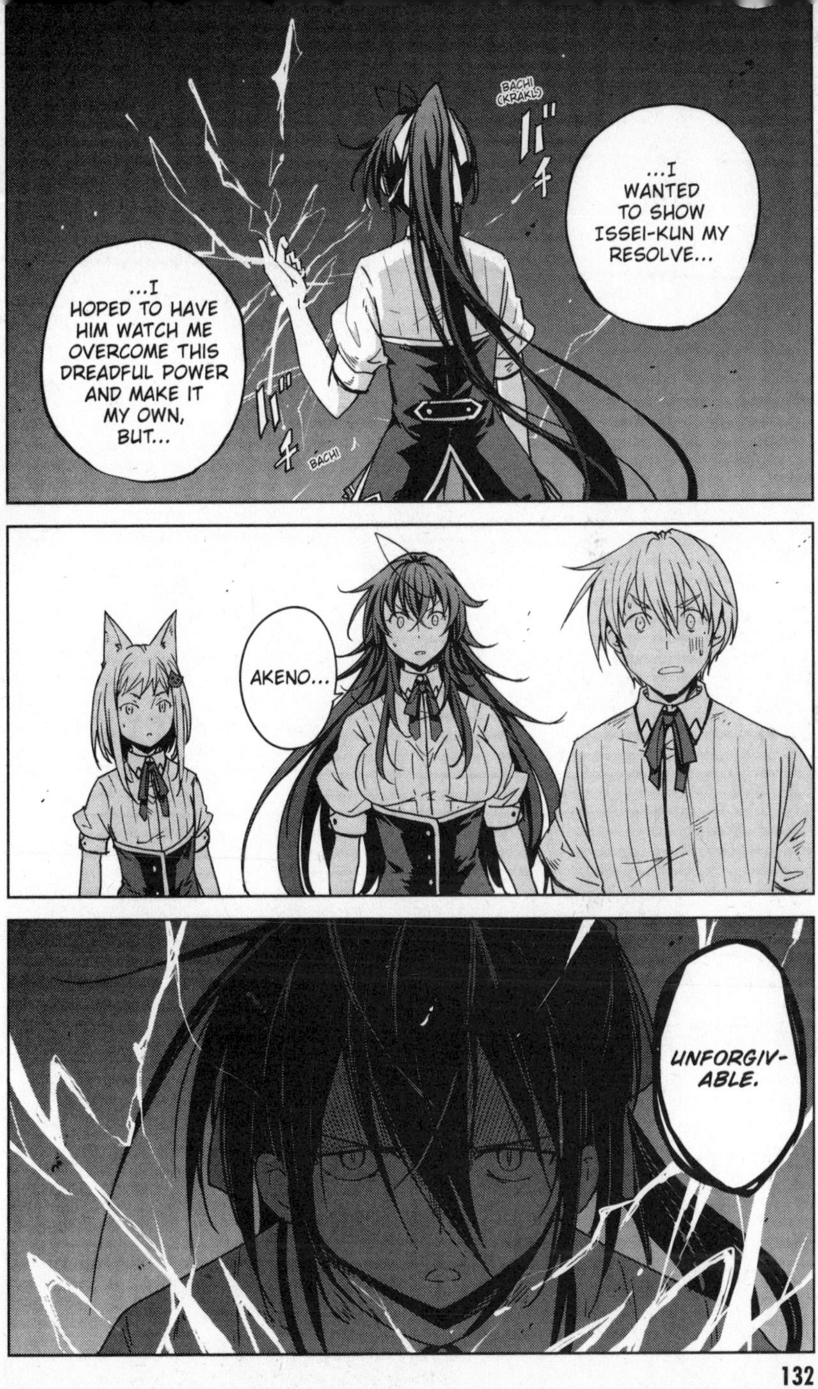
...I WANTED TO SHOW ISSEI-KUN MY RESOLVE...
BACHI (KRAKL)
...I HOPED TO HAVE HIM WATCH ME OVERCOME THIS DREADFUL POWER AND MAKE IT MY OWN, BUT...
BACHI
AKENO...
UNFORGIV-ABLE.

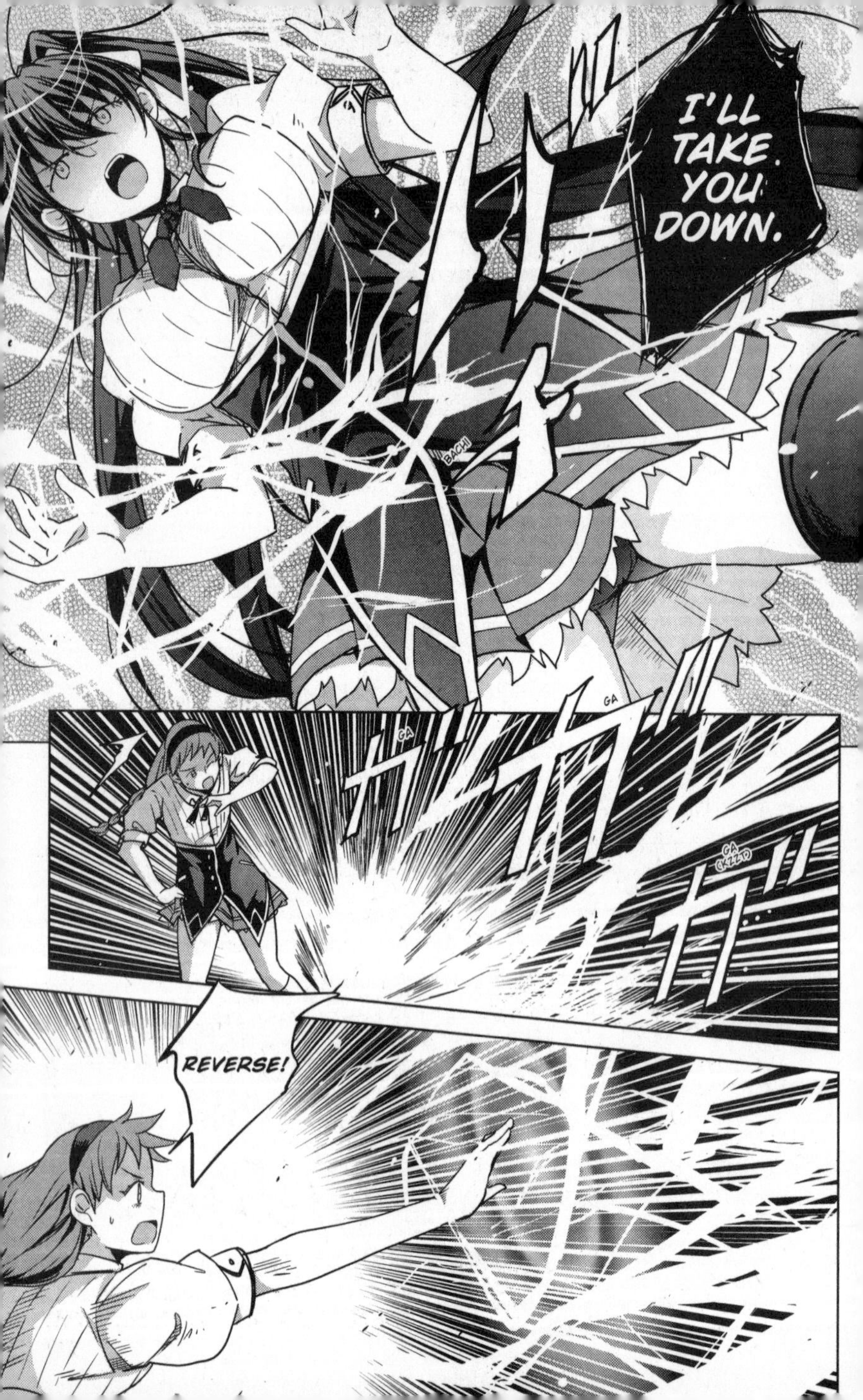

I'LL TAKE YOU DOWN.
BACHI
GA
GA
GA (KZZT)
REVERSE!

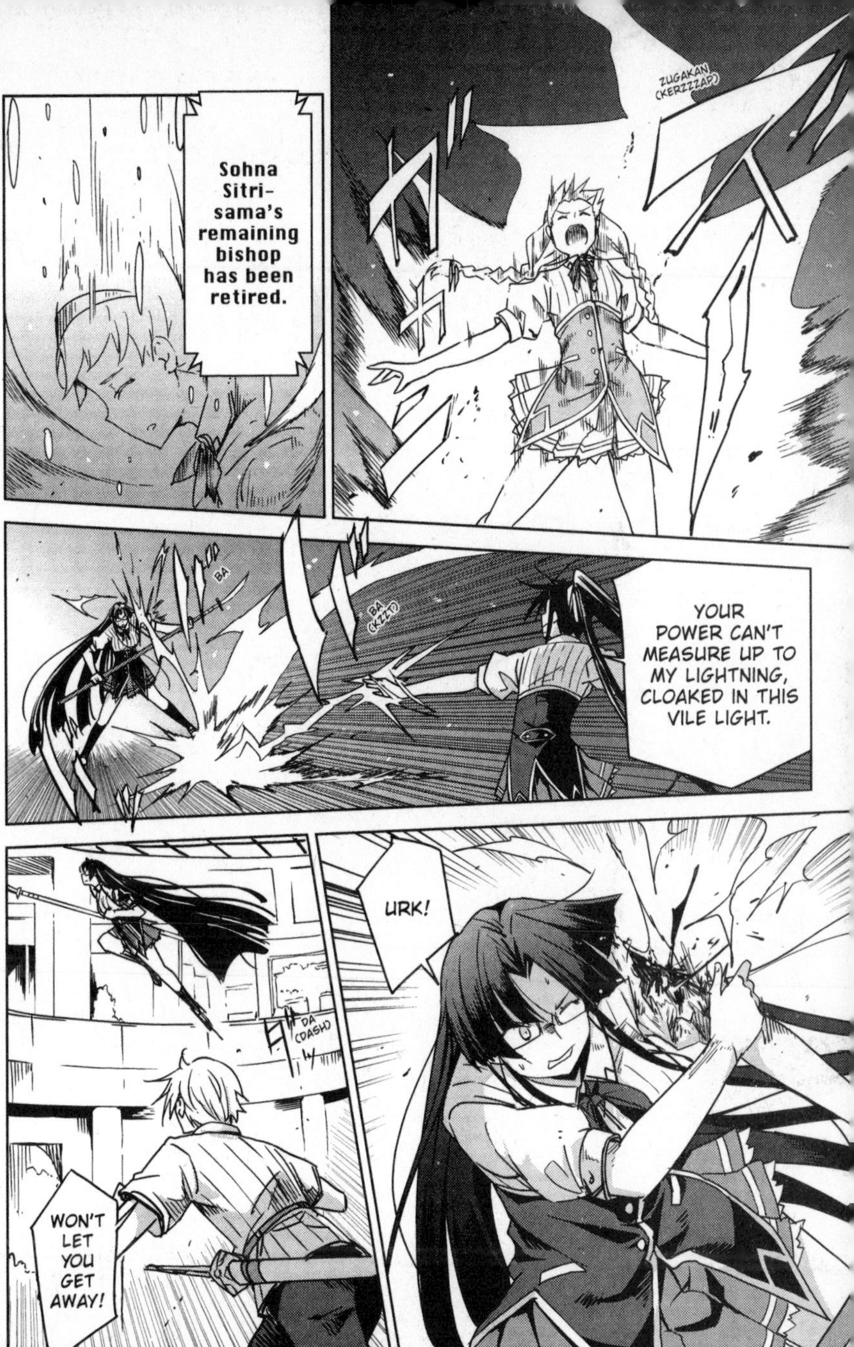

ZUGAKAN (KERZZZAP)
Sohna Sitri-sama's remaining bishop has been retired.
YOUR POWER CAN'T MEASURE UP TO MY LIGHTNING, CLOAKED IN THIS VILE LIGHT.
BA (KZZT)
BA
URK!
DA (DASH)
WON'T LET YOU GET AWAY!

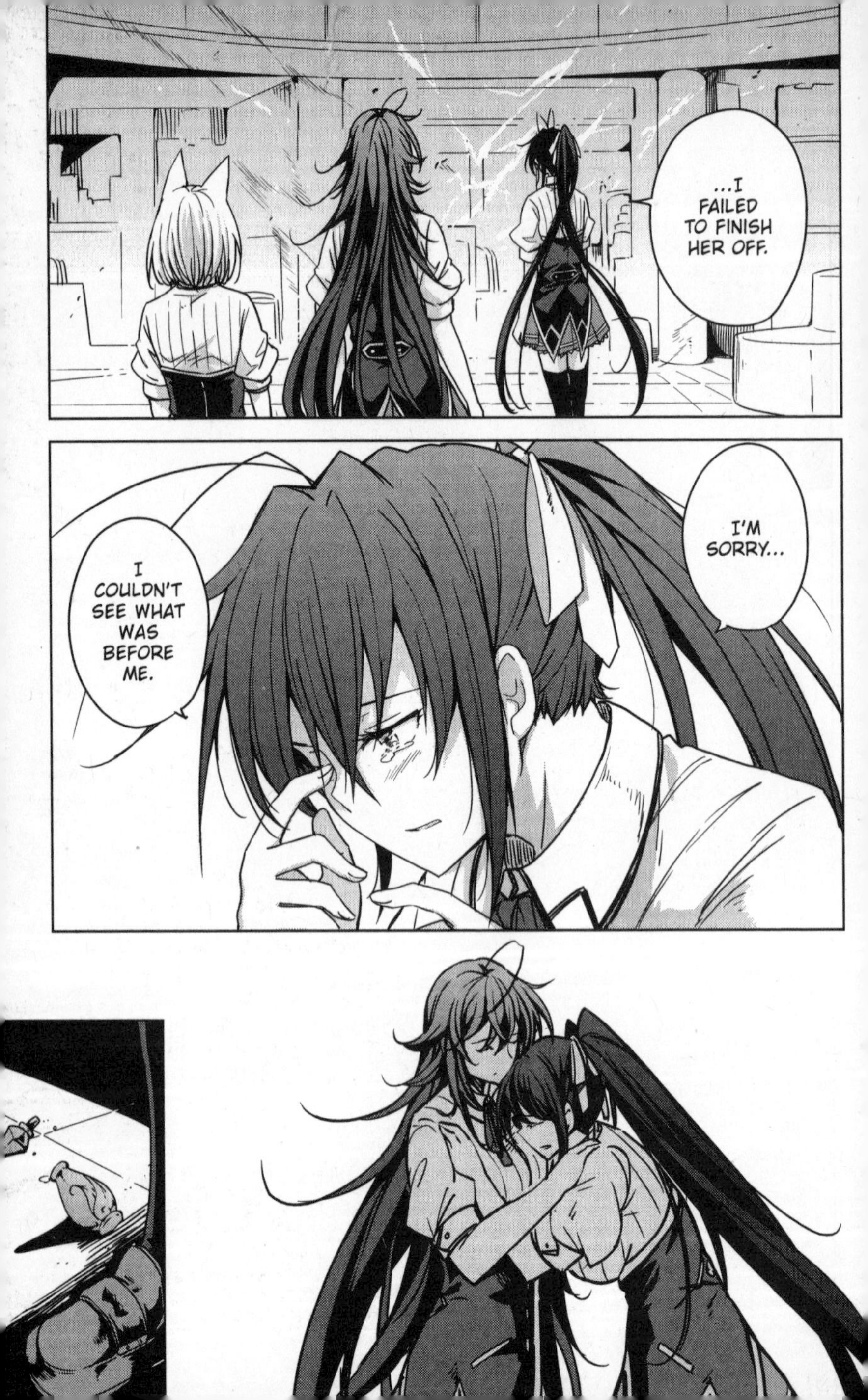
...I FAILED TO FINISH HER OFF.
I'M SORRY...
I COULDN'T SEE WHAT WAS BEFORE ME.

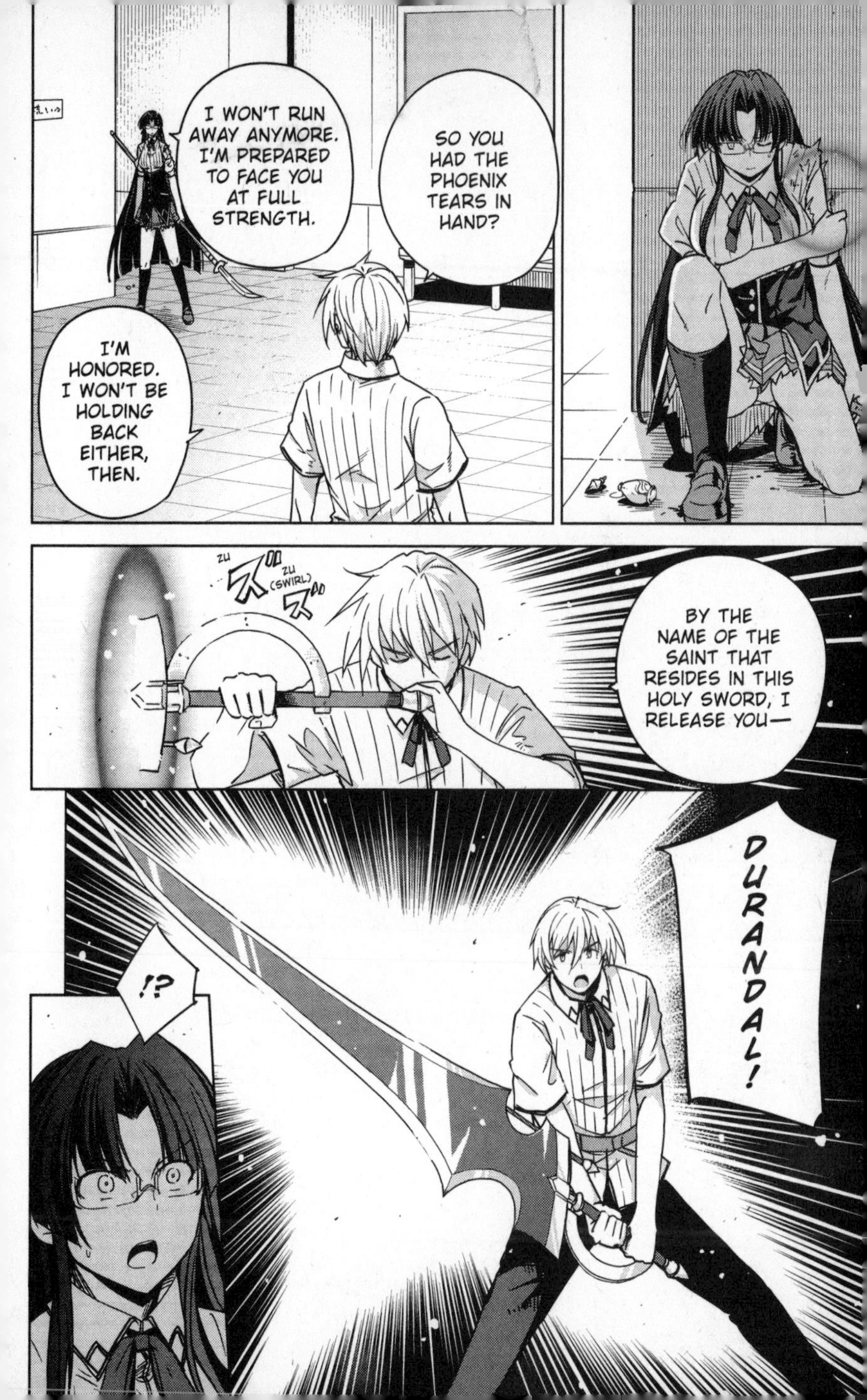
SO YOU HAD THE PHOENIX TEARS IN HAND?
I WON'T RUN AWAY ANYMORE. I'M PREPARED TO FACE YOU AT FULL STRENGTH.
I'M HONORED. I WON'T BE HOLDING BACK EITHER, THEN.
BY THE NAME OF THE SAINT THAT RESIDES IN THIS HOLY SWORD, I RELEASE YOU—
ZU ZU (SWIRL)
DURANDAL!
!?

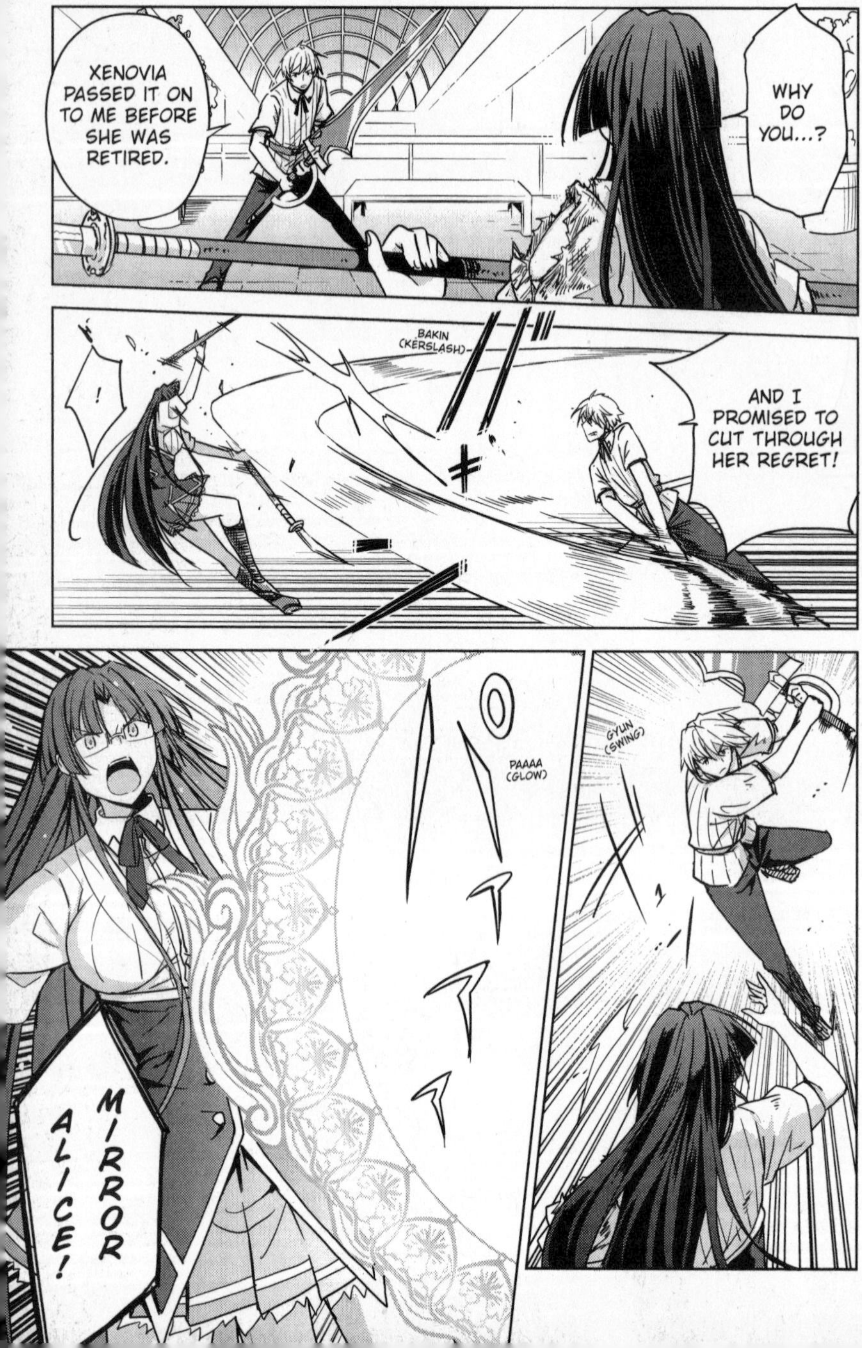
WHY DO YOU...?
XENOVIA PASSED IT ON TO ME BEFORE SHE WAS RETIRED.
AND I PROMISED TO CUT THROUGH HER REGRET!
BAKIN (KERSLASH)
!
GYUN (SWING)
PAAAA (GLOW)
MIRROR ALICE!

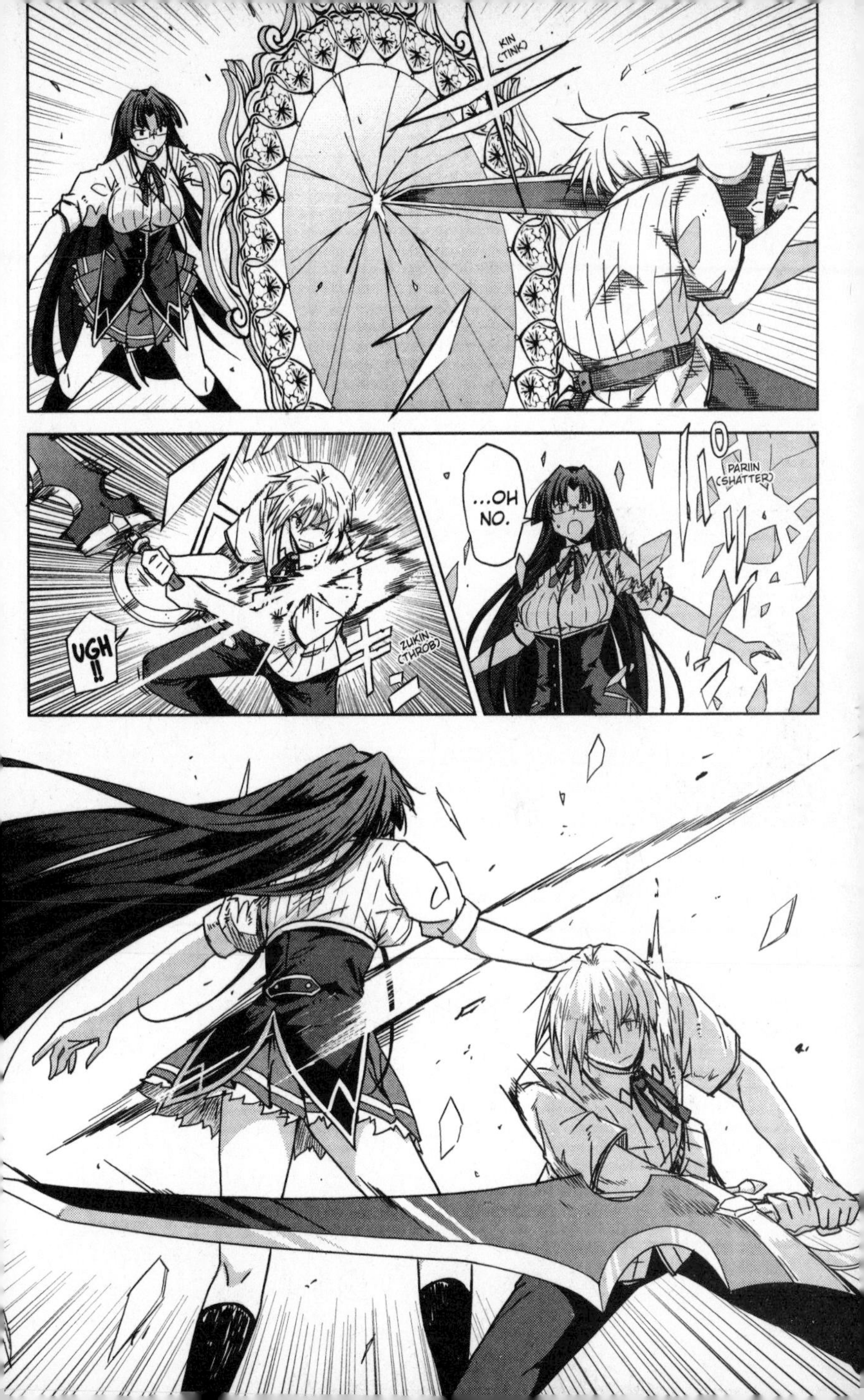
KIN
(TINK)
PARIIN
(SHATTER)
...OH NO.
UGH!!
ZUKIN
(THROB)

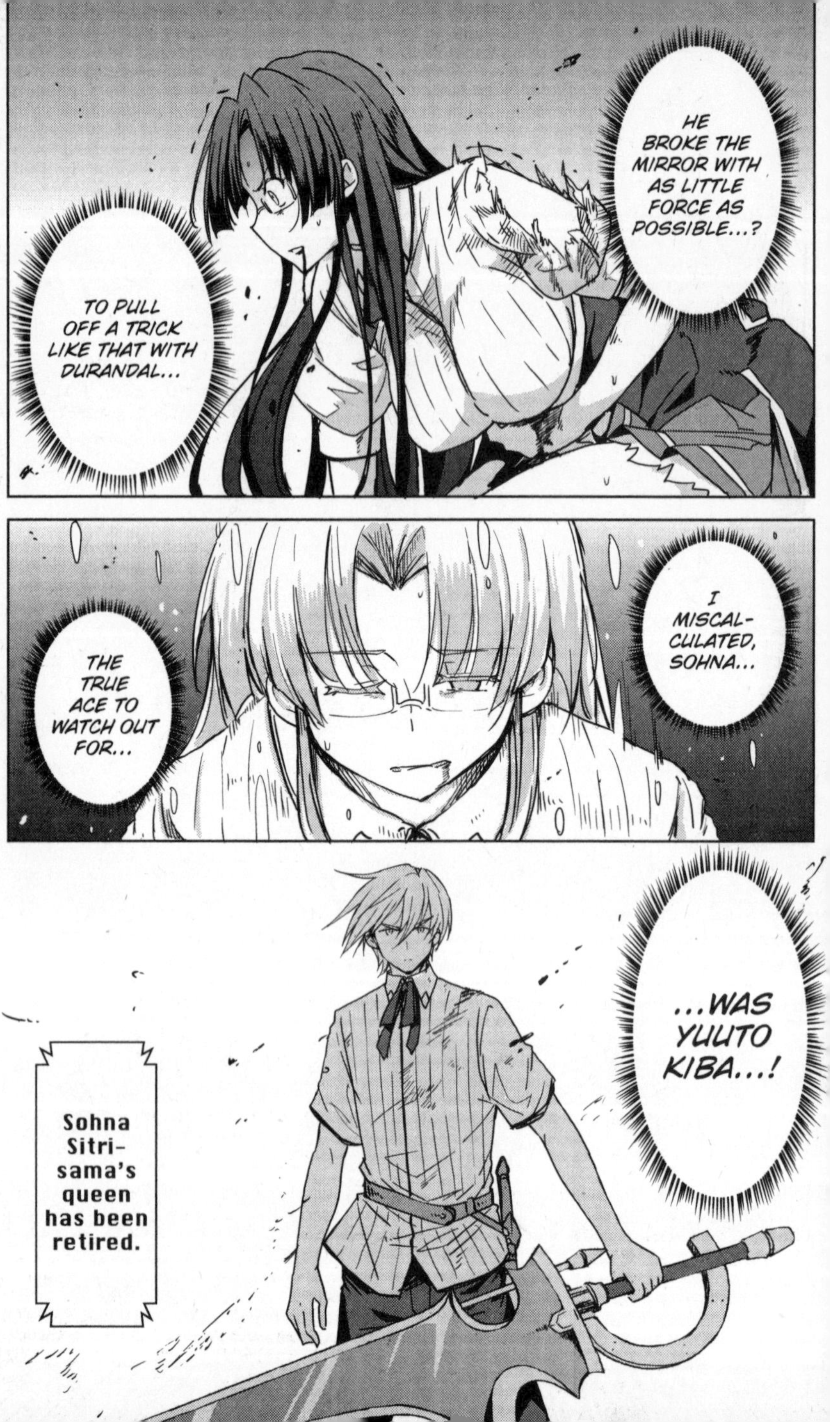
HE BROKE THE MIRROR WITH AS LITTLE FORCE AS POSSIBLE...?
TO PULL OFF A TRICK LIKE THAT WITH DURANDAL...
I MISCAL-CULATED, SOHNA...
THE TRUE ACE TO WATCH OUT FOR...
...WAS YUUTO KIBA...!
Sohna Sitri-sama's queen has been retired.

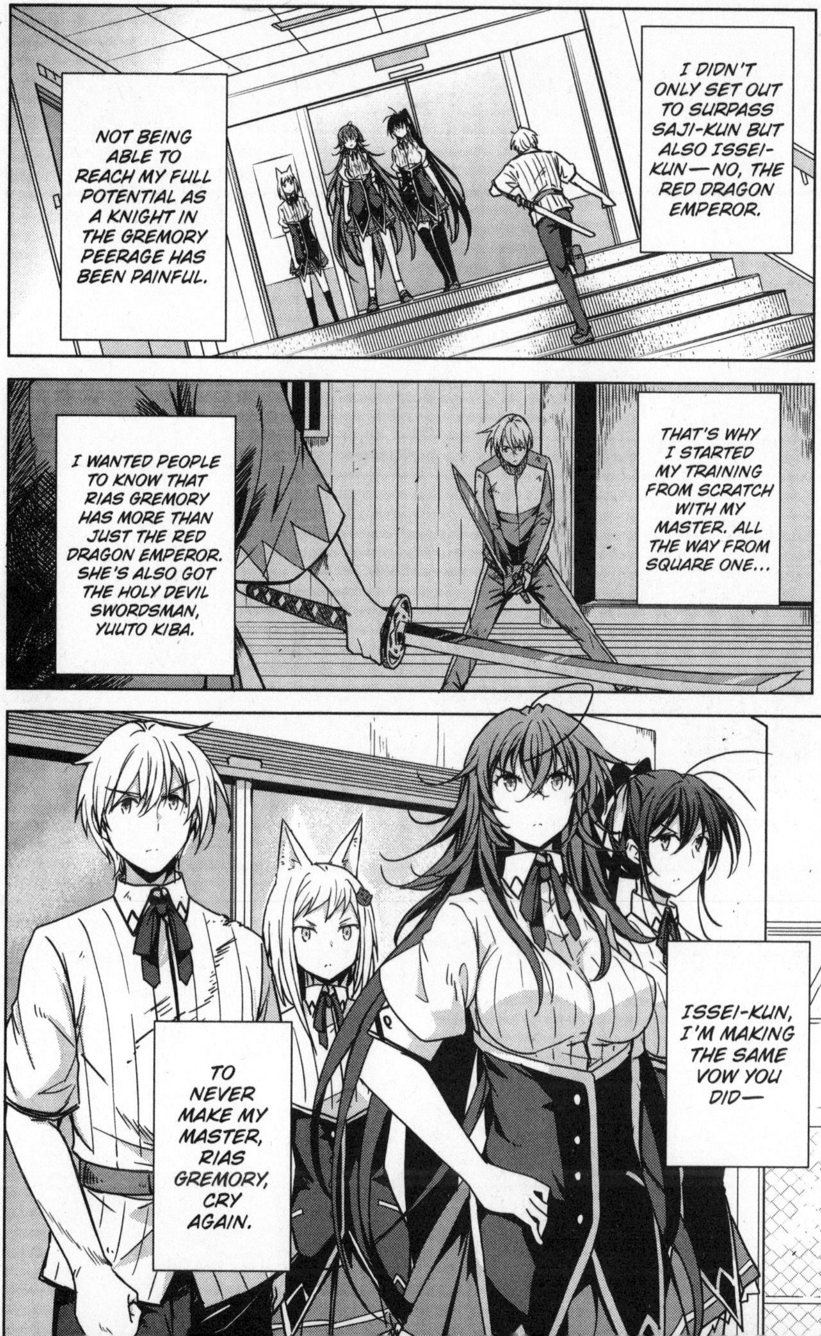
I DIDN'T ONLY SET OUT TO SURPASS SAJI-KUN BUT ALSO ISSEI-KUN—NO, THE RED DRAGON EMPEROR.
NOT BEING ABLE TO REACH MY FULL POTENTIAL AS A KNIGHT IN THE GREMORY PEERAGE HAS BEEN PAINFUL.
THAT'S WHY I STARTED MY TRAINING FROM SCRATCH WITH MY MASTER. ALL THE WAY FROM SQUARE ONE...
I WANTED PEOPLE TO KNOW THAT RIAS GREMORY HAS MORE THAN JUST THE RED DRAGON EMPEROR. SHE'S ALSO GOT THE HOLY DEVIL SWORDSMAN, YUUTO KIBA.
ISSEI-KUN, I'M MAKING THE SAME VOW YOU DID—
TO NEVER MAKE MY MASTER, RIAS GREMORY, CRY AGAIN.

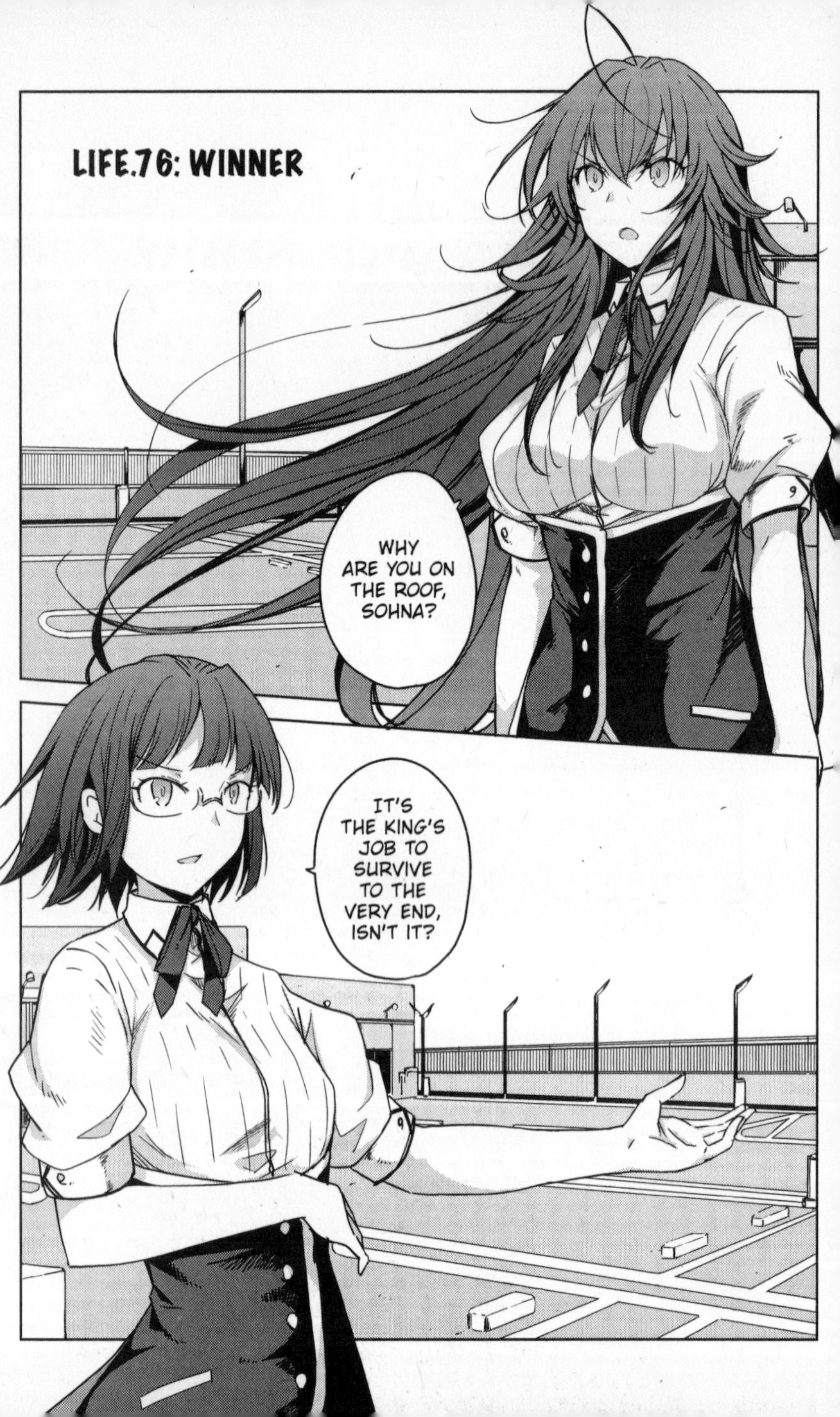
LIFE.76: WINNER
WHY ARE YOU ON THE ROOF, SOHNA?
IT'S THE KING'S JOB TO SURVIVE TO THE VERY END, ISN'T IT?

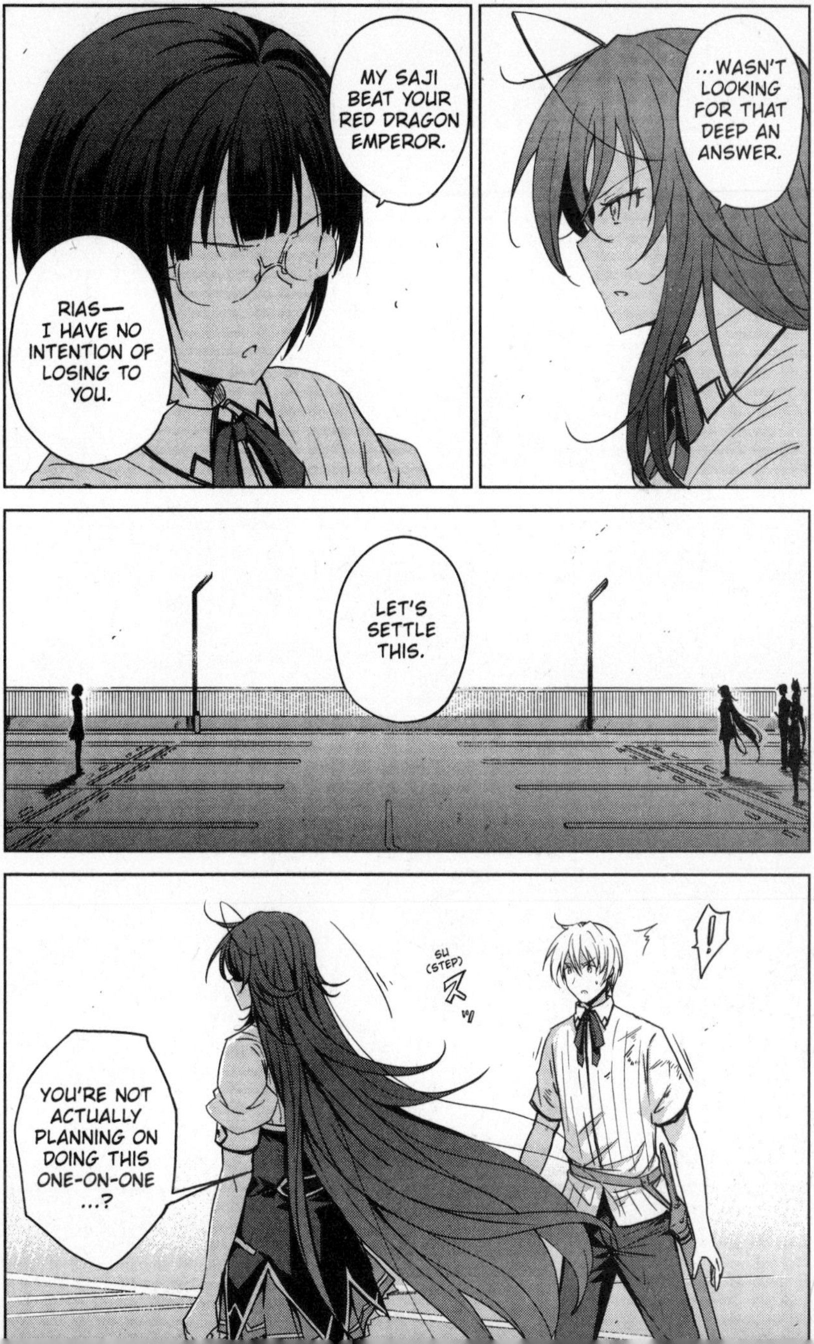
...WASN'T LOOKING FOR THAT DEEP AN ANSWER.
MY SAJI BEAT YOUR RED DRAGON EMPEROR.
RIAS— I HAVE NO INTENTION OF LOSING TO YOU.
LET'S SETTLE THIS.
!
SU (STEP)
ス
ッ
YOU'RE NOT ACTUALLY PLANNING ON DOING THIS ONE-ON-ONE ...?

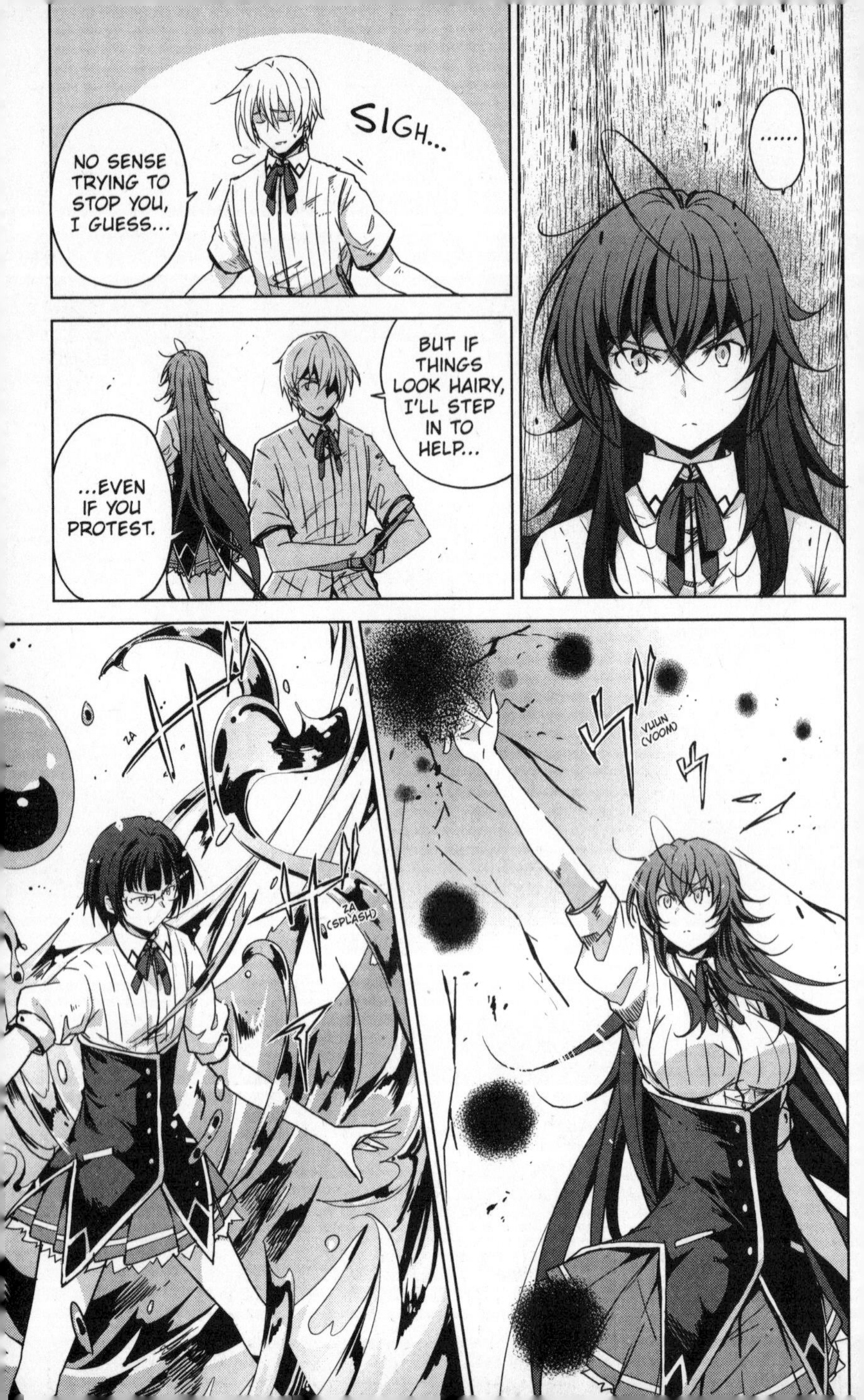
......
SIGH...
NO SENSE TRYING TO STOP YOU, I GUESS...
BUT IF THINGS LOOK HAIRY, I'LL STEP IN TO HELP...
...EVEN IF YOU PROTEST.
VUUN (VOOM)
ZA
ZA (SPLASH)

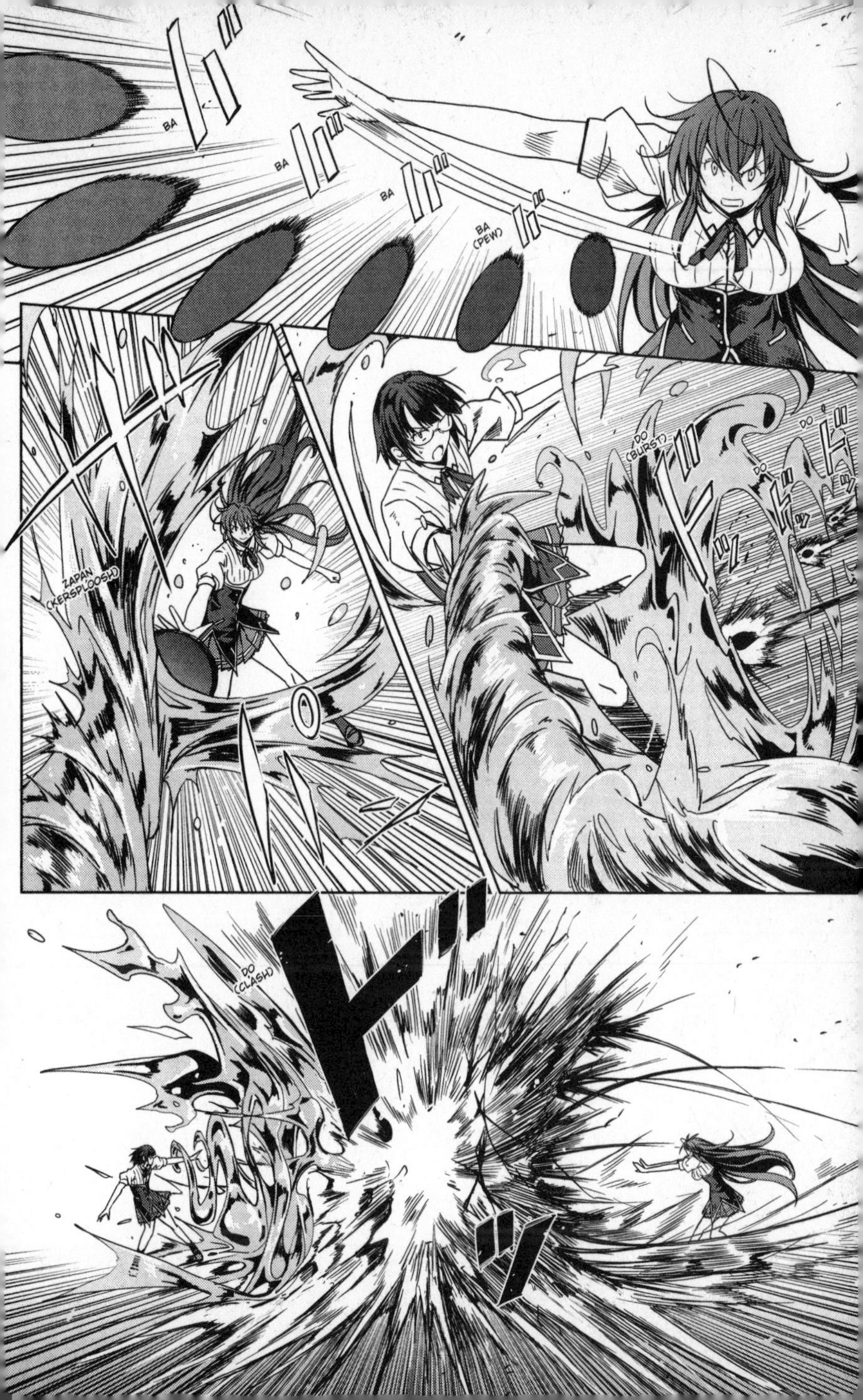

BA (PEW)
BA
BA
BA
DO
DO
DO (BURST)
ZAPAN (KERSPLOOSH)
DO (CLASH)

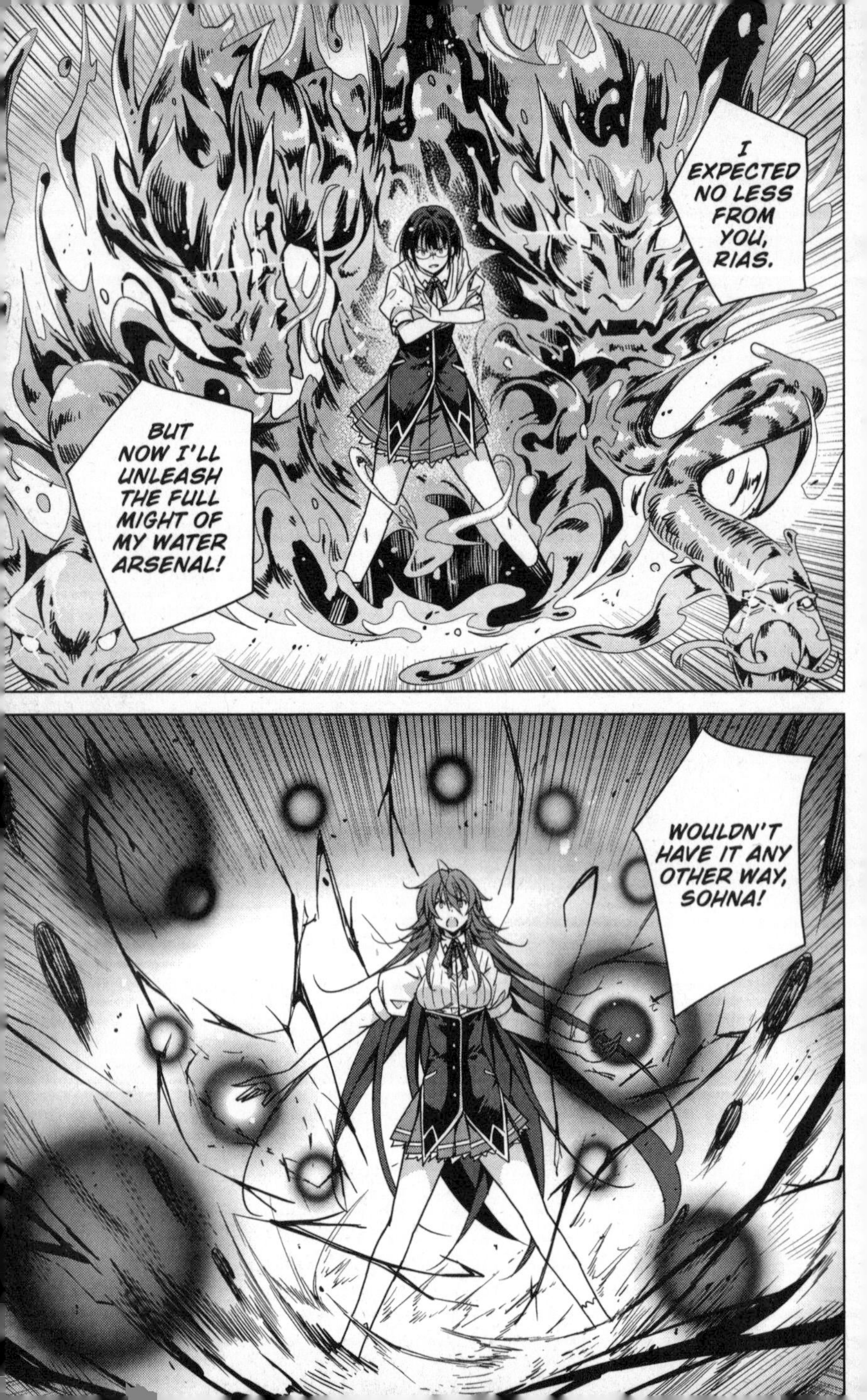
I EXPECTED NO LESS FROM YOU, RIAS.
BUT NOW I'LL UNLEASH THE FULL MIGHT OF MY WATER ARSENAL!
WOULDN'T HAVE IT ANY OTHER WAY, SOHNA!

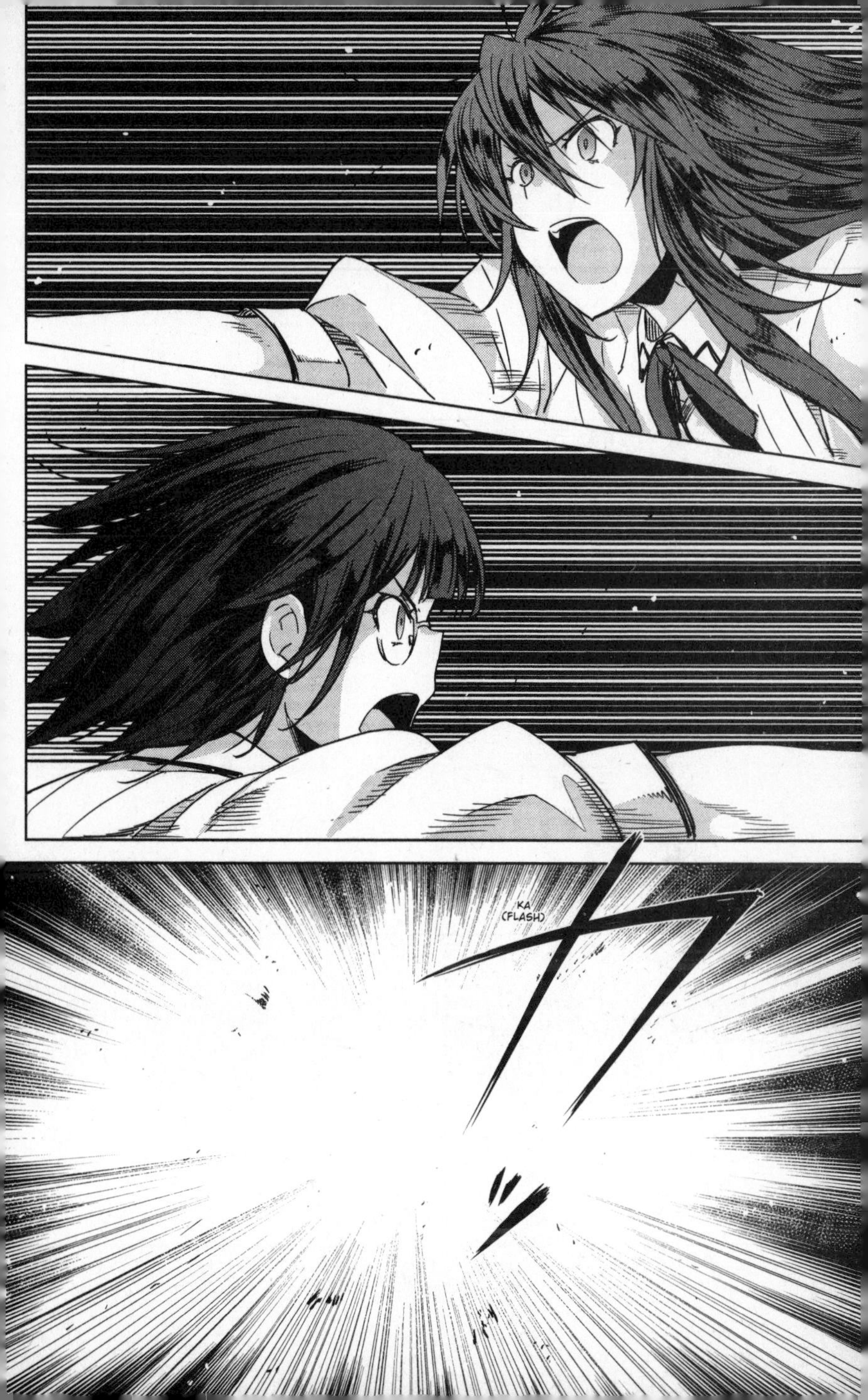
KA
(FLASH)

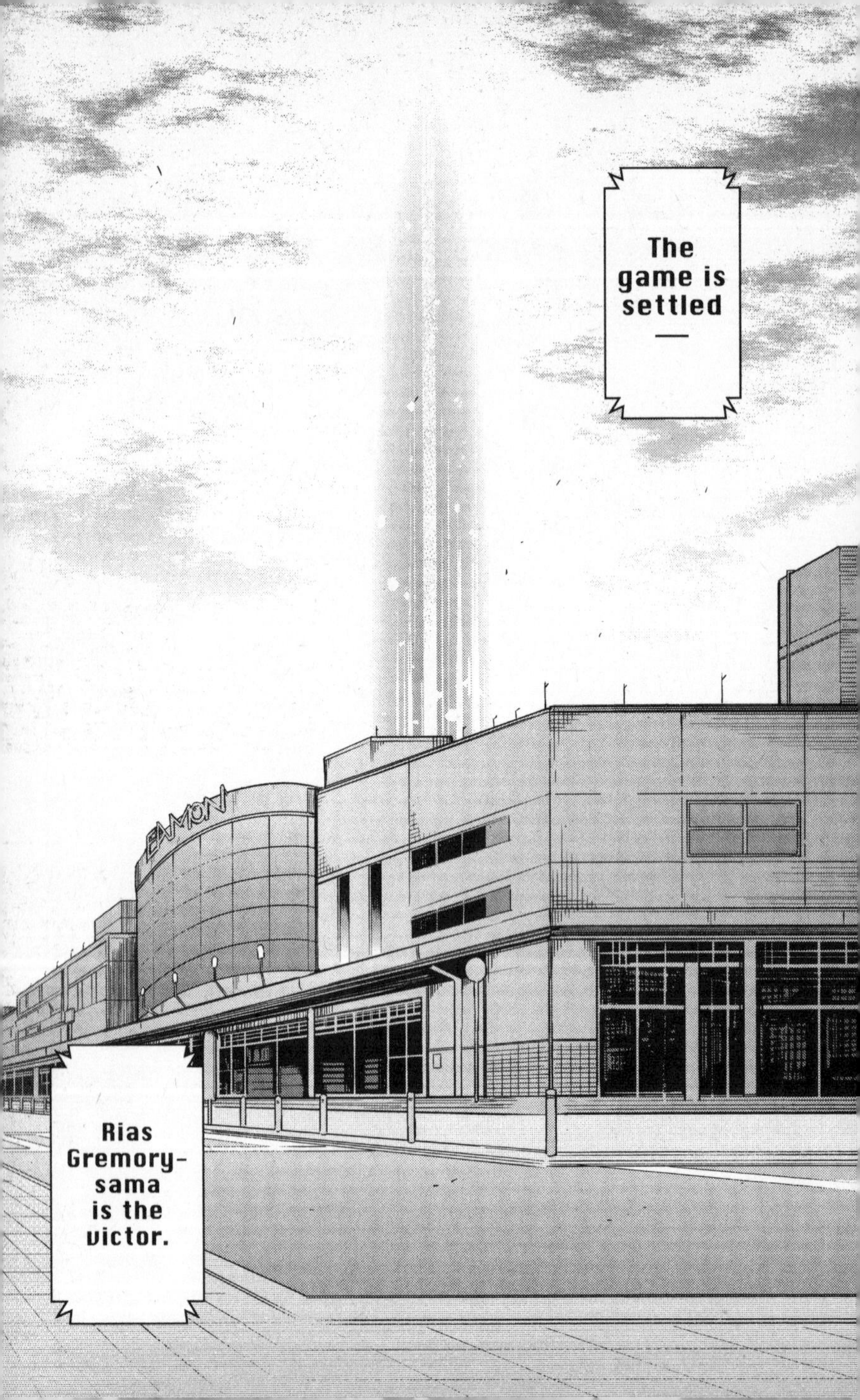
The game is settled —
Rias Gremory-sama is the victor.

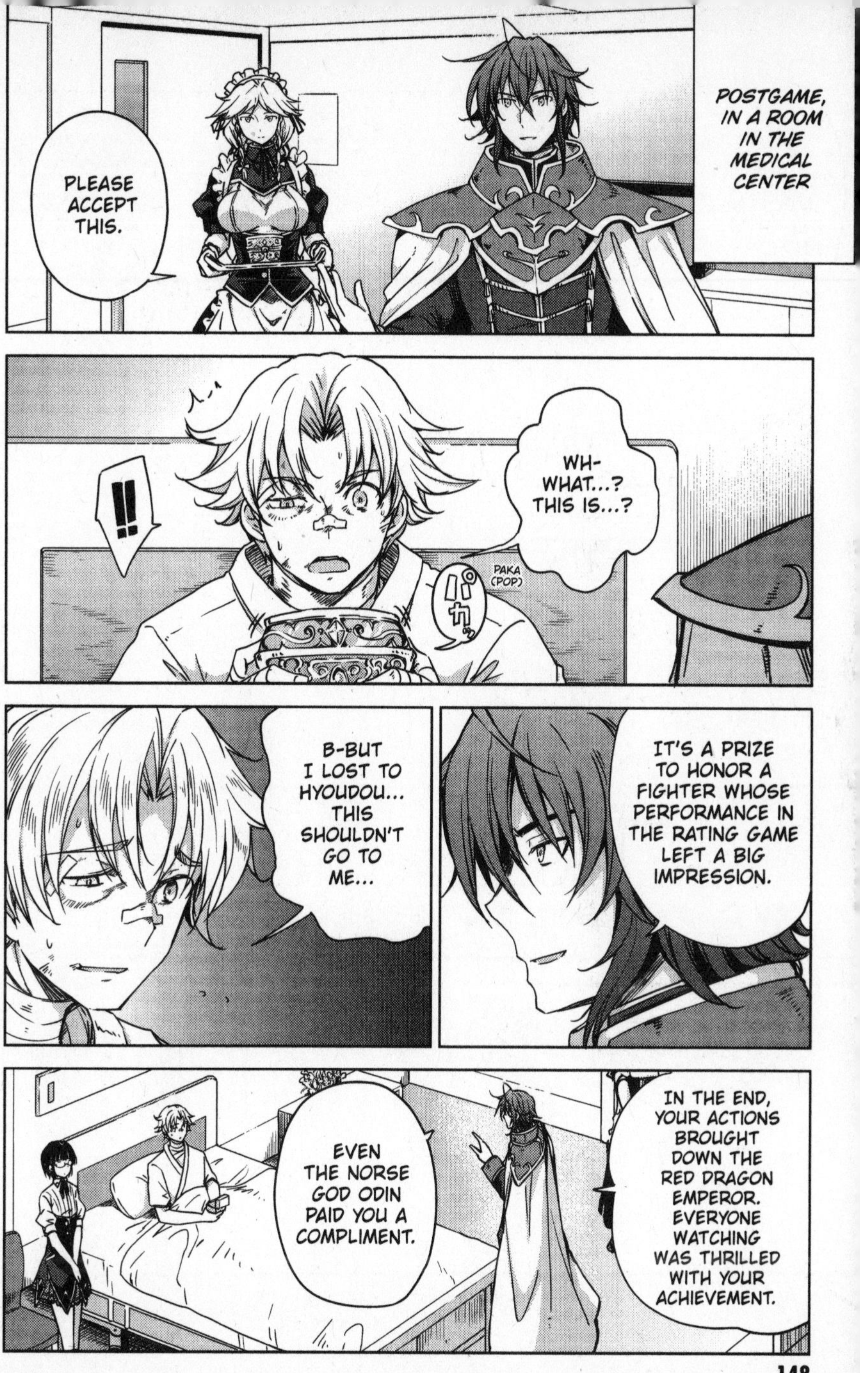
POSTGAME, IN A ROOM IN THE MEDICAL CENTER
PLEASE ACCEPT THIS.
WH- WHAT...? THIS IS...?
PAKA (POP)
パカッ
!!
IT'S A PRIZE TO HONOR A FIGHTER WHOSE PERFORMANCE IN THE RATING GAME LEFT A BIG IMPRESSION.
B-BUT I LOST TO HYOUDOU... THIS SHOULDN'T GO TO ME...
IN THE END, YOUR ACTIONS BROUGHT DOWN THE RED DRAGON EMPEROR. EVERYONE WATCHING WAS THRILLED WITH YOUR ACHIEVEMENT.
EVEN THE NORSE GOD ODIN PAID YOU A COMPLIMENT.

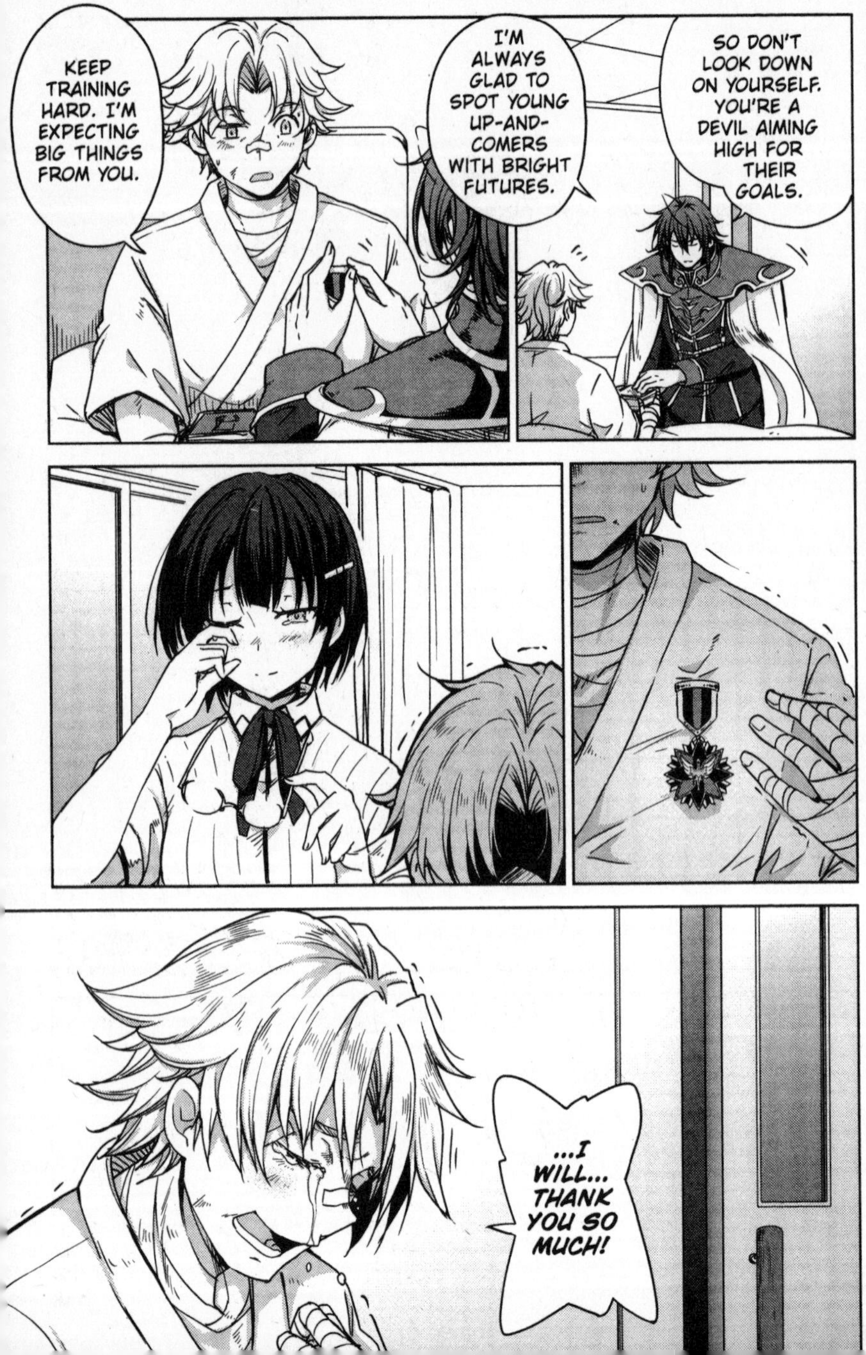
SO DON'T LOOK DOWN ON YOURSELF. YOU'RE A DEVIL AIMING HIGH FOR THEIR GOALS.
I'M ALWAYS GLAD TO SPOT YOUNG UP-AND-COMERS WITH BRIGHT FUTURES.
KEEP TRAINING HARD. I'M EXPECTING BIG THINGS FROM YOU.
...I WILL... THANK YOU SO MUCH!

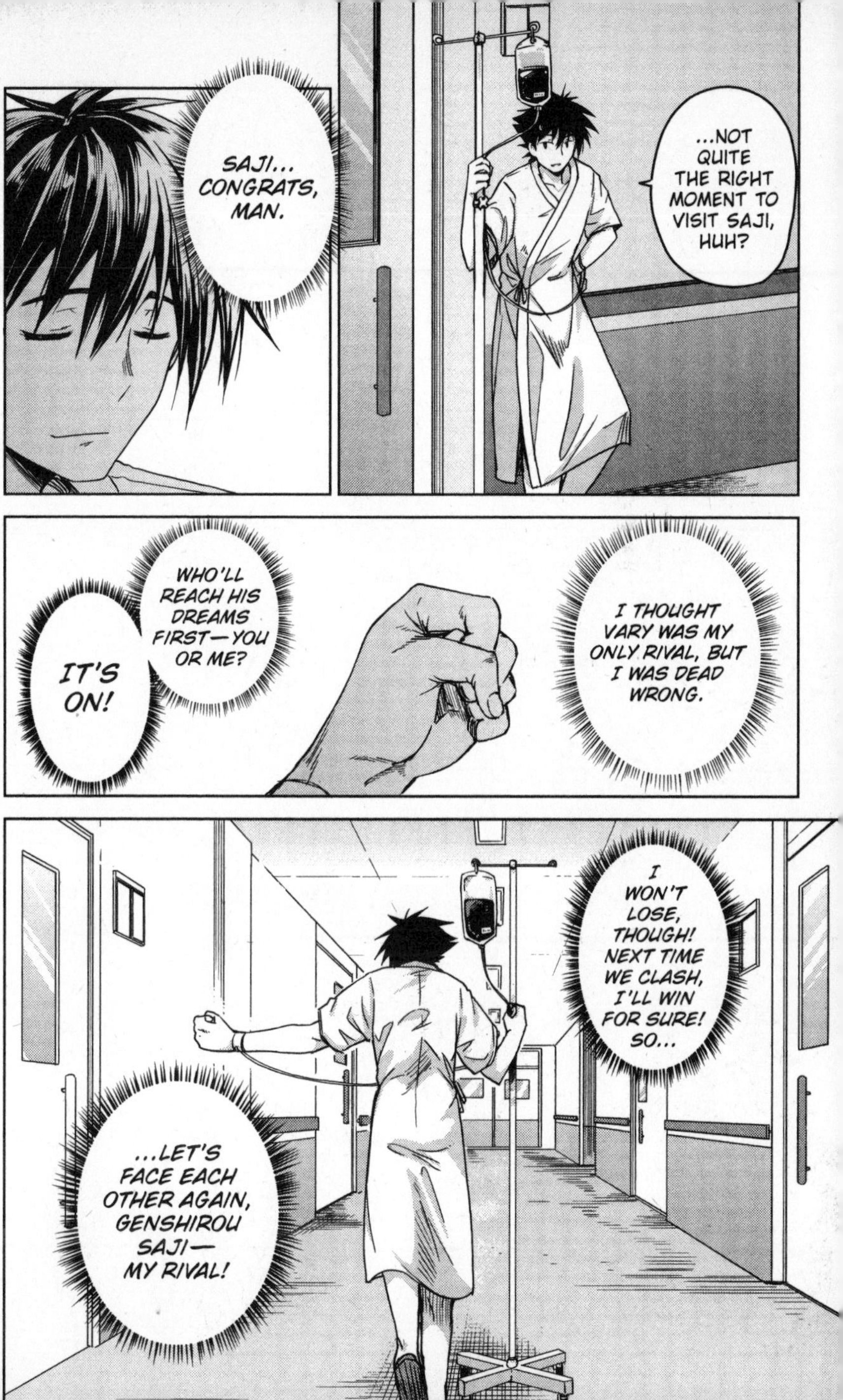
...NOT QUITE THE RIGHT MOMENT TO VISIT SAJI, HUH?
SAJI... CONGRATS, MAN.
I THOUGHT VARY WAS MY ONLY RIVAL, BUT I WAS DEAD WRONG.
WHO'LL REACH HIS DREAMS FIRST—YOU OR ME?
IT'S ON!
I WON'T LOSE, THOUGH! NEXT TIME WE CLASH, I'LL WIN FOR SURE! SO...
...LET'S FACE EACH OTHER AGAIN, GENSHIROU SAJI—MY RIVAL!

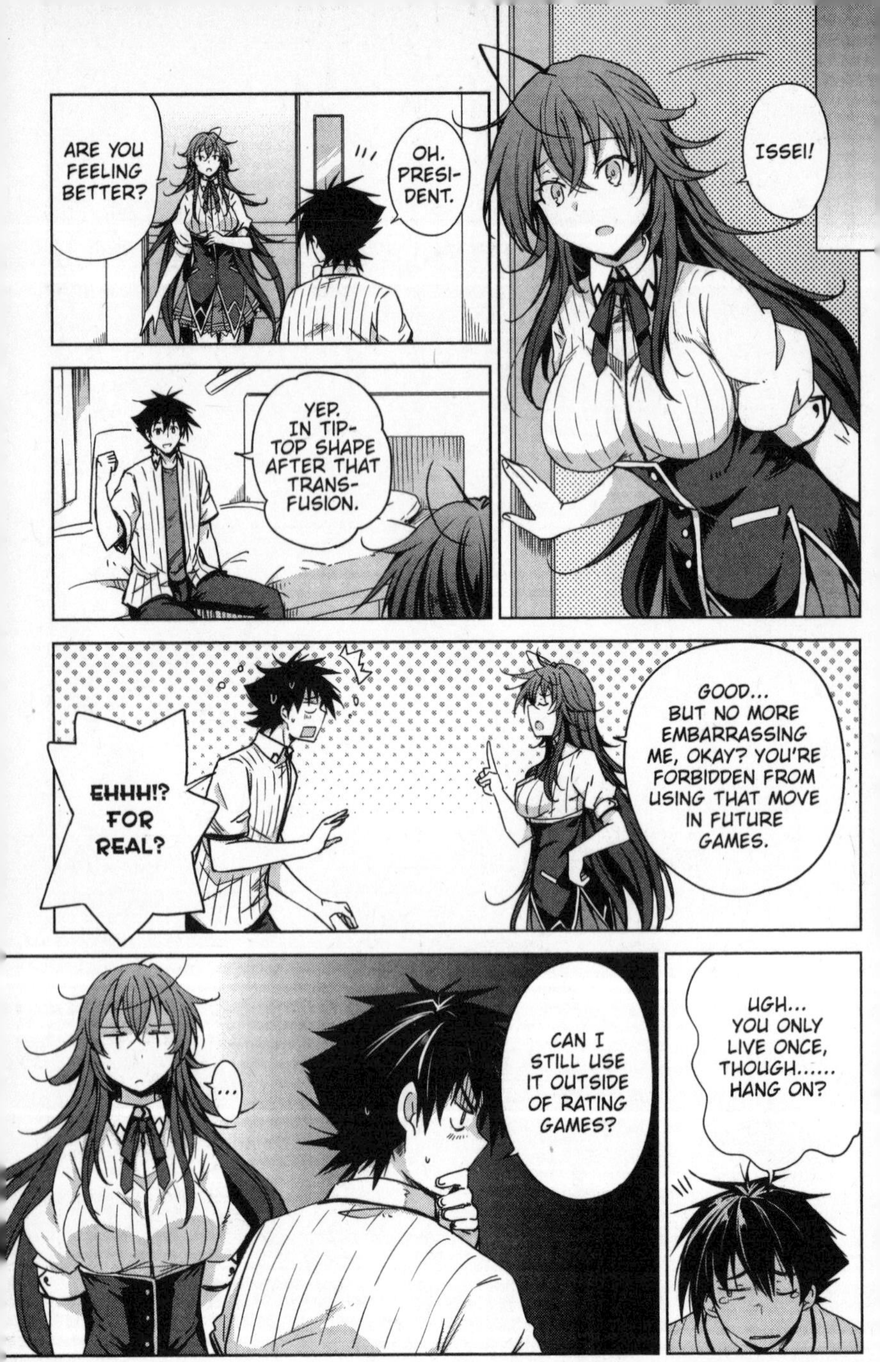
ISSEI!
OH. PRESIDENT.
ARE YOU FEELING BETTER?
YEP. IN TIP-TOP SHAPE AFTER THAT TRANSFUSION.
GOOD... BUT NO MORE EMBARRASSING ME, OKAY? YOU'RE FORBIDDEN FROM USING THAT MOVE IN FUTURE GAMES.
EHHH!? FOR REAL?
UGH... YOU ONLY LIVE ONCE, THOUGH...... HANG ON?
CAN I STILL USE IT OUTSIDE OF RATING GAMES?
...

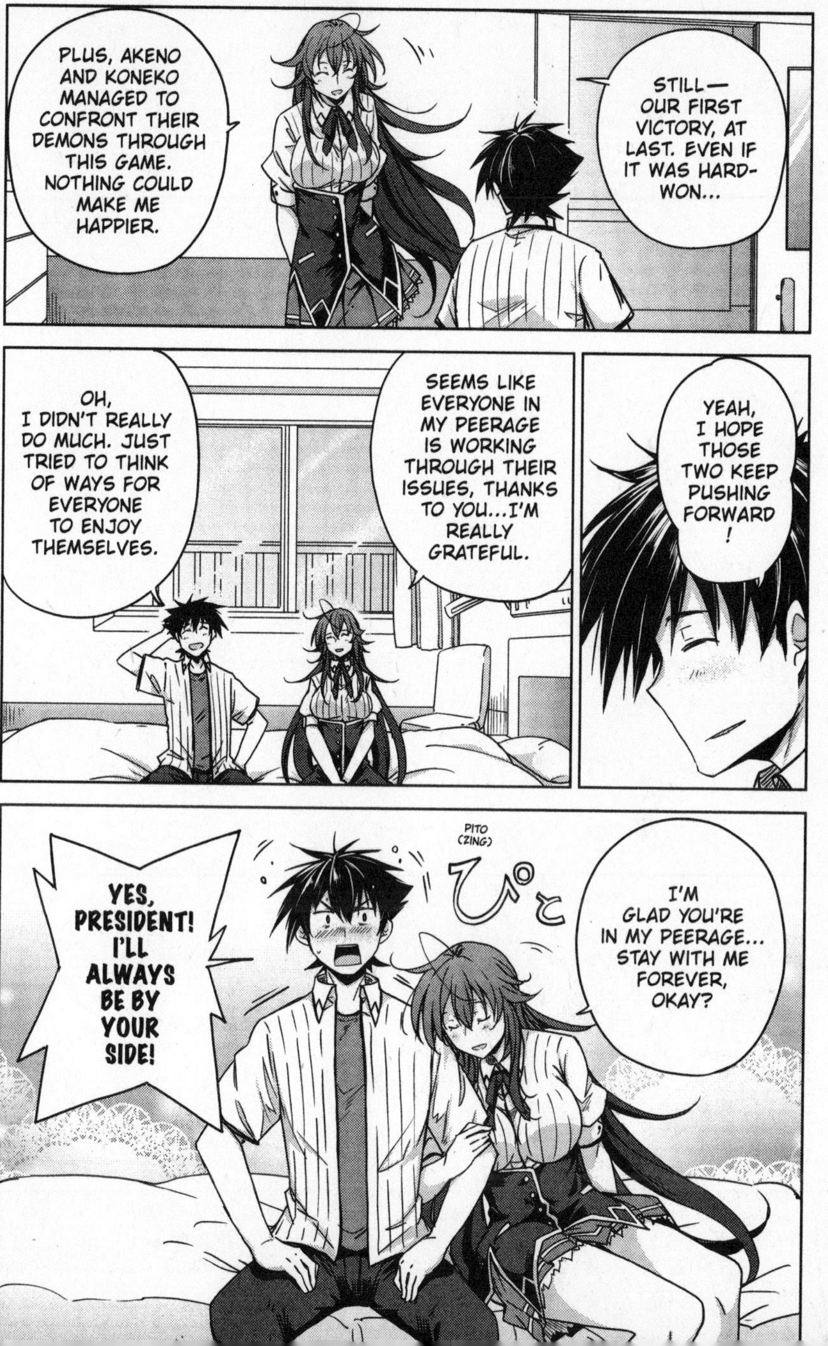
STILL— OUR FIRST VICTORY, AT LAST. EVEN IF IT WAS HARD-WON...
PLUS, AKENO AND KONEKO MANAGED TO CONFRONT THEIR DEMONS THROUGH THIS GAME. NOTHING COULD MAKE ME HAPPIER.
YEAH, I HOPE THOSE TWO KEEP PUSHING FORWARD!
SEEMS LIKE EVERYONE IN MY PEERAGE IS WORKING THROUGH THEIR ISSUES, THANKS TO YOU...I'M REALLY GRATEFUL.
OH, I DIDN'T REALLY DO MUCH. JUST TRIED TO THINK OF WAYS FOR EVERYONE TO ENJOY THEMSELVES.
I'M GLAD YOU'RE IN MY PEERAGE... STAY WITH ME FOREVER, OKAY?
ぴと
PITO (ZING)
YES, PRESIDENT! I'LL ALWAYS BE BY YOUR SIDE!

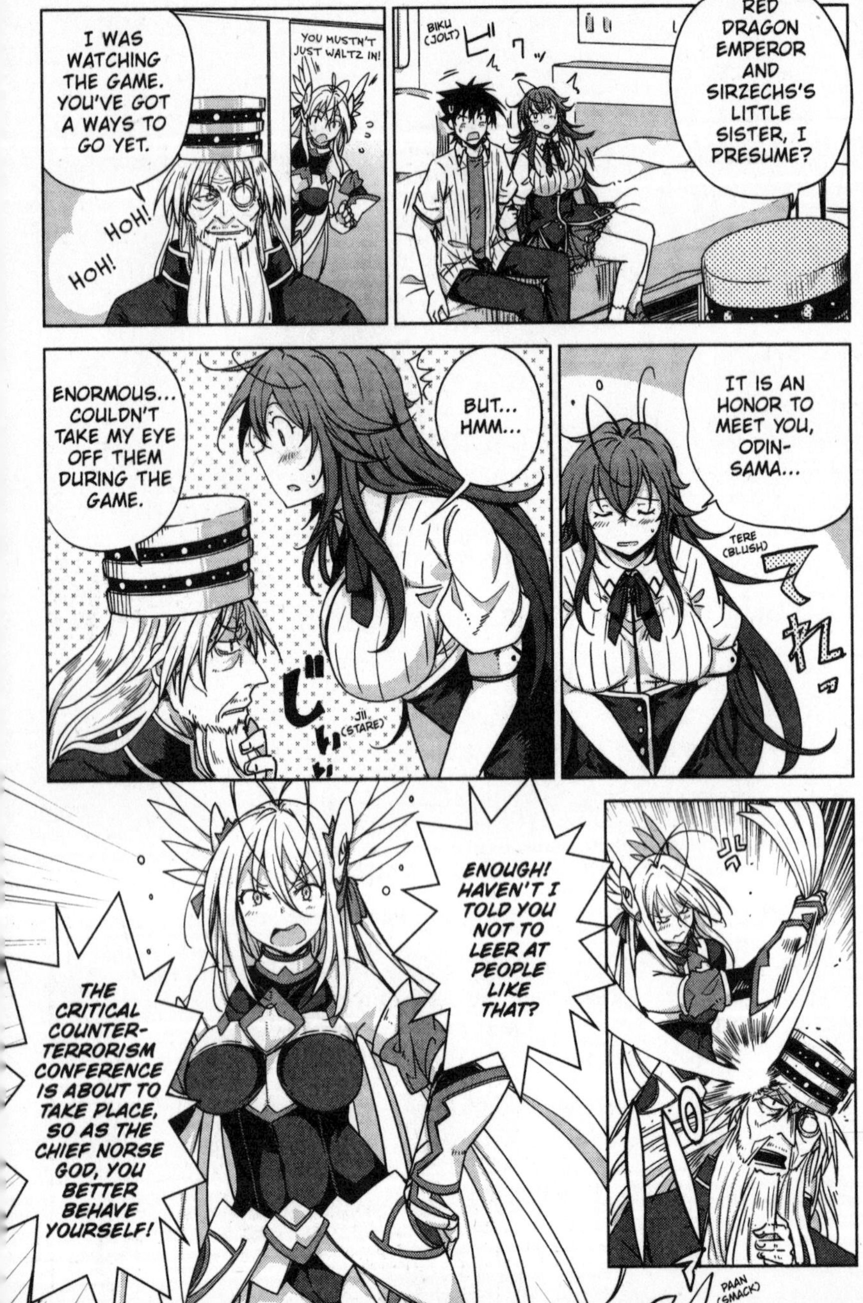
RED DRAGON EMPEROR AND SIRZECHS'S LITTLE SISTER, I PRESUME?
BIKU (JOLT)
YOU MUSTN'T JUST WALTZ IN!
I WAS WATCHING THE GAME. YOU'VE GOT A WAYS TO GO YET.
HOH! HOH!
IT IS AN HONOR TO MEET YOU, ODIN-SAMA...
TERE (BLUSH)
BUT... HMM...
ENORMOUS... COULDN'T TAKE MY EYE OFF THEM DURING THE GAME.
JII (STARE)
PAAN (SMACK)
ENOUGH! HAVEN'T I TOLD YOU NOT TO LEER AT PEOPLE LIKE THAT?
THE CRITICAL COUNTER-TERRORISM CONFERENCE IS ABOUT TO TAKE PLACE, SO AS THE CHIEF NORSE GOD, YOU BETTER BEHAVE YOURSELF!

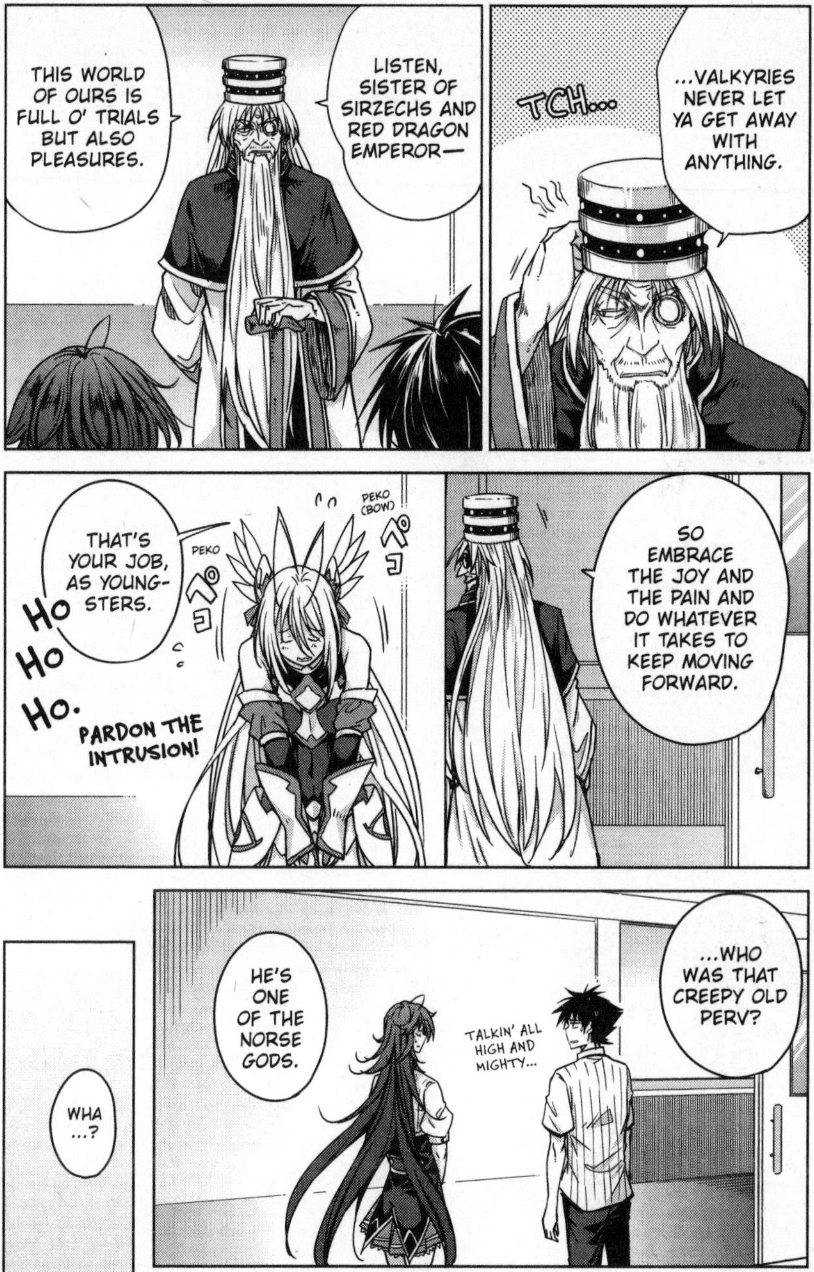
TCH...
...VALKYRIES NEVER LET YA GET AWAY WITH ANYTHING.
LISTEN, SISTER OF SIRZECHS AND RED DRAGON EMPEROR—
THIS WORLD OF OURS IS FULL O' TRIALS BUT ALSO PLEASURES.
SO EMBRACE THE JOY AND THE PAIN AND DO WHATEVER IT TAKES TO KEEP MOVING FORWARD.
PEKO (BOW)
ペコ
THAT'S YOUR JOB, AS YOUNG-STERS.
PEKO
ペコ
Ho Ho Ho.
PARDON THE INTRUSION!
...WHO WAS THAT CREEPY OLD PERV?
TALKIN' ALL HIGH AND MIGHTY...
HE'S ONE OF THE NORSE GODS.
WHA...?

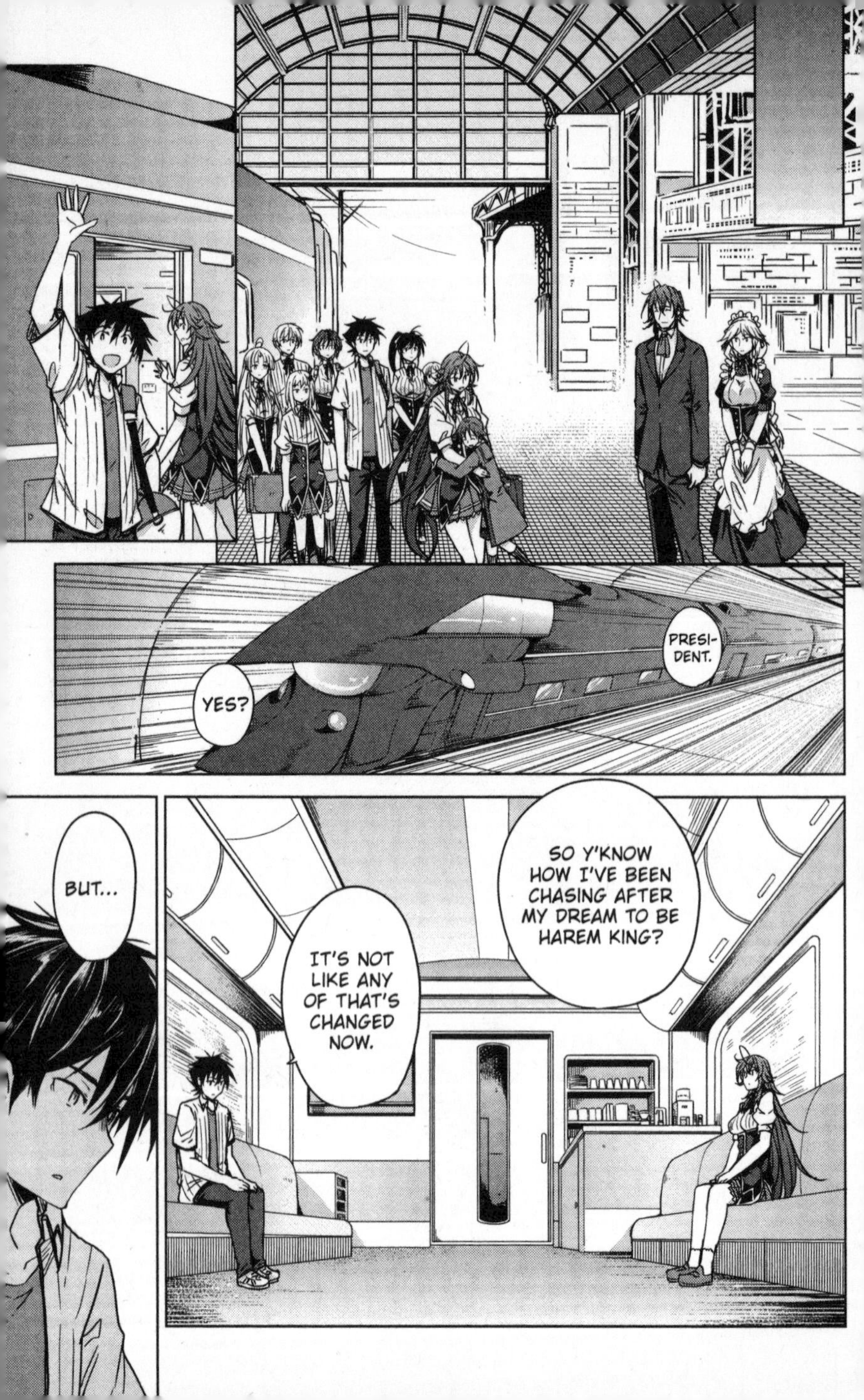
PRESI-DENT.
YES?
SO Y'KNOW HOW I'VE BEEN CHASING AFTER MY DREAM TO BE HAREM KING?
IT'S NOT LIKE ANY OF THAT'S CHANGED NOW.
BUT...

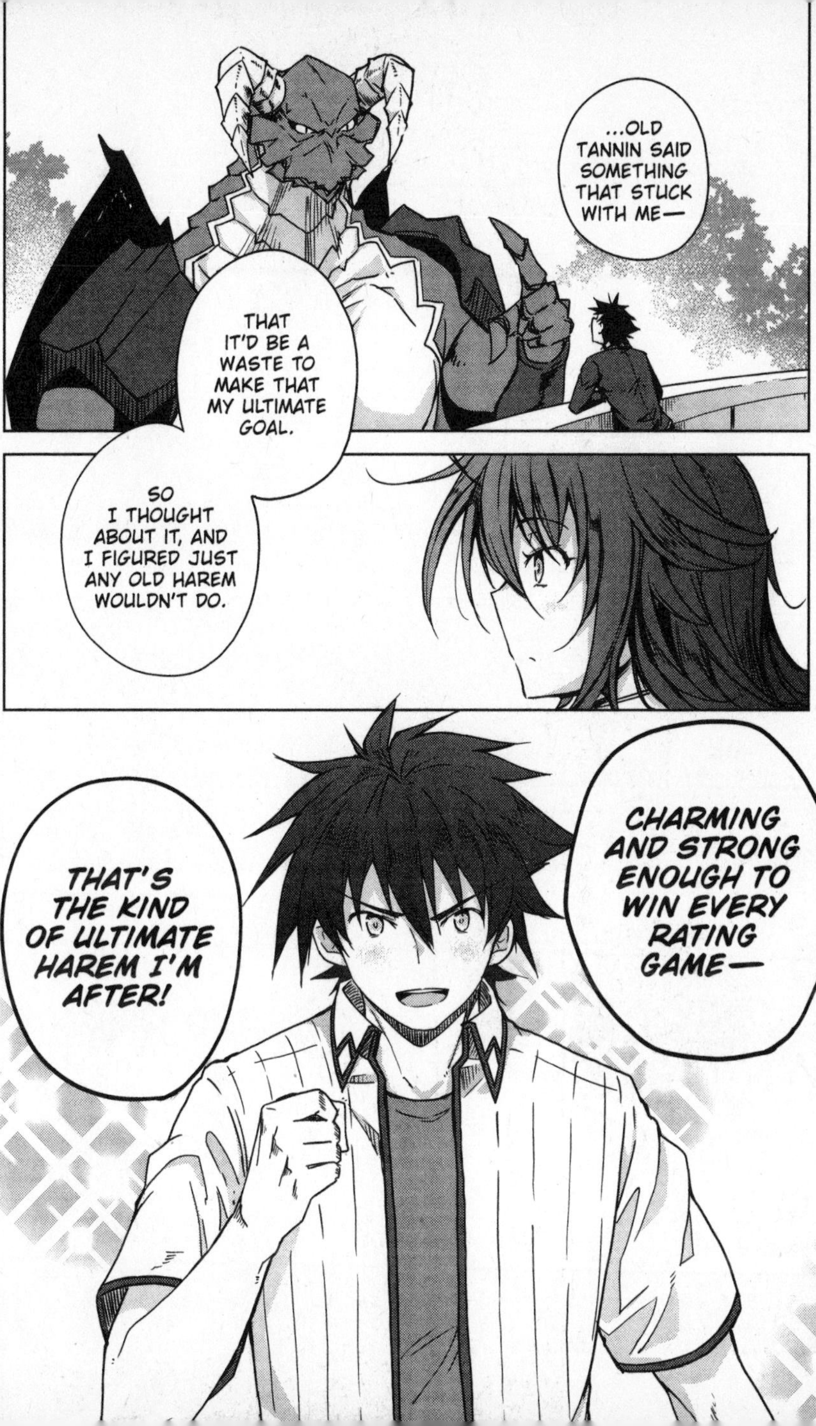
...OLD TANNIN SAID SOMETHING THAT STUCK WITH ME—
THAT IT'D BE A WASTE TO MAKE THAT MY ULTIMATE GOAL.
SO I THOUGHT ABOUT IT, AND I FIGURED JUST ANY OLD HAREM WOULDN'T DO.
CHARMING AND STRONG ENOUGH TO WIN EVERY RATING GAME—
THAT'S THE KIND OF ULTIMATE HAREM I'M AFTER!

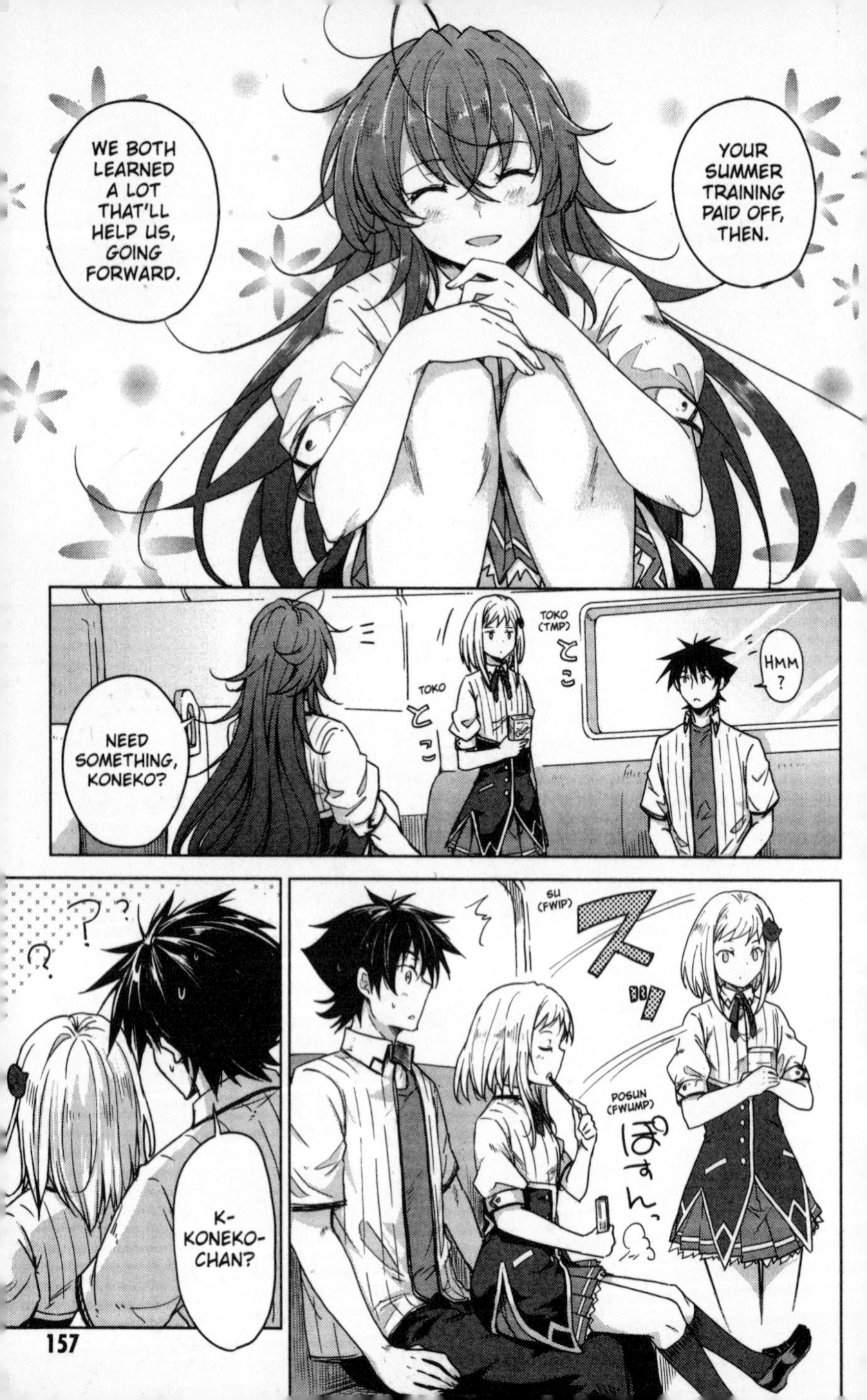
YOUR SUMMER TRAINING PAID OFF, THEN.
WE BOTH LEARNED A LOT THAT'LL HELP US, GOING FORWARD.
HMM ?
TOKO (TMP) とこ
TOKO とこ
NEED SOMETHING, KONEKO?
SU (FWIP) スッ
POSUN (FWUMP) ぽすん
K-KONEKO-CHAN?

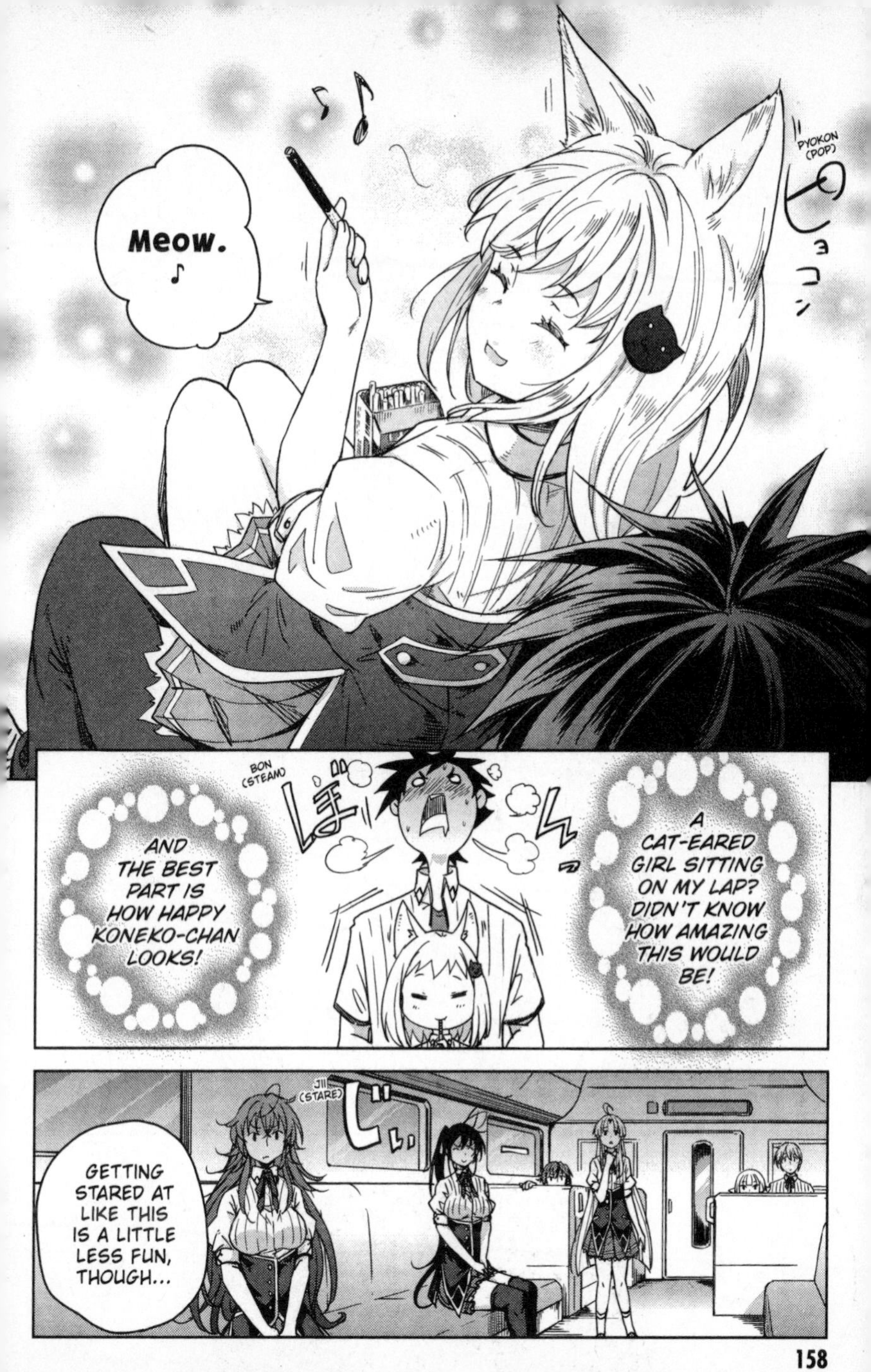
ピョコン
PYOKON (POP)
Meow. ♪
A CAT-EARED GIRL SITTING ON MY LAP? DIDN'T KNOW HOW AMAZING THIS WOULD BE!
ぼん
BON (STEAM)
AND THE BEST PART IS HOW HAPPY KONEKO-CHAN LOOKS!
JII (STARE)
GETTING STARED AT LIKE THIS IS A LITTLE LESS FUN, THOUGH...

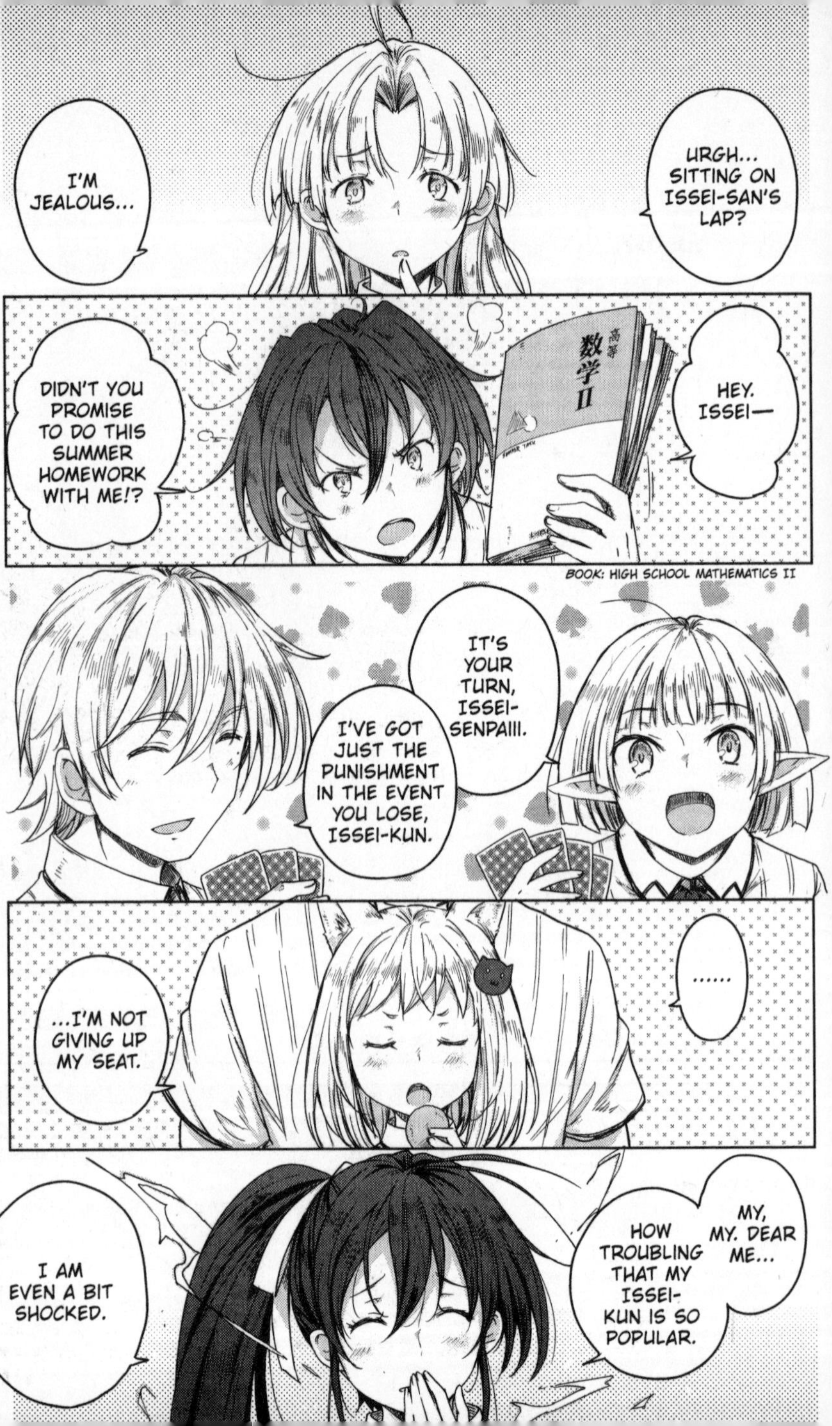
URGH... SITTING ON ISSEI-SAN'S LAP?
I'M JEALOUS...
HEY. ISSEI—
DIDN'T YOU PROMISE TO DO THIS SUMMER HOMEWORK WITH ME!?
高等 数学 II
BOOK: HIGH SCHOOL MATHEMATICS II
IT'S YOUR TURN, ISSEI-SENPAIII.
I'VE GOT JUST THE PUNISHMENT IN THE EVENT YOU LOSE, ISSEI-KUN.
......
...I'M NOT GIVING UP MY SEAT.
MY, MY. DEAR ME...
HOW TROUBLING THAT MY ISSEI-KUN IS SO POPULAR.
I AM EVEN A BIT SHOCKED.

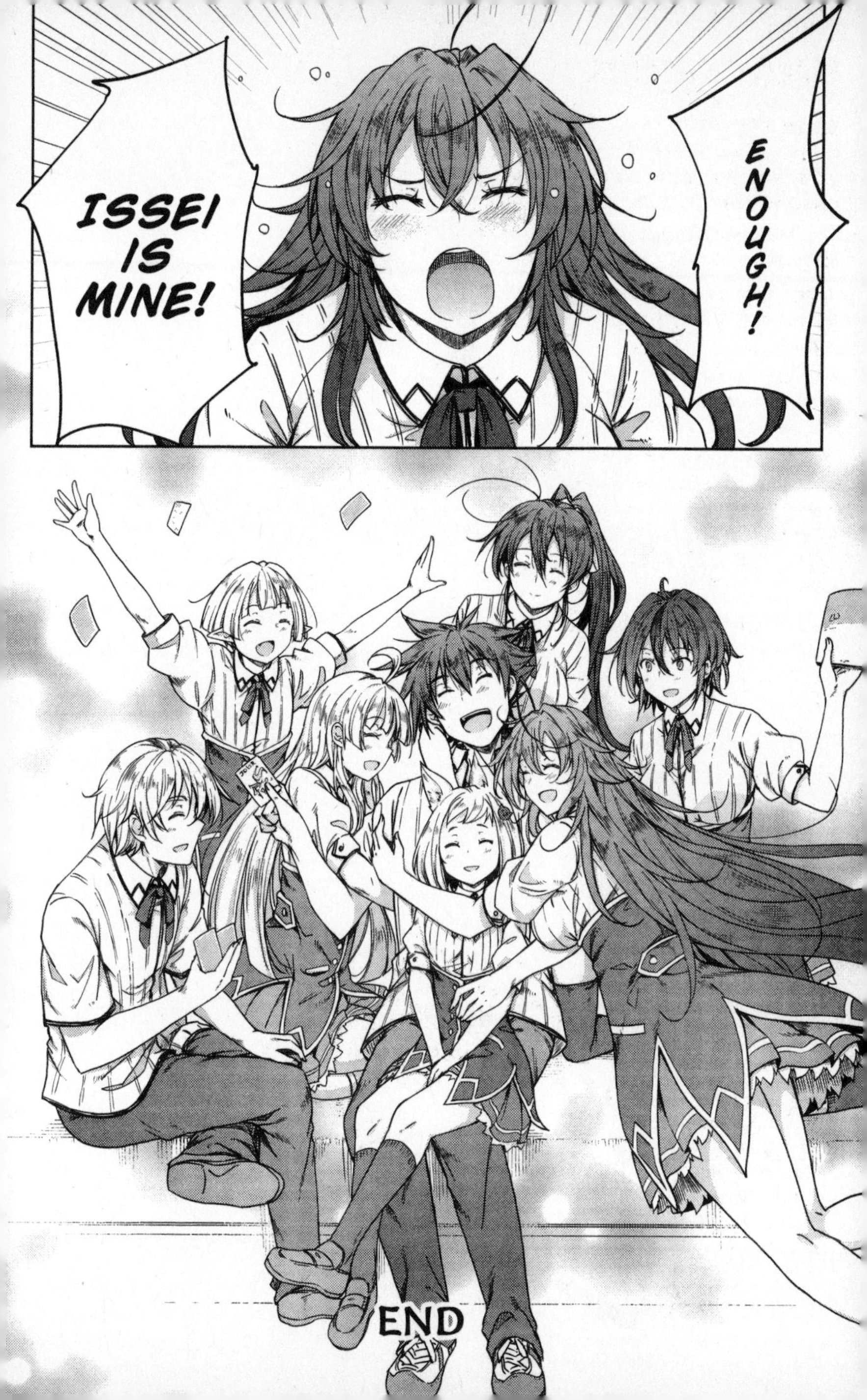
ENOUGH!
ISSEI IS MINE!
END

TRANSLATION NOTES

COMMON HONORIFICS

no honorific: Indicates familiarity or closeness; if used without permission or reason, addressing someone in this manner would constitute an insult.

-san: The Japanese equivalent of Mr./Mrs./Miss. If a situation calls for politeness, this is the fail-safe honorific.

-sama: Conveys great respect; may also indicate that the social status of the speaker is lower than that of the addressee.

-kun: Used most often when referring to boys, this indicates affection or familiarity. Occasionally used by older men among their peers, but it may also be used by anyone referring to a person of lower standing.

-chan: An affectionate honorific indicating familiarity used mostly in reference to girls; also used in reference to cute persons or animals of either gender.

-senpai: A suffix used to address upperclassmen or more experienced coworkers.

-sensei: A respectful term for teachers, artists, or high-level professionals.

HIGH SCHOOL DxD 11

BY:
HIROJI MISHIMA
ICHIEI ISHIBUMI
ZERO MIYAMA

Translation: Caleb D. Cook

Lettering: Anthony Quintessenza

HIGHSCHOOL DXD Volume 11
© HIROJI MISHIMA 2018
© ICHIEI ISHIBUMI • ZERO MIYAMA 2018
First published in Japan in 2018 by KADOKAWA CORPORATION, Tokyo.
English translation rights arranged with KADOKAWA CORPORATION, Tokyo, through TUTTLE-MORI AGENCY, INC., Tokyo.

English translation © 2018 by Yen Press, LLC

Yen Press
1290 Avenue of the Americas
New York, NY 10104

Visit us at yenpress.com
facebook.com/yenpress
twitter.com/yenpress
yenpress.tumblr.com
instagram.com/yenpress

First Yen Press Edition: November 2018

Yen Press is an imprint of Yen Press, LLC.
The Yen Press name and logo are trademarks of Yen Press, LLC.

Library of Congress Control Number: 2015960114

ISBNs: 978-1-9753-2807-8 (paperback)
        978-1-9753-8289-6 (ebook)

10 9 8 7 6 5 4 3 2 1

WOR

Printed in the United States of America